W9-CLG-176

COLLECTED WORKS OF ERASMUS

VOLUME 85

Erasmus
Engraving by Albrecht Dürer (1526)
Cabinet des Estampes, Bibliothèque Royale Albert I, Brussels

COLLECTED WORKS OF
ERASMUS

POEMS

translated by Clarence H. Miller

edited and annotated by Harry Vredeveld

University of Toronto Press

Toronto / Buffalo / London

The research and publication costs of the
Collected Works of Erasmus are supported by the
Social Sciences and Humanities Research Council of Canada.
The publication costs are also assisted by
University of Toronto Press.

Toronto / Buffalo / London
Printed in Canada

ISBN 0-8020-2867-5

Printed on acid-free paper

Canadian Cataloguing in Publication Data

Erasmus, Desiderius, d. 1536.
[Works]
Collected works of Erasmus

Includes bibliographical references.
Partial contents: v. 85–86. Poems / translated by
Clarence H. Miller; edited and annotated by
Harry Vredeveld.
ISBN 0-8020-2867-5

1. Erasmus, Desiderius, d. 1536. I. Title

PA8500 1974 876'04 C74-006326-X rev.

Collected Works of Erasmus

The aim of the Collected Works of Erasmus is to make available an accurate, readable English text of Erasmus' correspondence and his other principal writings. The edition is planned and directed by an Editorial Board, an Executive Committee, and an Advisory Committee.

Contents

Illustrations

VOLUME 86

Acknowledgments

We are deeply grateful to Nicolaas van der Blom and Daniel Kinney, as well as to the two readers for the University of Toronto Press, Alexander Dalzell and Terence Tunberg: they patiently studied our manuscript and gave us much invaluable advice. Mary Baldwin vigilantly watched over these volumes and guarded us from many an inconsistency and error; Jozef IJsewijn, Karin Tilmans, and Johannes Trapman obtained various source materials for us; Klaus-Dietrich Fischer and Marcus Haworth checked our Greek texts and translations; and David Carlson allowed us to use his as yet unpublished research on MS Egerton 1651. To each of them we offer our heartiest thanks.

Without Cornelis Reedijk's pioneering edition of Erasmus' poems our labours would have been immensely more difficult. We therefore gratefully acknowledge our many debts to him. We also wish to thank him for his generosity in sharing with us the many notes that he has been collecting since his edition appeared in 1956.

Our work on these volumes was generously supported by the National Endowment for the Humanities, which made possible a full sabbatical year for Clarence Miller in 1988–9, and by The Ohio State University, which granted Harry Vredeveld a Faculty Professional Leave for the academic year 1989–90. Harry Vredeveld also thanks the College of Humanities of The Ohio State University for a Special Research Assignment quarter in the winter of 1987 and for several grants-in-aid for photocopies. He also thanks the Center for Medieval and Renaissance Studies of The Ohio State University for providing him with numerous grants-in-aid for xeroxing research materials.

Finally we want to take this opportunity to express our gratitude to the Social Sciences and Humanities Research Council of Canada for its continuing support of the Collected Works of Erasmus.

CHM and HV

Introduction

I
ERASMUS' CAREER AS A POET

'From boyhood,' Erasmus told Cornelis Gerard in 1489, 'I have loved literature, and still love it, so much that it seems to me rightly to be preferred even to all the treasures of Arabia, and I would not give it up in exchange for Croesus' entire fortune, however great.'[1] And in his famous 'Poem on the troubles of old age,' composed in August 1506, he recalled how already 'as a beardless youth' he had been 'passionately devoted to reading and writing' and 'madly in love with the figures of the rhetoricians and the beguiling fictions of mellifluous poetry' (2.90–3). As a young man Erasmus found that his greatest strength lay in verse – a natural talent which, however, did not stop him from also writing in prose, even if it meant forcing himself to the task at first.[2] His teachers at 's-Hertogenbosch might frown on his avid studies and try to cool his enthusiasm for imitating the ancients;[3] his fellow monks at Steyn might look askance at his immoderate desire for assimilating all manner of books, both pagan and Christian, and for writing in all sorts of genres, both poetry and prose. And yet, as he told Johann von Botzheim many years later,[4] it was as if 'a kind of secret natural force' kept drawing him on to study literature and exercise his pen – all the more so, no doubt, because of his arduous struggles: *difficilia quae pulchra* 'all that is beautiful is difficult,' as he was fond of saying.

Why he might have been so attracted to literary studies Erasmus does not explain. A good part of this fascination must have been owing to his father Gerard, who knew Latin and Greek, had worked as a scribe in Italy, heard Guarino lecture in Ferrara, and copied out a small library of classical works with his own hand.[5] Erasmus' six years of schooling at Deventer (1478–84) and his two-odd years at 's-Hertogenbosch (1484–7) must also have inspired him more than he was afterwards prepared to admit. At Deventer he received instruction in the writing of Latin prose and poetry and learned the rudiments of Greek; and even at 's-Hertogenbosch, medieval-minded though it was, he found new books to read – works of excellent Latinity from which he was able to acquire some fluency of style.[6] Looking back at those early days, the mature Erasmus could discern only the bleaker picture of Dutch barbarism. But in Deventer he could admire, even if only from afar, the great humanist Rodolphus Agricola, who visited the school several times between his return from Italy in 1479 and his departure from Groningen to Heidelberg in April 1484. And in his last year at Deventer (1483–4) he could also look up to the school's new headmaster, the renowned scholar and poet Alexander Hegius, who lectured to all the boys on high days. Through them and the progressive teacher Jan Synthen, Erasmus found his imagination stirred by the new ideal of classical eloquence that the Italians were even then reviving.[7] Already at Deventer and later at 's-Hertogenbosch he tried his hand at imitating the writers of antiquity; but of his schoolboy exercises in poetry and prose nothing has survived.

AT STEYN, 1487–92

Erasmus joined the canons regular of St Augustine at Steyn, most probably in 1487, and took his vows there in late 1488. His older brother Pieter had entered the Augustinian monastery of Sion, near Delft. Erasmus had been ready for the university since leaving Deventer; but after his parents' death in the summer of 1484 his guardians steered him and his brother to the school of the Brethren of the Common Life in 's-Hertogenbosch instead. In later years he blamed all his troubles on the executors who had wasted the youths' patrimony, prevented them from attending university, and finally pressured them against their will into a monastic life for which Erasmus, at least, was quite unsuited.[8] We must be careful, however, not to take the piteous story completely at face value.[9]

For the twenty-one-year-old the probationary year was naturally a time of anxiety, but also of new friendships and intellectual ferment. After the depressing years spent with Pieter at 's-Hertogenbosch, Steyn must have seemed a very garden of the Muses. That, at least, is the phrase he uses in the letter to the papal official 'Lambertus Grunnius,' and that is how he idealized monastic life as late as 1491 in *De contemptu mundi*.[10] The library at Steyn was stocked not only with a wide range of Christian authors, but also with the principal ancient writers.[11] Here, for instance, he could read Terence, whom he had learned by heart along with Horace.[12] Moreover, there were at Steyn several young monks who, like him, had already tasted the old wine of classical learning. He 'greatly enjoyed the pleasant company of his contemporaries. They sang, they played games, they wrote verses in competition with one another.'[13] Among them were Cornelis of Woerden

– in the letter to Grunnius he is the *bête noire* 'Cantelius'[14] – and above all Servatius Rogerus. Initially Erasmus was allowed to spend much time reading and speaking with his friends night and day. Later, after he took the habit, this was apparently not always possible, since the house rules discouraged monks from conversing.[15] They were permitted to write as often as they pleased, however. Erasmus for one never tired of letter-writing. 'The more I write,' he used to say, 'the more I wish to write.'[16] And in letter after letter, couched in the florid rhetoric of passionate love, he strove first to win Servatius as a bosom friend and then to confirm him as a partner in his studies.

Erasmus' letters to Servatius are surely expressions of true friendship. 'It is not uncommon at [that] age to conceive passionate attachments [*fervidos amores*] for some of your companions,' he later told Grunnius.[17] That these same letters, which run the gamut of love's emotions, are undoubtedly also literary exercises – rhetorical *progymnasmata* – is by no means a contradiction to this. Rhetorical form colours, but does not necessarily exclude, sincerity and autobiographical authenticity. The fact is that the scholarly Erasmus could form no deep and lasting attachment except on the common ground of humanistic studies. 'In proportion to the intensity of my love for literature is the delight I take in the pursuits of literary men,' he once confided to Cornelis Gerard.[18] Having all things in common, reading and discussing the same works, composing verses together in friendly rivalry, writing elegant letters to each other when conversation was not possible: that was Erasmus' vision of friendship.[19]

For a while the course of true friendship did run smooth. In a letter to his brother Pieter, Erasmus praised Servatius as 'a youth of beautiful disposition and very agreeable personality and a devoted student in those branches of learning which have given the greatest delight to us both from our boyhood onwards.'[20] The two young men basked in each other's friendship and exchanged a series of letters, of which some of Erasmus' have survived. From these letters we gain the impression, however, that Servatius soon wearied of his friend's unbounded enthusiasm. He began to be slow in responding to Erasmus' letters, so full of the passionate eloquence that he could not and would not match. When pleading proved fruitless, Erasmus took to chiding Servatius for his laziness in not pursuing his studies more avidly and spontaneously.[21] He turned now to other monks more willing to match their pens with his, first and foremost Willem Hermans and Cornelis Gerard. It was to them above all that Erasmus was referring when he told Botzheim in 1523 how he loved to challenge his friends at the monastery in literary rivalry.

Like the early letters to Servatius, Erasmus' earliest poems are exercises in the rhetoric of friendship. Two of them are evidently intended to persuade a reluctant friend – quite possibly Servatius – to make the most of their youth and friendship. The 'Elegiac poem comparing sorrow and joy' (99) demonstrates the commonplace that joy – the joy of friendship shared – is the only thing that can extend the span of youth and increase the brilliance of intellect. The sorrow and cares of unrequited love, on the other hand, are detrimental to body and soul and hasten the onset of old age. Therefore the poet exhorts his friend to embrace joy together with him and to cast sorrow and grief into the underworld, where they belong. This poem of friendship is thus in essence a variation on the *carpe diem* theme. Another variation on this theme, the 'Elegiac poem complaining about grief' (101), goes a step further. Grief and sorrow, the young poet laments, have so worn him out that he expects to see all the signs of old age visited upon him before long. These verses, which are based on the elegy that opens Boethius' *Consolation of Philosophy*, may well have been intended to persuade the reluctant friend to convict himself of hard-heartedness, feel pity for the poet, and at last return his affection.

The bucolic poem (102), traditionally assigned to the period of Erasmus' schooldays at Deventer, should more probably be placed among the early poems to Servatius. When his love for Gunifolda is not returned, the shepherd Rosphamus loses all interest in what was once his only concern, his flock – just as the lovelorn Erasmus gives up reading and writing literature, formerly his only concern, when Servatius refuses to respond to his ardent appeals. And just as Gunifolda cannot be persuaded to love Rosphamus but would rather retire to the 'doggish embraces' of uncouth, cave-dwelling Polyphemus, so Servatius cannot bring himself to devote his heart to classical letters and prefers to take his ease among the 'barbarians' in the monastery. Rosphamus, therefore – like Erasmus in his letters to Servatius – laments that he is but ploughing the seashore and (quoting Virgil) prays for death to release him from his sorrows. If this interpretation is correct, the poem stands in the tradition of the allegorical eclogue. Indeed, though it also borrows eclectically from Ovid, Theocritus, and Boccaccio, it is at bottom an imitation of Virgil's second bucolic – a pastoral that Erasmus interpreted as a poem of disparate friendship.[22] But just as Virgil's second eclogue lets Corydon reject his unfulfillable passion at the end, so too the shepherd Rosphamus may yet come to his senses and reject the hard-hearted Gunifolda.

That obviously does not happen in the eclogue itself. The possibility, here only intimated by Corydon's example, is brought home in the 'Amatory ode' (103). This ode opens with a pastoral scene reminiscent of Virgil's second eclogue. Like Corydon, the hapless lover Amyntas wanders about disconsolately and laments his fate. And like Corydon, Erasmus' Amyntas rebels in the end against the tyranny of passion. In language closely following Horace's fifteenth epode, he warns the beloved to mend his ways. If not, so be it! The friend will learn to regret his hard-heartedness – if he does not relent before then.

Erasmus' rhetorical-literary attempts to induce Servatius to return his friendship in an exchange of letters and poems ended in failure. After berating him for his laziness and exhorting him to pursue his studies, Erasmus allowed his friendship to turn first into regretful defiance and finally into amiable indifference. Servatius' place in Erasmus' affections was soon occupied by another young monk at Steyn, his kinsman Willem Hermans, who had earlier studied with him at Deventer and was 'closely bound to [him] by friendship and literary studies.'[23] In the manuscript version of *Antibarbari* Erasmus praises him as 'the best and most learned of my contemporaries; you might wonder which to admire most, his charming character or his brilliant mind.'[24] And as late as 1496 he can still speak of him as 'a most delightful friend, a very Patroclus or Pirithous, in literary studies as in everything else.'[25] Willem, in short, fulfilled for a time Erasmus' dream of friendship based not merely on personal charm but also on a spirited intellectual and poetic rivalry. Beatus Rhenanus well describes their relationship: '[At Steyn] he had for several years as a companion in his studies Willem Hermans of Gouda, a youth deeply devoted to literature, whose *Sylva odarum* we still have ... They would spend day and night in literary pursuits. The time that other contemporaries spent lazily in trifles, sleeping, carousing, these two would spend in reading books and exercising their pen.'[26]

Among the fruits of their friendly competition we may certainly reckon the spring poem (106) in which Erasmus and Willem, like two shepherds in amoebean contest, strive mightily to outdo each other in alternating distichs praising the joys of springtime and youth. Another poem of this period, entitled simply 'To his friend' (109), is quite possibly also addressed to Willem. In these verses Erasmus depicts the cares and sorrows that incessantly burden his soul. For all its laments, however, this ode is an elaborate compliment to a new friend without whom, the poet confesses, he would long since have succumbed to grief. Shakespeare was to use the very same conceit in sonnet 30, the concluding lines of which read: 'But if the while I think on thee, dear friend, / All losses are restored and sorrows end.' The underlying pattern returns in later letters and poems to other new-found friends, beginning with the 'Ode to Cornelis' (93), written in the same metre as poem 109.

This 'Poem lamenting the neglect of the art of poetry: Ode to Cornelis,' as Erasmus seems to have entitled it originally,[27] was composed in early 1489 when Erasmus was very eager to get into contact with Cornelis Gerard, a learned monk in Hieronymusdal (Lopsen) outside the gates of Leiden. In the poem Erasmus recounts the many hardships that would surely have broken his spirit had not his new friend restored his soul. Erasmus' concerns, however, have evidently changed. Whereas the earlier ode 'To his friend' (109) still complains of the unabating madness (*furor*) of love, the 'Ode to Cornelis' laments the depression brought on by the 'barbarians' who constantly harass him in his classical studies and who condemn his fascination with pagan letters. Erasmus professes that these sorrows have forced him to abandon literature, formerly his greatest joy. But the report of Cornelis' enormous fame as a poet has so heartened him that he has once more taken up the pen to oppose the barbarians.

To Erasmus' delight Cornelis not only approved of the ode but also paid him the compliment of converting it into a dialogue by inserting three new sections of his own and adding an epilogue, written in hexameters. In this way the joint poem put into practice one of Erasmus' favourite maxims, later to be placed at the head of the *Adagia*: 'Between friends all is common.' The 'Ode to Cornelis' became an *Apologia adversus barbaros*, 'A defence taken up by Erasmus and Cornelis ... directed against the barbarous persons who scorn the eloquence of the ancients' (93, with the epilogue 135). Of course, in changing Erasmus' original ode of friendship into a dialogue, Cornelis also altered the poem's tone and emphasis. While Erasmus' exempla are drawn wholly from the sphere of classical poetry and mythology, Cornelis adds numerous examples from the Bible. He furthermore calls for a classicizing Christian poetry, garbed not in the cowl but in the toga, and so transforms Erasmus' ode into a manifesto hurled against the obscurantist enemies of biblical humanism.[28]

In 1489 Erasmus was not yet ready to follow Cornelis' lead and become a poet of Christian themes. His major concern for the time being remained the defence of classical eloquence and learning. We can see this concern clearly in his other works of that year. Closely recalling the terms employed in the 'Ode to Cornelis,' he hails the well-known (and well-to-do) scholar Engelbert Schut of Leiden as a bulwark against the forces of barbarism (poem 98). His *Conflictus Thaliae et Barbariei* pits the classical Muse Thalia against Barbarism, the anti-Muse of medieval learning.[29] And in the first draft of *Antibarbari*, which also dates from this period, Erasmus has his friend Cornelis declaim against the barbarians who in their ignorance and laziness deride the humanists for studying the ancient writers and emulating their eloquence.

Through Cornelis Erasmus became acquainted with at least some of the poetry of Girolamo Balbi. While he did not share Cornelis' enthusiasm for this expatriate Italian humanist, Erasmus thought well enough of him to take a *carpe diem* poem of his as the model for an elegy to a friend (perhaps Cornelis or Willem Hermans), urging him to take advantage of the spring of life, while it yet lasts, and to make good use of 'the time of youth, which is proper for the study of literature.'[30] He entitled it: 'On the mutability of time' (104). Evidently stimulated by Cornelis' ideals and by his own ever-widening circle of knowledge, Erasmus' thematic range began to broaden in 1490, first of all into the sphere of popular philosophy and moral satire. The 'Elegiac poem on patience' (105) was followed in the winter of 1490–1 by a series of hortatory elegies on false goals, lechery, and greed (94–6). These poems, to which Erasmus had planned to add two more elegies on worldly ambition and sinful curiosity, shortly afterwards became the core of his *De contemptu mundi* (c spring 1491), a *suasoria* addressed to a 'cousin' who is exhorted to disdain the stormy seas of this world and enter the tranquil harbour of the monastery.

The themes of these moral elegies – these *progymnasmata*, as Erasmus later termed them – do show the direction in which his interests were moving at the start of the decade. From writing sermons in verse to composing poems on sacred themes it is, after all, but a step. In Ep 28 (which is to be redated to c March 1491) Erasmus announces to Cornelis that he has taken that step.[31] Glancing back at the poetry that he wrote in the one or two years after he had entered Steyn, when he was only 'a youth and virtually still a layman,' he apologizes if any of the verses he is sending should be sentimental to a fault (*aequo mollius*). More recently, he says, he composed a verse satire – the tripartite satire on the folly of mankind (94–6). He had also written an *Oratio funebris* for Berta van Heyen along with two epitaphs (113–14). And at the moment he is working on a lyric ode. 'But, since you kindly remind me of this,' he tells his friend, 'I have decided for the future to write nothing which does not breathe the atmosphere either of praise of holy men or of holiness itself.'[32]

It is at least in part to Cornelis' influence, then, that we may attribute Erasmus' turn to moral-philosophical and sacred themes. In that most productive winter and spring of 1490–1 he wrote not only the three satires on vices and follies, but also a Christmas poem entitled 'On the shed where the boy Jesus was born and on the impoverished delivery of the Virgin Mary' (42), 'A rhythmical iambic hymn in praise of St Ann, the grandmother of Jesus Christ' (1), another hymn in praise of the patron saint of his monastery, Pope Gregory the Great (107), and a short meditation on the popular late-medieval theme 'The four last things' (108). 'The Saviour's earnest entreaty to mankind, perishing by its own fault' (117), which carries on a late-medieval tradition, may also have been written around that time. To Cornelis, who had earlier written a history of the civil war in the diocese of Utrecht, Erasmus furthermore dedicated a prose oration on peace, *Oratio de pace,* written in c 1489, during the civil war that had once again flared up in Holland in 1488 and was not to end until 1492. The theme of war and peace found its place also in poem 50, the 'Ode in praise of Michael and all the angels' (early spring 1491). The section devoted to St Michael, the 'angel of peace,' concludes with a prayer for an end to the bloody furore of war. The following two parts on the archangels Gabriel and Raphael likewise end with the thought of peace on earth. In his letter to Johann von Botzheim Erasmus does not mention the civil war, but he does recall that he wrote this sapphic ode at the insistence of the prior of a church dedicated to St Michael (probably the one at Den Hem near Schoonhoven and Gouda). It was a sign of the times, he says, that the man did not dare post it up in his church because it was so poetical as to seem Greek to him.[33]

FROM 1492 TO 1506

Erasmus' poetic output, as we have seen, peaked in the winter and spring of 1490–1. We shall have to wait until 1499 before we encounter another such efflorescence of poetry from him. Before that could happen, however, he had first to spread his wings and leave the small circle of friends he had been cultivating. On 25 April 1492 Erasmus was ordained priest. Some time thereafter, probably still in 1492, he was granted leave from the monastery to become secretary to Hendrik van Bergen, bishop of Cambrai and chancellor of the Order of the Golden Fleece. In this wider world he made many new friends, particularly Jacob Batt of Bergen op Zoom. Still, he took care to keep up contacts with the friends he had left behind in Holland. When he revised his *Antibarbari* in 1495, he named Willem Hermans and Jacob Batt – but not Cornelis – among the interlocutors.[34]

We know of no poetry written during these first years outside the monastery walls. Considering how little free time Erasmus enjoyed at the bustling court of a bishop who never stayed in any one place for long, this should not surprise us. He himself complained of being unable to 'attend at leisure to the Muse's task.'[35] It is not until early autumn 1495, after the bishop had given him permission to study theology at the Collège de Montaigu in Paris, that we find Erasmus the poet once more making an appearance.

Having arrived in Paris he immediately took the opportunity of introducing himself to Robert Gaguin, general of the Trinitarian order and the most prominent humanist in France. He did so both in poem 5 and in a now-lost prose letter, the effusive flattery of which Gaguin modestly declined. Impressed by Erasmus' genius, Gaguin quickly accepted the Dutchman into his literary circle and introduced him to the Italian expatriate poet Fausto Andrelini, with whose collection of amatory elegies, *Livia* (Paris: G. Marchant 1490), Erasmus had already become acquainted at Steyn. To both of these humanists Erasmus addressed a charming poem (no 6) – a dream-vision in which he lauds Gaguin's history of France, *De origine et gestis Francorum compendium* (Paris: P. Le Dru, 30 September 1495), and announces Andrelini's forthcoming *Eclogues*. He published the two complimentary poems 5 and 6 along with two of his earlier religious odes, 'On the shed where the boy Jesus was born' and 'In praise of Michael and all the angels,' in a little collection prefaced by Ep 47 and entitled *De casa natalitia Iesu* (Paris: A. Denidel [January 1496?]).

To his edition of Willem Hermans' *Sylva odarum* (Paris: G. Marchant, 20 January 1497), Erasmus contributed not only a prose letter of introduction to his tight-fisted patron Hendrik van Bergen (Ep 49), but also two new specimens of his own poetic skill: a liminary epigram commending the moral purity of his friend's work (30) and 'A lamentation about his fate, written when he was ill' (7). In spite of the title, the latter poem is not primarily concerned with Erasmus' low spirits during an illness, real as they no doubt were. Following a by now familiar pattern, Erasmus first rhetorically amplifies his unceasing hardships and then turns this long preamble into an elegantly understated compliment to Gaguin, now both friend and patron, without whom he must quickly sink into the slough of despond.

During his often interrupted theological studies in Paris Erasmus found time to produce a series of occasional poems, partly to exercise his pen, partly also to seek much-needed patronage: two epitaphs (14–15) for David of Burgundy, bishop of Utrecht, who died on 16 April 1496, a eulogy (38) for the singer and composer Jan Ockeghem, who had died on 6 February 1497, an epitaph for the otherwise unknown Margaret Honora (13), and three for the equally unidentified Odilia and her son (9–11). Patronage remained for the time being a most uncertain source of income. Like so many penniless poets before him, Erasmus could always take his revenge on a stingy patron in a sarcastic epigram (41); but whether he liked it or not, he had no choice but to go on looking for benefactors willing to give a little money in exchange for much praise. He worked especially hard to obtain the patronage of Anna van Borssele in the winter of 1498–9, churning out a 'Paean to the Virgin' in prose and several other prayers at her request when he stayed at her castle at Tournehem in February 1499.[36] To please her, Erasmus also expanded a hymn to St Ann (1) that he had written a decade earlier at Steyn and presented it to her on 27 January 1501. His verse paraphrase of the antiphon *Salve, regina* (118) may also have been intended for her.

After returning to Paris by way of Holland in early spring 1499, Erasmus found his zest for writing poetry reawakened. With an enthusiasm unmatched since the beginning of the decade he threw himself once more into the writing of verse. On 2 May 1499 he wrote Jacob Batt that he was now 'on very close terms indeed with Fausto [Andrelini] and a certain other poet, who is new.'[37] He goes on to say that he currently has 'a very keen contest afoot' with a poet named 'Delius.' This is most probably the theologian Gillis van Delft, who had arrived in Paris some years before. Erasmus' contribution to the contest was the lengthy 'Paean to St Mary' (110). Gillis' poem, also a sapphic ode, deals with 'The life of the Virgin Mary' and is addressed 'To the poet Erasmus.'[38]

In late spring 1499 Erasmus was invited by Lord Mountjoy, one of his pupils, to visit England. In that 'world apart' he made the acquaintance of men such as he had not met before: Thomas More and John Colet, William Grocyn and Thomas Linacre. The quickest and best way to impress them was undoubtedly through his verse. So it was that in the summer and autumn of that same year he composed a remarkable series of occasional and religious poems. As if to complete a cycle on the birth, life, and death of Christ begun with the ode 'On the shed where the boy Jesus was born' (42) and continued with the 'Paean to St Mary' (110), Erasmus now produced 'A poem on the preternatural signs that occurred at the death of Christ' (111) and a short epic 'On the feast of Easter and on the triumphant procession of the risen Christ and on his descent into hell' (112), the latter in imitation of Macarius Mutius' *De triumpho Christi* (Venice: F. Lucensis, 29 March 1499). Two other poems, composed in the autumn of 1499, are evidently the work of a young scholar eager to win powerful backers. The first was the admirable 'Ode in praise of Britain and of King Henry VII and the royal children' (4), which he offered as a token of his esteem to the eight-year-old Prince Henry. The second, 'An extemporaneous poem' (115), repays in kind the compliments that Henry's tutor, the poet-scholar John Skelton, had earlier paid Erasmus.

Between late January 1500, when he returned to Paris, and 4 September 1506, when he received a doctorate in theology at Turin, Erasmus' goals were becoming more sharply defined: he was going to aim at nothing less than the marriage of classical philology to Christian theology.[39] He was learning Greek night and day and composing his first translations of Euripides and Lucian. As the fruit of his theological and literary studies he published *Enchiridion militis christiani*, together with some other short works and a liminary poem (36), in *Lucubratiunculae aliquot* (Antwerp: D. Martens 1503).

In striving for his great goals he found himself, again and again, strapped for money. If only he had the resources to tide him over the lean years! In the meantime he did what he could to live by his pen. In addition to a series of epigrams (24–7) interpreting various mythological depictions either for some wealthy collector or, less probably, at the request of an artist, he wrote several brief poems to important personages. One of these epigrams (35) thanks a patron for a gift; another (65), accompanying his verse translations of Euripides' *Hecuba* and *Iphigenia in Aulis*, asks William Warham, archbishop of Canterbury, for his patronage; and a third (8) praises Hammes castle near Calais, where he stayed for a time as the guest of Lord Mountjoy in June 1506. His verse encomium of Archduke Philip the Handsome (64), which accompanied the longer prose *Panegyricus* of 1504, was no doubt written against the grain, as Erasmus sighed;[40] but his work did bring him fifty gold florins – a handsome gratuity indeed.[41]

Of the poems that Erasmus composed in the years following his second stay in England, one in particular merits attention: the 'Poem on the troubles of old age' (2). Erasmus wrote it in August 1506, a few months before his fortieth birthday, while he was travelling through the Alpine passes to Italy. In this *carpe diem* meditation on the flight of youth and the rapid approach of old age, Erasmus at the midpoint of life introduces as the central exemplum the story of his own career and concludes by exhorting himself to devote his life henceforth wholly to Christ, without whom all his studies and aspirations are vain.

FROM 1507 TO 1536

The publication of his collected verse in *Varia epigrammata*, printed together with the revised *Adagiorum collectanea* (Paris: J. Petit and J. Bade 1506/7), marks the end of the first half of Erasmus' career. For the last time poetry receives, so to speak, equal billing with his prose. Hitherto Erasmus' verse had always balanced out his prose in importance, if not necessarily in length. His need for friendship at Steyn had found expression in both poems and letters; the attacks on the monastic 'barbarians' occurred not only in the poems to Cornelis Gerard and Engelbert Schut of Leiden but also in *Conflictus Thaliae et Barbariei* and *Antibarbari*. His funeral oration for Berta van Heyen was accompanied by two verse epitaphs. The moral satires and poems on sacred themes had their counterpart in *De contemptu mundi*. And the theme of his *Oratio de pace* was reflected in the 'Ode in praise of Michael and all the angels.' This relative balance continued throughout the 1490s. Occasional poems were matched by the letters he was even then beginning to collect; the prose prayers to Christ and the Virgin and the paean to Mary of winter 1498–9 were counterbalanced by the hymn to Mary and the epyllion on Christ's descent into hell. Likewise the steady flow of original poems and the verse translations from the Greek between autumn 1499 and autumn 1506 corresponded to an equally steady output of prose works: *Adagiorum collectanea, Enchiridion, Panegyricus,* and, of course, the ever-growing body of letters. But after the publication of the *Adagia* and *Epigrammata* in the winter of 1506–7 the earlier balance between poetry and prose in Erasmus' writing shifts suddenly and dramatically in favour of prose. Henceforth, whether he was inserting metrical translations from Greek into the *Adagia,* writing complimentary poems or epitaphs, or recording his reaction to one event or another, poetry would be mostly reduced to a pastime for himself, a service to his friends, a handmaiden to his prose.

Erasmus' satirical bent, evident well before 1507 in his hammer-blows against Hemmerlin's edition of Virgil (116), his caustic epigrams on an uncourtly courtier who despised clerics (21–3), and his ridicule of the 'blind' corrector of his Euripides translations (33), naturally manifested itself also in the verses he wrote at the time of his *Moriae encomium* and *Julius exclusus*. One may well wonder if the three witty pasquinades on the rape of Europa by the monks (138–40) did indeed come from his pen while he was at Rome in 1509. Almost certainly, however, he was the author of one or two vitriolic epigrams against the warrior-pope Julius II. The first (119) must have been written in late spring 1511; the second (if Erasmus was indeed its author) came hard on the heels of news that the pope had recovered from a near-fatal illness in November of that same year (141). Two years later, in autumn 1513, Erasmus pleased his English friends by mocking the rout of the French in the Battle of the Spurs (58).

Closely related to satirical pieces like these are the tongue-in-cheek poems that Erasmus could write as well as any when the spirit moved him. His mock 'Epitaph for a drunken jokester' (52) – probably at the death of Henrique Caiado of Lisbon – dates from the summer of 1509. And in June 1515, after it had rained for months on end, he penned a note to the rain-god Jupiter (59), threatening to repeal his title of 'the best and the greatest' and replace it with 'the worst and the lowest of gods.'

Most of Erasmus' verse in the years of his greatest fame was written for his friends. His triumphal journey to Basel by way of Alsace in 1514 brought him much adulation, in prose and verse, which he had to repay in like coin: to the schoolmaster Johannes Sapidus (3), for example, or the famed humanist Sebastian Brant (54), and all the scholars of Sélestat (53). Almost overrun by Spanish visitors in Brussels during the winter of 1516–17, he was asked by Álvar Gómez to compose an epigram for his poem on the Order of the Golden Fleece (120). Not long afterwards, during a brief stay at London in April 1517, Erasmus wrote two more liminary epigrams, this time for Bernard André, Henry VII's poet laureate, for whom he did not care very much. One (121) compliments the blind scholar for shedding light on St Augustine's *City of God;* the other (67) praises his collection of hymns, which are Christian-medieval in content and (alas) also in style. Sometimes his verse serves as a kind of covering letter for a gift: the young Wilhelm Nesen receives an epigram (61) along with a reed pen; and a newly wed couple in Basel get some punning verses (80) along with a rooster, a hen, and their chicks – a joke that was frustrated when his housekeeper gave the birds away to someone else. And as the ageing humanist paid tribute to his friends in life, so he remembered them in death, in epitaph after epitaph: the theologian Maarten van Dorp (71), the printers Johann Froben and Dirk Martens (73–4 and 126), the councillors Nicolaas Uutenhove (78–9) and Antonius Clava (86), his patron Jérôme de Busleyden (68–9), his friend Bruno Amerbach and his young wife (70), the two wives of Pieter Gillis (83–5), and the legal scholar Ulrich Zasius (92).

New in Erasmus' poetry after 1507 are his original Greek verses. Before this time we possess from his pen only a two-line Greek epitaph for Jacob Batt (16) and a brief cento stitched together (not entirely according to the rules of the genre) from Homeric verses, half-lines, and verse-fragments (63). Longer Greek poems of his own composition make their first appearance in the votive poem to Our Lady of Walsingham (51), dating from spring 1512. Like the much later verses to Ste Geneviève, this votive poem presents itself as a model of how to venerate a saint without falling into popular superstition: not by expecting worldly rewards, but by praying for a clean heart devoted to Christ. Several other Greek poems were to follow: an epitaph for Jérôme de Busleyden (68), another for Johann Froben (74), and a third for Nicolaas Uutenhove (79). Among the poetic variations presented in the colloquy *Convivium poeticum* and dealing with the theme that one should first and foremost tend the garden of learning, there is also a four-line Greek epigram (130.34–7). Erasmus' last Greek poem – a 'Dialogue between a scholar and a bookseller' (87) – graced the title-page of Simon Grynaeus' edition of Aristotle's works (Basel: J. Bebel 1531).

Like so many of the complimentary epigrams and epitaphs of these years, a good deal of Erasmus' religious poetry in the latter half of his career was written at the request of friends. It was for John Colet's new school for boys that he composed the series of epigrams on the boy Jesus (44–8). Designed to inculcate the virtues of clean living and pure Latinity, they were first published together with *Concio de puero Iesu* ([Paris: Joris Biermans?] 1 September [1511?]). In the same collection he included a greatly expanded version of his 'Expostulation of Jesus with mankind' (43). His lengthy poem 'Basic principles of Christian conduct' (49) was also written at the request of John Colet; it was first published in a collection of ancient proverbs and maxims entitled *Opuscula aliquot Erasmo Roterodamo castigatore* (Louvain: D. Martens 1514). Actually it is not an original work as such, but a versification of Colet's English catechism. Half a decade later Jan van Merleberge asked Erasmus to write him a poem praising St Mary Magdalen and containing an acrostic of his name. Erasmus obliged the ageing monk with the epigram (124) in summer 1520. And the *Liturgy of the Virgin Mother as She is Venerated at Loreto*, with its exquisite verses in many different metres (133), was written in 1523 not on Erasmus' own initiative, but at the request of the Swiss priest Thiébaut Biétry.

Even Erasmus' last religious poem, the graceful 'Poem in fulfilment of a vow made to Ste Geneviève, whose protection freed him from a quartan fever' (88), is at least in part a tribute to Guillaume Cop – the same physician to whom he had earlier dedicated his 'Poem on the troubles of old age' (2). Perhaps it was the old Cop who gently prodded Erasmus to fulfil his vow after so many years.[42] Be that as it may, the poem, which describes his miraculous cure from a severe attack of quartan fever in the winter of 1496–7, is not an outpouring of devotion like that of the earlier 'Hymn in praise of St Ann' or the 'Paean to St Mary.' After so long a delay in fulfilling his vow, after so much harsh criticism of the popular cult of the saints, we can hardly expect such lyrics from him now. Instead, the votive poem is written in a measured, low-key style. Its metre, the dactylic hexameter, does not readily lend itself to lyric flights. So Erasmus' tribute to the saint is placed between a beautifully evocative description of the sacred landscape in which Geneviève once moved and a narration of the cure she performed. At the end of the poem the focus is not on Ste Geneviève, but on Christ. It is as if the old humanist is telling his readers one last time: this is how you should venerate a saint, by attributing all her glory to its true source, Christ.

II
IMITATION AND MODELS

In his handbook for preachers, *Ecclesiastes sive de ratione concionandi*, Erasmus makes one of his rare comments on the art of poetry. Poetry, he explains, is not just the art of versifying. The poet must also invest his words with dignity, gravity, charm, seductive imagery, and a certain divine inspiration or *enthousiasmos*. Only he who has universal knowledge can be a poet. 'True poetry,' he concludes, 'is like a pastry baked from the delicacies and the marrow of all branches of learning, or to use a better image: it is honey brought together from all the choicest flowers.'[43]

Erasmus' characterization of poetry as an erudite, highly refined compilation, drawn and distilled from many sources and models and presented in metrical form and eloquent language, should remind us of the gulf that separates Renaissance poetics from the romantic and neoromantic theories of poetry to which we are heir and from which we have only in the past few decades begun to break away. While the romantic tradition conditioned the reader to look for originality and individual genius, the Renaissance reader more often than not expected variations on commonplace themes, expressed in an elegant, classical style and modelled on the great masters of past and present. Writing poetry was, to be sure, considered an art that requires 'a certain divine inspiration or *enthousiasmos*.'[44] But the *poeta doctus* also understood that the Muses grant their aid only in exchange for hard work and consequently applied Varro's dictum to his own craft: 'Since, as they say, the gods help those who help themselves, I will invoke the gods first' (*Adagia* I vi 17). Poetry, in short, was not merely a matter of genius and inspiration, but had also to be learned by assiduous study of handbooks and by tireless practice in imitating the finest models that tradition had to offer.

The honey-bee image that Erasmus employs to describe the making of poetry has a long history.[45] It received its classic expression in Horace *Odes* 4.2.25–32. In this passage Horace likens Pindar to a swan and himself to a bee that flits from flower to flower, culling from them only the very best to make his own honey.[46] Later Seneca took up the image in *Epistulae morales* 84, a lengthy discussion of the process by which thinkers and writers gain their universal knowledge. Such erudition, Seneca explains, is acquired from many disparate sources just as the bee gathers nectar from flowers of all kinds. Once we have imbibed the nectar of learning, however, we must digest and transform it within us into honey of our own.

Imitation in Renaissance Latin verse takes many forms.[47] On the simplest level the poet follows one model throughout. Since this sort of imitation was considered apprentice work, the mature Erasmus tended to avoid it. But even he could make an exception when the pressure of the moment forced him to come up with an extempore composition. In a last-minute rush to fill a blank space in a copy of his translation of Euripides' *Hecuba*, which he wanted to present to William Warham, archbishop of Canterbury, he versified a brief letter by Angelo Poliziano to his patron Lorenzo de' Medici.[48] There Poliziano had used the learned conceit of the poet as a swan who can sing only when the fair breezes of patronage blow. Erasmus had already borrowed this argument once before, in one of his own letters (Ep 144). In poem 65 he does the same in verse, following his model freely, changing or adding details to suit the specific situation, adorning the material with poetic language and metre. To Renaissance thinking this was a fair use of existing literature, not plagiarism. Poliziano's letters were widely studied and imitated, and Erasmus could expect his well-read audience both to recognize the model and appreciate its transformation into poetry.

Closely related to this kind of adaptation from prose into verse is the transposition of material from one language into another or from one metrical pattern into another. Erasmus, in fact, recommended all three kinds of transformation as useful exercises for the aspiring writer:

> We shall add greatly to our linguistic resources if we translate authors from the Greek, as that language is particularly rich in subject-matter and vocabulary. It will also prove quite useful on occasion to compete with these Greek authors by paraphrasing what they have written. It will be of enormous value to take apart the fabric of poetry and reweave it in prose, and, vice versa, to bind the freer language of prose under the rules of metre, and also to pour the same subject-matter from one form of poetic container into another. It will also be very helpful to emulate a passage from some author where the spring of eloquence seems to bubble up particularly richly, and endeavour in our own strength to equal or even surpass it.[49]

One can see the results of such training in many Renaissance poems. Thomas More's translations from the *Greek Anthology* and Erasmus' verse translations of Euripides were, in part at least, exercises in competing with the Greek poets. Transpositions from one metre into another are very common in humanist poetry and may be frequently observed in Erasmus' practice as well. His *Precatio 'Salve, regina'* (118), for example, paraphrases the antiphon *Salve, regina* into elegiac distichs; and the 'Paean to St Mary' (110) includes several quite extensive adaptations from Prudentius' hymn on Christmas. Cornelis Gerard too, in one of his sections of the *Apologia adversus barbaros* (93), paraphrases a lengthy section of Silius Italicus' *Punica* while changing the metre from the epic hexameter into the second Asclepiadean strophe. And in the epilogue to the *Apologia* (135.29–33) his St Jerome urges the Christian poet to turn biblical stories into verse: 'Imitate the histories in Holy Scripture when you try to write.'

As the bee metaphor implies, the most widely practised and admired form of poetic imitation was the eclectic variety in which many models – some of them meant to be recognized by the reader, others consciously dissembled and estranged, still others followed more or less unconsciously – are reconstituted into a new, distinctively different whole. In composing this kind of recombinant poetry, the writer gathers together his themes, motifs, images, allusions, set phrases, and so forth, from the great storehouse of literature. This is the form of imitation that we find practically everywhere in Erasmus' poetry. The rule of thumb in successful imitations of this sort is to conceal the models carefully, by taking them out of their original context, for example, or by varying their phrasing and metre, or by overlaying them with other models.[50] But the sources need not always be so carefully hidden. Sometimes the poet wants them to be recognized, whether to demonstrate that he is outdoing a renowned master or to extend the resonance of his verse.

The 'Ode in praise of Britain and of King Henry VII and the royal children' (4) is a good example of eclectic imitation. During a dinner at Eltham Palace in early autumn 1499, the eight-year-old Prince Henry asked Erasmus to write some complimentary verses for him. Unable to produce them extempore, he spent the next three days (or so he says) sweating out this ode. The poem abounds in classical and contemporary reminiscences and allusions. Some of them serve as literary ornaments; others, alluding to great rulers of the past, are intended as extensions of the encomium; and still others are so dissembled that (as E.K. writes in his dedicatory epistle to Spenser's *The Shepheardes Calender*) only 'well scented' trackers can ferret them out.[51]

Among the associations for which Erasmus could count on recognition, if not from the young Henry, then at least from his more cultivated audience, is his choice of the second Pythiambic strophe. The metre is clearly meant to remind the reader of Horace's sixteenth epode.[52] In that poem Horace expresses his revulsion at the civil wars and his longing for the fabled Isles of the Blessed in the western ocean – a realm that Jupiter has reserved for the pious remnant of the golden age. Erasmus' choice of metre thus links Rome's civil wars, finally ended by Caesar Augustus, with Britain's Wars of the Roses, ended by Henry VII, and identifies the Blessed Isles of ancient myth with its modern realization in the British Isles. The theme of the golden age renewed, subtly suggested by the choice of metre, is amplified by verbal allusions within the poem itself. Here Erasmus reminds the reader primarily of Virgil's fourth eclogue – the famous prophecy of the return of the golden age that is to be inaugurated with the birth of a marvellous baby. Under Henry VII, he assures us, England is enjoying a renewed golden age. The iron race which for so many years battled in the Wars of the Roses has been vanquished. The goddess of justice, Astraea, has come back, and Henry VII, an Augustus redivivus, is inaugurating a new era of peace. At this point the associations with Virgil's 'messianic' eclogue begin to blend with some verbal reminiscences of Horace's *Odes* that in their original context refer to Augustus.[53] At the end of the poem, however, Erasmus returns to the theme of the golden age as developed in Virgil's fourth eclogue. The baby hailed by Virgil is here associated with Edmund. Erasmus describes him as lying in a cradle that is to be sprinkled with the very same flowers that the earth is to lavish on the child in Virgil's prophecy.

To the flowers listed in Virgil's fourth eclogue Erasmus adds white and red roses. The symbolism, of course, recalls Henry VII's union of the red rose of Lancaster with the white rose of York and the end of the Wars of the Roses. Earlier in the poem Erasmus elaborated on this symbolism in an allegory portraying the king's five children as red or white roses in various stages of growth and development. Here he borrows extensively from one of his favourite poems: *De rosis nascentibus*, formerly attributed to Virgil but much more probably the work of Ausonius.

It should by no means be imagined, as people sometimes do, that Erasmus imitated only the ancient poets. Just as he was no Ciceronian in his prose but drew eclectically on the whole range of Latin vocabulary,[54] so in his poetry he often availed himself of medieval and contemporary models. We have already noted his imitation of Poliziano in the poem to Archbishop William Warham. The 'Ode in praise of Britain' provides us with a further instance. For in the passage where the personified Britain praises herself by comparing herself to other countries, Erasmus is in fact imitating a section in Willem Hermans' *Hollandia* – a passage that in its turn is partially modelled on a description of Italy in Virgil's *Georgics*.

Allusions to and borrowings from the great works in the literary canon add lustre to neo-Latin poetry and increase its resonance. But there are also numerous cases of imitation that are not to be regarded as deliberate on the part of the poet or recognizable in cursory reading. Many phrases, images, figures of speech, and the like, whose pedigree may be traced, say, to Virgil, Horace, or Ovid, must have become almost second nature to Erasmus over the years. They were part and parcel of the treasure-house of his mind, ready to be retrieved when needed, without necessarily conjuring up a specific model. As he himself explains in *De copia*: 'We must keep our eyes open to observe every figure of speech that [the great authors] use, store it in our memory once observed, imitate it once remembered, and by constant employment develop an expertise by which we may call upon it instantly.'[55] The modern commentator duly records such borrowings, in part to demonstrate the imitative eclecticism of neo-Latin poetry, in part to show the reader from which gemstones the Renaissance poet put together the mosaic of his verse, in part also to shed light on the precise meaning of this phrase or that.

Who were Erasmus' favourite poets? In *Ciceronianus* Bulephorus-Erasmus says: 'When I was young I adored all the poets, but as soon as I became better acquainted with Horace, the others by comparison began to stink in my nostrils, though marvellous enough in absolute terms.'[56] Elsewhere he speaks of a certain mysterious affinity between himself and Horace when he was still young.[57] What drew him so much to Horace? Erasmus himself singles out the ancient poet's elegant simplicity of style. In a letter written in 1495 he says that he is personally more attracted to 'the direct, spare style of Horace' than to the more exalted, learned, and fluent style of Virgil, Lucan, Ovid, or Baptista Mantuanus.[58] And in *Virginis et martyris comparatio* he praises Horace's 'inimitable elegance.'[59] We should not make too much of this preference, however, and start thinking of some problematic kinship between Erasmus' personality and that of the pagan-epicurean Horace.[60] To him Horace was the supreme lyric poet and satirist. Naturally he was the one to imitate if you wanted to write odes or satires, as Erasmus liked to do in his youth. But if you were writing pastoral or epic, you would want to imitate Virgil, the king of Latin poets.[61] Later Erasmus also reserved a special place in his heart for 'the prince of poets,' Homer.[62]

As early as 1489 Erasmus confided to Cornelis Gerard that his 'authorities in poetry' were 'Virgil, Horace, Ovid, Juvenal, Statius, Martial, Claudian, Persius, Lucan, Tibullus, and Propertius.'[63] This canon of poets, evidently arranged in order of their importance rather than chronology, would remain fairly constant throughout his life. In *De ratione studii* he still commends Virgil and Horace as models of pure Latin speech – after Terence and Plautus, who as writers of comedy are naturally superior in everyday language.[64] And in *Ciceronianus* he suggests that the best Latin poets are 'Virgil, Horace, Ovid, Lucan, and Persius.' Later in the same dialogue he lists 'the most famous and most gifted of all: Virgil, Horace, Ovid, Lucan, and Martial.'[65]

These, then, are the poets whom Erasmus acknowledged as guiding stars in his own writing. As we have noted, however, it would be erroneous to assume that Erasmus looked only to the ancients for inspiration and guidance. He himself argued that modern poets should not hesitate to model themselves also on biblical and early Christian writers. In a letter written in 1496 to Bishop Hendrik van Bergen, he says that one should as a matter of course avoid imitating the erotic poems of Catullus, Tibullus, Propertius, and Ovid and look instead to St Ambrose, Paulinus of Nola, Prudentius, and Iuvencus, as well as to the Old Testament poets Moses, David, and Solomon.[66] The Christian, to be sure, may borrow from even the most lascivious of the pagan poets, just as the Hebrews at their exodus took with them the treasures of Egypt. 'I am myself happy to be of my friend Gaguin's opinion in thinking that even ecclesiastical subjects can be splendidly adorned with native treasures provided the style is pure. And I would not reprehend anyone for applying Egyptian trimmings, but I am against the appropriation of Egypt in its entirety.'[67] Of the Christian poets Prudentius was Erasmus' favourite. He praised him as 'the one really stylish poet among Christian authors,' and frequently imitated him.[68] But he also drew on Sedulius' *Paschale carmen* and the poems of Venantius Fortunatus, especially the latter's well-known poem on Easter (*Carmina* 3.9). And of course he admired the verses in Boethius' *Consolation of Philosophy* and liked to borrow from them, even in his earliest work.

Among the modern Italian poets Erasmus singled out Baptista Mantuanus, praising him as a 'Christian Virgil.'[69] He thought well enough of Boccaccio's first two eclogues to imitate them in his own bucolic poem (102). In this same youthful effort he also borrows from other Italian works, including Antonio Geraldini's sacred eclogues of 1485 and Angelo Poliziano's *Ambra*, the third of his *Sylvae*, first printed in 1485. From Marcantonio Sabellico's elegies on the birth of the Virgin Mary he later adopted many phrases and motifs, especially in his 'Paean to St Mary' (110). Macarius Mutius' short epic on the harrowing of hell (Venice 1499) inspired Erasmus to write an epyllion on the same subject (112). With Cornelis Gerard he discussed the merits of the expatriate Italian poet Girolamo Balbi (see Epp 23, 25, and 27, written in 1489). Another Italian poet living in Paris was Fausto Andrelini. Erasmus borrowed phrases from the latter's collection of amatory poems, *Livia* (Paris 1490), as early as the winter of 1490–1. In autumn 1495 he acclaimed Andrelini's allegorical eclogues for their moral purity (poem 6) – so much in contrast with the lascivious tone of his *Livia*.

But there were many other modern poets for the young Erasmus to read and admire. We should, of course, not fail to mention Rodolphus Agricola, whom he hailed as 'a second Virgil' in *Adagia* I iv 39 and with whose poem on St Ann (Deventer 1484) he was much impressed.[70] Alexander Hegius of Westphalia, Agricola's disciple and headmaster of St Lebuin's school in Deventer during Erasmus' last year there, also wrote much lyric poetry, which Erasmus appreciated, even in later years.[71] At Steyn there was his friend Willem Hermans, whose odes he was to edit at Paris. Erasmus lauds him in poem 30 and Ep 49 as a truly Christian writer and praises him in *Ciceronianus* as 'a sound poet.'[72] He also approved of Cornelis Gerard's poems and welcomed his long *Mariad* on the life of the Virgin (Ep 40). Among the neo-Latin poets of Germany he deeply respected the learned Sebastian Brant, author not only of *Das Narrenschiff* (translated into Latin hexameters by Jacob Locher) but also of a collection of miscellaneous poems, entitled *Varia carmina* (Basel 1498).[73]

Apart from such early-medieval Christians as Ambrose, Iuvencus, Paulinus of Nola, Prudentius, and Arator, Erasmus only rarely mentions medieval poets. In his youth he held Geoffrey of Vinsauf's *Poetria nova* in high esteem;[74] and in later years he commended Jean Gerson's writings, in particular his prosimetric *Consolatio theologiae*.[75] Among the medieval poets whom Erasmus never mentions but from whom he did borrow on occasion we may point, for example, to Walther of Châtillon, author of the greatest medieval Latin epic, the *Alexandreis*. He was also thoroughly familiar with the very popular eleventh-century medical poem *Regimen sanitatis Salernitanum* and the twelfth-century play *Pamphilus*, whether in one of the many manuscripts then circulating or in an early printed edition. There are, moreover, indications that he was acquainted with at least some of Alcuin's poems, with John of Salisbury's *Entheticus maior* and *minor*, and with Alain de Lille's prosimetric work *De planctu Naturae*. And of course he knew many medieval hymns and sequences by heart and often used them in composing his own sacred verse.

Just as Erasmus flitted bee-like through the gardens and meadows of his predecessors, so too his admirers sought out his poetic flowers and distilled from them a honey of their own. The German humanist Helius Eobanus Hessus (1488–1540), for instance, frequently looked to Erasmus' poems for themes, motifs, and phrasing.[76] In 1515 Eobanus published two mock epitaphs for a drunkard that are plainly variations on Erasmus' 'Epitaph for a drunken jokester' (52). And in one of his heroic epistles, a verse letter from St Paula to St Jerome at Bethlehem, first published in *Heroidum christianarum epistolae* (Leipzig 1514), he closely imitates portions of Erasmus' ode 'On the shed where the boy Jesus was born' (42). Another German who imitated parts of this same ode in a poem on the nativity was the Baroque poet Paul Fleming (1609–40).[77] Erasmus' friend Andrea Ammonio was sufficiently impressed by the 'Ode in praise of Britain' (4) to draw on it for his own praises of Henry VII and Henry VIII.[78] Other contemporaries – Philip Melanchthon among them – seem to have been deeply moved by the 'Poem on the troubles of old age' (2).[79] Indeed, no less a poet than Janus Secundus borrowed phrases from it and praised it as exquisitely Horatian, worthy of comparison with the song of the dying swan.[80]

III
POETRY AND RHETORIC

To Erasmus and his fellow humanists, poetry and rhetoric were so closely interconnected as to seem inseparable. 'I take the greatest pleasure in rhetorical poems and in poetical rhetoric,' he once wrote, 'such that one can sense poetry in the prose and the style of a good orator [*rhetoricam phrasin*] in the poetry.'[81] And in a letter to Cornelis Gerard he maintains that only he who has mastered the art of rhetoric can compose good poetry:

> In writing poetry a great many points have to be watched if the result is to be creditable. Of the first importance are these: a lively power of inventing themes [*inventio*], clever arrangement [*dispositio*], harmony of style [*elocutio*], a retentive memory [*memoria*]. We must add to them the brilliant effect created by rhetorical devices [*colorum splendor*] ... But why should I attempt to include the whole world in a small map, as it were – to embrace the entire science of rhetoric and its rules within the compass of a short letter? Why should I endeavour to teach Minerva, as the saying goes, or carry wood into a forest? You know your Cicero, your Quintilian, your Horace, your Geoffrey of Vinsauf, and you are certainly not unaware of the abundance of excellent advice on the art of poetry which they contain; whoever keeps their advice faithfully is bound to fulfil to perfection his function as a poet.[82]

If, then, we are to understand Renaissance poetry on its own terms in the way that an Erasmus or a Cornelis understood it, we ought to have some insight into the art of rhetoric.

Rhetoric, as traditionally defined, is the art of speaking or writing effectively and eloquently. Its aim is threefold: 'to inform, to give pleasure, to influence.'[83] The subjects on which speakers and writers discoursed were likewise divided into three main classes, judicial, deliberative, and demonstrative, each of which had its own set of goals and precepts.

Judicial or forensic rhetoric is primarily concerned with questions of guilt and innocence. This class was originally at home in courts of law. Its range was later extended so that it comprised not only 'accusation, complaint, defence,' but also 'protest [*expostulatio*], justification [*expurgatio*], reproach, threat, invective, and entreaty.'[84] Among Erasmus' poems that may be classified as 'judicial' we should certainly include 'The expostulation of Jesus with mankind' (43), in which the Saviour accuses man of wilfully seeking his own damnation. In this category we may also reckon such early work as the elegy 'On the overmastering power of Cupid' (100), the 'Amatory ode' (103), in which the poet accuses his friend of being 'deafer than any sea cliff' and threatens to break the bonds between them, as well as the 'Elegiac poem complaining about grief' (101), which tacitly reproaches a marble-hearted friend for making the poet 'bear the afflictions of old age during [his] tender years.' Several of Erasmus' laments, whether occasioned by unrequited love (109), the envy of the barbarians (93), or his fate (7), begin in the judicial genre, but, by a surprising twist, are in the end turned into a compliment and so ultimately belong to the demonstrative kind of rhetoric.

Deliberative rhetoric urges the audience to take one course of action rather than another. This type has as its model the speeches in a legislative assembly. Erasmus subdivides the deliberative class of rhetorical writing into 'conciliation, reconciliation, encouragement, discouragement, persuasion, dissuasion, consolation, petition, recommendation, admonition, and the amatory letter.'[85] A good number of Erasmus' poems belong to the deliberative type. His elegy on long-suffering (105) and his 'Basic principles of Christian conduct' (49) come to mind at once. But we must not forget the variations on the *carpe diem* theme (99, 104, 95, and 2) that urge the reader to make good use of life's brief spring before the winter of old age draws near.

Demonstrative or epideictic rhetoric, being either encomiastic or satiric, dispenses praise or censure. Its natural setting is the royal court, where a trained orator delivers a panegyric of the ruler. 'In the demonstrative category,' says Erasmus, 'belong accounts of persons, regions, estates, castles, springs, gardens, mountains, prodigies, storms, journeys, banquets, buildings, and processions.'[86] Much of Erasmus' poetry – as indeed a great deal of Renaissance poetry – falls into this class. His encomium of Great Britain and her royal family (4) and of Archduke Philip the Handsome (64) have their place here, as do the poems in praise of the Virgin (42, 51, 110, 133), St Michael and all the angels (50), and saints Ann (1), Gregory (107), Mary Magdalen (124), and Geneviève (88). The short epic on the harrowing of hell (112) celebrates Christ as Saviour and so may be classified among the encomiastic poems. The *carmina scholaria* that Erasmus wrote for the edification of the boys of Colet's school (44–8) likewise praise Christ, though they naturally shade off into the hortatory poem. In the encomiastic category we may furthermore place all the epigrams to patrons and fellow humanists, as well as the numerous epitaphs, which are in effect brief eulogies. Here too we should put the epigrams lauding Sélestat and her learned sons (53), Hammes castle (8), Meersburg castle (125), and the structural framework at Calais (123), as well as the amoebean poem in which Willem Hermans and Erasmus celebrate the arrival of spring (106). Satiric poetry forms a subcategory of demonstrative rhetoric, though there is often considerable overlap with the judicial and deliberative genres. The moral satires on false goals, lechery, and avarice (94–6) belong partly to the demonstrative category, partly to the deliberative type of rhetoric. The epigrams that mock the power of money (97), a bad corrector of some tragedies (33), a perverse editor of Virgil (116), and the flight of the French at the Battle of the Spurs (58) are unambiguously demonstrative, as are the virulent verses that attack an irreverent courtier (21–3), a stingy patron (41), and the warrior-pope Julius II (119 and 141).

How was one to go about writing such poems? Medieval and Renaissance poetics, drawing on ancient theory, isolated four elements or stages in the process of composition and gave detailed prescriptions for each. Erasmus' letter to Cornelis, as we saw, lists them as follows: finding the material (*inventio*), arrangement (*dispositio*), style (*elocutio*), and memory (*memoria*).

The poet must first gather together the arguments, circumstances, and evidence of all sorts that make his case plausible (*inventio*). Elaborate methods were developed to help orators and writers find such materials efficiently. Arguments were classified according to 'places' or topoi where they might be easily discovered. Topoi that could be used in arguing both for and against a case were called 'common places.' Much of the eclecticism of medieval and Renaissance writing, with its incessant borrowing from the most varied sources, is a concomitant of the habit, inculcated in the schools from the beginning, of compiling and searching storehouses of images, figures of speech, maxims, anecdotes, and commonplaces. Erasmus' *Adagia*, *De copia*, and *Parabolae* are essentially contributions to such thesauruses.

Once the material has been found and gathered together it has to be organized in an effective way (*dispositio*). Since judicial oratory was the oldest and formally most consistent class of rhetoric, its structure traditionally received the closest attention. The judicial speech is typically made up of five sections, for each of which rhetorical theory provides much guidance. The *exordium* or introduction has the function of making the judge sympathetic to the speaker's case, arousing his attention, and making him eager to learn more. Next comes the *narratio*, which lays out the facts basic to the case and thus provides the foundation for the argumentation. In complex cases a speaker is advised to conclude his narrative by way of a *propositio* reviewing the facts just presented and introducing the argumentation proper. The *argumentatio* is often subdivided into the positive arguments (*probatio*) and the rebuttal of the opponent's arguments (*refutatio*). The speaker's last chance to persuade the judge is the *peroratio* or epilogue. Here he should sum up his arguments and pull out all the emotional stops. These five sections suit judicial rhetoric very well indeed. For deliberative and demonstrative speeches and poems other structures apply. A panegyric, for instance, might be divided into *exordium*, *divisio*, and *peroratio*, the division being subdivided into external circumstances (for example parentage, education, wealth), physical attributes (such as agility, strength, good looks), and qualities of character (in particular wisdom, justice, courage, and temperance).[87]

After the poet has gathered together and organized his material, he must go on to clothe the ideas in words chosen to delight and move the reader (*elocutio*). Thus rhetorical language differs from ordinary speech in its calculated intensity to provoke the desired response in the audience. A large proportion of rhetorical theory is devoted to an analysis of the various tropes or figures of speech that arouse either the calmer feelings (*ethos*) or the more powerful emotions (*pathos*), and when and how such devices may be used with aptness (*decorum*).[88]

Writers had to have at their fingertips not only the cyclopaedia of knowledge, but also a vast array of ready-made epithets, phrases, metaphors, stories, myths, arguments (*memoria*) – in fact, the whole treasure-house of materials on which *inventio* and *elocutio* could draw. When praising his learned friends Erasmus would often single out their retentive memory. Thomas More, for example, had 'his memory always at his elbow, and as everything in it is held, so to say, in ready cash, it puts forward promptly and without hesitation whatever time or place demands.'[89] Complicated systems were devised to train speakers and writers in the art of instant recall. Erasmus himself, like Quintilian before him, was sceptical of the more elaborate mnemonic schemes. He did, however, recommend a series of practical techniques to help imprint the essential rhetorical tools in the memory.[90]

As an example of the rhetorical poetry that Erasmus had in mind when he wrote Cornelis, we may take his early elegy 'On the overmastering power of Cupid' (100). The poem begins on a personal note and so arouses in the modern reader the expectation that Erasmus will pour out his deepest feelings: 'Now I know what love is: love is a madness in the mind.' Our humanist, however, is not writing a romantic poem expressive of his own, private distress; his verses are audience-centred. Like a lawyer in a court of law, he intends to prove that Love is guilty as charged. Having suffered the overwhelming power of love, the rhetorical poet sets out to persuade us that his sufferings reflect an eternal truth. He therefore immediately universalizes the experience, tying it to traditional wisdom and literary models by borrowing his first half-line from one of Virgil's eclogues: 'Now I know what love is.' The second hemistich is also not Erasmus' own, but is taken word for word from a medieval adage: 'love is a madness in the mind.' The next verse likewise presents the feeling that love is an overpowering force by expressing it in a traditional image coupled with a proverbial comparison: love is a fire hotter than Aetna. In these ways the private experience that gave rise to the poem – quite possibly Erasmus' friendship for Servatius – is raised to the level of universal experience and placed in a literary, gnomic tradition.

The opening two lines indeed serve as a *propositio* to the poem as a whole. They accuse passionate love of being a madness of the mind, a burning fire in the heart.[91] In the following verses the poet-litigant will prove his case to the reader-judge by means of a series of commonplace arguments and mythological or biblical exempla, carefully arranged along the lines of a judicial speech. The *narrative* outlines the basic facts: it tells how love begins innocuously enough but in the end consumes body and mind (lines 3–18). The *argumentation* proves that love is all-powerful by adducing a series of classical and biblical exempla (lines 19–48). The *peroration* or epilogue sums up the argument and repeats the charge: love, which causes so much pain and suffering, is both wicked and cruel (lines 49–52). Thus the opening thesis is rhetorically amplified in order to arouse fear and loathing against *Amor*. Such amplification, as Erasmus says elsewhere, is 'the chief – indeed almost the only – dominating factor' in stirring up emotions.[92]

Of course Erasmus could not be content simply to instruct and persuade. He was not presenting a lawyer's brief but a rhetorical poem, and such poetry requires that the subject be treated in a way that gives readers pleasure and excites their admiration. To avoid tedium, therefore, the commonplace arguments, drawn from the storehouse of literary tradition and arranged according to the pattern of a forensic speech, had now to be embellished with elegant language, learned allusions, and rhetorical figures. A few instances may give the reader some appreciation of the laboured quality of these verses. Very prominent are the devices of reiteration. Even at first reading one cannot fail to notice the replication of phrases and half-lines from distich to distich or line to line (*anadiplosis*, lines 6–7, 8–9, 16–17, 32–3, and 50–1), or within the distich itself (*epanadiplosis*, lines 15–16, 31–2, and 51–2), or at the beginning of two consecutive distichs (*anaphora*, lines 19–21 and 35–7). This, however, by no means exhausts the variety of repetition in the elegy. Each of the pentameters up to line 48 ends with the word *amor* (*epiphora*). There is chiastic arrangement of words in lines 13–14: *unus amor ... duo / duo ... unus amor*, in lines 41–2: *amor temnit / temnit amor*, and in lines 51–2: *Seva parens ... puer improbus ille / Improbus ille puer ... seva parens*. Nor is the repetition always verbally exact. As in the Psalms we find here much parallelism of thought and language from verse to verse within the distich (*interpretatio*), for instance in lines 7–8, 13–14, and 31–2. These devices of repetition have the dual function of driving home the poet's charge against *Amor* and of adorning the expression through an artful arrangement of the words. There are many other figures of speech as well: *antithesis* in lines 17–18 and 35–40, *apostrophe* in lines 47, 50, and 52, and play on the root of words (*annominatio*), as for example in line 22 *domat indomitos non domitandus*, line 26 *vincere, vicit*, and line 38 *amarus amor*. Rhetorical questions (*interrogatio*) enliven the argument in lines 27–8, 29, 43, and 49 and arouse pathos. Indignation against love's power is also stirred by the device of *dubitatio* (line 51).[93] The device of passing over (*praeteritio*) in line 49 (*Singula quid memorem?*) demonstrates that the poet knows the virtue of making a long story short. There is no lack of telling epithets, in particular those for *amor*, varied from distich to distich. Other devices flatter the reader's ability to recognize classical and biblical allusions and reminiscences of Virgil, Ovid, Statius, Juvenal: Virgilian metaphors like *pascuntur* 'are nourished,' applied to love's fire in line 3, or maxims like those in the opening half-line or in lines 19 and 21: *Omnia vincit amor* 'Love conquers all,'[94] or the Ovidian adage half-hidden in line 7: *tacitisque edit intima flammis* 'eats away the innards with silent flames.'[95] The poem concludes with an extensive borrowing from Virgil's eighth eclogue that serves as an *epiphonema* – a figure that Erasmus defines as 'anything in the closing section of an utterance which strikes on the ear as shrewd and pungent.'[96]

This early elegy, which Erasmus to his credit never published, strikes us as little more than a rhetorical exercise. An apprentice in the workshop of the masters, the poet is only beginning to learn his craft. Lacking a personal voice to express universal experience in a compelling way, he appears to manipulate language as an end in itself. His rhetoric, too much in love with itself, fails to kindle our indignation against Love. But as we judge work like this, we should remember that it fails as a rhetorical poem, not as a romantic elegy wanting romance.

Rhetorically far more successful is no 104, 'On the mutability of time.' A *carpe diem* poem, this elegy begins by describing the flight of time and the imagined onset of wintry old age and then urges a friend to take advantage of youth while it lasts: 'Therefore, while the fierce goddess of fate still permits it, while the years still allow it, while youth rejoices and flourishes in its own season, let us make use of this time in our lives, lest we lose it in vain through our own lethargy. Let us seize, sweet friend, the days of our youth.' To convince the friend to whom these verses are addressed, the poet amplifies the infirmities of old age. But we should observe in passing that the old-age theme is here introduced primarily for rhetorical purposes, not because the poet wishes to demonstrate some 'neurasthenic fear of becoming old.'[97] His purpose is to persuade his friend to join him in taking advantage of fleeting youth; and to this end he amplifies the *incommoda* of old age.

The very same *carpe diem* theme – or so it would seem at first reading – also occurs at the beginning of the hortatory 'Elegy against a young man dissipating himself in lust' (95). Lines 7–20 of this poem present the classic structure of the argument that Erasmus is combatting: the hedonistic philosophy that we should 'eat, drink, and be merry, for tomorrow we shall die.' Here then is the foolish young man exhorting himself and his companions: 'While the propitious fates allow it, while we are in the bloom of youth, let us gratify our voluptuous desires in agreeable ways ... Let us make use of this time in our lives, while joyful youth still blooms on our tender cheeks, lest we lose it in vain through our own lethargy.' In this passage Erasmus recycles many lines from the somewhat earlier poem on the mutability of time. Reedijk remarks that it is 'curious' that our poet should have used the very same lines in arguing first for the premise that we should enjoy youth while it lasts, and later against the same point of view.[98] The repetition will appear less curious when we remember that a *locus communis* or 'common place' is, rhetorically speaking, an argument that can be used *in utramque partem*, both for and against. The two poems are directed at different readers and have dissimilar intentions. In the earlier poem Erasmus exhorts his friend to make good use of the springtime of life, while in the moral elegy he is inveighing against the pleasures of the flesh. The first is a poem of friendship, the second a sermon in verse, which does not just reject the epicurean *carpe diem* argument but proceeds to turn that argument around to argue that, since decrepit old age is inevitable, we should use our youth wisely and meditate on death so as to prepare ourselves for the life hereafter.

We may go further yet. The 'Elegiac poem on the mutability of time' does indeed stand in the tradition of the *carpe diem* exhortation as exemplified by Erasmus' putative model, a poem by Girolamo Balbi. Yet the resemblance is quite superficial. For how are we to imagine Erasmus and his friend making good use of life's spring? Most certainly not in lechery, drinking, and merrymaking like the dissipated young man addressed in poem 95. When Erasmus counsels his friend to 'make use of this time in our lives, lest we lose it in vain through our own lethargy,' he can hardly be speaking as a hedonist. He must be urging his friend to take advantage of youth by studying the ancients, by imitating and emulating the masters, by rivalling each other in writing letters and verses and prose works. In effect, he is turning the *carpe diem* argument topsy-turvy in this poem too: we should devote our youth to studies, while it lasts, for soon enough old age and death will befall us.

Within the context of Erasmus' other writings, then, the poem on the mutability of time is at bottom very similar to the paraenetic 'Elegy against a young man dissipating himself in lust.' Both present an inverted *carpe diem* argument in which the hedonistic exhortation is turned on its head – as an argument against lethargy and hedonism and for a life of studies, virtue, and godliness. Erasmus himself analysed this inversion of the *carpe diem* argument many years later in his *Ecclesiastes*.[99] In a lengthy discussion of rhetorical figures useful in sermons he mentions among others the device of βιαιου (in Latin *violentum, reflexio*). He explains this figure as wresting the opponent's weapon out of his hands and using it against him.[100] The example he offers is the Christian inversion of the hedonistic *carpe diem* theme: 'Horace frequently exhorts us to enjoy the pleasures of life with this argument, that man's life is both short and uncertain. But on the contrary: for that reason we should not waste any part of life in debauchery; rather we should devote it instead wholly to virtue, precisely because life is brief and uncertain.'

The inversion of the *carpe diem* argument is a very ancient device. Ecclesiastes 12:1–7 lists the disasters of old age in order to admonish the young to 'remember also your Creator in the days of your youth, before the evil days come, and the years draw nigh, when you will say, "I have no pleasure in them."' Ovid uses the same inverted argument in his *Ars amatoria* 2.113–22 to exhort the young to cultivate the intellect by studying the humanities and the two languages, Latin and Greek. He reminds them that they must not rely on youthful beauty, for good looks will soon wilt and give way to the grey hair and wrinkles of old age. Only the things of the mind can last a lifetime:

> Beauty is a fragile good. It diminishes with increasing age and is destroyed by the passage of time. Violets and opened lilies do not bloom forever, and the thorn is left bare after it loses the rose. Your hair too, handsome youth, will soon turn grey. Soon wrinkles will furrow your body. Now shape your mind, so that it may last, and add it to your good looks, for it alone endures until death. Strive to cultivate the intellect with the liberal arts and to learn both Latin and Greek.

Ovid's argument resurfaces from time to time during the Middle Ages and the early Renaissance, for instance in the poetry of Alcuin and the correspondence of Enea Silvio de' Piccolomini.[101] In Erasmus' educational and moral writings it becomes a leitmotiv. At Steyn he urges Servatius to shake off his sluggishness, pursue literary studies, and start writing: 'Before fleeting youth departs, therefore, acquire for yourself now the means of enjoying old age.' And quoting Ovid he adds: 'Now shape thy mind to last, and mould its beauty; / Only man's mind endures until his end.'[102] He gives the same advice to Sasbout: 'I could name to you ... very many persons ... who ... are bitterly remorseful, when it is too late, because they see that the time of youth, which is proper for the study of literature, has slipped away between their fingers. So, my sweetest Sasbout, while your age is strong and fresh follow the ant in garnering for yourself that which may delight and nourish your old age: amass in youth what you would enjoy as an old man.'[103] In a letter of spring 1497 he advises his pupil Christian Northoff: 'Always keep fixed in your heart Pliny's dictum that all the time which one fails to devote to study is wasted, and reflect that youth is the most fleeting thing on earth, and that when once it has fled away it never returns.'[104] And in *De pueris instituendis*, written in Italy around 1509, he once again takes up the argument in words that closely recall the ones he had employed a few years earlier in his 'Poem on the troubles of old age' (2):

> Once our years have flown by – and how swiftly they fly! – they cannot be recalled by any magic spell. Poets talk nonsense when they speak of a fountain from which the aged can draw, as it were, a second youth, and doctors practise deception when they promise a renewed vitality to the old through some mysterious quintessence. There is no remedy to restore wasted years; we must husband them, therefore, with the utmost care.[105]

IV
THE 'POEM ON THE TROUBLES OF OLD AGE'

Written in August 1506 not long before his fortieth birthday, when the humanist was on his way to Turin to receive the degree of doctor of theology, the 'Poem on the troubles of old age' (2) has always been Erasmus' best known and best loved poetic work. In our own century it has received special attention, not only for its aesthetic qualities but also for its unusually personal tone and autobiographical character. Indeed, some modern critics have hailed the work as a romantic poem before romanticism: introspective and melancholy at the thought of fleeting youth, centred on the poet rather than the audience, lyrical rather than rhetorical.[106] We do well to recall, however, that Erasmus in the *Varia epigrammata* of January 1507 entitled it 'Poem on the flight of human life.' And in later years, when he began to arrange his writings in preparation for a complete edition, he wanted the poem placed in the fourth group, among the moral works that contribute to the building of character. Philip Melanchthon understood this when he urged young people to commit it to memory.[107] The church historian Ernst-Wilhelm Kohls understood this when he recognized that the poem is in part a meditation on death and the life to come.[108] We too should move beyond our interest in the autobiographical and psychological elements to see the poem within the broader context of Erasmus' rhetorical poetics and paraenetic intentions. Approaching the halfway point in life's arc, the nearly forty-year-old poet meditates on the rapid approach of old age and on the flight of youth. He thereupon exhorts himself – and implicitly his reader as well – to make good use of the time left to him. While he is still of sound mind and body, before the winter of decrepit old age arrives, he resolves henceforward to devote himself wholly to Christ.

True to its author's character, the 'Poem on the troubles of old age' is a deeply Christian and profoundly experienced piece of work. As in his earlier poetry, however, Erasmus' personal experience is realized in conventional rhetorical structures and is universalized by being cast in a traditional literary mould. The poem's opening passage detailing the horrors of decrepitude confesses, to be sure, a very human fear at the approach of old age; Reedijk even senses here something like a 'sudden panic' on the poet's part.[109] But that fear, precisely by being both personal and universal, lends this passage its profoundly rhetorical pathos, and by that token its power to attract our attention and open our eyes to the brevity of youth. The description of decrepitude, in other words, plays an important functional role within the poem. From a rhetorical perspective, the section is not so much an unbosoming of private emotion as an argument calculated to move the reader to take advantage of what is left of youth and life and use it wisely. The old-age theme thus becomes once again the fundamental argument in an inverted *carpe diem* poem. It is thematically no different from the argument Erasmus had offered fifteen years earlier in his hortatory elegy urging a dissipated young man to meditate on old age and death, so as to commit himself henceforth to a life of Christian piety. The difference between the two poems is not in theme or argument, but rather in the greater intensity of Erasmus' language and above all in the far deeper subtlety of his rhetorical technique. Instead of berating the foolish readers who slumber in their belief that youth will last forever and that they will never grow old and die, as he did in the earlier paraenetic poem,[110] Erasmus now shrewdly introduces himself as one of those fools caught up in the dream of eternal youth. But having been roused at last from his delusion by being confronted with the horrors of old age, the poet as exemplary Everyman also shows us the way out. Converted, he exhorts himself to give up the trifling pleasures of youth and devote himself to Christ.

STRUCTURE

In keeping with the inverted *carpe diem* argument, the poem is divided into two main parts. The first may be labelled the *dissuasio*, for here the poet dissuades himself from staying on his present course. The second is the *exhortatio*, in which the speaker urges himself (and, through his own example, the reader) to make up for lost time and use it wisely. These two central sections are framed by a brief introduction addressed to the physician Guillaume Cop and an equally brief epilogue directed to Christ.

Exordium (lines 1–9)

The poem is in the first instance addressed to Guillaume Cop and seeks to gain his attention and favour (*captatio benevolentiae*) through hyperbolic praise: Cop is able to cure all diseases save one – old age, the only disease for which medicine has found no cure. The compliments to Cop are not superfluous to the argument, as is sometimes asserted, and cannot be dropped from the poem without doing violence to its rhetorical structure and argument.[111] The famed physician, Erasmus assures us, will vouch for the accuracy of his description of the aetiology, symptoms, and course of the disease known as old age and will moreover attest that it is incurable. As the poet reminds us in the epilogue, only the heavenly physician, Christ, can grant us eternal youth.

Dissuasio (lines 10–185)
In this section, the first of the poem's two main parts, Erasmus seeks to awaken his readers from their lethargy and persuade them to abandon their present way of thinking. He does this by relentlessly listing the *incommoda* of old age and thereupon disabusing his shocked readers of any and all false hopes that youth can be eternal. In order to gain our confidence and cure us of our delusion that we will not grow old and die, Erasmus throughout this section wears the mask of Everyman. He thus pretends that he is suffering from the same delusion of which he is trying to cure his reader. In this regard it is worthwhile to study the enlightening passage in *De conscribendis epistolis* where Erasmus explains his rhetorical strategy as follows: 'those who are eager to cure [victims of delusion] sometimes pretend that they themselves are victims of the same evil. Then once they have gained their good will, they easily convince them of the cure, and by this gradual approach remove the false imaginings in the end.'[112] He recommends the same technique in *Ecclesiastes,* adding that wearing a mask like this is not hypocrisy, but Christian charity.[113]

We might add parenthetically here that Boethius' *Consolation of Philosophy* uses essentially the same device of insinuation. Languishing in his jail cell, Boethius finds himself aged prematurely because of his sorrows. And while lamenting his fate, this Everyman is confronted by Philosophy, who gradually opens his eyes and wakes him out of his slumber and delusions. Erasmus follows the same underlying strategy also in his *Praise of Folly,* though of course the personae are in each case quite different. There too he wears a mask – the mask of folly – in order to reach and cure the deluded. And by slowly, humorously, paradoxically unmasking the wisdom of man, which is mere foolishness in the eyes of God, he ultimately leads his readers to see the wisdom of God, which is folly to unredeemed mankind.[114]

Because Erasmus adopts the persona of Everyman – the fool caught up in the pleasures and ambitions of youth – the tone in this portion of the poem is that of a melancholy lament for the rapid flight of life's springtime.[115] He thus amplifies a commonplace expressed succinctly in Virgil's famous complaint: *Sed fugit interea, fugit inreparabile tempus, / singula dum capti circumvectamur amore* 'But meanwhile time flies away unrecoverable while we, enthralled by love of our theme, make the rounds of all things'[116] – a passage to which he pointedly alludes in line 101.

The dominant emotions that Erasmus intends to arouse in the *dissuasio* are fear and a sense of hopelessness.[117] In accordance with these goals the section is subdivided further, the first part amplifying the proverbial thought that youth flies, the second elaborating the maxim that youth, once lost, is irrecoverable.

In the first part (lines 10–114) Erasmus artfully amplifies the commonplace that youth flies by focusing first on the loss of youth's blessings in old age and then, in a twofold variation of perspective, on the rapidity with which youth is lost. The dominant emotion that Erasmus intends to arouse is fear.

1/ Since the poem began by addressing a physician, Erasmus goes on to describe the aetiology, symptoms, and course of that dread disease, old age (lines 10–29). The troubles of old age, presented as the progressive loss of the blessings of youth, are listed cumulatively to increase the pathos. For the positive aspects of ageing, of which Erasmus was well aware, this is clearly not the place.[118] The catalogue of the ills of decrepitude, based on numerous literary models, culminates in a rhetorical question: should we not call this decline a slow death? The Ovidian phrase 'a slow death' recalls similar definitions of old age in ancient and medieval literature.

2/ Envious Fates! Unlike the deer and the crow, man soon grows old. Old age attacks the body at thirty-five, the mind at forty-nine, according to Aristotle. The poet's own experience confirms the ancient philosopher's observation: at nearly forty Erasmus is indeed beginning to see the effects of old age on his own body. His spring has come to an end, his winter is about to begin (lines 29–69).

3/ The theme already amplified in the preceding section is now restated through a change of perspective, from the point of view of youth. How youth flies! (lines 70–114) The commonplace is amplified rhetorically (lines 70–8): 'youth' is restated five times, 'flies' two times. A series of comparisons follows (lines 79–88). The first series is negative ('not so fast are ...'), with two similes; the second series is positive ('just so fast are ...'), with two more similes. Like the preceding one, this segment concludes with an exemplum: Erasmus' youth has been flying away all the while; old age has been creeping up on him as he was growing up and becoming a scholar.

The second section of the *dissuasio* (lines 115–85) also amplifies the commonplace that time flies, but with emphasis on the fact that time, the greatest treasure, can never be recovered once it has been lost. One by one our foolish fancies are stripped from us. In the end we must admit with the poet: there can be no hope of eternal youth. The basic emotion aroused in this section is hopelessness. The argument is threefold.

1/ Youth is a treasure (lines 115–25). It is more valuable than all the purple, gems, and gold in the world. Why do we waste youth, our 'golden age,' on trifles?

2/ Youth cannot be recovered once lost (lines 126–71). While other treasures can be restored or recovered, nothing can bring back our youth once it has passed: no sorceresses, no gods and goddesses, no demigod-physician like Chiron. Magic rings, drugs, and incantations are of no avail against old age. Sun and moon and spring return in their cycles and are perpetually renewed. But once man's brief spring is over, he grows old and dies.

3/ We realize these facts too late (lines 172–85). Only when youth has flown do we become aware of its value. Then we suddenly discover that we have squandered a treasure we should have invested wisely. The section concludes with an exemplum: Erasmus has been caught unawares by the stealthy advance of time. He has spent the first half of his life on trifles.

Exhortatio (lines 186–242)

The exhortation amplifies the adage: use your time wisely. Erasmus continues to wear the mask of Everyman by urging himself to action. The dominant emotion to be aroused in the exhortation is hope: it is not too late to mend our ways. This second main section of the poem is subdivided into three parts.

1/ Wake up, Erasmus, while there is still time! (lines 186–210) While you still have breath in you, strive with might and main to make up for lost time. You are only on the threshold of old age! The symptoms of old age are still only very slight. You have only begun the autumn of life, but remember that your winter is drawing ever closer.

2/ Therefore use your time wisely by devoting the remainder of your life to Christ, not the things of this world (lines 211–32). Farewell to the pleasures and pursuits of youth! These have no meaning except through Christ. Make him your all in all, let him be your Muses, your honour, your delight! Devote yourself wholly to Christ!

3/ Do not worry about the body (lines 233–42). Christ will be your all in all. The body will be of no concern (as they say) to Hippocleides, as long as the soul remains pure. The body will be reunited with the mind on Judgment Day, at the resurrection of the dead. Then we shall enjoy spring eternal.

Epilogus (lines 243–6)
The epilogue is in the form of a prayer. May Christ, the true author and redeemer of life, the giver of strength, make these resolutions come true.

MODELS AND TRADITIONS
Like almost all neo-Latin poetry, Erasmus' 'Poem on the troubles of old age' stands squarely within literary tradition. Its structure, as we saw, is that of the traditional *carpe diem* argument, inverted to Christian use. In its rhetorical strategy it follows Boethius' *Consolation of Philosophy*. But in its use of autobiographical elements, so captivating to the modern reader, it is modelled above all on Prudentius' *Praefatio*.

Prudentius' *Praefatio* is a poetic foreword to an edition of his collected poems. Its argument develops along the following lines: I have lived fifty-seven years and am on the threshold of old age. What profitable thing have I done in all this time? I went to grammar school and then studied rhetoric. As a young man I indulged in the pleasures of the flesh. After that I became a lawyer eager for victory. I twice rose to the rank of governor of famous cities and later became an important member of the emperor's court. And while I was thus engaged in all kinds of activities, white-haired old age suddenly stole upon me. Now I realize how life has sped away. What will these things profit me after I am dead? My sinning soul must put off her folly. Let me henceforth devote myself wholly to God and write only on sacred themes. And while I write or speak of these themes, O may I fly forth in freedom from the bonds of the body to heaven![119]

Here, if anywhere, is the inspiration for the 'Poem on the troubles of old age.' The conventional inverted *carpe diem* argument had, of course, been in Erasmus' mind for a long time already. He may well have been involuntarily reminded of the theme as he rode through the Alps in that August of 1506 and listened in dismay to the foolish quarrels of his companions. Withdrawing from them, he began to meditate on the delusions of mankind, so oblivious to life's flight into old age and death. He thought of his own studies thus far, the flight of his own youth, the great goals he had set for himself. And then it must have come to him in a burst of creative insight. Upon the stock of the inverted *carpe diem* exhortation he would graft the outline of Prudentius' 'Preface.' Like Prudentius he would use the details of his own life's story as an exemplum of the flight of human life and the need to make wise use of it, while there is still time. And like Boethius he would make himself a fool in order to cure the delusions of his readers.

Erasmus' main problem in adapting Prudentius' *Praefatio* to his own use must have lain in the fact that the early Christian poet was fifty-seven years old at the time of writing and actually, according to classical terminology, on the threshold of old age. Erasmus, on the other hand, was just approaching his fortieth birthday. By the classical and patristic standard of the four seasons or ages of man – the system he uses everywhere else in his writings – Erasmus was just then about to leave the summer of life (*iuventus* 'youth') and enter its autumn (*virilitas* 'manhood'). By that standard, of course, he could not very well use himself as the exemplum of a man on the threshold of old age. But there were other traditions on which he could fall back. The simplest scheme of all was the division of life into two parts: youth, up to age thirty-five or forty, followed by old age until age seventy or eighty (Ps 90:10). This division of life into two halves also underlies the late-medieval nomenclature for the four ages of man. In this originally Arabic scheme, widely diffused since its introduction into the Latin West in the eleventh century, the autumn of life was said to begin at either age thirty-five or forty and was called *senectus* 'old age.' The winter of life, known as *senium* 'decrepitude,' set in at age sixty.[120]

Thus, by replacing the standard ancient terms for the autumn and winter of life with the corresponding late-medieval ones, Erasmus was able to introduce himself not only as an example of the flight of life but also of the sudden transition from youth to old age. At nearly age forty he could now offer himself as proof that life's spring and summer pass all too quickly into autumn and winter. In other words, he was not at all *fancying* himself across the threshold of old age, as Huizinga once put it,[121] but was describing an objective, inevitable, irreversible event. Ageing, he says, is an insidious process that no one can escape. It must of necessity befall every one of us – even you, dear reader of this poem, who may still be caught up in your slumber. Therefore, wake up! Youth does not last. No miracle drugs, no fountain of youth, no magic arts can bring it back once it is gone. Therefore make good use of it while you still may, before old age comes and death. Devote your life to Christ!

Horace, in his *Ars poetica* 102–3, tells writers that 'if you would have me weep, you must first feel grief yourself.' Erasmus held the same opinion. A preacher who wishes to convert his flock must have a pure and Christian heart himself, for the word is the mirror of the soul.[122] Of Erasmus' sincerity in expressing his disdain for the world and meditating on the hereafter there can be no question: these are the cardinal themes of his writings throughout his career,[123] beginning with his turn toward sacred poetry in the winter of 1490–1. When he says that he will give up everything that has been dear to him – his secular studies and ambitions, philosophy, poetry, and rhetoric – he is using the language of the *contemptus mundi* tradition to say that he will not see these pursuits as ends in themselves, but will, like Prudentius before him, put his talents wholly in the service of Christ, to adorn his temple. Christ will be his all in all: his studies, his Muses, his Apollo, his Peitho.[124] It is a pledge he had made years before at Steyn; it is a commitment he hereby exemplarily renews. For, as he declares in his *Ciceronianus*: 'This is the purpose of studying the basic disciplines, of studying philosophy, of studying eloquence, to know Christ, to celebrate the glory of Christ. This is the goal of all learning and all eloquence.'[125]

V
ARRANGEMENT, TEXTS, AND EDITORIAL PRINCIPLES

In 1524 Erasmus took stock of his writings and arranged them into volumes in case someone should wish to do for him what Tiro had done for Cicero. 'Miscellaneous poems, on other than religious subjects' were to be included in the first volume of his works concerning 'literature and education.' The 'Poem on the troubles of old age' (2) was to be placed in the fourth volume devoted to those 'works which contribute to the building of character.' The fifth volume was to be 'allocated to works of religious instruction.' Among the devotional poems that belong in this class he singled out 'The expostulation of Jesus with mankind' (43), 'On the shed where the boy Jesus was born' (42), and the 'Ode in praise of Michael and all the angels' (50).[126]

These suggestions were faithfully carried out in the *Opera omnia* published by Hieronymus Froben and Nicolaus Episcopius at Basel in 1538–42 and again in the *Opera omnia* edited by Jean Leclerc and printed by Pieter vander Aa at Leiden in 1703–6. Naturally, only the poems published by Erasmus himself were included in volumes I, IV, and V of the Basel and Leiden editions. By 1706, however, Leclerc had come into possession of a hitherto unpublished manuscript copied in 1570, formerly belonging to Petrus Scriverius and containing among other writings of Erasmus a series of his early poems. These works, both secular and religious in theme, were published in volume VIII of the Leiden edition.[127]

Since 1706 many more of Erasmus' juvenilia have come to light – poems that the mature humanist would certainly have preferred to keep slumbering in oblivion.[128] Preserved Smith, for example, printed three unpublished poems from MS Egerton 1651 (British Library) in Appendix III of his *Erasmus* (1923; repr New York 1962) 453–7. Albert Hyma published five others from Gouda MS 1323 (Town Archives of Gouda) in Appendix A of *The Youth of Erasmus* (Ann Arbor 1930) 221–37. These and other poems not included in the Leiden edition were subsequently gathered together in Wallace K. Ferguson *Erasmi opuscula: A Supplement to the Opera omnia* (The Hague 1933) 1–37 and 362–7. It was not until 1956, however, that Cornelis Reedijk took the momentous step of collecting all the known poems in his doctoral dissertation, a critical and annotated edition of *The Poems of Desiderius Erasmus* (Leiden 1956). This book has been the standard edition of Erasmus' poetry ever since. Recently, however, Dr Reedijk's text has been criticized for a number of editorial lapses.[129] The present volume, accordingly, offers a new text of the poems, in an arrangement quite different from the one adopted by the Basel and Leiden editions on the one hand and Reedijk's edition on the other.

Whereas the basic organizing principle in Erasmus' own scheme was thematic, Reedijk arranged the poems according to the dates of their composition. This chronological arrangement was intended to give the reader a clearer picture of Erasmus' development as a poet. 'For,' as Reedijk put it, 'apart from their literary qualities ... Erasmus' poems may prove to have a certain value as documents marking the successive phases of his intellectual and spiritual development and of his relations with his contemporaries.'[130] In practice, the chronological arrangement of the poems has been fraught with problems. Like many of the early letters, the poems are largely undated. The provisional datings assigned to them are subject to sometimes quite drastic revision as research uncovers further evidence. For example, the 'Paean to St Mary,' the 'Poem on the preternatural signs that occurred at the death of Christ,' and the 'Heroic poem on the feast of Easter' (Reedijk nos 19–21 / CWE nos 110–12) have now been redated from 1489 to 1499. The bucolic poem, which Reedijk placed at the head of his edition as the oldest of Erasmus' poems (Deventer 1483), was more probably written at Steyn in 1487; and his turn to paraenetic and sacred poetry seems to have taken place in winter 1490–1 rather than in 1489. Such revisions in the chronology seriously dislocate Reedijk's chronological numbering.

Erasmus himself published less than half of his total poetic output. Many of his early poems were *progymnasmata* that he had no intention of ever publishing. Accordingly, when such poems as the defence against the barbarians (93) and the three moral satires (94–6) were printed at Gouda by Reyner Snoy in 1513, Erasmus was understandably embarrassed and offended. Even though Reedijk takes considerable pains to point out circumstances like these, the chronological principle forces him to disregard Erasmus' discomfiture. Hence poems that Erasmus was loath to see printed now stand next to those that he gladly published of his own accord. In Reedijk's edition, for instance, we have to work our way through a sizeable number of juvenilia before we come to an ode like 'On the shed where the boy Jesus was born' (Reedijk no 33), the first poem that Erasmus published. That the mass of apprentice works has tended to cloud the modern reader's judgment of Erasmus' more finished and mature pieces is as undeniable as it is unfortunate.

To avoid difficulties of the sort just described, we have adopted the following arrangement. We begin with the poems printed during Erasmus' lifetime and then present those published after his death. These two main groups are divided into the following categories: poems in *Epigrammata* (Basel: J. Froben, March 1518); poems not in the 1518 *Epigrammata* but published by Erasmus elsewhere; poems published in Erasmus' lifetime without his prior consent; poems published after Erasmus' death. To these four groups, which constitute the main body of his poems, we append two others: poems embedded in Erasmus' prose works; and poems dubiously ascribed to Erasmus.

1/ Poems in *Epigrammata* (Basel: J. Froben, March 1518): nos 1–61

Either before travelling to Italy in August 1506 or later that autumn, while he was already in Italy, Erasmus collected a number of his previously published and unpublished poems and had them printed at Paris by Jean Petit and Josse Bade. The slim volume of devotional and occasional verse was published under the title *Varia epigrammata* on 8 January 1507. It was bound together with his *Adagiorum collectanea* (24 December 1506), though the two parts also circulated as separate books.

Almost a decade later, in 1515, Erasmus seems to have been planning to update his collected poems and publish them in conjunction with epigrams by Andrea Ammonio.[131] If so, nothing came of the project. During 1517, however, Erasmus oversaw the publication of Thomas More's *Utopia* and epigrams together with some of his own works.[132] The fruits of this planning were two handsome volumes, published at Basel by Johann Froben in 1517–18. Froben had originally intended to publish a single volume including translations of Lucian by More and Erasmus, Erasmus' *Querela pacis, Declamatio de morte*, and epigrams, and More's *Utopia* and epigrams. But as the volume grew too large, it had to be divided into two parts, the first of which was published in December 1517. The second part, which included *Utopia* and the two sets of epigrams, came out in March 1518 under the following title: *De optimo reip. statu deque nova insula Utopia libellus vere aureus, nec minus salutaris quam festivus, clarissimi disertissimique viri Thomae Mori inclytae civitatis Londinensis civis et vicecomitis. Epigrammata clarissimi disertissimique viri Thomae Mori, pleraque e Graecis versa. Epigrammata Des. Erasmi Roterodami.*[133]

Nowhere in the extant correspondence does Erasmus specifically mention that he was planning to include a new collection of his own poems. In fact Froben's preface says that in response to popular demand it was he who gathered up Erasmus' poems with the assistance of Beatus Rhenanus and Bruno Amerbach. Erasmus follows the same line in his letter to Johann von

Botzheim: 'In no kind of verse have I had less practice than in epigrams; yet sometimes while out walking, or even over the wine, I have at different times thrown off a certain number, some of which have been put together by friends over-zealous for my reputation, and published in Basel; and to make them even more ridiculous, they appended them to the epigrams of Thomas More, who is a master of the art.'[134] That Erasmus' *Epigrammata* were published by over-zealous friends without his express approval is almost certainly a fiction. It is a formula of affected modesty that he uses as early as November 1495 in Ep 47, the preface to his first collection of verse, *De casa natalitia Iesu*.[135] Considering his deep involvement in the publication of the joint volume, there can be no doubt that Erasmus had, at the very least, a hand in selecting and arranging his own poems.[136] At no time did he express regret or dismay at their publication, neither in March 1518 nor in November–December of the same year, when Froben published a second edition of the volume.

The *Epigrammata* of 1518, in any case, incorporates most of the poems that Erasmus had already published of his own accord and adds seven previously unpublished ones. We print the poems here in the order of *1518*. The backbone of this collection is a reprint of the *Varia epigrammata* of 8 January 1507 (poems 2 and 4–42 in the present edition). Following this series are 'The expostulation of Jesus with mankind' (43), the epigrams written for John Colet's school for boys at St Paul's (44–8), and the 'Epitaph for a drunken jokester' (52), which were first published in *Concio de puero Iesu* (Paris 1511?). 'Basic principles of Christian conduct' (49) was originally published in *Opuscula aliquot Erasmo Roterodamo castigatore* (Louvain: D. Martens 1514). Next comes the 'Ode in praise of Michael and all the angels' (50), which had been printed in Erasmus' *De casa natalitia Iesu* (Paris: A. Denidel [1496?]), but had not been included in the *Varia epigrammata*, perhaps because of its length. The 1518 volume then adds a series of poems more recently published. The Greek 'Votive offering to the Virgin of Walsingham in Britain' (51) comes from *Lucubrationes* (Strasbourg: M. Schürer 1515). The 'Praise of Sélestat' (53) was first printed with four of Erasmus' letters in *Iani Damiani Senensis ad Leonem X. Pont. Max. de expeditione in Turcas Elegeia* (Basel: J. Froben 1515). The epigrams for the Alsatian humanists Johannes Sapidus, Sebastian Brant, and Thomas Vogler (3 and 54–5) had earlier appeared together with *De duplici copia verborum ac rerum commentarii* (Strasbourg: M. Schürer 1514). Seven of the poems in the 1518 *Epigrammata* had never been printed before. To underline their newness – and to help the book sell better – they were placed at the beginning and end of the collection: the 'Hymn in praise of St Ann' (1), probably written in the winter of 1490–1 and revised a decade later, and six epigrams (56–61) composed between 1511 and 1516.

2/ Poems not in *1518*, but published by Erasmus elsewhere: nos 62–92
Our copy-text for the poems in this section is their first edition. They are arranged in chronological order, according to their dates of composition. Four of them were already in print before the *Varia epigrammata* of 8 January 1507 but were not included in that collection. The poem to Antoon van Bergen on the death of his brother Hendrik (62) may have been omitted because of Antoon's stinginess as a patron. The cento from Homer (63) and the welcome-back poem to Archduke Philip the Handsome (64), printed at Antwerp in early 1504, were too closely associated with the *Panegyricus* to be separated from it; the encomiastic poem, like the prose panegyric, was in any case written against the grain and not to Erasmus' taste. The verses to Archbishop William Warham (65) had just been printed by Bade in September 1506 and did not need to be reprinted in the *Varia epigrammata*. The epitaph for Jacques de Croy (66), though written in c November 1516(?), was first published in *Auctarium selectarum aliquot epistolarum* (Basel: J. Froben, August 1518). No 67, a liminary poem for Bernard André's collection of hymns, which had been published by Bade in Paris in July 1517, may have been deliberately excluded from the *Epigrammata* of March 1518.[137] The remaining poems in this section – mainly epitaphs and occasional verses, but also the votive poem to Ste Geneviève (88) – were composed after the publication of the March 1518 edition of the *Epigrammata*.

3/ Poems published without Erasmus' consent: nos 93–7
This group comprises five early poems originally published without Erasmus' consent by Reyner Snoy in *Silva carminum antehac nunquam impressorum* (Gouda: A. Gauter 1513). They are: no 93, written half by Erasmus, half by his friend Cornelis Gerard, against the barbarians who decry ancient eloquence; nos 94–6, three hortatory elegies or 'satires' on false goals, lechery, and greed; and no 97, a poem on the power of money. Erasmus later revised nos 94–7 slightly and published them, albeit with a show of embarrassment and reluctance, in *Progymnasmata quaedam primae adolescentiae Erasmi* (Louvain: D. Martens 1521). We have adopted the authorized edition of 1521 as the copy-text of the three hortatory elegies (94–6) and *De nummo* (97). The *Apologia Herasmi et Cornelii adversus barbaros* (93) is not included in the authorized edition. We therefore print it according to Snoy's text.

4/ Poems published after Erasmus' death: nos 98–127
Here we include poems that Erasmus for one reason or another did not publish himself. Most of them have come down to us in sixteenth-century manuscripts; several are known only in editions printed in the first hundred years after Erasmus' death. Poems found in the three principal manuscripts are reprinted in the same order in which they occur there; the remaining

poems have been arranged in chronological order, according to the conjectural or known dates of composition. The section is arranged as follows:
– Poems in Gouda MS 1323: nos 98–102. This manuscript, which is kept in the Town Archives of Gouda (Librije coll. 1323), contains a miscellany of letters and poems by Erasmus, Cornelis Gerard, Willem Hermans, and others, as well as extracts from books by various authors. The first third of it was written by a monk at Steyn monastery ('Hand A') in about 1520, while the remaining two-thirds were written by another monk ('Hand B') in about 1590. The earlier part, written by Hand A, is our only source for poems 98–101 and offers a version of *Carmen buccolicum* (102) that appears to be closer to the archetype than that given in the later MS Scriverius. It also contains the epigram to Johannes Sapidus (3), first published in 1514. The manuscript has been described in some detail by Allen; further information is provided by J.W.E. Klein.[138] After Steyn burned down in 1549 the monks moved the monastery library to Gouda. For a time the library was kept at the house of one of the last monks from Steyn, Herman Jacobsz Blij. After Blij's death in 1599 the town magistrates confiscated the library and had a catalogue drawn up. They left the books and manuscripts for the time being in the charge of the last canon regular from Steyn, Cornelis Adriaensz Diephorst. Part of this library, as Klein notes, was moved to the Librije, the Gouda Town Library, in 1611. When Diephorst died in 1637, a new inventory was drawn up; in 1641 the remainder of the old Steyn library was moved to the Gouda Librije. Among the manuscripts of Erasmus' works transferred in 1641 were Gouda MS 1323 as well as Gouda MS 1324 (Librije coll. 1324), copied by Hand A around 1524. The poems by Erasmus (98–102) and two poems by Willem Hermans were first published from Gouda MS 1323 in Hyma *Youth* Appendix A, 221–37.
– Poems in MS Scriverius: nos 103–14. This manuscript, formerly in 's-Hertogenbosch but now in the library of the Katholieke Universiteit Brabant, Tilburg, contains a revised version of *Carmen buccolicum* (102) and is our only source for nos 103–14. It also offers a text of *Apologia Herasmi et Cornelii adversus barbaros* (93), earlier printed in Snoy's *Silva carminum* (Gouda 1513), together with the epilogue by Cornelis Gerard (135), which Snoy did not include, as well as numerous letters to and from Erasmus, his *Oratio de pace et discordia, Oratio funebris* (followed by poems 113–14), and *Conflictus Thaliae et Barbariei* (see headnote on poem 128 below). MS Scriverius is a copy, made by the Dutch scholar Bonaventura Vulcanius in 1570, of a manuscript that he had acquired from the library of the Court of Holland.[139] Vulcanius' 1570 copy subsequently came into the possession of Petrus Scriverius (1576–1660) and later served as Leclerc's copy-text for poems 102–14,

93, and 135 in LB VIII. The manuscript was rediscovered in 's-Hertogenbosch and thoroughly described by A.A.J. Karthon.[140]

– Poems in British Library MS Egerton 1651: nos 115–17. Besides being our only source for nos 115–17, this manuscript contains Ep 104 (the dedicatory letter for Erasmus' poem in praise of Britain and her royal family, no 4) as well as nos 1, 5, 6, 7, and 50, with numerous minor and major deviations from the texts already published or printed later. Allen suggests that this 'illuminated MS ... is very likely a special copy of some of Erasmus' poems prepared for presentation to Prince Henry' after Erasmus' visit to Eltham Palace in the autumn of 1499.[141] But the manuscript, despite Allen's assertion, is not illuminated; indeed, it is so carelessly written that the scribe even began copying out the poem to Skelton (115) that he had already finished a few leaves before. It is therefore quite unlikely that the manuscript was ever intended to be a presentation copy. The fact that the poem in praise of Britain (4) is missing also argues against Allen's assumption. Moreover the manuscript contains two poems addressed to Gaguin (5 and 6) as well as an epigram by Gaguin who, as Erasmus must surely have known, had written a Latin epigram in early 1490 rudely accusing the English and Henry VII of deceitfulness, ingratitude, and bellicosity, and warning them to prepare for war. Gaguin, in turn, had been severely taken to task for this by Bernard André and other writers at the English court.[142] Since we may assume that Erasmus would not have wanted to raise memories of that incident at the royal court in 1499, the manuscript as we have it cannot have been intended for presentation to the prince. It begins with what is evidently an early version of Ep 104 (written and sent to Prince Henry in early autumn 1499 and first printed in revised form in c July 1500). From these dates it appears that the manuscript was copied between October 1499 and July 1500 from a manuscript that Erasmus had circulated among his friends (at Oxford?) before his return to the Continent in late January 1500.[143]

– Poems from other sources: nos 118–27. These have been arranged in chronological order, according to their conjectural or known dates of composition. Their provenance is described in the headnotes to each of the poems.

5/ Poems embedded in Erasmus' prose works: nos 128–34

In this section we gather together the verses that occur in *Conflictus Thaliae et Barbariei*, *Colloquia* (in the order of their publication), the introit and sequence of *Virginis Matris apud Lauretum cultae liturgia*, and *Responsio ad Petri Cursii defensionem*. Like Reedijk, we have excluded the series of isolated verses in the colloquy *Impostura* (ASD I-3 601–2), written in different metres but disguised as prose; we have also excluded the countless verse translations that Erasmus inserted into his *Adagia* and other prose works.

6/ Poems dubiously ascribed to Erasmus: nos 135–44

These are poems that have been ascribed with varying degrees of probability to Erasmus. They are arranged in their presumed chronological order of composition.

Several poems that Erasmus mentions in his correspondence seem to have disappeared without a trace. Cornelis Reedijk has catalogued them in 'Verdwenen poëzie van Erasmus' *Het boek* 31 (1952–4) 113–20 and in *The Poems* Appendix IV, 397–400. Some of these poems, discussed in two letters exchanged between Johannes Sixtinus and Erasmus in late October 1499 (Epp 112–13), have now been identified with extant ones and can thus be struck from Reedijk's list.[144] A few others hitherto regarded as lost were in all likelihood never written:

– Both Allen and Reedijk suggest that Allen Ep 28:18–23 / CWE Ep 28:18–22 might refer to 'some verses to win the favour of David of Burgundy, Bishop of Utrecht.'[145] The context of the letter, however, does not bear this out. Erasmus says only that a number of his poems were taken partly to Alexander Hegius and Bartholomäus Zehender in Deventer and partly to Utrecht (presumably to the bishop).

– Reedijk further assumes that the reference to an *epitaphium* for Archduke Philip the Handsome in Allen Ep 205:24–6 / CWE Ep 205:27–9 means that Erasmus must have been composing a verse epitaph: 'Ye gods, how many panegyrics I then promised myself, and full of matter too! And now, behold, by this sudden change of fortune I sadly write his epitaph [*epitaphium*] instead.' But the word *epitaphium* here means 'eulogy,' not 'epitaph in verse.' Thus St Jerome's famous letter eulogizing St Paula (108) is entitled *Epitaphium sanctae Paulae*. Erasmus uses this term also in Allen Ep 1991:3 to describe his prose eulogy for Albrecht Dürer in *De recta pronuntiatione* ASD I-4 40:887–905 / CWE 26 398–9. The word *epitaphium* in Ep 205 thus may be safely taken to mean the letter itself. First published in 1506 as a preface to some of Lucian's dialogues, this letter is indeed a eulogy for the archduke. Caspar Ursinus Velius *Genethliacon Erasmi*, reprinted among the *Encomia in laudem Erasmi* in LB I, does mention Erasmus' lament for the archduke on page (20) column 2, as Reedijk points out; but Ursinus does not say that it was written in verse. Indeed, his catalogue of Erasmus' writings nowhere singles out a specific poem.

– The same reasoning may serve to dismiss the idea that Erasmus might have written an epitaph for Peace. In the colloquy *Charon* ASD I-3 578:47–8, written in 1523 but not printed until March 1529, it is said that Erasmus once wrote a 'Lament of downtrodden Peace' (the *Querela pacis*). Now that Peace has perished, however, he is writing her *epitaphium*. Dekker *Janus Secundus* 120 and 135 assumes that this must refer to a verse epitaph entitled *Epitaphium Pacis extinctae*. But the 'epitaph' to which Erasmus is referring is undoubtedly the colloquy *Charon* itself.

Thus only the following poems are at present known to be lost:
1/ In *Adagia* II v 74 (LB II 574B) Erasmus quotes five hendecasyllables from an otherwise unknown epigram of his: *Nos item in epigrammate quodam ad hanc paroemiam sic allusimus*:

> Non stulti[146] usque adeo sumus futuri, ut
> Gustatum toties voremus hamum,
> Unco plus semel aere sauciati.
> Vel sero sapiemus, et nocentem
> Tandem carpere desinemus escam.[147]

> I too in one of my epigrams have alluded to this proverb in the following words: 'I will not go on being so foolish as to swallow the hook that I have nibbled at so often, since I have been wounded by the barbed bronze more than once before. I will be wise, though it is late to do so, and now at last I will stop taking the bait that will hurt me.'

Since Erasmus does not mention these verses in his discussion of the adage in *Adagiorum collectanea* (Paris: J. Philippi 1500) and first quotes them in *Adagiorum chiliades tres* (Venice: Aldo Manuzio, September 1508) we may assume that they were written between 1500 and 1508. They probably derive from some epigram in which the Christian humanist expresses his disdain for the pleasures of the flesh. In his *Enchiridion*, written in 1501–2, Erasmus describes the fatal attraction of erotic love, which the wise man avoids, in words strongly reminiscent of the poem fragment: 'Such and such a sensual gratification had such dire consequences, brought me so much harm, so much disgrace, weariness, trouble, and sickness, and shall I be stupid enough to swallow the hook again wittingly [*et iterum stultissimus hamum vorabo prudens*]?'[148]
2/ In Allen Ep 129:62–4 / CWE Ep 129:72–4, written at Paris in early September 1500, Erasmus mentions a *carmen in Delium* 'a poem on Delius.' This Delius may be identified as Gillis van Delft, the same theologian with whom Erasmus had engaged in a poetic contest (*certamen*) in April–May 1499; see the headnote on poem 110 below. Reedijk infers from the Latin preposition *in* that the poem may have been a piece of invective verse. This preposition

is, however, very commonly used in a neutral sense, to inform the reader about the theme of the poem, and need not suggest any animadversion against the poem's subject.
3/ Of the four epitaphs for Hendrik van Bergen only two have survived; see the headnotes on nos 39 and 137 below. The Greek epitaph and one of the three Latin epitaphs are lost.
4/ A passage in *De conscribendis epistolis* mentions that Erasmus once wrote a letter to Thomas Linacre in trochaic tetrameters disguised as prose. The learned English physician did not notice the trick that was being played on him until Erasmus pointed it out to him. This verse letter has not come down to us.[149]
5/ A similar letter, also written in a trochaic metre, is mentioned in Allen Ep 2241:21–2, dated 10 December 1529.
6/ In Allen Ep 1239:2 / CWE Ep 1239:4, dated 14 October [1521], Erasmus wrote the Carthusian Gabriël Ofhuys: 'I send you your verses.' Ofhuys had apparently asked Erasmus to contribute a metrical inscription for an engraving of some biblical scene on which he was working. On Ofhuys see CEBR III 28.

This volume, unlike the others in CWE, includes the original Latin and Greek texts. A prose translation of Erasmus' elegant, vibrant prose can hope to do some justice to both the sense and the style. But a prose translation of Erasmus' verse must inevitably fall far short of capturing the flavour of his various metres and rhythms, the sonorities of his poetic idiom, and the rich allusiveness of his style, in which the trained ear may hear the whole gamut of poetry resound – ancient, medieval, and Renaissance.

The text here presented is in some respects quite different from that offered in Dr Reedijk's edition. As we have noted, Reedijk placed the poems in chronological order; in so doing he also took them out of the textual context in which they occur, whether it be manuscript or printed book. Having thus isolated the poems and put them in a different, chronological arrangement, he then tended to present a composite text drawn from different textual strata. The present edition bases itself on the copy-texts described in general above and more specifically in the headnotes to the individual poems. It should be noted that we are not presenting a critical edition. Readers who desire information on the details of the textual tradition should consult Reedijk's critical apparatus and Vredeveld 'Edition.' A new critical text of the poems, edited by Harry Vredeveld, is to appear in Ordo I of ASD. It will follow the organization adopted in the present volume, so that the numbering of the poems in CWE and ASD will be the same.

To make the Latin and Greek texts conform to the requirements and expectations of modern readers, we have normalized them according to the following principles:
1/ Punctuation has been consistently modernized.
2/ The orthography of the copy-texts has been retained except in the following instances. Consonantal and vocalic *u* and *v* have been distinguished; *j* (generally in capital letters and in *ij*) has been printed as *i*. The genitive singular and nominative plural ending *-e* has been changed to *-ae*; *e* caudata (ę) has been written as *ae*. Contractions have been expanded. Ligatures and diacritical marks or accents have not been reproduced. The Latin enclitics *-ne* and *-ve*, often written as separate words in the copy-texts, have been joined to the preceding word. Capitalization has been modernized. Obvious printing errors have been corrected. Greek texts have been printed according to modern conventions.
3/ The various verse forms used in Erasmus' poetry have been indented according to present practice. The indentation in poem 112, used to indicate the start of new sections, derives from the copy-text. The editor is responsible for the indentation in poems 64, 88, 102, and 111, and in the prose prefaces.
4/ In the copy-texts many poems have a postscript indicating 'The end' in either Latin or Greek. Such postscripts have been omitted in the present edition.
5/ Sidenotes and marginalia have not been reprinted. They are noted in the commentary only when they help elucidate the meaning of the text itself.
6/ The poem and line numbers have been added. For a table of corresponding poem numbers in Reedijk's edition see pages 390–3 in this volume. Cross-references to LB, ASD, Allen, and Reedijk (R) are also given before each of the headnotes in CWE 86.
7/ Wherever possible we have added at the head of each poem the known or conjectural date of composition, followed by the date of its first publication. For a list of the poems in the order of their composition see pages 382–5 in this volume.

HV

POEMS

translated by CLARENCE H. MILLER
edited by HARRY VREDEVELD

POEMS IN
EPIGRAMMATA DES. ERASMI ROTERODAMI

(Basel: Johann Froben, March 1518)

IOANNES FROBENIUS CANDIDO LECTORI S.D.

Accepimus iam pridem, Erasmi Roterodami compatris nostri epigrammata a studiosis summopere flagitari. Proinde dedimus operam, ut quicquid illius versiculorum aut apud Beatum nostrum Rhenanum esset aut Brunonem Amorbacchium, id omne uno complexi libello typis nostris excuderemus. Quanquam intelligebamus, plurimum nos hac re studiosis, Erasmo vero minimum gratificaturos. Nam magnam horum epigrammatum partem non in hoc scripsit ut aederentur, sed ut amiculis suis (ut est minime morosus) obsequeretur. Quin ipsi vidimus, cum abhinc sesquiannum apud nos ageret, evangelica et apostolica monumenta partim Latine vertens, partim recognoscens, et doctissimas illas in Novum instrumentum annotationes nec non in divum Hieronymum scholia scriberet – deum immortalem, quam laboriosis lucubrationibus, quam pertinaci studio, quantum sudoris illi cotidie exhauriebatur! – ipsi, inquam, vidimus non defuisse e magnatibus, qui virum occupatissimum (si quisquam in literis unquam fuit occupatus) interpellare de nugis auderent, aliquod epigrammation aut epistolium eblandientes. Sed enim quid ageret vir suavissima morum facilitate praeditus? Negaret? Incivile hoc exigentibus videretur. Scriberet? At animus aliis cogitationibus impediebatur nec ab inceptis laboribus quicquam respirare licebat. Nihilo secius scribebat, sed ex tempore et obiter ad Musarum sacra divertens. Quanquam huius extemporalia plane talia sunt, ut aliorum diu meditatis anteponi mereantur. Et veniet nunc triobolaris aliquis paedagogulus, qui instar Momi tantum carpendi studio singulis curiosissime exploratis verbulum aliquod reperiet quod sibi non probetur ut non Baptistinianicum aut Faustinum aut

POEMS IN *THE EPIGRAMS OF DESIDERIUS ERASMUS OF ROTTERDAM*

(Basel: Johann Froben, March 1518)

JOHANN FROBEN TO THE FAIR-MINDED READER, GREETINGS

For some time now I have heard that the epigrams of my compatriot Erasmus of Rotterdam are in great demand among intellectuals. And so I have taken the trouble to gather together and print at my press in one small book whatever poems were in the possession either of my friend Beatus Rhenanus or of Bruno Amerbach. Of course I was aware that this would please the intellectuals a good deal but Erasmus himself hardly at all. For he wrote most of the epigrams not to publish them but to comply with the wishes of his friends, since he is a very obliging person. Indeed I myself observed, when he was staying with us a year and a half ago, devoting himself partly to editing, partly to translating into Latin the Gospels and the writings of the apostles, and composing those very learned annotations of his on the New Testament as well as his commentary on St Jerome – good lord, how much sweat was drained from him by toiling far into the night and studying with no let-up day after day! – I myself observed, I say, that there was no lack of great men who dared to interrupt him with some trifles even as he was so very immersed in his writing (and if anyone ever has been so immersed, he was), just to wheedle some little epigram or letter out of him. But what was such an agreeable and obliging person to do? Was he to refuse? He would seem impolite to those who were making these demands. Was he to write what they wanted? But his mind was preoccupied by other thoughts, nor could he allow himself any breather from the work he had begun. Nevertheless he wrote what they wanted, but only on the spur of the moment and by the by, making a detour to the temple of the Muses – though even his extemporaneous pieces are clearly such as to be worthy of a higher place than the carefully thought out writing of other men. And now along comes some two-bit little schoolmaster, who like Momus examines every detail very carefully but only out of a desire to find fault, and when he finds some little word of which he disapproves as not in the vein

denique, si diis placet, Marullicum, hic statim succlamabit: 'O virum carminis
25 indoctum!' Regererem in illum ego, si quem superbe sic ineptientem audirem:
'O nebulonem, o furciferum, tune tantum tibi tribuis, ut tanti viri censorem
agas? Decem totis mensibus non posses vel unum versiculum scribere, caput
scabens et arrosis ante digitis, quod genus hic multos (ut Horatius inquit)
stans pede in uno, minima parte horae, amanuensi suo dictat.' Sed haec in
30 malignos istos. Candidi vel infeliciora boni consulunt, tantum abest ut quae
docta sunt vellicent.

Bene vale.

Basileae Cal. Martiis, anno M.D.XVIII.

of Mantuan or Fausto or, for lord's sake, Marullus, then right away he pipes up: 'Oh, this man knows nothing about poetry.' If I ever heard such an arrogant fool, I would come right back at him: 'You buffoon, you rascal, how can you take it upon yourself to play the judge over such a man? In ten whole months, scratching your head and chewing your fingernails to the quick, you couldn't write even one little verse to match the quality of poetry he dictates in abundance to his secretary in the smallest fraction of an hour, standing on one foot (as Horace says).' But so much for these spiteful carpers. Fair-minded readers, far from ripping to shreds what is written learnedly, make the best of what is not so happily put.

Farewell.

Basel, 1 March 1518

DE OPTI
MO REIP.STATV DEQVE
noua insula Vtopia libellus uere aureus, nec minus salutaris
quàm festiuus, clarissimi disertis
simiq; uiri THOMAE MORI in
clytæ ciuitatis Londinensis ciuis
& Vicecomitis.
EPIGRAMMATA clarissimi
disertissimiq; uiri THOMAE
MORI, pleraq; è Græcis uersa.
EPIGRAMMATA. Des. Eras
mi Roterodami.
Apud inclytam Basilea

Title-page of Thomas More *Utopia* and the two sets of *Epigrammata*
by More and Erasmus
Basel: Froben, March 1518
Beinecke Rare Book and Manuscript Library, Yale University

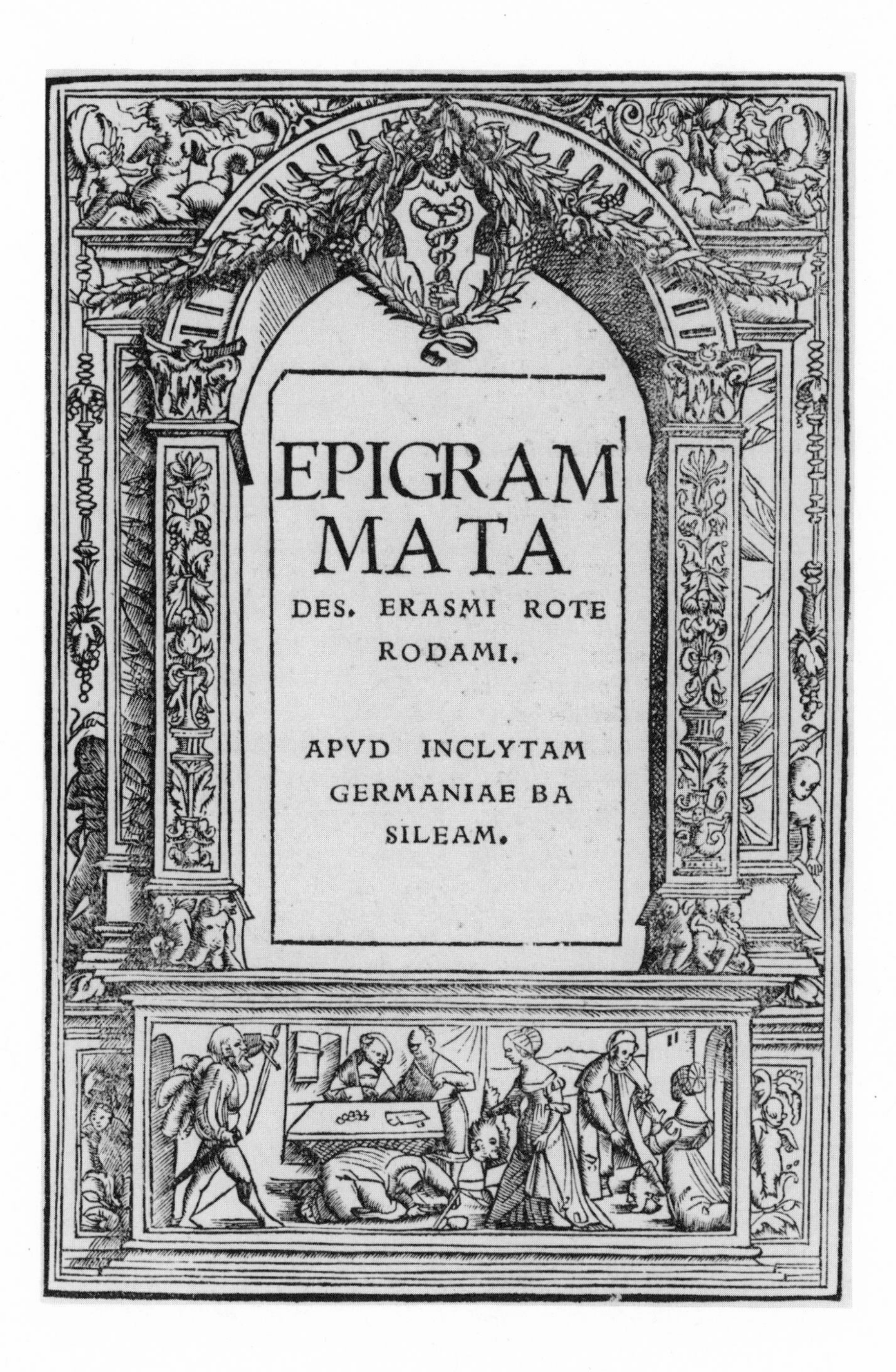

Second title-page of Erasmus *Epigrammata*
Basel: Froben, March 1518
Beinecke Rare Book and Manuscript Library, Yale University

1 Des. Erasmi Roterodami rhythmus iambicus in laudem Annae, aviae Iesu Christi [winter 1490–1? / 1518]

Salve, parens sanctissima,
Sacro beata coniuge,
Sacratiore filia,
Nepote sacratissimo.
5 Domo quid hac illustrius
Ornatiusve? Quae altera
Tam multiplex habuit decus,
Tantum una monstrorum tulit?
Hic hic maritum annis gravem
10 Effoeta anus facit patrem.
Est virgo foeta filia,
Nepos dei verbum ac deus.
Gener pudicus se negat
Partus parentem uxorii.
15 At integram iurat, neque
Rivale pallet suspicax.
Ergo, Anna, mater optima,
Cumulatius multo tuas
Lachrymas deus solatus est
20 Quam vel Rebeccae vel Sarae
Vel illius quae te refert
Et rebus et vocabulo,
Quae dum silenter anxii
Proferret aestus pectoris
25 Visa est Heli multo mero
Amens parumque sobria.
At te pio cum coniuge
Amore prolis annua
Templis ferentem munera
30 Procax sacerdos reppulit.
'Heus,' inquit, 'hinc mihi ocyus
Prophana vota tollite.
Ipsi simul procul procul
Aris sacris absistite.
35 Vestran' deo donaria
Futura grata creditis
Quorum pudendae nuptiae

1 A rhythmical iambic hymn by Desiderius Erasmus of Rotterdam, in praise of St Ann, the grandmother of Jesus Christ

Hail, most saintly mother, blessed in having a holy spouse, an even more holy daughter, a most holy grandchild. What home has ever been more famous or more eminent than this one? What other home ever had such manifold glories or produced, all by itself, so many marvellous prodigies? Here, here in this place an old woman past childbearing makes a father of a husband weighed down by years. The daughter becomes pregnant but remains a virgin. The grandchild is the Word of God and God himself. The chaste son-in-law denies that he is the father of the child borne by his wife; yet he swears that she is inviolate and does not grow pale out of fear and suspicion of a rival.

And so, Anna, best of mothers, God consoled you in your tears far more abundantly than he did either Rebecca or Sarah or the one who reminds us of you, both in her circumstances and her name, the one who, as she was silently expressing the turmoil and anxiety in her heart, seemed to Eli to be distraught and drunk with too much wine. But the arrogant priest rejected you when you came to the temple with your pious spouse, bearing the gifts you offered every year out of a longing for offspring. 'Ho there,' he said, 'get your unholy offerings out of here and be quick about it! And you also, get away, far far away, from the sacred altar. Do you think that God will be pleased by gifts from the likes of you, whose shameful marriage has produced

Praeter libidinem nihil
Luxum et senilem scilicet
40 Tanto tulere tempore?'
Quo se locorum verterent
Vultus pudentum coniugum,
Repulsa quos tam foeda, tam
Insignis exanimaverat?
45 Ioachim pudorem non ferens
Gregum ad suorum pascua
Se proripit, tristis suam
Recepit Anna se domum.
Largis uterque fletibus
50 Votisque pertinacibus
Orare non cessat deum
Ut prole probrum tolleret.
Caelum penetrarunt preces.
Adest ab astris angelus
55 Qui prole promissa graves
Luctus iuberet ponere.
Surgunt alacres, invicem
Narrare visa gestiunt.
Porta maritus aurea
60 Se quaeritantem coniugem
Offendit. Hic laetus stupor
Dulces utrique lachrymas
Excussit. Hinc modicos lares
Iunctis revisunt gressibus.
65 Haud vana vox oraculi
Lusit piam senum fidem.
Bis luna nata quinquies
Anum videt puerperam.
Tanto quidem felicius
70 Foecunda quanto serius
Fit Anna filiae parens,
Nec filiae cuiuslibet,
Sed filiae, quae fertilis
Eademque virgo gigneret.
75 At quem beata gigneret?
Summi parentis filium,
Qui sceptra terrae et aetheris
Cum patre habet communia,
Qui, deus et idem homo, necis

nothing after all this time except debauchery and lust, and senile lust at that?' Where could the bashful couple hide their faces, drained of life as they were by such an ugly and open repudiation? Joachim, unable to bear the shame, hurries away to the pastures of his flocks; Anna, in her sadness, makes her way to their house. With copious tears and steadfast prayers, both of them call on God incessantly to take away their reproach by giving them offspring. Their prayers pierce the heavens. An angel comes down from the stars and, promising them offspring, tells them to put away their heavy grief. Each of them arises happily and sets off eagerly to tell the vision to the other. At the Gate of Gold the husband encounters his wife, who is looking for him. Here, joyful amazement draws tears of happiness from both of them. From here they walk back side by side to their modest hearth.

The words of the prophecy were not illusory and did not mock the pious faith of the old couple. The tenth new moon saw the old woman give birth. And certainly the longer her pregnancy was delayed, the more auspicious it was for Anna to become the mother of a daughter, and not just any daughter, but a daughter who would be fertile and give birth while still remaining a virgin. And to whom would this blessed lady give birth? The Son of the highest Father, who in union with his Father holds sway over heaven and earth alike, who, being God and likewise man, conquered

80 Autore victo per necem
Vitam reduxit mortuis,
Aperuit in caelos iter.
O terque quaterque et amplius
Parens beata, nam potes,
85 Iuva preces mortalium
Tuo vacantum cultui,
Nam te patrona quidlibet
Speramus assequi, modo
Voles voletque et filia.
90 Nec huic petenti pusio
Negare quicquam noverit.
Amat parentem filius,
Neque filio negat pater,
Amans et ipse filium.

Amen.

2 Des. Erasmi Roterodami carmen ad Guilielmum Copum Basileiensem de senectutis incommodis, heroico carmine et iambico dimetro catalectico

[August 1506 / 13 November 1506]

Unica nobilium medicorum gloria, Cope,
Seu quis requirat artem
Sive fidem spectet seu curam, in quolibet horum
Vel iniquus ipse nostro
5 Praecipuos tribuit Gulielmo livor honores.
Cedit fugitque morbi
Ingenio genus omne tuo. Teterrima porro
Senecta, morbus ingens,
Nullis arcerive potest pellive medelis.
10 Quin derepente oborta
Corporis epotet succos animique vigorem
Hebetet, simul trecentis
Hinc atque hinc stipata malis, quibus omnia carptim
Vellitque deteritque
15 Commoda, quae secum subolescens vexerit aetas,
Formam, statum, colorem,
Partem animi memorem cum pectore, lumina, somnos,

the originator of our death, and by his death gave life to the dead and opened up a way to heaven.

O mother blessed, thrice blessed and more, give aid – for you can – to the prayers of us mortals who honour you devoutly on this holyday, for under your patronage there is nothing we do not hope to obtain, as long as you wish it and your daughter also wishes it; and when she asks for anything, her little boy will not know how to refuse her. The Son loves his mother, nor will his Father refuse his Son, for he, too, loves his Son.

Amen.

2 A poem by Desiderius Erasmus of Rotterdam, addressed to Guillaume Cop of Basel, on the troubles of old age, written in hexameters and iambic dimeters catalectic

Cop, the unparalleled glory of the noble medical profession, whether someone needs skill or is looking for trustworthiness or careful treatment, in all these respects even malicious envy herself yields the highest honours to our Guillaume. Faced with your genius, every kind of disease gives way and flees. But then no medicines can stave off or drive away hideous old age, that monstrous disease. Indeed, she rises up suddenly to drink up the juices of the body and blunt the powers of the mind, surrounded on all sides by a host of afflictions, through which she snatches away one by one and wears down all the benefits which growing up brought with it: beauty, posture, colouring, the part of the mind which remembers, understanding, eyesight, sleep, strength,

Vires, alacritatem.
Autorem vitae igniculum decerpit et huius
20 Nutricium liquorem,
Vitaleis adimit flatus, cum sanguine corpus,
Risus, iocos, lepores.
Denique totum hominem paulatim surripit ipsi,
Neque de priore tandem
25 Praeterquam nomen titulumque relinquit inanem,
Cuiusmodi tuemur
Passim marmoreis inscalpta vocabula bustis.
Utrum haec senecta, quaeso,
An mors lenta magis dicenda est? Invida fata et
30 Impendio maligna,
Ut quae deteriora labantis stamina vitae
Pernicitate tanta
Accelerare velint rapidisque allabier alis,
At floridam iuventam
35 Usqueadeo male praecipiti decurrere filo,
Ut illius priusquam
Cognita sat bona sint, iam nos fugitiva relinquant,
Et citius atque nosmet
Plane vivere senserimus, iam vivere fracti
40 Repente desinamus.
At cervi volucres et cornix garrula vivunt
Tot saeculis vigentque.
Uni porro homini post septima protinus idque
Vixdum peracta lustra
45 Corporeum robur cariosa senecta fatigat.
Neque id satis, sed ante
Quam decimum lustrum volitans absolverit aetas,
Tentare non veretur
Immortalem hominis ductamque ex aethere partem
50 Et hanc lacessit audax
Nec timet ingenii sacros incessere nervos,
Sua si fides probato
Constat Aristoteli. Sed quorsum opus, obsecro, tanto
Autore, quando certam
55 Ipsa fidem, heu nimium facit experientia certam?
Quam nuper hunc Erasmum
Vidisti media viridem florere iuventa!
Nunc is repente versus

enthusiasm. She pinches the little flame which is the source of our life and dries up the moisture which nourishes it. She robs us of the vital spirits, of blood and body, of laughter, wit, charm. In a word, bit by bit she steals the whole man away from himself and finally leaves behind nothing of what he was except a name and an empty inscription, such as we see everywhere in the epitaphs carved on marble tombs. I ask you, should we call her old age or rather death long drawn out?

The Fates are envious and enormously malicious: they choose to give immense speed to the thinning thread of our declining time of life and to make it glide toward us on swift wings, while they make the thread of flourishing youth slide away with such untoward and headlong speed that before we are really aware of its advantages they have fled away, leaving us behind, and before we fully realize that we are alive we are suddenly enfeebled and we cease to live. Yet the swift stag and the chattering crow live for so many centuries with full vigour, but man alone, after three and a half decades, and those hardly lived out at all, is thenceforth worn out and deprived of bodily strength by withered old age. Nor is that enough, but before his fleeting years have finished the fifth decade, old age does not hesitate to assail the immortal part of a man, the part descended from the heavens; even this she boldly challenges and has no fear of assaulting the sacred sinews of his inner nature – if we give credence to the esteemed Aristotle.

But what need is there, I beg you, for such a great authority when experience itself establishes our credence firmly, all too firmly, alas! How short a time ago did you see this Erasmus flourishing amidst the greenery of his youth! Now this man, by a sudden change,

Incipit urgentis senii sentiscere damna
60 Et alius esse tendit
Dissimilisque sui, nec adhuc Phoebeius orbis
Quadragies revexit
Natalem lucem, quae bruma ineunte Calendas
Quinta anteit Novembreis.
65 Nunc mihi iam raris sparguntur tempora canis,
Et albicare mentum
Incipiens, iam praeteritis vernantibus annis,
Vitae monet cadentis
Adventare hyemem gelidamque instare senectam.
70 Eheu fugacis, ohe,
Pars veluti melior, sic et properantior aevi,
O saeculi caduci
Flos nimium brevis et nulla reparabilis arte,
Tenerae o viror iuventae,
75 O dulces anni, o felicia tempora vitae,
Ut clanculum excidistis,
Ut sensum fallente fuga lapsuque volucri
Furtim avolastis, ohe!
Haud simili properant undosa relinquere cursu
80 Virideis fluenta ripas.
Impete nec simili fugiunt cava nubila, siccis
Quoties aguntur Euris.
Sic sic effugiunt tacitae vaga somnia noctis
Simul avolante somno,
85 Quae desyderium curas et praeter inaneis
Sui nihil relinquunt.
Sic rosa, quae tenero modo murice tincta rubebat,
Tenui senescit Haustro.
Atque ita, me miserum, nucibus dum ludo puellus,
90 Dum literas ephebus
Ardeo, dum scrutor pugnasque viasque sophorum,
Dum rhetorum colores
Blandaque mellifluae deamo figmenta poesis,
Dum necto syllogismos,
95 Pingere dum meditor tenueis sine corpore formas,

begins to feel the damage thrust upon him by the onset of old age. He is getting to be someone else, different from himself, and the circle of Phoebus has not yet reverted forty times to the day of his birth, which comes at the onset of winter on the fourth day before the beginning of November. Now a few white hairs are already sprinkled on my temples, and the hair on my chin, which is just beginning to get white, reminds me that the years of my springtime are already gone by as the winter of my declining lifetime approaches and freezing old age presses upon me.

Hold, O better part of our fleeting life span! Alas, the better part is the very part that hurries away faster! O flower of a perishing lifetime, blossom all too brief which no skill can restore, O tender green of youth, O sweet years, O blissful time of life, how secretly you have departed! With what swift and furtive flight, deceiving our senses, you have slipped away! Hold! Not so rapidly in their course do surging streams rush to leave the green banks behind them. Not so forcibly in their flight are the hollow clouds driven before the dry winds of the east. Just so, just so the shifting dreams of noiseless night-time flee as soon as sleep flies away, leaving behind nothing of the dreams but longing and empty anxiety. Just so a rose, which even now was flushed with a fresh and deep-dyed crimson, grows old under a faint breeze from the south.

And just so, woe is me, while as a little boy I was playing with nuts, while as a beardless youth I was passionately devoted to reading and writing, while I examined the controversies and the schools of the philosophers, while I was madly in love with the figures of the rhetoricians and the beguiling fictions of mellifluous poetry, while I wove together syllogisms, while I concentrated on drawing

Dum sedulus per omne
Autorum volvor genus, impiger undique carpo
Apis in modum Matinae,
Paedias solidum cupiens absolvere cyclum,
100 Sine fine gestienti
Singula correptus dum circumvector amore,
Dum nil placet relinqui,
Dumque prophana sacris, dum iungere Graeca Latinis
Studeoque moliorque,
105 Dum cognoscendi studio terraque marique
Volitare, dum nivosas
Cordi est et iuvat et libet ereptare per Alpeis,
Dulceis parare amicos
Dum studeo atque viris iuvat innotescere doctis,
110 Furtim inter ista pigrum
Obrepsit senium, et subito segnescere vireis
Mirorque sentioque
Vixque mihi spatium iam defluxisse valentis
Persuadeo iuventae.
115 Quur adeo circumspecte parceque lapillis,
Quur purpuris et ostro
Mortales utuntur, et aetas aurea, tanto
Preciosior lapillis
Et quovis auro, quovis preciosior ostro,
120 Prodigitur inque nugis
Conteritur miseris nullo vecorditer usu
Siniturque abire frustra?
Adde quod illa queant sarciri perdita, Crassos
Spires tibi licebit
125 Et Lydos spires Croesos, iam Codrus et Irus.
Sed quod semel severa
Pensilibus fusis Clotho devolverit aevum,
Id nec venena Circes
Nec magicum, Maia nati gestamina, sceptrum
130 Neque dira Thessalorum
Medeae succis revocare precamina possint,
Non si vel ipse divum

abstract and incorporeal diagrams, while I painstakingly wended my way through each class of writers, everywhere drawing indefatigably from them like the bees of Mount Matinus, longing to complete the whole, unbroken circle of learning, while I made the rounds of each separate subject, driven by endless enthusiasm and love, while I was loath to leave anything unattempted, while I was striving and struggling to combine secular with sacred studies and to join Greek with Latin, while in the pursuit of knowledge I eagerly flitted about over land and sea, while I joyed and delighted in clambering over the snowy Alps, while I strove to acquire sweet friends and took pleasure in becoming well known to learned men, all the while sluggish old age stole imperceptibly over me, and I feel – with amazement I feel – my strength suddenly slacken, and I can hardly believe that the time of my vigorous youth has already slipped by.

Why do mortals handle gems so cautiously and sparingly, why are they so careful about rich garments dyed in purple and crimson? And the golden age of their lives, so much more precious than gems, more precious than any gold or any purple garments, they madly squander and waste in miserable trifles of no use whatever and let it pass away in vain. Then too, when such riches are lost they can be replaced; even if you are now as poor as Codrus or Irus, you can still give yourself the airs of a Crassus or a Croesus of Lydia. But whatever of your lifetime strict Clotho has once and for all spun off from her hanging spindles can never be recalled, not by the potions of Circe, not by the magical sceptre borne by the son of Maia, not by the dire incantations of Medea together with the magic potions of the Thessalians – not even if the father of the gods himself were to sate you

Nectare te saturet pater ambrosioque liquore
(Nanque his ali iuventam
135 Arceri senium scripsit nugator Homerus),
Non si tibi efficaci
Rore riget corpus Tithoni lutea coniunx,
Non si ter octiesque
Phaon per Chias Venerem transvexeris undas,
140 Non si tibi ipse Chiron
Omneis admoveat quas tellus proserit herbas.
Nec anulus nec ulla
Pharmaca cum nervis annos remorantur eunteis.
Atqui ferunt magorum
145 Monstrifico sisti torrentia flumina cantu.
Iisdem ferunt relabi
Praecipites amnes verso in contraria cursu,
Et Cynthiae volucres
Et rapidas Phoebi sisti figique quadrigas.
150 Sed ut haec stupenda possint
Carmina, non speres tamen improbus ut tibi quondam
Aut iam peracta vitae
Saecla iterum referant aut praetereuntia sistant.
Sol mergitur vicissimque
155 Exoritur novus et nitido redit ore serenus.
Extincta luna rursum
Nascitur inque vices nunc decrescente minuta
Sensim senescit orbe,
Nunc vegeta arridet tenero iuveniliter ore.
160 Redit ad suam iuventam,
Bruma ubi consenuit, Zephyris redeuntibus annus,
Et post gelu niveisque
Ver nitidum floresque reversa reducit hirundo.
At nostra posteaquam
165 Fervida praeteriit saeclis labentibus aestas,
Ubi tristis occupavit
Corpus hyems capitisque horrentia tempora postquam
Nive canuere densa,
Nulla recursuri spes aut successio veris,
170 Verum malis supremum
Imponit mors una, malorum maxima, finem.

with nectar and ambrosial draughts (for Homer, that teller of tall tales, says that these nourish youth and ward off old age), not if the saffron consort of Tithonus should steep your body in invigorating dew, not if you, like Phaon, should ferry Venus three or even eight times from Chios across the waves, not if Chiron himself should apply to you all the herbs which the earth brings forth. No ring, no drugs hold onto our strength and keep back the passing years.

But they say that the miraculous incantations of the magicians stop the flow of torrential rivers. They say such charms make plunging streams reverse their course and flow backwards and cause the winged team of Cynthia and the swift steeds of Phoebus to stop fixed in their tracks. But even if incantations could perform such prodigious feats, still do not presume to hope that they can ever bring back parts of your life that are finished or halt what is now passing onward. The sun sinks and rises in turn, returning renewed and clear, with a shining countenance. The extinguished moon is born once again and changes by turns: now, as her circle gradually wanes, she shrinks and grows old; now she is reinvigorated, with a tender and youthful smile on her face. When winter grows old, the year returns to its youth as the western winds return, and after the ice and snow the returning swallow brings back the bright spring and the flowers. But after our hot summer has passed in the course of our declining years, when gloomy winter has taken possession of our body, and after the stubble on our temples has gone white under a heavy snowfall, there is no hope that a past spring will return or that a new one will follow. Instead our afflictions will finally be brought to an end only by death, the greatest of afflictions.

More Phrygum inter ista
Incipimus sero sapere et dispendia vitae
Incogitanter actae
175 Ploramus miseri et consumptos turpiter annos
Horremus, execramur.
Quae quondam heu nimium placuere et quae vehementer
Mellita visa dudum,
Tum tristi cruciant recolentia pectora felle,
180 Frustraque maceramur
Tam rarum sine fruge bonum fluxisse, quod omni
Bene collocare cura
Par erat et nullam temere disperdere partem.
At nunc mihi oscitanti
185 Qualibus heu nugis quanta est data portio vitae!
Satis hactenus, miselle,
Cessatum, satis est dormitum! Pellere somnos
Nunc tempus est, Erasme,
Nunc expergisci et tota resipiscere mente.
190 Velis dehinc equisque
Et pedibus manibusque et totis denique nervis
Nitendum, ut anteacti
Temporis et studio iactura volubilis aevi
Vigilante sarciatur,
195 Dum licet ac dum tristis adhuc in limine primo
Consistimus senectae,
Dum nova canicies et adhuc numerabilis et dum
Pilis notata raris
Tempora duntaxat spatium effluxisse virentis
200 Iam clamitant iuventae,
Nec tam praesentem iam testificantur adesse
Quam nunciant citatum
Ferre gradum et sterilem procul adventare senectam.
Cuiusmodi videtur
205 Tum rerum facies, quum autumni frigore primo
Iam vernus ille pratis
Decessit decor ac languescunt lumina florum,
Iam iam minus nitenteis
Herbas affirmes Boreasque geluque nocentis
210 Iam praetimere brumae.

In such circumstances, we begin, like the Trojans, to grow wise when it is too late, and we miserably bewail the waste of a life lived unthinkingly, we abhor and shudder at the shamefully spent years. What once pleased us – alas, only too much so – what formerly seemed sweet beyond all honey sweetness, now, as our hearts recall it, tortures us with bitter gall, and we are vainly tormented by the thought that such a rare resource has slipped away fruitlessly, a resource which we should have taken every conceivable care to invest well, so as to lose no part of it through recklessness.

But now, how large a part of my life have I drowsily given over to trifles – and such trifles, alas! Enough now of this dallying, poor wretch, enough of this slumbering! Now is the time, Erasmus, to shake off sleep; now is the time to wake up and come to your senses with your mind totally alert. From now on, with all sails set and riding full tilt, with tooth and nail, with every ounce of strength, we must strive by vigilant effort to make good the loss of time past, to make up for the years that have rolled away, to do so while we still can and while we are standing only at the very threshold of gloomy old age, while this new greyness which can still be counted, these temples marked with only a few white hairs, are still proclaiming only that the time of vigorous youth has slipped away, while they do not so much testify that barren old age is actually present as announce that it has speeded up its pace and is approaching from afar. This is the way things seem at the first frost of autumn when that springtime beauty of the meadows has already departed, and the splendour of the flowers has waned, and you would swear that the grass, already less glossy, has forebodings of the north wind and the ice of destructive winter.

Ergo animus dum totus adhuc constatque vigetque
    Et corporis pusillum
Detrimenta nocent, age iam meliora sequamur.
    Quicquid mihi deinceps
215 Fata aevi superesse volent, id protinus omne
    CHRISTO dicetur uni,
Quo, cui vel solidam decuit sacrarier, ut cui
    Bis terque debeatur,
Principio gratis donata, hinc reddita gratis
220 Totiesque vindicata,
Huic saltem pars deterior breviorque dicetur.
    Posthac valete, nugae
Fucataeque voluptates risusque iocique,
    Lusus et illecebrae,
225 Splendida nobilium decreta, valete, sophorum,
    Valete, syllogismi,
Blandae Pegasides animosque trahentia Pithus
    Pigmenta flosculique.
Pectore iam soli toto penitusque dicato
230 Certum est vacare CHRISTO.
Hic mihi solus erit studium dulcesque Camoenae,
    Honos, decus, voluptas.
Omnia solus erit, neque quicquam ea cura (quod aiunt)
    Movebit Hippoclidem,
235 Terrea si moles compagoque corporis huius
    Marcescet obsolescens,
Mens modo pura mihi scelerumque ignara per illum
    Niteatque floreatque,
Donec summa dies pariter cum corpore mentem
240 Ad pristinum novata
Convictum revocabit et hinc iam vere perenni
    Pars utraque fruetur.
Haec facito ut rata sint, vitae exorabilis autor
    Vitaeque restitutor,
245 Quo sine nil possunt unquam mortalia vota et
    Vires labant caducae.

Therefore, while the mind is still intact, firm, and strong, and the weaknesses of the body do only a little harm, come, let us now pursue a better course. Whatever remaining time the Fates wish to allot me, let it be from now on dedicated to Christ alone, so that he, who should have had my whole life consecrated to himself, who can claim it twice and thrice over, who bestowed it freely in the beginning and then restored it freely and rescued it so often, may at least have the poorer and shorter part of it dedicated to him. From now on, farewell, trifles and spurious pleasures, laughter and jests, frivolity and enticements. Farewell, brilliant dogmas of eminent philosophers. Farewell, syllogisms, delightful Muses, mind-winning colours and flowers of the goddess Persuasion. Now I am firmly resolved, with all the dedication of my heart and soul, to have time only for Christ. To me he alone will be study and sweet Muses, honour, glory, pleasure. He alone will be all things, and (like Hippocleides, as they say) I will not be at all concerned if the earthly bulk and the fabric of this body shrivels as it fades away, as long as through him I have shining and flourishing within me a pure mind and a sinless conscience, until the last day renews both body and mind and makes them live together as intimately as they once did long ago, so that thenceforth both parts together will enjoy a perpetual springtime.

Grant that these things may happen in due course, O creator of our life who hears our prayers, O restorer of our life, without whom the desires of mortals can do nothing and their powers collapse and fall.

3 Erasmus ad Ioannem Sapidum suum, in discessu

[August 1514 / December 1514]

Quando distrahimur, absens absentis amici,
  Candide Ioannes, hoc tibi pignus habe,
Quoque magis spatium seiunget corpora nostra,
  Mutuus hoc propius pectora iungat amor.

[Dedicatory letter to poem 4]

ILLUSTRISSIMO PUERO DUCI HENRICO
ERASMUS ROTERODAMUS S.P.D.

Meminisse debes, Henrice Dux illustrissime, eos qui te gemmis aurove honorant, dare primum aliena, quippe fortunae munera, praeterea caduca, deinde qualia quam plurimi mortales possint elargiri, postremo quae tibi ipsi domi abundent quaeque donare aliis quam accipere magno 5 principi longe sit pulchrius. At qui carmen suo ingenio, suis vigiliis elucubratum nomini tuo dicat, is mihi non paulo praestantiora videtur offerre; utpote qui non aliena, sed propria largiatur, nec paucis annis intermoritura, sed quae gloriam etiam tuam immortalem queant efficere, tum ea quae perquam pauci possint donare (neque enim pecu- 10 niosorum et bonorum poetarum par copia), denique quae non minus sit regibus pulchrum accipere quam remunerari. Et opibus quidem nemo non regum abundavit, nominis immortalitatem non ita multi sunt assequuti; quam quidem illi pulcherrimis facinoribus emereri possunt, at soli vates eruditis carminibus praestare; siquidem et ceras et imagines 15 et stemmata et aureas statuas et incisos in aes titulos et operosas pyramidas longa annorum series demolitur, sola poetarum monumenta ipsa aetate, quae res omneis debilitat, invalescunt. Quod prudenter intelligens Alexander ille, cognomento Magnus, a Cherylo, poeta non admodum sane bono, singulos versiculos tolerabileis singulis Philip- 20 picis ex pacto redimebat. Prospiciebat nimirum et Apellis tabulas et

3 Erasmus to his friend Johann Witz, at their parting

Now that we are torn apart, my sincere friend Johann, in your absence keep this token of your absent friend. The wider the distance that separates our bodies from each other, the more closely may our mutual love join our hearts together.

[Dedicatory letter to poem 4]

TO THE MOST ILLUSTRIOUS BOY, DUKE HENRY,
FROM ERASMUS OF ROTTERDAM, GREETINGS
You ought to remember, most illustrious Duke Henry, that those persons who honour you with jewels or gold are giving you, first, what is not their own, for such gifts belong to Fortune and are, moreover, perishable; further, they are such as very many mortals can amply bestow; and lastly they are things which you yourself possess in abundance and which it is much finer for a great prince to give than to receive. But someone who dedicates to you a poem which is the fruit of his own talent and sleepless toil offers, it seems to me, a present that is more distinguished by far, since he lavishes upon you what belongs to himself, not to another, something which will not fade away in a few years but can even bring you everlasting renown and which few indeed can bestow (for the supply of good poets by no means matches that of wealthy men) and which, finally, it is as fine for kings to receive as to reward. And while there never was a king who was not overflowing with riches, not so many have achieved immortal fame. Kings can indeed earn such fame by their glorious deeds, but poets alone can confer it through their learned lays, for waxen effigies and portraits and genealogies and golden statues and inscriptions on bronze and pyramids laboriously reared, these things decay in the long course of the years; only the poets' memorials grow strong with the lapse of time, which weakens everything else. The Alexander surnamed the Great showed a wise understanding of this fact when he purchased merely tolerable verses at a *Philippus* apiece, as he had agreed, from Choerilus, not a very good poet, to be sure. He foresaw, doubtless, that the paintings by Apelles and the statues by Lysippus would be

Lysippi statuas paucis annis interituras, nec quicquam omnino fortium virorum memoriam aeternam posse reddere praeter immortalitate dignas eruditorum hominum literas, nec ullum esse gloriae genus syncerius ac praestantius quam quod a posteris virtuti datur hominum, non fortunae, non ab amore, non a metu, non ab assentatione, sed libero iudicio profectum. Age iam, qui malos versus tam chare prodigus emit, nonne optet Homericos non singulis aureis, sed singulis urbibus emercari? Quem quidem poetam et in delitiis habuisse et Achilli invidisse legitur, beatum illum pronuncians non solum virtute, sed potissimum tali virtutum suarum praecone.

Quanquam non me clam est hac nostra memoria principes plerosque literis tam non delectari quam eas non intelligunt; qui utrunque iuxta ineptum existimant, imo pudendum, optimatem virum vel scire literas vel a literatis laudari, quasi vero sint ipsi vel cum Alexandro, vel cum Caesare, vel omnino cum ullo veterum aut gravitate aut sapientia aut benefactorum gloria conferendi. Ineptum putant a poeta laudari, quia desierunt facere laudanda, nec tamen a gnatonibus suis laudari refugiunt; a quibus rideri se aut sciunt, aut id si nesciunt, stultissimi sint oportet. Quos quidem ego vel ipso Mida stolidiores iudico, qui asininis auriculis deturpatus est, non quod carmina contemneret, sed quod agrestia praeferret eruditis. Midae itaque non tam animus defuit quam iudicium; at his nostris utrunque. A quorum stultitia quum intelligerem generosam tuam indolem vehementer abhorrere, dux clarissime, eoque iam nunc a puero tuos conatus spectare, ut non tam tuorum temporum quam veterum similis evadere cupias, non veritus sum hunc qualemcunque panegyricum nomini tuo nuncupare. Qui si tuae celsitudini longe impar (ut est) videbitur, memineris facito et Artaxersem, regem praestantissimum, aquam a rusticano quodam operario, quam ille manu utraque haustam obequitanti obtulerat, hilarem subridentemque accepisse, et eiusdem nominis alium (ut opinor) pro malo a pauperculo quopiam allato perinde ut pro magnificentissimo munere gratias egisse, ratum videlicet non minus esse regale parva prompte accipere quam magna munifice elargiri. Quid? Nonne etiam superi ipsi, qui nullis mortalium opibus egent, ita muneribus huiusmodi delectantur ut contempta interim divitum hecatombe rusticana mica et thusculo paupere

destroyed in a few years and that nothing on earth could make a brave man's memory live forever except those learned authors' writings which were themselves worthy of immortality and that there was no purer or more brilliant fame than that which posterity attributes to men's courage, not to their fortune, fame that proceeds from untrammelled judgment, not from affection or fear or flattery. Tell me now, would not a man who so wastefully purchases bad verses at such a high price be glad to contract for lines by Homer not at a gold coin apiece but at a city apiece? And indeed we read that Alexander delighted in Homer and envied Achilles, declaring that he was blessed not only in his valour but also in having such a one as Homer to sing its praises.

At the same time I am not unaware that in our times most princes lack the enjoyment of literature in proportion to their failure to understand it. They think it equally foolish, equally shameful indeed, for a nobleman either to know literature or to be praised by men of letters, though, of course, they are not to be compared with Alexander or Caesar or any of the ancients at all, either in dignity or wisdom or in glorious services to mankind. They think it is foolish to be praised by a poet for the simple reason that they have ceased to do praiseworthy deeds, though they do not shrink from the flattery of their toadies. Either they know such flatterers are mocking them – that is, they do if they have any sense – or if they do not, they are perfect fools themselves. In my opinion at least, they are stupider than Midas himself, who was disfigured with ass's ears not because he despised poetry but because he preferred crude to polished verse. Thus Midas was not so much mindless as tasteless; the nobles of our time are both. Because I am aware that your noble nature, most illustrious Duke, recoils from such folly and that from boyhood onward you have made it the goal of your endeavours to model your life on ancient rather than modern ideals, I have ventured to dedicate this laudatory poem, such as it is, to you. And if it should seem far inferior to your royal dignity, as indeed it is, pray remember the smiling good humour with which Artaxerxes himself, mightiest of kings, accepted the water that a country workman lifted up in his cupped hands for him to drink on horseback, or how another king of the same name, I believe, expressed his thanks for an apple brought to him by a poor little man in exactly the same terms he might have used for a sumptuous gift, evidently thinking that it is a no less royal trait to accept small gifts readily than to bestow great gifts generously. Indeed, do not the powers above, who have no need for the wealth of mortals, take such pleasure in these small gifts that upon occasion they spurn the rich man's offering of a hundred

placentur, animo nimirum offerentis, non rerum precio, nostra donaria metientes.

Et haec quidem interea tanquam ludicra munuscula tuae pueritiae dicavimus, uberiora largituri ubi tua virtus una cum aetate accrescens 60 uberiorem carminum materiam suppeditabit. Ad quod equidem te adhortarer, nisi et ipse iam dudum sponte tua velis remisque (ut aiunt) eo tenderes et domi haberes Skeltonum, unum Britannicarum literarum lumen ac decus, qui tua studia possit non solum accendere sed etiam consummare. Bene vale, et bonas literas splendore tuo illustra, auto- 65 ritate tuere, liberalitate fove.

4 Ode Erasmi Roterodami de laudibus Britanniae Regisque Henrici septimi ac regiorum liberorum, carmine hexametro et iambico trimetro acatalectico

[late September? 1499 / 1500]

Britannia loquitur.

Si iactare licet magnorum munera divum
    Sibique veris fas placere dotibus,
Quur mihi non videar fortunatissima tellus?
    Digna est malis, bona quae parum novit sua.
5 Ultima lanigeris animosa est India lucis,
    Suis superbus est Arabs odoribus,
Thuriferis gaudet Panchaia dives harenis,
    Ibera flumen terra iactat aureum,
Aegypto faciunt animos septem ostia Nili,
10 Laudata Rheni vina tollunt accolas,
Laeta nec uberibus sibi displicet Africa glebis,
    Haec portubus superbit, illa mercibus.
At mihi nec fontes nec ditia flumina desunt
    Sulcive pingues prata nec ridentia.

oxen and are satisfied with the peasant's pinch of salt, the poor man's fragment of incense? – for they doubtless assess what we give not by the value of the offering but by the intention of the offerer.

And so for the time being I have dedicated this small gift to you as a toy suited to your boyish age, intending to bring richer offerings when your powers, increasing with your years, will furnish me with richer themes for my verse. Certainly I would urge you on toward this goal, except that you yourself, of your own accord, are already making your way there by sail and oar, as the saying goes, and that you have living with you Skelton, the great light and ornament of English letters, who can not only inspire but also perfect your studies. Farewell. May you make learned writing illustrious by your own splendour, defend it by your authority, and encourage it by your generosity.

4 An ode by Erasmus of Rotterdam in praise of Britain and of King Henry VII and the royal children, in hexameters and iambic trimeters acatalectic

Britannia speaks.

If it is permissible to boast of the gifts
bestowed by the mighty gods and if it is right
to have a favourable opinion of oneself
because of genuine endowments, why should I
not think I am the most fortunate land of all?
A country that does not recognize its
advantages deserves its afflictions. India, at the
very edge of the world, takes pride in her
cotton-bearing groves; Arabia is proud of her
perfumes; wealthy Panchaia rejoices in her
incense-bearing sands; Iberia vaunts its golden
river; Egypt glories in the seven mouths of the
Nile; the inhabitants of the Rhine valley exult
in its famous wines; and Africa takes no little
pleasure in the rich farmlands with which she
is blessed. One land is proud of its ports,
another of its commerce. But I have no lack of
springs and wealthy rivers or of rich furrows or
of laughing meadows. I am teeming with men,

15 Foeta viris, foecunda feris, foecunda metallis,
Ne glorier quod ambiens largas opes
Porrigit Oceanus, neu quod nec amicius ulla
Caelum nec aura dulcius spirat plaga.
Serus in occiduas mihi Phoebus conditur undas,
20 Sororque nocteis blanda ducit lucidas.
Possem ego laudati contemnere vellera Betis:
Ubi villus albis mollior bidentibus?
Et tua non nequeam miracula temnere, Memphi,
Verum illa maior iustiorque gloria,
25 Quod Latiis, quod sum celebrata Britannia Graiis,
Orbem vetustas quod vocavit alterum.
Non tamen haec iacto, nam sunt antiqua, sed inde
Attollo cristas ac triumpho serio,
Quod mihi rex pulchri pars est pulcherrima regni,
30 Rex unicum huius saeculi miraculum.
Instructus pariter Martisque et Palladis armis,
Belli peritus, pacis est amantior.
Indulgens aliis, sibi nil permittit; habenas
Suis relaxans civibus, stringit sibi.
35 Hoc regnum ille putat: patriae charissimus esse,
Blandus bonis, solis timendus impiis.
Non Deciis sua Roma, suo non Attica Codro
Pluris fuit, fatis redempta mutuis.
Numinis ac caeli tanta est reverentia, quanta
40 Nec erat Metello nec marito Aegeriae.
Non mellita magis Pylio facundia regi,
Nec Caesari mens maior aut sublimior,
Nec Mecoenati vel dextra benignior unquam
Vel sanguinis tam magna parsimonia.
45 Creditus Aeneas Veneris de semine cretus,
Dictus parente Scipio satus Iove.

abundant with game, abounding in metals – not to boast of the copious riches proffered by the surrounding ocean or of friendlier skies and balmier breezes than in any other region. For me Phoebus vanishes late under the western waves and his charming sister brings on bright nights. I could scorn the fleeces of much-praised Baetica; where do the white sheep have softer wool than mine? And I could scorn your wonders, too, Memphis, not without good grounds, but there is more ample and more genuine glory in this fact: I, Britannia, was celebrated among the Latins and the Greeks, and the ancients called me a second world.

But still, I do not boast of these things, for they are ancient history, but rather I plume myself and triumph in earnest because of this: my king is the most beautiful part of a beautiful kingdom, a king who is the unparalleled wonder of these times. Equally trained in the weapons of both Mars and Athena, he is an expert in warfare, but an even greater lover of peace. Indulgent to others, he is strict with himself; giving his citizens free rein, he keeps a tight rein on himself. He thinks that kingship consists in this: to be most beloved in the eyes of his native land, to be mild to good men, to be feared only by the wicked. To the Decii their Rome was not more dear, nor Athens more dear to her Codrus – men who gave their lives to save their fatherlands. And he has more reverence for the God of heaven than Metellus or the husband of Egeria. In honeyed eloquence he is not surpassed by the king of Pylos; in greatness and loftiness of mind he is a match for Caesar; nor was Maecenas ever more open-handed in patronage or as parsimonious in bloodshed. Aeneas was thought to be sprung from the seed of Venus; Scipio was said to be begotten by his true father Jove. What if ancient ages

Quid si prisca meum vidissent saecula regem,
    Hoc ore tam decente, tali pectore?
Nonne Iovem humanis ipsum succurrere rebus
50   Nostro latentem credidissent corpore?
Atque hic semper erit magni mihi numinis instar,
    Meus hic Apollo saeculi pater aurei.
Hoc oriente meis gens ferrea cessit ab oris,
    Fraudes reversa Astrea distulit malas,
55 Non secus ac toto vanescunt sydera caelo
    Simul ore Titan emicavit igneo.
Claudere iam Ianum fas est, iam ducere longas
    Custode rerum tam potente ferias.
Me miseram, quur huic aeternos Iuppiter annos
60   Non addidisti, cuncta quum donaveris?
Nolunt nostra suis aequari numina regnis.
    At si qua magnos vota tangunt caelites,
Serus sydereas certe referatur in arces,
    Fatale sera stamen amputet Atropos.
65 Finiit Alcides speciosos morte labores,
    Debetur altum regibus caelum bonis.
Hunc repetant superi, sed tum, quum Nestoris aevum,
    Ubi senectam vicerit Tithoniam.
Et vivet tamen usque mihi, dum regia proles
70   Referet parentis nomen, os et indolem.
Quae mihi purpureis iam quina adolescit in aulis,
    Regum futuri tres patres, matres duae.
Non aliter pictis Pesti vernantis in hortis
    Almo nitentes rore pubescunt rosae,
75 Formosae Veneri flos acceptissimus, et quo
    Nec spirat alter aut renidet blandius,
Nec cui nexilibus sit gratia tanta coronis,
    Ambire solus regiam dignus comam.

could have seen my king, this handsome countenance, such a noble heart? Would they not have thought Jove himself had come to aid mankind, disguising himself in a body like ours? And to me certainly this king will always be the counterpart of a mighty god; he will be my Apollo, the father of the golden age. When this king rose, the race of iron departed from my shores. Astraea returned and drove away malicious deceit, just as the stars vanish from the whole sky as soon as the fiery face of Titan flashes forth. Now it is right to close the doors of Janus; now is the time, under such a powerful guardian of our affairs, to take a long holiday. Ah, woe is me, Jupiter, since you endowed this man with all gifts, why did you not add an endless lifetime? The gods do not wish our kingdoms to be equal to theirs. But if any prayers can touch the hearts of the great powers on high, may it be a long time indeed before he is taken back to the palaces among the stars, a long time before Atropos cuts off his fatal thread. Hercules capped his splendid labours with his death; good kings deserve their reward in the heights of heaven. Let the powers above take back this king, but not until his life has grown longer than Nestor's and he has surpassed the old age of Tithonus.

But even then he will still go on living for me as long as his royal offspring reflect the name, the features, and the character of their father. I have five of them now growing up at the resplendent court, three who will be fathers of kings, two who will be royal mothers. They are growing up like roses in the bright-coloured gardens of Paestum in the springtime, glowing with life-giving dew, like the favourite flower of fair Venus, the rose, which surpasses all flowers in fragrance and seductive hue, of which the most beautiful wreaths are woven, which is the only flower worthy of aspiring to

Hic ubi cultoris lasciva industria docti
80 Miscere gaudet punicanteis candidis
Plurimaque in spina rutilat rosa et albicat una,
Ut lacteum si murici iungas ebur,
Omnibus idem odor est, ros omneis educat idem,
Eadem iuventa, forma par, idem frutex,
85 Atque eadem tellus succo nutricat eodem,
Foventur auris iisdem, eodem sydere.
Sunt duo quae variant cognataque germina pulchro,
Aetas colorque, dividunt discrimine.
Haec modo nata latet prope cortice tota virenti,
90 Tenuique rima tenera lucet purpura.
Haec nivei tantum fastigia protulit oris,
Sensim at dehiscens turgidos rumpit sinus.
Exerit haec totum discissa veste mucronem,
Clausas minata iam comas evolvere.
95 Illaque lacteolos nondum exinuavit amictus,
Vix credit auris tam rudeis adhuc opes,
Candida sed tenui suffunditur ora rubore,
Seu fratris hic est sive syderis color.
Maxima bis seno foliorum gaudet honore,
100 Tyrio micantes explicans ostro comas.
Non sic lana rubet bis concha imbuta marina,
Non sic Eois Phoebus emergens aquis.
Nec solum arridet pulchro venientibus ore,
Luteola sed iam pollicetur semina.
105 Hic meus Arcturus qui nominis omine felix
Virtute reddet quem refert vocabulo.
Aspice quod specimen generosae frontis in illo est,
Ut lucet oculis vividus mentis vigor.

crown the locks of kings and queens. Here, where the expert gardener, amusing himself at his task, delights in mingling the red with the white, where many roses glow red and white on one thorny stem, like crimson stain applied to milk-white ivory, they all have the same fragrance, all are fostered by the same dew; they share the same youth, the same beauty, the same stem; the same plot of earth nourishes them all with the same moisture, the same breezes cherish them, the same sunlight warms them. There are two things that distinguish them from each other, making a beautiful contrast among kindred buds: their age and their colour.

This newborn bud is almost totally concealed by its green sheath; only a thin slit lets the tender red shine out. This one displays its snow-white countenance only at the topmost tip, gradually splitting open and breaking forth from the swelling fold of its garment. This one has torn open its clothing and unsheathed its whole bud, giving signs now of unfolding its closed petals. That one has not yet unfolded its milk-white vesture, hardly entrusting to the breezes such riches as yet unripened, white but with a slightly flushed countenance, whether in this she has something of her brother's colouring or has it from the star. The largest rose exults in the glory of twelve petals, unfolding its gleaming, bright-red locks, more glowing red than wool twice steeped in dye made from molluscs or than Phoebus when he emerges from the waters of the dawn. Its fair countenance not only smiles on those who approach it, but its yellow down already gives promise of seed.

This is my Arthur, whose name is a happy omen and who makes good the valour ascribed to him by that appellation. Behold what a noble forehead he has! See how the lively

Praecoqua nec tardam expectat sapientia pubem,
110 Praevertit annos indoles ardens suos.
Talis Iesides illique simillima proles,
Hic quum timendas dissecat puer feras,
Haec quando ancipitem potuit dissolvere litem
Malamque fraudem fraude docta prodere.
115 Proxima consequitur nymphe quae nomina ducit
Ab unione, Persici foetu maris.
Omine delector: blando candore lapillus
Placet, pudore Margarita lacteo.
Hic teres est nec inaequali levore rotundus,
120 In Margaritae moribus scabrum nihil.
Est nova cum liquido gemmae cognatio caelo:
Claret sereno sole, pallet nubilo.
At mea virgo piis est addictissima divis
Caelumque mavult quam vagum pelagus sequi.
125 Hanc qui cum sociis vidisset ludere nymphis
Habilique fratrem tela torquentem manu,
'Aureus hic Phoebus, soror haec argentea Phoebi est,'
Per ipsa iuret alma Phoebi lumina.
Iam puer Henricus genitoris nomine laetus,
130 Monstrante fonteis vate Skeltono sacros,
Palladias teneris meditatur ab unguibus arteis.
Quam multus illi lucet in vultu pater!
Talis in Ascanio renitebat imago parentis,
Sic pulchram Achilles ore reddebat Thetin.
135 Nescio quid Maria praeclari spondet ab ipso
Nunquam occidentis syderis cognomine.
Sed cunas, Edmonde, tuas quo carmine dicam?
Adeste plectris huc, sorores, aureis
Et puero fidibus placidos accersite somnos

vigour of his mind shines in his eyes. Wisdom cannot wait for the slow years to make him a man but comes to him early; his fervent nature outstrips his years. He is like the son of Jesse and most like the offspring of David: like David when as a boy he cut terrifying wild beasts to pieces; like Solomon when he was able to resolve a doubtful case, skilful in using wise deception to expose malicious deceit. Next after him comes a maiden who takes her name from a pearl, such as is produced by the Persian sea. I am delighted by the omen of her name: the gem pleases us with its winning whiteness; Margaret, with her milk-white modesty. A pearl is smooth, evenly and perfectly round; Margaret's character is without any rough blemishes. The gem has a strange affinity with the open sky: it is bright if the sun is clear, pale if the sun is overcast. So too my maiden is most devoted to the holy saints and prefers to conform to heaven rather than to follow the shifting currents of the sea. Anyone who has seen her playing with her maiden companions and observed her brother shooting shafts with his expert hand would swear 'He is the golden Phoebus and she the silver sister of Phoebus' – would swear it by the bountiful light of Phoebus himself. Now comes the boy Henry, who rejoices in having his father's name; guided to the sacred springs by the poet Skelton, he has trained himself in the arts of Athena from his tenderest years. How much of his father shines forth in his countenance! So in Ascanius shone the image of Aeneas; so the face of Achilles reflected the beauty of Thetis. Mary gives promise of something quite splendid by the very fact of her name, taken from the star that never sets under the sea. But what cradle-song shall I sing for you, Edmund? Come, O Sisters, with your golden plucks and summon calm sleep for the

140 Ac fesceninis insonate versibus.
Muneribus blandis cunabula spargite, nymphae,
Aggerite, quicquid est odori graminis:
Ambrosiam, casiam calthamque thymumque crocumque
Et Syra amoma nec insuavem amaracum,
145 Tum florum mille species ac mille colores,
Sed plurima omneis inter ardeat rosa.
Hanc rubram, hanc niveam pulchris miscete corollis;
Gaudet paternis parva proles floribus.
Vos precor o puero date vellera candida, Parcae,
150 Eatque fausto molle stamen pollice.

5 Des. Erasmi Roterodami ad Gaguinum nondum visum, carmen hendecasyllabum

[c September 1495 / January 1496]

Alloquitur Musas suas.

Quid dum mittimini verenda ad ora
Gaguini, lacerae ac leves Camoenae,
Restatis trepidaeque pallidaeque
Nec non Parmeno uti Terentianus
5 Causas nectitis: 'ecquis? ecquid? ecquo?'
Vos solas adeo fugit Roberti
Nomen, scripta diserta cuius ingens
Novit, suspicit, ac adorat orbis?
'Ergo nos humilesque barbaraeque
10 Ad tanti patris irruemus altas
Docti, nobilis, ac potentis aedes?'
Magna est rusticitas, nihil pudere;
Summa est rusticitas, nimis pudere.
Ecquem fingitis, obsecro, Robertum?
15 Personam tragicam? Cavete cultum
Tam raris studiis et expolitum
Vulgi moribus aestimare pectus.
Sunt fastidia tetra barbarorum.

boy with your lyres and sing lullabies to him. Sprinkle the cradle, O nymphs, with sweet gifts, bring hither all fragrant herbs: tansy, lavender, and marigolds, both thyme and saffron, and Assyrian cardamom and delightful marjoram. Then bring flowers of a thousand kinds and a thousand colours, but among them all let the glowing rose be the most plentiful. Mingle now a red rose, now a white, in pretty garlands; the little child delights in the flowers of his forebears. And you, O Fates, I beg you, give the boy white wool for the thread of his life and let it run softly and smoothly over your thumb.

5 A hendecasyllabic poem by Erasmus of Rotterdam to Robert Gaguin, whom he had not yet met

He speaks to his Muses.

When you are sent to see the venerable countenance of Gaguin, O ragged and trifling Muses, why do you just stand there, trembling and pale, making up a chain of excuses like Terence's Parmeno: 'Who? What? Where?' Are you the only ones who are unaware of the name of Robert, whose learned writings the whole wide world knows, admires, and reveres?

'Are we lowly and barbarous creatures, then, to go rushing off to the lofty residence of this great father, so learned, noble, and mighty?'

It is very boorish to have no shame; it is most boorish of all to have too much. I ask you, what kind of person do you think Robert is? A stuffed shirt? Be careful not to follow vulgar standards in judging a mind cultivated and polished by such exceptional studies. Such harsh standoffishness is to be found among

Sunt commercia Gratiis solutis
20 Cum blando Aonidum choro sororum.
Vanum ponite pectoris timorem
Et doctum celeres adite vatem.
Vos quamvis humilesque barbarasque
Blando comiter ille candidoque
25 Exceptabit (ut est benignus) ore.
Si dictaque salute redditaque
Percontabitur illico 'unde, cuiae?'
Ne crassum pudeat solum fateri
Obscurive vocabulum magistri.
30 Si quid veneritis rogabit, hoc o-
ratum carminis huius ut poetam
Commendatum habeat suumque scribat.

6 In Annales Gaguini et Eglogas Faustinas, eiusdem carmen ruri scriptum et autumno

[autumn 1495 / January 1496]

Nuper quum viridis nemoroso in margine ripae
Irrigua spatiarer in herba,
Errabam tacitae per amica silentia sylvae,
Dulci tactus corda furore.
5 Iam nemora et fontes, iam rustica vita placebat
Turbam et fumida tecta peroso.
Cumque Marone meo gelidis in vallibus Hemi
Sisti terque quaterque precabar,
Quum subito affulgens Venerique simillima pulchrae
10 Obvia fit tua, Fauste, Thalia.
Protinus illa oculis est eminus agnita nostris,
Comi arrisit molliter ore.
Ut coram stetit, 'ecquid agit meus,' occupo, 'Faustus?
Quidve decus commune Gaguinus?'

barbarians. The untrammelled Graces associate with the winsome choir of the Heliconian sisters. Put this empty fear out of your hearts and hurry off to visit the learned poet. However lowly and barbarous you may be, he will receive you with a genial, courteous, and frank look, because he is kind. After you have exchanged greetings, if he goes right on to ask 'Where do you come from? To whom do you belong?' do not be ashamed to confess the uncultivated soil you come from or the obscure name of your master. If he asks why you have come, say you come to beg that he might consider the writer of this poem as commended to his service and might enroll him as one of his own.

6 A poem by the same author on the *Annals* of Gaguin and the *Eclogues* of Fausto, written in the countryside during the autumn

Recently, as I was strolling on the well-watered grass among the trees along the edge of the green bank of a stream, as I roamed in the friendly quiet of the silent trees, my heart was touched by a sweet rapture. Now I took pleasure in the groves and springs, now I enjoyed the life of the countryside, detesting the crowds and the smoky houses. And like my dear Virgil I was begging again and again to be set down in the cool valleys of the Haemus mountains, when suddenly, Fausto, I encountered your Muse Thalia, radiant and almost as beautiful as Venus herself. Even at a distance my eyes recognized her instantly; her face had a kind and tender smile.

When she stood before me, I spoke first: 'What is my friend Fausto doing, and Gaguin, the glorious friend we have in common, what is he about?'

15 'Vivit uterque, et uterque suo devinctus Erasmo
Aut eadem aut meliora precatur.'
'Gaudeo. Verum age dic, quidnam molitur uterque
Quod cantet schola Franca legatve?
Quae, reor, a tam ditibus atque feracibus arvis
20 Iamdudum annua munera sperat
Autumnumque suum.' 'Primum tuus ille Robertus
Exaequat sermone soluto
Stemmata Francorum et decus et fera praelia regum.
Iam nihil est, quod Gallia docto
25 Invideat Latio, suus ipsi contigit alter
Livius ac Salustius alter.'
'Quid tuus ille parat vates? Quonam monumento
Faustum nigris invidet umbris?
An silet, alterna cupiens recreare quiete
30 Longis hausta laboribus arva?'
'Ille quidem felix agit ocia, qualia quondam
Scipiades agitare solebat
Urbe procul tacitis solus, neque solus, in agris,
Ocia pulchri plena negoci.
35 Quippe inter colles vinetaque Gallica solus,
Parrisiis vagus errat in agris.
Sunt comites pingui gaudentes rure Camoenae.
Illic raptus Apolline toto
Et sese et Musis dignum Phoeboque poema
40 Agresti meditatur avena,
Quale nec aequari doleat sibi Tityrus ipse
Qui patulae sub tegmine fagi
Sylvestrem tenui tentabat arundine Musam,
Quale trahat camposque pecusque,
45 Quale queat rigidas deducere montibus ornos,
Sistere flumina, flectere saxa,

'Both are alive and well and both of them, devoted as they are to their Erasmus, hope that he is the same, or even better off.'

'I am delighted to hear it. But come now, tell me, what compositions have they undertaken for the learned community of France either to sing or to recite? For France, I imagine, has been expecting for some time the annual autumn harvest from such rich and fertile fields.'

'First, your friend Robert is doing justice in prose to the dynasties and glories and fierce battles of the French kings. Now France has no reason to envy learned Rome: she has another Livy, another Sallust of her own.'

'What is that poet of yours working on? With what literary monument does Fausto begrudge his name to the dark shades of the underworld? Or is he keeping silent out of a desire to reinvigorate, by means of a fallow interval, the fields exhausted by long labours?'

'He is indeed enjoying a happy time of leisure, as Scipio once enjoyed such a time of leisure, far from the city, alone – and yet not alone – in the silent fields, a leisure full of noble activity. In fact he is roaming and roving alone among the hills and vineyards of France, in the fields outside Paris. He is accompanied by the Muses, who delight in the fertile countryside. There, totally enraptured by Apollo, he is working out on his rustic oaten flute a poem worthy of himself and the Muses and Phoebus, a poem which Tityrus himself would not be sorry to see compared even with his own poems – the same Tityrus who tried out the thin reed-pipe of his rustic Muse under the shade of a spreading beech tree – a poem which draws to itself the fields and the cattle, which can draw the unbending ash trees down from the mountain slopes, stop rivers, move

Reddere quale queat placidos tigresque luposque,
Quale feros evincere manes,
Denique (quod proprie tecum laetabere) castum:
50 Nulla hic Livia, nulla Columba,
Nusquam hic formosum Corydon ardebit Alexin,
Phyllis toto in carmine nulla,
Quod neque Sorbonae nequeat censura probare
(Et multos habet illa Catones),
55 Quod neque grammaticus tenerae dictare iuventae
Plagoso vereatur in antro,
Nec tetrico Hippolytum pudeat recitare parenti.
Felicem ter et amplius illum,
Quisquis Faustina dicetur arundine Gallus,
60 Vel Varus vel Pollio quisquis,
Vivet et aeternum pulchro cum carmine notus
Quadrifido cantabitur orbe.'

7 Eiusdem in morbo de fatis suis querela

[spring? 1496 / 20 January 1497]

Miror, quae mihi sydera
Nascenti implacido lumine fulserint,
O Gaguine meum decus.
Nam seu iure aliquo nostra negotia
5 Ignes aetherei regunt,
Me primum teneras lumen ad insolens
Aedentem querimonias
Nec mitis rutilo sydere Iuppiter
Aspexit, neque prospera
10 Arrisit radiis mi Venus aureis.
Tantum Mercurius celer
Adfulgens nitidis eminus ignibus
Adflarat sua munera,
Sed stella vetuit falcifer invida

stones, a poem which can render tigers and wolves tame, which can conquer the fierce shades in the underworld, and finally – something you will find especially delightful – a poem which is chaste: no Livia here, no Columba, no Corydon burning with love for the beautiful Alexis, not a Phyllis in the whole poem. It is a poem which even the censors of the Sorbonne could not help approving – and there's many a Cato among them – a poem which no schoolmaster would fear to recite to the tender youths in that den of his, full of the sound of whippings, a poem which Hippolytus would not be ashamed to recite to his stern father. Blessed, thrice blessed and more, is any Gallus who is celebrated by the pipe of Fausto, or any Varus or Pollio; he will live and, together with the beautiful poem, he will be known and sung forever to the four corners of the earth.'

7 A lamentation by the same author about his fate, written when he was ill

I am amazed at whatever stars shone down on me at my birth with such harsh light, O Gaguin, my glory. For if the fires in the heavens do rule our affairs with some binding law, the glittering star of Jupiter did not look kindly on me when I first uttered my feeble complaints at the unaccustomed light, nor did Venus smile favourably on me with her golden rays. Only swift Mercury, shining from afar with his clear beams, breathed his gifts into me, but he was thwarted by the baleful star

15 Vulcanique minax rubens
Rivalis, calidus cum gelido sene.
Seu tres terrigenum deae
Fortunas triplici numine temperant,
Sum durissima stamina
20 Sortitus. Volucrem seu potius deam
Versare omnia credimus,
Hanc in perniciem certe ego deierem
Coniurasse meam miser.
Felicis mihi nec fata Polycratis
25 Nec Scyllae precor improbus.
Arpinas toties consul iniquius
Fortunam insimulat suam,
Quae tot prospera, tot dulcia paululo
Fermento vitiaverit.
30 Ingrate ille quidem rusticus ac foro
Rerum nescius utier,
Alternas dominae qui queritur vices.
Sat felicem ego iudico,
Qui praesentia lenire potest mala
35 Actis prosperius memor
Ac sperare iterum iam fore, quod fuit.
At me matris ab ubere
Fati persequitur tristis et asperi
Idem ac perpetuus tenor.
40 In me, crediderim, proruit improbi
Pixis tota Promethei
Et quicquid stabulat triste vel asperum
Nigri in limine Tartari.
Heu quod simplicibus vatibus invidum
45 Numen, quis genius malus
Quaeve infesta novem Iuno sororibus
Sic nostrum caput impetit?
O fatis genite prosperioribus,
Bis, Gaguine, meum decus,
50 Hunc si tu minime temnis amiculum,
Non totus fuero miser,
Nec cedent gravibus pectora casibus.

with his sickle and by the threatening red rival of Vulcan, the hot-blooded god together with the cold old man.

Or if the three goddesses control the fortunes of earthborn men with their threefold divinity, I was allotted a very cruel thread of life.

Or if instead we believe that the winged goddess whirls everything around, I would certainly swear that she has plotted to destroy me in my misery.

I am not so outrageous as to ask for the fate of the fortunate Polycrates or Sulla. The Arpinate who so often became consul was wrong to assail Fortune just because she soured her many favours and sweet successes with a little touch of displeasure. Anyone who complains about the vicissitudes of lady Fortune is ungrateful and naive and does not know how to take the market as he finds it. I judge a person to be happy enough if he can mitigate present evils by remembering past successes and can hope that things will once again be what they were.

But from my mother's breast I have been dogged by the same unceasing round of sad and harsh misfortune. I have been assaulted, I would think, by the whole box of the wicked Prometheus and the kennel of sad and harsh afflictions at the threshold of the black underworld. Alas, what god hostile to simple poets, what evil genius of mine, what Juno full of hatred for the nine sisters pours down these troubles on my head?

O born to a happier fate, O Gaguin, my glory twice over, if you do not scorn this humble friend of yours, I will not be completely miserable, nor will my heart collapse under the burden of its misfortunes.

8 **Arx vulgo dicta Hammensis** [June 1506? / 8 January 1507]

Me, quia sim non magna, cave contempseris, hostis:
   Arx Tarpeia Remi non mage tuta fuit.
Quam bene defensat primum hic qui sustinet agger,
   Tum quae me cingit non inamoena palus!
5 Ista quidem omnigenos mihi commoda servit in usus,
   At subito infusis, quum volo, stagnat aquis.
Iam vero ut cesset vigilum custodia pernox,
   Stertat ut aerea Lynceus in specula,
Attamen excubias grus officiosa diurnas
10 Intus, nocte foris pervigil anser agit.
Grus neque docta nec admonita, speculantis ad aera
   Responsans, acri clangit in astra tuba.
Et procul insidias (nam praesentire videtur)
   Fida sono vigili prodit et arcet avis.
15 Anser item non doctus obit sua munia; quum fas
   Pabulat, et nota ad symbola rursus adest.
Ast ubi vicino se condidit aequore Titan,
   Milite tum denso moenia nostra subit,
Partiturque aliquis mira arte locosque vicesque
20 Quive aetate prior sorteve lectus erit.
Nec cedunt statione sua, dum rursus ab undis
   Emicet et clarum lux agat alma diem.
Adde quod hic miles tam fidus et impiger annos
   Complures nullo iam meret aere mihi.

8 The castle commonly called Hammes

Take care, enemy, not to hold me in contempt because I am not large. The Tarpeian citadel of Remus was not more safe than I am. How well am I defended, first of all by these ramparts which uphold me and then by the not unpleasant marsh which encircles me! Indeed this marsh is advantageous to me in all sorts of useful ways, but, whenever I wish, it can suddenly be flooded with water and become a standing lake. Even if the nightly watch should grow slack and the sharp-eyed sentinel should snore in the lofty watch-tower, the dutiful crane forms a guard within by day, and outside the wakeful goose keeps watch by night. The crane, neither instructed nor admonished, corresponding to the watchman's horn, sends his shrill trumpet notes up to the stars. This faithful bird betrays and wards off even distant infiltrators with his vigilant sound, for he seems to know about them ahead of time. The goose, likewise uninstructed, fulfils his duties. When it is proper he feeds, and at the well-known signals he is back once again. But when Titan disappears beneath the neighbouring ocean, then like dense soldiery they come up under my walls and one of them, chosen either by seniority or by lot, assigns with wondrous skill their stations and their turns at watch. Nor do they leave their posts until the sun springs up once more from the waters and everything becomes clear in the refreshing daylight. On top of that, this loyal and zealous soldiery has served me for many years without pay.

9 Epitaphium Odiliae figendum in cimiterio sub signo crucifixi [July 1498? / 8 January 1507]

Sepulta vivum te salutat Odilia.
Quid ad sepultae verba mox fugit color?
Vivum saluto viva. Quur lubitum est rei
Placidae bonaeque dira dare vocabula?
5 Mala vita mors est et sepulchrum et inferi.
Una haec tibi timenda, si mortem times.
Nam quod vocant mori, est piis renascier.
Nostri peribit nihil et haud pilus, nisi
Perit feraci semen abditum scrobe,
10 Mox se benigno redditurum foenore.
Si rem putaris, quid mori est nisi seri?
Condi sepulchro, quid nisi occari sata?
Iamque in propinquo est ille fatalis dies,
Quum vere nostro flantibus Favoniis
15 ⟨Haec ossa sicca, siccus hic cinisculus,⟩
Rediviva putri pullulabunt e cavo
Moxque emicabit laeta corporum seges,
Quorum viror perennis haud unquam amplius
Marcescet. Hanc in spem fidelis interim
20 Sopita gremio terra servat fragmina.
At mens caducis expedita vinculis,
Invisa quanquam, vivit ac te cominus
Sentit videtque, triplici discrimine
Vitae anteactae merita carpens praemia
25 Messemque pro semente quam fecit metens.
⟨Sua cuique nostrum nota sors, at vos latet.⟩
Bona pars relictis artubus circumvolans
Captat pias hac commeantium preces,
Ut a luendis expiata noxiis,
30 Quas terreo contraxit e contagio,

9 An epitaph for Odilia, to be set up at her burial place under a crucifix

You who are alive, Odilia greets you from her tomb. Why do you suddenly grow pale when you hear words spoken from the tomb? I who am alive greet you who are alive. Why do we decide to assign fearful names to something that is peaceful and good? A bad life is death and tomb and hell. If you fear death, this is the only death you should fear. For to the good what is called death is a rebirth. Nothing of us perishes, not a single hair, unless a seed perishes when it is hidden in a fruitful furrow, soon to return with a generous increase. If you consider the matter, what is it to die except to be planted? What is it to be laid away in the tomb except for the planted seeds to be harrowed? And even now that fated day is not far off when our springtime will come, the west wind will blow, and these dry bones, this handful of dry ashes, will return to life and sprout up from the mouldering hollows, and then the joyful crop of bodies will spring up forever strong and nevermore to wither.

Toward this hope, in the meanwhile, the faithful earth keeps in her lap the unconscious fragments. But the mind, freed when these shackles fall away, lives, though it is unseen. It perceives you, it sees you from close by. It receives its reward in one of three ways, according to the merits of its past life, and it will reap its harvest according to what it sowed. Each of us knows his lot, but it is hidden from you. A good number of us hover about the limbs we have left behind, longing to get the pious prayers of those who come and go here, so as to be purged of the offences that need to be expiated, offences contracted by earthly contagion, and to be able to rise

Iam pura purum adire possit aethera.
Has flagitato subleva precamine,
Memor vices te mox manere mutuas.
Pendentis alto victimae de stipite
35 Mors obsecranda est, obsecranda vulnera.
Hoc fonte si quod efficax piaculum
Vivisque manat, manat hinc et mortuis.
Si porro properas, tum precatus verbulo
Lucem et quietem, perge cursum. Te quoque
40 Para sepulchro, mox sequuturus. Vale.

10 Eiusdem querela de filio superstite [July 1498? / 8 January 1507]

Dictum erat ad sacras mihi nomen Odilia lymphas,
  Idque mei solum iam superesse vides.
Caetera mors rapuit, cineres atque arida tantum
  Terra parens gremio confovet ossa suo.
5 Quid tibi te dignum nisi te, mors saeva, precemur,
  Scindere cui cordi est quae bene iunxit amor?
Iam nihil est charam a membris discerpere vitam;
  Quiddam etiam dulci dulcius est anima.
Tu potes a gnato dilectam avellere matrem,
10 Impia, vel centum rumpere vincla potes.
Quos natura potens, te praeter in omnia victrix,
  Mutua quos pietas, quos ita rara fides,
Quos mores placiti et dulcis concordia vitae
  Tam bene, tam multis nexibus unierant,
15 Hos tu ut distraheres tollis sine pignore matrem,
  Atque ita pars melior orba relicta mei est.
Sed bene, quod mors nostra scidit, tua, CHRISTE, resarcit,
  Plusque boni reddit quam dedit ista mali.

pure into the pure heavens. Lift them up through the prayers they beg for. Remember that the same fate lies in store for you. Pray by the death of the victim hanging on the lofty tree, pray by his wounds. If from this fountain flows powerful expiation for the living, from there it also flows for the dead. And so, if you are in a hurry, say a little prayer for light and rest and go on your way. Prepare yourself, too, for your tomb, for you will soon follow after us. Farewell.

10 The same lady's lament about her son, who was still alive

I was given the name Odilia at the sacred font and, as you see, that is all that is left of me. Death has snatched away the rest, and mother earth fondles in her lap nothing but ashes and dry bones. O cruel Death, what fitting gift should we pray for you to have except yourself, since it is your pleasure to split what love has joined so well? Now it does not matter that my limbs have been bereft of life. For there is something that is sweeter than the sweet breath of life. You, O impious Death, have the power to tear a beloved mother from her son, the power to break innumerable bonds. Those who were joined by mighty nature (who conquers everything but you), those who were so firmly united by so many links, mutual affection, extraordinary faithfulness, agreeable habits, the harmony of a sweet life, those two you tore apart by taking the mother without the son and thus leaving my better part orphaned and bereft of me. But what was slashed apart by my death, your death, Christ, heals completely, and the evil done by that death, yours more than outweighs in good.

11 Respondet filius sub pictura Christi crucifixi, Moysi, et serpentis. [July 1498? / 8 January 1507]

Vita fugax haud longa dedit divortia nostri:
En mors aequa tibi quod tulit ipsa refert.
Una duos pietas vivos bene iunxerat, ut nunc
Amborum cineres una recondit humus.
5 Amborum vultus tabula visuntur eadem;
Subripuit leto hoc ingeniosa manus.
At tu spectator, sortis memor omnibus aequae,
Haec saltem ex animo fundito vota sitis:
'CHRISTE, necis domitor ac vitae perpetis autor,
10 Iugem animis vitam morte repone tua.
Tu sacra illa silex, teretis quae verbere virgae
Vitaleis scatebras gentibus icta dedit,
Tuque salutiferum serpentis in arbore signum,
Quod veteris colubri cuncta venena domat.
15 Quin hodieque piis vitae fons ille perennis
Pectore defosso sanguis et unda scatet.
Ille dat exanimes reduci recalescere flatu,
Haec animae maculas abluit omnigenas.
His age muneribus dulci cum pignore matrem
20 In dextrum referens assere, CHRISTE, gregem.'

12 In filiam Bekae, quod sonat rivum lingua nostrate [1502–4 / 8 January 1507]

Sum Gulielma, patre Arnoldo cognomine Beka; is
Iuris fons gemini, non modo rivus erat.
Cui, gener Antoni, placuisti ex omnibus unus,

11 The son replies from under a picture representing Christ crucified, Moses, and the serpent.

Fleeting life did not keep us separated for long. Behold, what death took from you it justly gives back. Single-hearted affection joined the two of us firmly in life, just as a single plot of earth now conceals the ashes of us both. Both our faces are seen in one and the same painting; this much was snatched from death by the skilful hand of the craftsman. But you, O onlooker, remember the fate that comes equally to all. At least pour forth from your heart this prayer for those buried here: 'O Christ, victor over death and source of everlasting life, restore by your death perpetual life to their souls. You are that rock which gave forth living streams to the nations when it was struck by the polished staff. You are the salvific sign of the serpent on the tree, which overcomes all the venom of the ancient serpent. Indeed, to this very day you are for the faithful that perennial fountain; from your pierced side flow blood and water. That blood makes the dead grow warm again and restores the breath of life; this water washes from the soul all manner of stains. Come then, by these gifts of yours, Christ, when you raise up the mother and her sweet son, claim them for the flock at your right hand.'

12 On the daughter of Beka, which in our language means 'brook'

I am Wilhelmina, surnamed Beka after my father Arnold. In his mastery of the twin laws he was not only no mere brook: he was a spring. You, Antoon, as his son-in-law, were the one who pleased him above all the others;

Isbrandum referens ore animoque patrem.
5 Nec minus est mea vita tibi quam forma probata;
Templa, domus, proles, haec mea cura fuit.
Quatuor enixam pueros totidemque puellas
Mors rapit intra aevi septima lustra mei.
Lector, age huic requiem cinerique animaeque precatus
10 Vive diu, imo diu est hic nihil, ergo bene.

13 Epitaphium Margaretae Honorae [1497–9? / 8 January 1507]

Hic sita Margareta est, merito cognomine Honora,
Fiscini, tedis digna, Guihelme, tuis.
Quam bene congruerant et forma et pectus et anni
Et ne morte quidem dissoluendus amor.
5 Rapta sed est viridis primaevo in flore iuventae,
Ut rosa lacteolis semadaperta comis.
Dimidius superest dulci sine coniuge coniunx,
Moerens ut viduus compare turtur ave.

14 Episcopo Traiectensi David, notho Philippi ducis Borgondionum [May? 1496 / 8 January 1507]

Hic situs est praesul, non tantum nomine, David,
Digna patre proles, magne Philippe, tua.
Iste gregem plusquam patria pietate fovebat,
Pacis amans, virtuti ingeniisque favens.

you bring to mind your father Ysbrandtsz, both in looks and temperament. You approved no less of my way of life than of my person; church, home, children – these were my concerns. After I had borne four boys and as many girls, death snatched me away in the first half of my fourth decade. Come now, reader, when you have said a prayer for the rest of both my ashes and my soul, live long – nay, nothing here is long – therefore live well.

13 An epitaph for Margaret Honora

Here is Margaret laid to rest, deserving of her surname Honora, worthy of your hand in marriage, William Fiscinius. In her how well were matched beauty and understanding and years and love, love which not even death can dissolve. But she was snatched away in the first flowering of her vigorous youth, like a rose that has only half opened its milk-white petals. Without his sweet wife her husband remains behind, half what he was, mourning like a turtle-dove bereaved of its mate.

14 For David, bishop of Utrecht, the illegitimate son of Philip, duke of Burgundy

Laid to rest here is David, who was a bishop in more than name. Mighty Philip, he was a worthy scion of you, his father. He cherished his flock with a more than fatherly devotion. He was a lover of peace and a patron of virtue and of gifted men.

15 Eidem [May? 1496 / 8 January 1507]

Hic David ille, duci proles iactanda Philippo.
Commissum patrio fovit amore gregem.

16 Iacobo Batto, Graeco dimetro iambico [1502 / 8 January 1507]

Ἰάκωβε Βάττε, θάρσεο,
Καλῶς θανὼν παλιμφύει.

17 Iidem Latini versus [1502 / 8 January 1507]

Iacobe Batte, ne time,
Bene moriens renascitur.

18 In tergo codicis Battici [before 1502 / 8 January 1507]

Sum Batti. Qui me manibus subduxerit uncis,
Huic ne quo Battus defuat opto loco.

19 Duo salina argentea abbati cuidam dono missa a monialibus monasterii vulgo dicti Vallis virginum [autumn 1497? / 8 January 1507]

Virginea de valle duo sine labe salilla
Adsumus; hanc mensam non nisi pura decent.

In altero salino

Virginitas nitor argenti, sapientia sal est.
Virgo dat argentum, tu, pater, adde salem.

15 For the same man

Here lies David, a scion of whom Duke Philip should be proud. With fatherly love he cherished the flock committed to his charge.

16 To Jacob Batt, in Greek iambic dimeters

Jacob Batt, take heart; whoever dies well is born again.

17 The same verses in Latin

Jacob Batt, have no fear; whoever dies well is born again.

18 On the back of a codex belonging to Batt

I belong to Batt; if anyone takes me away in his grasping claws, I hope that, wherever it may be, he may not lack a Battus.

19 Two silver salt-cellars, sent as a gift to a certain abbot by the nuns of the convent commonly called Maidendale

Here we are, two salt-cellars without flaw, come from Maidendale. For this table only the pure is fitting.

On the second salt-cellar

Shining silver stands for maidenhood; salt, for wisdom. A maiden gives the silver; you, father, add the salt.

20 In sex tintinabula restituta, quae fulmine conflagrarant

[1497–1501? / 8 January 1507]

Concinimus sex aera, at ego cui maxima vox est
Alpha et ω Triadi rite dicata vocor.
Nos aedemque sacram Scasti pia cura Girardi
Praesulis absumptam fulmine restituit.

In tintinabulum Mariae sacrum

5 Aenea mi vox est, ac sic nulla aenea vox est,
Ut par Christiparae laudibus esse queat.

In idem

Maria nomen inditum est mihi mutuum,
Qua trinitati nil sedet vicinius.

Tertium Baptistae sacrum

Vox clamantis erat, cuius gero nomina; plebem
10 Ad CHRISTI cultum nocte dieque voco.

Quartum Petro sacrum

Petro sacra fugo cacodaemonas, arceo fulmen,
Funeraque et festos cantibus orno dies.

Quintum Magdalenae sacrum. Scazon

Sum Magdalenae; iuvit impium fulmen,
Meliora quando cuncta dat pius praesul.

20 On six bells that were recast after they were ruined in a fire caused by lightning

We six bronze bells ring together in harmony, but I who have the biggest voice am called the alpha and the omega and am rightly dedicated to the Trinity. We and the holy church building destroyed by lightning were restored through the pious solicitude of the prelate Gerard Scastus.

On the bell sacred to Mary

I have a voice of bronze, but there is no voice of bronze that can be equal to the task of praising her who gave birth to Christ.

On the same

The name I have been given is borrowed from Mary, for no one has a seat closer to the Trinity than she does.

The third, sacred to the Baptist

I bear the name of one who was a voice crying out; I call the people night and day to the worship of Christ.

The fourth, sacred to Peter

Sacred to Peter, I put the evil demons to flight; I ward off lightning; with my song I adorn both funerals and feast-days.

The fifth, sacred to the Magdalen, in scazons

I belong to the Magdalen; the wicked lightning bolt had a good effect, since the pious prelate renders everything better than before.

Sextum omnibus sanctis sacrum

15 Exilis mihi vox, sed quae ferit eminus aures;
Dat mihi caelicolum nomina tota cohors.

Aliter

Non mihi Dodones, non aera prophana Corinthi
Certent, nam cunctis tinnio caelitibus.

21 In aulicum quendam clero infestum [8 January 1507]

Ursalus ecce Midas, sed Lydo stultior illo,
Se properat quovis nobilitare modo
Et furit in clerum; capit hinc exordia famae
Eque Mida subito vertitur in Phalarim.
5 Sic quondam exusto peperit sibi nomina templo,
Credo, autor generis Graeculus ille mali.
Tam stolidam mentem nullis aboleveris undis,
At rabiem solus tollere mucro queat.

22 In eundem [8 January 1507]

Tam stolidum, credo, nec te, Mida, pectus habebat,
Malce, nec in clerum tam violentus eras,
Quam quidam – non est sententia dicere nomen,
Nam famam affectat qualibet ille via.
5 Huic utinam aut aliquis asininas addat Apollo
Aut ambas Petrus demetat auriculas,
Aut certe crepet ipse magis faciatque paterni
Quod cognomenti syllaba prima monet.

The sixth, sacred to all the saints

My voice is thin but it strikes the ear from afar; the whole host of saints in heaven give me their names.

Another

Not the bronze of Dodona, not the unhallowed bronze of Corinth can vie with me, for I ring out for all the saints in heaven.

21 On a certain courtier who is anticlerical

See how Ursalus, a Midas but more stupid than that Lydian, is trying to become well known in short order, by any means whatever. And so he rages against the clergy, thinking to make this the starting point of his fame, and from a Midas he has suddenly changed into a Phalaris. In the same way, I believe, that Greekling once got himself a great name by burning a temple – he was the originator of a vicious race. You could not do away with such a stupid mind as Ursalus' with floods of water; only a sword-point could put down his rage.

22 On the same man

I don't think that even you, Midas, had as stupid a mind or that you, Malchus, were as violent against the clergy, as a certain person – I don't intend to tell you his name, for this man pursues fame by any means whatever. Would that some Apollo would give him ass's ears or some Peter would lop off both his ears. Or rather let him burst and so do what is meant by the first syllable of his father's family name.

23 **In eundem** [8 January 1507]

Bacchanti in clerum tibi dixerat, Ursale, quidam
Et ius Caesareum laedier atque sacrum.
Hic tu ridebas hominem multumque diuque –
Et merito, quid enim hoc stultius ac levius? –
5 Qui praeter tibi iura coqui notissima iuris
Auditum nomen crederet esse aliud.

24 **In picturam fabulae Giganteae** [8 January 1507]

En stolida sine patre sati tellure Gigantes
Montibus accumulant montes ipsumque minantur
Caelicolum regem supera detrudere ab arce.
Sed male vaesanae cedent sine pectore vires.

25 **In eosdem fulmine depulsos** [8 January 1507]

Iuppiter extructas disturbat fulmine moles,
Ignibus involvens rapidis monteisque virosque.
Sic sic vis sine consilio, sic impia facta
Praecipitata ruunt superis ultoribus usque.

26 **In tabulam Penthei trucidati** [8 January 1507]

Penthea cernis Echioniden,
Hospitis orgia qui Bromii
Spreverat. Impius ecce deo
Vindice iam malefacta luit.
5 Matris enim Orgiadumque manu,

23 On the same man

When you were raging against the clergy, Ursalus, someone said to you that to do so is an offence against the legal saws of the emperor and the church. Thereupon you laughed long and loud at the man, and rightly, for what could be more stupid and empty-headed than to think that to your ears the word 'saws' means anything other than the sauce of the cook, which you know very well indeed?

24 On a picture based on the story of the Giants

See how the Giants, born of the senseless earth with no father, are piling mountains on top of mountains and threatening to cast down from his lofty palace the very king of the heaven-dwellers. But mere mad power without intelligence will fail.

25 On the same Giants, cast down by lightning

With lightning Jupiter shatters the massive structure they have built up, enveloping both mountains and men in raging flames. So it is that force without deliberation, so it is that wicked deeds are constantly hurled down headlong by the avenging gods.

26 On a picture of the slaughtered Pentheus

You are looking at Pentheus, the son of Echion, who scorned the wild rites of the foreign god Bacchus. See how the wicked man, struck by the vengeance of the god, now pays for his crimes. For he perishes at the hands of

Dum fera creditur esse, perit.
Quam sceleri bene poena suo
Congruit et mala digna malis!

27 In picturam Europae stupratae [8 January 1507]

Hic qui a monte boves ad proxima littora vertit,
Aurea te quis sit virga monere potest.
Tum testes alae neque non talaria, testis
In flavo bicolor crine galerus erit.
5 Si rogitas quid agat, patrio subservit amori
Inscius, obsequio furta dolosa tegens.
Raptor enim nivei latitat sub imagine tauri
Improbus ac praedam per freta longa vehet.
Ut Cretam attigerit, mox taurus desinet esse
10 Iuppiter, et virgo non erit ista diu.
Quid non caecus amor mortalia pectora cogat,
Si taurum aethereum non piget esse Iovem?
Aut quae formosis satis est cautela puellis,
Hic quoque stuprator si metuendus erat?

28 In fronte libelli dono missi episcopo Atrebatensi. Scazon [autumn 1503 / 8 January 1507]

Avibus sequundis vade, charteum munus,
Exile quanquam te brevis dicat vates.
Liceat modo placere praesuli docto,
Precio lapillos viceris et Erithreos.

his mother and the bacchantes, who think he is a wild beast. How well the punishment fits the crime and the evil inflicted matches the evil committed!

27 On a picture of the rape of Europa

Who this person is that is making the oxen veer from the mountain toward the nearby shore, you can tell by his golden wand. Other marks of his identity are the wings on his sandals, and also the two-coloured hat on his blond hair. If you ask what he is doing, he is accommodating himself to his father's amorous passion, though he is unaware of this, even as he obediently conceals the treacherous theft. For the outrageous ravisher is hiding under the appearance of a snow-white bull, and he will carry his prey far across the sea. As soon as he reaches Crete, Jupiter will cease to be a bull, and she will no longer be a virgin. To what lengths does blind passion goad the hearts of mortals, if even heavenly Jupiter was not ashamed to be a bull? Or what precautions can be sufficient to protect beautiful girls, if even such a god as this must be feared as a ravisher?

28 At the beginning of a little book sent as a gift to the bishop of Arras, in scazons

Go, paper gift, with favourable omens, even though you are a meagre work dedicated by a slight poet. If only you can manage to please the learned prelate, you will be more valuable than pearls, even those from the Persian Gulf.

Elegās libellus ac nūc primū impressus/de pcellētia pote
statis imperatorie. i quo plurima lectu vehemēter tū vtilia
tū amoena ex variis authorib⁹: de ortu/gradib⁹/& discri
mīe dignitatū ciuiliū & ecclesiasticarū cōscript⁹ a viro vn
decūq; doctissimo Iacobo middelburgeñ. iuris pōtificii p
fessore. Hērici de Bergis epi Cameraceñ. vicario generali

Ad lectores distichon.
Christianum orbem tuenti/qui fauetis Caesari
Huic fauebitis libello: qui tuetur Caesarem.

J. Anthoniszoon *De praecellentia potestatis imperatoriae*, title-page
Antwerp: Dirk Martens 1502 (NS 1503)
Courtesy The Newberry Library, Chicago

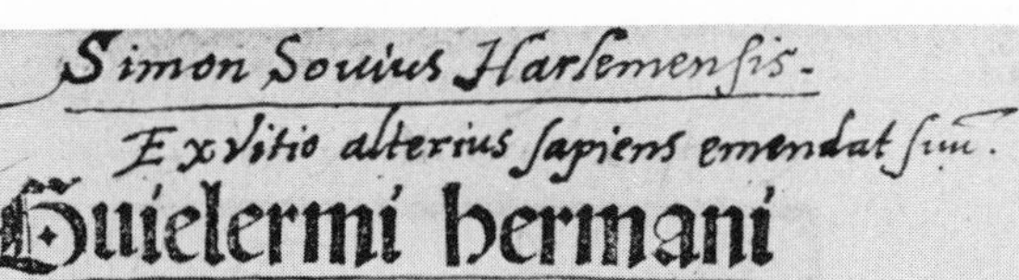

Simon Souius Harlemensis.

Ex vitio alterius sapiens emendat suum.

Guielermi hermani

Goudensis Theologi ac Poetae clarissimi Sylua Odarum.

¶ Hendecasyllabum herasmi ad studiosos.

Huc si quem pia si pudica musa
Delectat: nihil hic vel inquinatum
Vel quod melle nocens tegat venenum
Christum tota sonat Chelis Guielmi.

Erasmus.

Queritur unde tibi sit nomen Erasmus? Eras Mus.

Resp.

Si sum Mus ego, te judice, Summus ero.

Willem Hermans *Sylva odarum*, title-page
Paris: G. Marchant, 20 January 1497
Gemeentebibliotheek, Rotterdam

29 In fronte libelli de imperatoria maiestate

[13 February 1503 / 1 April 1503]

Christianum orbem tuenti qui favetis Caesari,
Huic favebitis libello qui tuetur Caesarem.

30 In fronte Odarum Guilielmi

[20 January 1497]

Huc, siquem pia, si pudica Musa
Delectat: nihil hic vel inquinatum
Vel quod melle nocens tegat venenum.
CHRISTUM tota sonat chelis Guihelmi.

31 In fronte libelli Buslidio dono missi

[November 1503? / 8 January 1507]

Non ego Buslidiae decus adfero bibliothecae,
  Sed decus apponit bibliotheca mihi.

32 In fronte alterius

[November 1503? / 8 January 1507]

Non equidem ornabis tu Antoni bibliothecam,
  Te magis ornabit bibliotheca, liber.

33 In caecum tragoediarum castigatorem

[autumn 1506 / 8 January 1507]

Quur adeo, lector, crebris offendere mendis?
  Qui castigavit, lumine captus erat.

29 On the title-page of a little book on the majesty of the emperor

If you are well disposed toward the emperor, who defends the Christian world, you will be well disposed toward this little book, which defends the emperor.

30 On the title-page of Willem's *Odes*

Come hither, all you who delight in a pious and chaste muse. There is nothing here that is either defiled or that covers deadly poison with honey. The lyre of Willem resounds with nothing except Christ.

31 On the title-page of a little book sent as a gift to Busleyden

I bring no honour to Busleyden's library. Rather, the library confers honour on me.

32 On the title-page of another

No, book, you will not grace the library of Antonius. Rather, the library will grace you.

33 On a blind corrector of some tragedies

Why, reader, are you so offended by the frequent errors? The man who did the correcting was quite blind.

34 Sub pictura vultus Christi [1503? / 8 January 1507]

Hic intuetur et intimos mentis sinus.
Fac tota niteant pectoris penetralia.

35 Agit carmine gratias pro misso munere [1505–6 / 8 January 1507]

Antistes sacer elegantiorum ac
Princeps, Carmiliane, literarum,
En versus tenuis tibi poeta
Hos pro munere splendido rependit.
5 Hoc est scilicet, aere mutat aurum.
At quid tandem aliud deis vel ipsis
Gratus sed tenuis referre vates
Possit quam numeros modosque? Verum
Largiri numeros tibi, Petre, hoc est
10 Sylvae ligna, vago mari addere undas.

36 In fronte Enchiridii [15 February 1503]

Nil moror aut laudes levis aut convicia vulgi:
  Pulchrum est vel doctis vel placuisse piis.
Spe quoque maius erit mihi si contingat utrunque;
  Cui CHRISTUS sapit, huic si placeo, bene habet.
5 Unicus ille mihi venae largitor Apollo,
  Sunt Helicon huius mystica verba meus.

37 Libellus dono missus [1 January 1506? / 8 January 1507]

Mittere quur verear magno leve munus amico,
  Quum capiant summos thuscula pauca deos?

34 Under a picture of Christ's face

This man looks into the innermost recesses of the mind. See to it that the secret places of your heart are all bright and shining.

35 A poem offering thanks for a gift sent to him

Carmeliano, holy high priest and prince of literary refinement, here are some verses from an impoverished poet, sent to you in repayment of your splendid gift – that is, here is bronze in exchange for gold. But after all, what can a poet who is grateful but poor offer even to the gods themselves except verses and songs? But to bestow such lines on you, Pietro, is like bringing logs to a forest or adding water to the shifting sea.

36 On the title-page of *Enchiridion*

I do not care about the praise or the insults of the superficial mob. The fine thing is to please either the learned or the pious. If I happen to do either of these, it is more than I hoped for. If I please someone who relishes the wisdom of Christ, it is well. Christ alone is my Apollo, the source of my vein; his mystic words are my Helicon.

37 A little book sent as a gift

Why should I be afraid to send a little gift to a lofty friend, since even the highest gods are captivated by a few bits of incense?

38 Ioanni Okego musico summo epitaphium [c February 1497 / 8 January 1507]

Ergone conticuit
Vox illa quondam nobilis,
Aurea vox Okegi?
Sic musicae extinctum decus?
5 Dic age, dic fidibus
Tristes, Apollo, naenias.
Tu quoque, Calliope
Pullata cum sororibus,
Funde pias lachrymas.
10 Lugete, quotquot musicae
Dulce rapit studium,
Virumque ferte laudibus.
Artis Apollineae
Sacer ille Phoenix occidit.
15 Quid facis, invida mors?
Obmutuit vox aurea,
Aurea vox Okegi,
Vel saxa flectere efficax,
Quae toties liquidis
20 Et arte flexilibus modis
Per sacra tecta sonans
Demulsit aures caelitum
Terrigenumque simul
Penitusque movit pectora.
25 Quid facis, invida mors?
Vel hoc iniqua maxime,
Aequa quod omnibus es.
Sat erat tibi promiscue
Tollere res hominum.
30 Divina res est musica.
Numina quur violas?

39 Henrici episcopi Cameracensis epitaphium [autumn 1502 / 8 January 1507]

Henricus hic est, Bergicae stirpis decus,
Qui laude morum avita vicit stemmata.

38 An epitaph for the superlative musician Jan Ockeghem

Has it fallen silent then, that voice once so renowned, the golden voice of Ockeghem? Is the glory of music thus snuffed out? Sing, Apollo, come sing a sad dirge to your lyre. You also, Calliope, clad in mourning together with your sisters, pour forth loving tears. Mourn, all who are enraptured by the sweet pursuit of music, and extoll this man with your praises. That sacred Phoenix of Apollo's art is dead.

What are you doing, O envious Death? The golden voice has been silenced, the golden voice of Ockeghem, the voice that could move even stones, the voice that so often resounded in the vaulted nave with fluid and subtly modulated melodies, soothing the ears of the saints in heaven and likewise piercing the hearts of earthborn men.

What are you doing, O envious Death? You are unjust precisely because you deal justly with everyone. It would be enough for you to take away indiscriminately the things that belong to mankind. Music is something divine. Why do you violate the divine?

39 An epitaph for Hendrik, bishop of Cambrai

Here is Hendrik, the splendour of the Bergen lineage, who surpassed his ancestral pedigree

Gregis salute nil habuit antiquius,
In quem pius paterna gessit viscera.
5 Hic incitatus amore miro caelitum,
Iacobe, sedem visit impiger tuam,
Arcemque Petri visit et Solymas sacras.

40 De eodem [autumn 1502 / 8 January 1507]

Berganae stirpis septem de fratribus unum
 Condidit Henricum hoc invida Parca loco.
Ille gregis Cameracini praesulque paterque,
 Cui simul et patriae, non sibi natus erat,
5 Bisque Iacobaeam visit pius advena sedem,
 Dehinc Romam et Solymas vectus adusque sacras.
Sic pietate vagus, virtute gravissimus, aevum
 Exegit felix et sine labe suum.

41 In magnatem quendam, sed ficto nomine, qui laudes suas exiguo munusculo pensarat [1498–1500? / 8 January 1507]

Correxit errorem meum
Lepide Marullus, nam mihi
Laudatus aequo largius
Nimium pusillo prodigum
5 Vatem redonat munere.
O pectus, o memorabilem
Huius modestiam viri!
Non vult cani quae non facit,
Vult et sileri quae facit.
10 Proin pudendis praemiis
Invitat ad palinodiam,
Invitat ad silentium.
Non suadet hoc frugalitas
Tenaxque parsimonia,

through praiseworthy conduct. He considered nothing more important than the salvation of his flock, to whom he devoted his heart like a loving father. Aroused by a marvellous love of the saints in heaven, this man zealously visited your shrine, James, and he visited the citadel of Peter and holy Jerusalem.

40 On the same man

Of the seven brothers from the lineage of Bergen, envious Fate buried one, Hendrik, in this place. He was the bishop and the father of the flock of Cambrai. For them and for his fatherland he was born, not for himself. And as a pious pilgrim he twice visited the shrine of James. Afterwards he travelled to Rome and all the way to holy Jerusalem. Wandering thus out of piety, most steadfast in virtue, he finished his life a happy and a blameless man.

41 On a certain magnate (under a fictitious name) who rewarded a eulogy of himself with a very small remuneration

Marullus corrected my mistake neatly, for when I had praised him too much, he rewarded his prodigal poet by paying him too little. O the insight, the remarkable modesty of the man! He does not want to be celebrated in verse for what he does not do; he also wants what he does do to be passed over in silence. And thus by shameful rewards he invites me to recant what I have said; he invites me to be silent. He is not motivated to do this by thriftiness and tight-fisted stinginess, since at

15 Quum sannionibus quoque
Foedisque morionibus
Prolixa donet munera.
Quod ista donat vatibus,
Quae dare minus quam nil dare est,
20 Pudore, non vitio facit.

42 Ode dicolos, distrophos, altero versu heroico hexametro, altero iambico dimetro. De casa natalitia pueri IESU deque paupere puerperio virginis deiparae Mariae

[c Christmas 1490? / January 1496]

Ecquid adhuc veterum sequimur spectacula rerum?
Huc huc frequentes currite.
Haec casa, quae lacera et stat agrestibus horrida culmis,
Novum dabit spectaculum,
5 Quale nihil saeclis proavi videre vetustis,
Nihil videbunt posteri.
Hic cuius tonitru tellusque tremiscit et aether
Teneris crepat vagitibus.
Hic orbis magni moderator maximus infans
10 Virginea mulget ubera.
His ego non stabulis augusta palatia Romae
Feliciora iudicem,
Non (operosa licet) Solomonia templa nec auream
Lydi tyranni regiam.
15 Salve, clara domus caeloque beatior ipso,
Partus sacrati conscia.
Iure tibi Iovis invideant Capitolia falsi,
Divis superba saxeis.
Aegyptus sancta invideat cunabula, monstris
20 Finem datura turpibus.
Nec minus apta deo es, quod hiantibus undique rimis
Imbres et Euros accipis,
Quod lodicis egens rigidoque incommoda foeno
Foetus rubenteis excipis.
25 Talia nascentem decuere cubilia CHRISTUM, ut
Qui dedocere venerit

the same time he lavishes gifts on buffoons and filthy fools. He rewards poets by giving them less than nothing, not out of stinginess but out of shame.

42 An ode in couplets alternating between two kinds of lines, heroic hexameters and iambic dimeters. On the shed where the boy Jesus was born and on the impoverished delivery of the Virgin Mary, the mother of God

Why do we still search out the marvels of ancient times? Hither, come crowding hither! This shed, which stands dilapidated and bristling with rustic thatch, will provide a new marvel, the likes of which our forefathers never saw in past ages, nor will posterity see the like. Here the one whose thunder makes heaven and earth tremble puts forth his weak cries. Here the almighty ruler of the universe is a baby sucking his milk from virgin breasts. This stable is more fortunate, in my judgment, than the august palace of Rome or the temple of Solomon (though it was indeed elaborate) or the golden palace of the Lydian tyrant. Hail, splendid dwelling, more blessed than heaven itself, since you experienced this sacred birth. The Capitoline temple of the false god Jupiter, proud of its stone deities, should rightly envy you. Egypt should envy the holy cradle which will put an end to its shameful and monstrous gods.

You are no less suitable to God because on all sides your gaping cracks let in the wind and rain or because you lack a coverlet and so receive the ruddy child into your stiff and disagreeable hay. Such a bed was suitable for the newborn Christ, since he came to preach

Fastum nullaque non suadentem turpia luxum.
Non hic renident purpurae
Sertave frondea, non imitantes fulmina taedae,
30 Non mensa sumptuosior,
Nec strepit officiis domus ambitiosa, nec alti
Fovent puerperam thori.
Pannosus iacet in duris praesepibus infans,
Divinus attamen vigor
35 Emicat et patrios vagitu dispuit ignes.
Sensere praesentem deum
Quodque licet puero iumenta tepentibus auris
Frigus decembre temperant.
Upilio calamis iisdem, quibus ante capellis,
40 Agreste, sed pium canit,
Aethereique chori volitant cunabula circum.
Ut mensibus vernis apum
Degenerem simul ac pepulere examina regem,
Regi novo faventibus
45 Applaudunt alis sublimemque agmine tollunt:
Sic turma caelitum, duci
Circumfusa suo, gaudens stupet atque iacentem
Pronis adorat vultibus
Et natalitium sonat ad praesaepia carmen.
50 Coniux pudicus interim,
Fusus humi, magnum trepidus veneratur alumnum.
Porro puella, nobilis
Pars bona spectacli, defixis haeret ocellis
Primumque sese non capit
55 Seque suumque stupens genitrix virguncula partum,
Nulli marito debitum.
At simul eiecit pietas materna stuporem,
Praedulce pignus corripit
Ac modo porrectis prohibet vagire papillis,
60 Modo tepente frigidum
Blanda fovet gremio parvisque dat oscula labris.
Nunc pectori adprimit suo,
Nunc bleso teneros invitat murmure somnos.
Amabili invicem modo
65 Laetam prole deo videas gestire parentem,
Prolem parente virgine.

against pride and luxurious excesses that lead to all sorts of shameful vice. Here there is no splendour of purple cloth, no wreaths woven from leafy boughs, no torches emulating flashes of lightning, no sumptuous banquet tables, no showy house full of the busy hum of servants, no lofty bed to comfort the lady in labour. Swaddled in rags, the babe lies in the hard manger. But nevertheless a divine force flashes forth from him and his cries spew forth his Father's fires. The beasts of burden sense that God is present there, and they do what they can for the boy to temper the December cold with their warm breath. The herdsman, on the same reed-pipe he has just before played for his goats, plays a rustic but loving song. The heavenly choirs fly around the cradle. Just as in the spring months a swarm of bees, as soon as they have expelled their unworthy king, applaud the new king with their buzzing wings and lift him up with their moving mass: just so the troop of angels surround their commander in joyful amazement, and with lowered faces they adore the child lying there and sing his birthday song at the manger. Meanwhile the chaste husband, lying prostrate on the ground, fearfully venerates his mighty fosterling. And then the girl, an important part of the noble spectacle, cannot take her eyes off the babe, and at first she is at a loss, a virgin mother amazed at herself and her offspring, one born with no help from her husband. But as soon as motherly love has overcome her amazement, she picks up the sweet child and then she stops him from crying by giving him her breast, and then she holds the cold babe gently in her warm lap and kisses his little lips. Now she presses him to her bosom; now with a murmuring lullaby she invites gentle sleep. It is a lovely sight: by turns the joyful mother delighting in her divine child and the child in his virgin mother.

43 Des. Erasmi Roterodami expostulatio IESU cum homine suapte culpa pereunte

[1510–11? / 1 September 1511]

Cum mihi sint uni bona quae vel frondea tellus
Vel Olympus ingens continet,
Dicite, mortales, quae vos dementia cepit,
Haec aucupari ut unde vis
5 Malitis quam de proprio deposcere fonte,
Adeo benigno et obvio,
Mendacesque iuvet trepido miseroque tumultu
Umbras bonorum persequi,
Pauci me, qui sum verae largitor et autor
10 Felicitatis, expetant?
Forma rapit multos: me nil formosius usquam est,
Formam ardet hanc nemo tamen.
Suspiciunt ceras antiquaque stemmata multi,
At me quid est illustrius,
15 Ut qui sim genitore deo deus ipse profectus,
Genitrice natus virgine?
Unde fit, ut mecum vix gestiat unus et alter
Affinitatem iungere?
Maximus ille ego sum caelique solique monarcha:
20 Servire nobis cur pudet?
Dives item et facilis dare magna et multa roganti,
Rogari amo: nemo rogat.
Sumque vocorque patris summi sapientia: nemo
Me consulit mortalium.
25 Ipse ego sum aetherei splendorque decusque parentis:
Me nemo stupet aut suspicit.
Sum firmus iuxta ac iucundus amicus amico,
Me pariter ac meas opes
Candidus atque lubens charis impertio: nemo hanc
30 Ambit necessitudinem.
Sum via qua sola caeli itur ad astra, tamen me
Terit viator infrequens.
Cur tandem ignarum dubitat mihi credere vulgus,
Aeterna cum sim veritas?
35 Pollicitis cur, stulte, meis diffidere perstas,

43 The expostulation of Jesus with mankind, perishing by its own fault, by Desiderius Erasmus of Rotterdam

Since all the good things to be found in the greenery of the earth or in the vastness of the sky belong to me alone, tell me, mortals, what fit of madness makes you prefer to hunt for them anywhere else rather than ask for them from their source, so generous and accessible, and makes you eager to pursue the deceptive shadows of good things with such anxiety and miserable agitation, while few seek after me, the source and giver of true happiness? Many are obsessed with beauty: nothing anywhere is more beautiful than I am, yet no one burns with love for this beauty. Many admire ancestral statues and ancient pedigrees, but what can be more illustrious than I, since I who am myself God was begotten by God the Father and born of a virgin mother? How is it that only one or two are eager to ally themselves with me by marriage? I am that greatest monarch of heaven and earth: why are people ashamed to serve us? I am rich as well and quick to give many great gifts to anyone who asks – I love to be asked: no one asks. I am and I am called the wisdom of the highest Father: no one among mortals asks me for advice. I myself am the splendour and the glory of the heavenly Father: no one looks up to me with amazement. As a friend I am equally faithful and genial to my friend; openly and willingly I share both myself and my resources with those who are dear to me: no one seeks this bond of friendship. I am the only way that leads up to the stars in the heavens, but rarely am I trodden by any traveller. Why in the world does the ignorant mob hesitate to believe me, since I am eternal truth? Fool, why do you persist in not trusting

Cum sit nihil fidelius?
Autor ad haec vitae cum sim unicus ipsaque vita,
Cur sordeo mortalibus?
Lux ego sum: cur huc vertunt sua lumina pauci?
40 Dux: cur gravantur insequi?
Vivendi recte certissima regula solus:
Aliunde formas cur petunt?
Ipse ego sum solus vera et sine felle voluptas:
Quid est quod ita fastidior?
45 Unica pax animi: quin huc deponitis aegri
Curas edaces pectoris?
Si benefacta truces etiam meminere leones
Referuntque beluae vicem,
Respondere feri merito didicere dracones,
50 Si meminit officii canis,
Si redamant aquilae, redamant delphines amantem,
Cur efferacior feris
Me me non redamas homo, cui semel omnia feci,
Quem condidi, quem sanguine
55 Asserui proprio propriaeque a morte recepi
Dispendio vitae volens?
Si bos agnoscit dominum, si brutus asellus
Agnoscit altorem suum,
Cur me solus, homo, male gratus nosse recusas
60 Et conditorem et vindicem?
Unus ego hic tibi sum cunctorum summa bonorum:
Quid est quod extra me petas?
Quorsum distraheris per tot dispendia, grassans
Laboriosa inertia?
65 Sum placabilis et pronus miserescere: quin hoc
Miser ad asylum confugis?
Idem iustus et implacabilis ultor iniqui:
Cur non times offendere?
Corpus ego atque animum nutu sub Tartara mitto:
70 Nostri metus vix ullum habet.
Proinde, mei desertor homo, secordia si te
Adducet in mortem tua,
Praeteritum nihil est. In me ne reiice culpam,
Malorum es ipse autor tibi.

my promises, since no one is more trustworthy? Since I am also the only source of life, since I am life itself, why do mortals think me so paltry? I am the light: why do so few turn their eyes hither? I am the leader: why are they so reluctant to follow? I alone am the most reliable rule of right living: why do they seek their patterns elsewhere? I myself am the only true pleasure, with no admixture of bitterness: why is it that I am found so distasteful? I am the only peace of mind: why do you not come hither and lay down the cares eating at your troubled hearts? If even savage lions remember good deeds and wild beasts repay them, if fierce snakes have learned to do a good turn to someone who has earned it, if a dog remembers its duty, if eagles and dolphins return love for love, why, oh why do you not return my love, O man more beastly than the beasts, for whom I made all things once for all, whom I created, whom I freed with my own blood, whom I saved from death by willingly giving up my own life? If an ox recognizes its master, if a dumb ass recognizes the man who feeds it, why are you alone, O mankind, so ungrateful that you refuse to recognize me, both your creator and your redeemer? For you I alone am the sum of all good things here: what is there for you to seek apart from me? What good is it to be torn among so many pursuits, wasting your energy in toilsome idleness? I am forgiving and quickly moved to mercy: in your misery why do you not take refuge in this sanctuary? I am also a just and implacable punisher of evil: why do you not fear to offend me? With a nod I send body and soul together down to hell: hardly anyone is constrained by fear of me. And so, O mankind, if you desert me and stupidly cause your own death, there is nothing I have not done. Do not put the blame on me; you yourself are the

75 Nam quid adhuc superest si te neque provocat ardens
Suique prodiga charitas,
O bis marmoreum pectus, neque mitigat unquam
Adeo profusa benignitas,
Si neque tantarum vel spes certissima rerum
80 Expergefacit et allicit,
Si neque Tartareae cohibet formido gehennae,
Nec ullus admonet pudor,
Immo si durant magis haec adduntque stuporem
Tam multa tamque insignia,
85 Ut facile immanesque feras chalybemque petramque
Rigore victo molliant,
Quid faciat pietas, quibus artibus abstrahat ultro
Devota morti pectora?
Invitum servare nec est mentis, puto, sanae
90 Et patria prohibet aequitas.

44 Carmen iambicum [1510–11 / 1 September 1511]

Non invenusto antiquitas aenigmate
Studii magistram virginem
Finxit Minervam, ac literarum praesides
Finxit Camoenas virgines.
5 Nunc ipse virgo matre natus virgine
Praesideo virgineo gregi,
Et sospitator huius et custos scholae.
Adsunt ministri virgines,
Pueros meos mecum tuentes angeli.
10 Mihi grata ubique puritas,
Decetque studia literarum puritas.
Procul ergo sacro a limine
Morum arceant mihi literatores luem,
Nihil huc recipiant barbarum.
15 Procul arceant illiteratas literas,
Nec regna polluant mea.

source of your own afflictions. For what is there still left to do if you are neither aroused by burning and self-sacrificing charity, O heart twice as hard as marble, nor are ever softened by such abundant kindness, if you are not awakened and allured even by the firmest hope for such great rewards, not restrained by fear of the depths of hell, not prompted by shame, nay, if you are hardened and numbed by these things, so numerous and so extraordinary that they would easily overcome the hardness of monstrous beasts and soften steel and stone – if this is so, what can kindness do, with what other devices can it hold back hearts willingly devoted to death? To save someone against his will is not, I think, a sane thing to do, and the justice of my Father forbids it.

44 A poem in iambic metre

In an allegory not without elegance, the ancients imagined the virgin Minerva as the mistress of study, and they imagined the virgin Muses as the guardians of reading and writing. Now I, myself a virgin born of a virgin mother, am the patron of a virgin flock, the preserver and guardian of this school. My assistants are virgins, angels who join me in guarding my boys. Purity is everywhere pleasing to me and purity is an appropriate goal for literary studies. Therefore let my teachers of reading and writing keep all moral filth far from this sacred threshold; let them admit nothing barbarous here. Let them keep far hence all illiterate literacy and let them not defile my kingdom.

45 Sapphicum [1510–11 / 1 September 1511]

Coeperit faustis avibus precamur,
Semper augescens meliore fato,
Hic novae sudor novus officinae,
  Auspice IESU.
5 Hic rudis (tanquam nova testa) pubes
Literas Graias simul et Latinas
Et fidem sacram tenerisque CHRISTUM
  Combibet annis.
Quid fuit laeta sobolem dedisse
10 Corporis forma, nisi mens et ipsa
Rite fingatur studiisque castis
  Culta nitescat?
Stirpe ab hac sensim nova pullulabit
Civium proles, pietate iuxta ac
15 Literis pollens breviterque regno
  Digna Britanno.
Ludus hic sylvae pariet futurae
Semina, hinc dives nemus undequaque
Densius surgens decorabit Anglum
20   Latius orbem.

46 Imago pueri IESU in ludo literario, quem nuper instituit Coletus [1510–11 / 1 September 1511]

Discite me primum, pueri, atque effingite puris
  Moribus, inde pias addite literulas.

47 Carmen phalecium [1510–11 / 1 September 1511]

Sedes haec puero sacra est IESU,
Formandis pueris dicata. Quare
Edico procul hinc facessat aut qui
Spurcis moribus aut inerudita
5 Ludum hunc inquinet eruditione.

45 A poem in sapphic metre

We pray that all may augur well as the new labours of this new workshop begin and that they may ever grow and prosper under the auspices of Jesus.

Here the raw young men, like a new earthenware jar, will soak up from their tender years Greek as well as Latin learning, and the holy faith, and Christ.

What good is it to have produced offspring who rejoice in beautiful bodies if the mind itself is not also properly shaped and cultivated and brought to a gleaming polish by studies that are spotless and pure?

From this stock a new progeny of the citizens will gradually sprout up, flourishing in holiness as well as learning and worthy before long of the British realm.

This school will bring forth the seeds of a future forest. From here a rich grove, springing up thicker and thicker on all sides, will adorn the world of England more and more widely.

46 An image of the boy Jesus in the elementary school recently established by Colet

Learn me first of all, boys, and make an image of me by your pure conduct. Then add to that the rudiments of holy reading and writing.

47 A poem in phalaecian metre

This building is consecrated to the boy Jesus and dedicated to forming the character of boys. Therefore I banish far hence anyone who would defile this school either by impure conduct or by uninstructed instruction.

48 Aliud [1510–11 / 1 September 1511]

Quin hunc ad puerum, pueri, concurritis omnes?
Unus hic est vitae regula fonsque piae.
Hunc qui non sapiat, huius sapientia stulta est,
Absque hoc vita hominis mors (mihi crede) mera est.

49 Christiani hominis institutum Erasmi Roterodami. Ad Galat. quinto: Valet in CHRISTO fides, quae per dilectionem operatur. [1513–14 / September 1514]

Fides

Credo. Primus articulus

Confiteor primum ore pio venerorque fideli
Mente deum patrem vel nutu cuncta potentem,
Hunc qui stelligeri spaciosa volumina caeli
Et solidum omniparae telluris condidit orbem.

Et in IESUM. II

5 Eius item gnatum IESUM, cognomine CHRISTUM,
Quem dominum nobis agnoscimus ac veneramur.

Qui conceptus. III

Hunc MARIA afflatu divini numinis alvo
Concepit virgo, peperit purissima virgo.

Passus sub Pontio. IIII

Et grave supplicium immeritus damnante Pilato
10 Pertulit, infami suffixus in arbore mortem

48 Another poem

Why, boys, do you not all rush together to this boy? He alone is the rule and the source of a holy life. If anyone is not wise enough to know this boy, his wisdom is foolish. Without him human life, believe me, is death pure and simple.

49 Basic principles of Christian conduct by Erasmus of Rotterdam. Based on Galatians 5: What counts is faith in Christ that works through love.

Faith

The Creed. The first article

First of all, I profess with a pious mouth and I venerate with a faithful mind God the Father, who rules all things at his slightest nod, the same God who created the vast spheres of the starry heavens and the solid orb of the all-fruitful earth.

And in Jesus. The second article

And also his son Jesus, surnamed Christ, whom we acknowledge and venerate as our lord.

Who was conceived. The third article

By the breath of the Divine Spirit Mary conceived him in her womb, still remaining a virgin, and brought him forth, still a most pure virgin.

Suffered under Pontius. The fourth article

And, though innocent, he was condemned by Pilate and suffered a heavy punishment. He

Oppetiit, tumulatus humo est claususque sepulchro.
Interea penetrat populator ad infera regna.

Tertia die. V

Mox ubi tertia lux moesto se prompserat orbi,
Emersit tumulo superas redivivus in auras.

Ascendit. VI

15 Inde palam aetheream scandit sublimis in arcem.
Illic iam dexter patri assidet omnipotenti.

Iterum venturus est. VII

Idem olim rediturus ut omnem iudicet orbem,
Et vivos pariter vitaque ac lumine cassos.

Credo in spiritum. VIII

Te quoque credo fide simili, spirabile numen,
20 Halitus afflatusque dei sacer, omnia lustrans.

Sanctam ecclesiam. IX

Et te confiteor, sanctissima concio, qua gens
Christigena arcano nexu coit omnis in unum
Corpus et unanimis capiti sociatur IESU.
Hinc proprium nescit, sed habet communia cuncta.

Remissionem peccatorum. X

25 Hoc equidem in coetu sancto peccata remitti
Credo, vel iis sacro fuerint qui fonte renati

underwent his death fixed to a tree of infamy. He was buried in the earth and shut up in a sepulchre. In the meantime he invaded and plundered the kingdom of hell.

On the third day. The fifth article

As soon as the third day dawned on a grieving world, he rose from the grave, alive once more in the air above.

He ascended. The sixth article

Then he rose in full view high up to the heavenly palace. There he now sits at the right of his almighty Father.

He will come again. The seventh article

The same Christ will one day return to judge the whole world, both the living and those deprived of life and light.

I believe in the Spirit. The eighth article

With a similar faith I also believe in you, O life-sustaining divinity, Holy Spirit and Breath of God, illuminating all things.

In the holy church. The ninth article

And I profess you, most holy assembly, in which the whole family of Christ comes together by a secret bond into one body and with one soul is joined to its head, Jesus. Hence it knows nothing of what is private but holds all things in common.

In the forgiveness of sins. The tenth article

In this holy gathering, indeed, I believe that sins are forgiven, both of those who have been reborn through the holy font or of those who

Vel qui diluerint ultro sua crimina fletu.

Carnis resurrectionem. XI

Nec dubito quin exanimata cadavera sursum
In vitam redeant, animas sortita priores.

Vitam aeternam. XII

30 Utraque pars nostri, corpusque animusque deinceps
Iuncta simul vitam ducent sine fine perennem.

Sacramenta VII

Hoc quoque persuasum est, ecclesia mystica septem
Munera dispensat, quae sacramenta vocantur.
Hinc variae dotes et gratia plurima menti
35 Caelitus inseritur, si quis modo sumpserit apte.

Ordo. I

Ordine nanque sacro confertur sacra potestas
Ut fungare ministeriis CHRISTO auspice sanctis.

Matrimonium. II

Munere coniugii nati hunc prodimus in orbem,
Usque adeo pulchri pulcherrima portio mundi.

Baptismus. III

40 Munere baptismi longe felicius iidem
Quam prius in te, CHRISTE, renascimur atque novamur.

of their own accord have washed away their offences with their tears.

In the resurrection of the flesh.
The eleventh article

I have no doubt that soulless corpses will arise once more to life, each being allotted the soul it had before.

In life everlasting. The twelfth article

Thenceforth both parts of us, body and spirit joined together, will lead an endless and everlasting life.

The seven sacraments

I am also persuaded of this: the church dispenses seven mystical gifts, which are called sacraments. By them various gifts and an abundance of grace from heaven are implanted into the mind, if only they are received fittingly.

Holy orders. The first sacrament

For holy orders bestows the holy power to exercise the sacred ministries under the auspices of Christ.

Matrimony. The second sacrament

By the gift of marriage we are born and come forth into this world, ourselves the most beautiful part of a world so beautiful.

Baptism. The third sacrament

By the gift of baptism we become far more blessed than we were before because in you, Christ, we are reborn and renewed.

Confirmatio. IIII

Deinde in amore dei nos confirmatio sacra
Constabilit mentemque invicto robore durat.

Eucharistia. V

Mysticus ille cibus (Graeci dixere synaxin),
45 Qui panis vinique palam sub imagine CHRISTUM
Ipsum praesentem vere exhibet, intima nostri
Viscera caelesti saginat et educat esca
Inque deo reddit vegetos et reddit adultos.

Poenitentia. VI

Si quem forte deo capitalis reddidit hostem
50 Noxia, continuo metanoea medebitur illi.
Restituet lapsum rescissaque foedera rursum
Sarciet, offensi placabit numinis iram,
Commissi modo poeniteat pigeatque nocentem
Isque volens peragat praescripta piamina culpae.

Unctio. VII

55 Unguinis extremi munus nos munit et armat
Migrantemque animam per summa pericula tuto
Transmittit patriae et superis commendat euntem.

Amor dei

Haec est indubitata fides. Cui pectore certo
Nixus amabo patrem super omnia cunctipotentem,
60 Qui me condideritque et in hunc produxerit orbem.
Rursus amore pari dominum complectar IESUM,
Qui nos asseruit precioque redemit amico,
Spiritum item sanctum, qui me sine fine benigno

Confirmation. The fourth sacrament

Then holy confirmation makes us firm in the love of God and hardens the spirit with invincible strength.

The Eucharist. The fifth sacrament

That mystical food (the Greeks call it 'synaxis'), which under the outward appearance of bread and wine clearly tenders to us Christ himself truly present, fattens and fosters our inmost hearts with heavenly food and makes us vigorous and mature in God.

Penance. The sixth sacrament

If perhaps a mortal sin makes someone God's enemy, a change of heart will immediately heal him. It will reinstate the fallen and restore the broken covenant; it will placate the anger of the offended Deity, provided that the sinner repents and is sorry for his transgression and that he willingly carries out the prescribed expiation of his guilt.

Anointing. The seventh sacrament

The gift of the last oil fortifies and arms us and through the greatest dangers safely conveys the travelling soul over to its homeland, and, as it goes, commends it to the powers above.

Love of God

This is the undoubted faith. Relying on it with a firm heart, I will above all love the omnipotent Father, who has all power over all things, who created me and brought me forth into this world. Moreover, I will embrace with an equal love the Lord Jesus, who set us free and paid our ransom like a friend. Likewise I will love the Holy Spirit, who warms me

Afflatu fovet atque animi penetralia ditans
65 Dotibus arcanis vitali recreat aura.
Atque hic ternio sanctus et omni laude ferendus
Toto ex corde mihi, tota de mente, supremis
Viribus, obsequio meritoque coletur honore.
Hunc unum reverebor et hoc semel omnis in uno
70 Spes mea figetur, hoc omnia metiar uno,
Hic propter sese mihi semper amabitur unus.

⟨Amor sui⟩

Post hunc haud alia ratione ac nomine charus
Ipse mihi fuero, nisi quatenus omnis in illum
Ille mei referatur amor fontemque revisat.

Fuga peccati

75 Culpam praeterea fugiam pro viribus omnem,
Praecipue capitale tamen vitavero crimen,
Quod necat atque animam letali vulnerat ictu.

Superbia. Invidia. Ira

Ne fastu tumeam, ne vel livore maligno
Torquear aut bili rapiar fervente, cavebo.

Gula. Luxuria. Pigritia

80 Ne vel spurca libido vel insatiabilis alvus
Imperet, enitar, ne turpis inertia vincat,

Avaritia

Ne nunquam saturanda fames me vexet habendi,
Plus satis ut cupiam fallacis munera mundi.

endlessly with his kind breath and, enriching the innermost recesses of my mind with secret gifts, recreates me with his life-giving spirit. And this Trinity, holy and worthy to be exalted with all praise, I will obey and worship and deservedly honour with all my heart, with all my mind, with my utmost strength. I will revere only this triune God; on him only all my hope will be fixed once for all; by him only will I measure all things. Only him will I always love for his own sake.

⟨Love of self⟩

Next to him, I will be dear to my own self, but only provided that and in so far as all that love of myself is referred to him and goes back to its source.

Fleeing from sin

Moreover, I will flee all guilt to the best of my ability; but I will especially avoid mortal sin, which kills the soul and wounds it with a lethal stroke.

Pride. Envy. Anger

I will take care not to swell with pride or to be tormented with malicious envy or to be carried away by seething anger.

Gluttony. Lust. Sloth

I will struggle not to be subject to impure desires or an insatiable stomach or to be conquered by shameful laziness.

Avarice

I will try not to be plagued by an insatiable hunger for possessions so as to desire more

Fuga malorum hominum

Improba pestiferi fugiam commertia coetus
85 Omnia summo animi conatu proque virili.

Studium pietatis

Atque huc incumbam nervis ac pectore toto,
Ut magis atque magis superet mihi gratia, virtus,
Augescatque piae divina scientia menti.

Oratio

Orabo superosque precum libamine puro
90 Placare adnitar, cum tempore sedulus omni,
Tum vero eximie quoties lux festa recurret.

Frugalitas victus

Frugales epulae semper, mensaeque placebit
Sobria mundicies et avari nescia luxus.

Ieiunium

Servabo reverens quoties ieiunia nobis
95 Indicit certis ecclesia sancta diebus.

Mentis custodia

Sancta uti sint mihi secretae penetralia mentis,
Ne quid eo subeat foedumve nocensve, studebo.

Linguae custodia

Ne temere iuret, ne unquam mendacia promat,

than enough of the gifts of this deceiving world.

Fleeing from evil men

With the greatest effort of my mind and with all my strength I will avoid all dealings with wicked and corrupting company.

The pursuit of holiness

And I will strain every nerve and try with all my heart to be more and more ruled by grace, by virtue, and to enlarge the holiness of my mind by the knowledge of God.

Prayer

I will pray and will strive to win over the powers above by a pure libation of prayers, zealous in such prayer at all times, but especially when their holydays recur.

Temperance in eating

My feasts will always be frugal and I will find pleasure in meals marked by a sober elegance, with no trace of greedy luxury.

Fasting

I will reverently observe fasts on those fixed days which holy church has indicated to us.

Guarding the mind

I will take pains to keep the secret recesses of my mind holy, so that nothing filthy or harmful may approach there.

Guarding the tongue

I will take care to keep my tongue from

Turpia ne dictu dicat mea lingua, cavebo.

Manus custodia

100 A furto cohibebo manus, nec ad ulla minuta
Viscatos mittam digitos, et si quid ademptum
Cuiquam erit, id domino properabo reddere iusto.

Restitutio rei forte repertae

Id quoque restituam, si quid mihi forte repertum est;
Me penes haud patiar prudens aliena morari.

Amor proximi

105 Nec secus atque mihi sum charus, amabitur omnis
Proximus (est autem, ni fallor, proximus ille
Quisquis homo est), ac sic ut amor referatur amici
In CHRISTUM vitamque piam veramque salutem.
Huic igitur, fuerit quoties opus atque necesse,
110 Sedulus officio corpusque animumque iuvabo,
Ut mihi succurri cupiam, si forsan egerem.
Id tamen in primis praestabo utrique parenti,
Per quos corporeo hoc nasci mihi contigit orbe.
Tum praeceptori, qui me erudit instituitque,
115 Morigerus fuero ac merito reverebor honore.
At rursus dulcisque scholae studiique sodales
Semper (uti par est) syncero amplectar amore.

Assidua confessio

Si quando crimen fuero prolapsus in ullum,
Protinus enitar, pura ut confessio lapsum

swearing thoughtlessly, from ever putting forth lies, from saying what it is shameful to say.

Guarding the hands

I will restrain my hands from stealing, and I will not lay sticky fingers on the slightest thing whatsoever; and if anything has been taken away from someone, I will hasten to return it to its rightful owner.

Giving back something found by chance

I will also give back whatever I might happen to find; I will be too prudent to allow the property of others to remain in my possession.

Love of neighbour

And just as I am dear to myself, I will love all my neighbours – and unless I am mistaken, anyone who is a human being is my neighbour – and I will do so in such a way that my love for a friend is referred to Christ and to a holy life and to true salvation. Therefore, whenever it is needful and necessary, I will assist him in body and mind, eagerly and dutifully, just as I would wish to be helped if I should lack for something. But I will especially do this for both my parents, through whom I happened to be born into this corporeal world. Next I will be obedient to my teacher, who instructs and trains me, and I will give him the obedience and honour he deserves. Then, too, I will always, as is fitting, embrace with a sincere affection the companions of my studies in this sweet school.

Frequent confession

If I should ever fall into any sin, I will immediately make an effort to recover from my

120 Erigat ac iusta tergatur noxia poena.

Sumptio corporis CHRISTI in vita

Ast ubi sacrati me ad corporis atque cruoris
Caelestes epulas pietasque diesque vocabit,
Illotis manibus metuens accedere, pectus
Ante meum quanta cura studioque licebit
125 Purgabo maculis, virtutum ornabo nitelis.

Morbus

Porro ubi fatalis iam terminus ingruet aevi
Extremumque diem cum morbus adesse monebit,
Mature sacramentis me armare studebo
Atque his muneribus quae ecclesia sancta ministrat
130 Christigenis: reteget confessio crimina vitae
Sacrifico, sumam CHRISTI venerabile corpus.

Mors

Quod si vicinae propius discrimina mortis
Urgebunt, supplex accersam qui mihi rite
Oblinat ac signet sacro ceromate corpus.
135 Atque his praesidiis armatus, sic uti dignum est
Christicola, forti ac fidenti pectore vita
Decedam, bonitate dei super omnia fretus.

Hoc fac et vives.

fall by a sincere confession and to wipe away the damage by performing a just penance.

Receiving the body of Christ during my lifetime

But when piety and the proper day call me to the heavenly banquet of the consecrated body and blood, fearing to approach with unwashed hands, I will purge my heart beforehand of its stains with all the care and diligence I can muster, and I will adorn it with the scintillating brightness of the virtues.

Illness

Then, when the fated limit of my lifetime thrusts itself upon me and illness warns that my last day is at hand, I will take care to arm myself betimes with the sacraments and with those gifts which holy church ministers to the family of Christ: in confession I will reveal the sins of my life to a priest, and I will receive the venerable body of Christ.

Death

But if the dangers of approaching death draw near and press upon me, I will humbly summon someone who will anoint me according to the proper rites and make the sign of the cross on my body with holy oil. And armed with these defences, I will depart from this life in a manner worthy of a Christian, with a strong and trusting heart, relying above all on the goodness of God.

Do this and you will live.

50 In laudem Michaelis et angelorum omnium, ode dicolos hendecasyllaba sapphica, suffigenda in templo Michaeli sacro

[early spring 1491? / January 1496]

Caelitum princeps, Michael, et omnes
Spiritus sacri, libeat precamur
Supplicum votis tribuisse pronas
  Caelitus aures.
5 Sordidae sed ne merito canentum
Sordeant odae, citus huc ab arce
Devolet fulgente Seraph decoris
  Igneus alis,
Qui foco sacro usque calentis arae
10 Calculum vivum rapiens (ut olim)
Applicet nostris placidus labellis
  Oraque tergat.
Luridae quicquid maculae perurat,
Desidem pellens animo teporem.
15 Igneas cantent acies (ut aequum est)
  Ignea verba.

⟨De Michaele⟩

Porro tu primas tibi vendicato
Carminis partes, Michael beate,
Primipilari duce quo triumphant
20 Agmina caeli.
In quibus luces, itidem ut pyropus
Nobiles inter radiat lapillos,
Utve formosus socia inter ardet
  Lucifer astra.
25 Ius tibi summum necis atque vitae
Tradidit magni moderator orbis,
Tu potes servare probos et idem
  Perdere sontes.
Tu piorum tutor et advocatus,
30 Tu dei in templo nitidas ad aras
Visus es dextra tenuisse plenam
  Thuris acerram.
Inde surgens fumus odore multo
Ibat ad summi solium tonantis,
35 Ac dei nares liquidi iuvabant
  Dona vaporis.

50 A hendecasyllabic sapphic ode, containing two kinds of lines, in praise of Michael and all the angels, to be hung up in a church dedicated to Michael

Prince of the heavenly hosts, Michael, and all you sacred spirits, deign, we beseech you, to bend down from heaven and give ear to the prayers of your suppliants.

But lest the unclean hymns of the singers should rightly be deemed unworthy, let a burning seraph swiftly fly hither from the shining citadel on his comely wings.

Let him seize a live coal from the holy fire of the ever-burning altar, as once before, and let him calmly place it on our lips and cleanse our mouths.

Let him burn away any ugly spots, driving from our hearts all lukewarm sluggishness. Let the fiery ranks, as is fitting, be celebrated in words of fire.

⟨Michael⟩

And so, blessed Michael, claim for yourself the first share in the song, a captain who leads the heavenly hosts in triumph.

You shine out among them just like a fiery ruby among precious stones, or like Lucifer burning in his beauty amid his fellow stars.

To you the ruler of the whole world handed over the final right to judge life and death. You have the power to save the upright and likewise to destroy the guilty.

You are the protector and advocate of the good. You appeared by the shining altar in the temple of God, holding the thurible full of incense in your right hand.

From it rose fragrant fumes up to the throne of the all-highest, the wielder of thunder, and the offering of the billowing exhalation pleased the nostrils of God.

Tu pias laetis animas reponis
Sedibus, cantu procul audiendo
Squalidis olim gelida exciebis
40 Funera bustis.
Quam dedit laetos pia turba plausus,
Cum gravi caelum quateret ruina
Hostis et serpens veterator, acri
Non sine pugna.
45 Ille sublimes subito sub auras
Emicans septem (stupuere cuncti)
Ora tollebat, colubris tumebant
Colla trecentis.
Flammeis ardens oculis, Avernum
50 Virus efflabat furiale monstrum
Fulminisque instar piceos vomebat
Faucibus ignes.
Te nihil terret rabies minacis
Beluae, sed vi domitam superna
55 Cogis absorptam superas ad auras
Reddere praedam.
Quae tuas fulvas fugitat sub alas
Laeta, praesenti sed adhuc periclo
Palpitans, elapsa velut rapaci
60 Ales ab ungui.
Ergo ne quid iam trepident, cadaver
Triste deturbas. Labat, ac labantis
Pondus exhorrens aperit profunda
Tartara tellus.
65 Non secus quam si Siculo Peloro
Pendulum in fluctus abeat cacumen,
Territum cedit refluumque late
Dissilit aequor.
Ferreis illic domitus catenis
70 Horridum quassat caput, ac minatus
Multa nequicquam, furibundus iras
Volvit inanes.
Te manet palma, o Michael, suprema,
Te novi plausus. Tibi non iniquas
75 Impius poenas dabit Antichristus,
Orbe levato.

You bring pious souls to their blissful abode. With a trumpet blast that will be heard even from far away, you will one day rouse up the cold bodies of the dead from the squalor of their graves.

How joyfully the holy throng applauded when the enemy, the sly old serpent, after a fierce struggle, came crashing down and shook heaven itself!

Suddenly he sprang forth (everyone was astounded) and he lifted up his seven mouths high into the air, the necks swollen with hundreds of snakes.

His eyes aflame, the raging monster breathed out a hellish poison. His jaws spewed out pitch-black flames, flashing like bolts of lightning.

For you the rage of the threatening beast holds no terrors: you defeat him with power from on high and force him to bring up into the air the prey he has swallowed.

Joyfully they flee to take refuge under your tawny wings, panting at the prospect of still-present danger, like a bird that has escaped from grasping talons.

To dispel any fear, you thrust down the miserable hulk. It falls and, in terror of the falling weight, the earth opens up the abyss of hell.

Just so, if the overhanging crag of Pelorus in Sicily should fall into the waves, the surface of the terrified sea gives way, splits, and draws back, leaving a wide chasm.

Subdued there with iron chains, he shakes his bristling head, making many vain threats, thrashing about in furious and futile rage.

The final palm of victory, O Michael, is still in store for you. You will be applauded yet once more. When the world has been relieved, you will exact just punishment from the wicked Antichrist.

Laetus idcirco meritos uterque
Orbis en hymnos canit, altus aether
Inclyto gaudet duce, gaudet aeque
80 Praeside tellus.
At meri cantus celebrantur isthic,
Hic (uti res sunt variae atque mixtae)
Reddimus proni querulis remixta
Carmina votis.
85 En vides quantis miseri premamur
Cladibus (nostro merito, fatemur),
Tota proh caeci terimus nefandis
Saecula bellis.
Si tibi haud frustra data cura nostri est,
90 Si tibi pax non temere vocablum
Mutuat, belli procul o cruentos
Pelle furores.
Fac tua lenis prece rex Olympi
Vindicem condat miseratus ensem,
95 Ferias donet referatque fessis
Ocia terris.

De singulari laude Gabrielis angeli

Te quibus digne recinemus odis,
Gabriel, quem rite chorus supernus
Proximum primo colit? O tonantis
100 Armiger alti,
Illius tu strennuus administras
Bella, nec quisquam melior piorum
Castra tutari et rabidas nocentum
Frangere vires.
105 Tu tenes oracula sacra. Te olim
Nuncio casus didicit futuros
Ille quem insonti leo gaudet atrox
Lambere rictu.
Tu Zachariae vetulo marito,
110 Thura dum festis adolet sacellis,
Pignoris seri subitus stupenti
Nuncius adstas.

Behold, therefore, both worlds rightly sing joyful hymns. Heaven above rejoices in its glorious leader; the earth likewise rejoices in its guardian.

But there the celebratory songs are unqualified and pure. Here, where affairs are mixed and various, we bow down and sing hymns intermingled with wailing supplications.

Behold, you see how many disasters overwhelm us in our misery – through our own fault, we confess. Whole ages, alas, we wear away in blind and wicked warfare.

If it is not in vain that you have been assigned the task of taking care of us, if it is not for nothing that peace has lent you her name, oh, drive far from us the bloody rage of war!

Through your prayers, make the mild king of heaven take pity on us and sheathe his avenging sword, make him grant us a holiday and give the weary world a rest.

The special praise of the Archangel Gabriel

With what hymns shall we celebrate you worthily, Gabriel, whom the choir of heaven venerates as second only to the supreme captain? O armour-bearer of the Thunderer on high,

you conduct his wars vigorously, nor is anyone better at defending the camps of the pious or at breaking the savage forces of their assailants.

You have charge of the sacred prophecies. Once as a messenger you revealed future events to the man whom the fierce lion licked with delight, baring his teeth in a harmless grin.

You appeared to the aged husband Zachary as he was burning incense on a feast-day in the temple; you suddenly stood before him and

Cuncta quid frustra sequimur canendo?
Illius dulce est meminisse nunci,
115 Laetius quo nil lachrymosus unquam
Audiit orbis.
Nec salus olim neque spes salutis
Ulla erat, sed mors Stygiis profecta
Sedibus gentem rapiebat omnem
120 Vindice nullo.
Tum novas autor meditatus artes,
Ipse ut invisat homo factus orbem,
Te rei tantae, Gabriel, ministrum
Deligit unum.
125 'Advola terris,' ait, 'et saluta
Virginem, matrem mihi mox futuram.
Fac sacramentum tege, ne ille sciscat
Callidus hostis.
Sic opus facto.' Neque plura fatus
130 Ille, tu lapsu placido volucres
Dissecas nubes decorasque pictis
Aethera pennis,
Qualis adversos feriente nimbos
Sole resplendet, monumenta pacti,
135 Iris, antiqui, varioque caelum
Cingit amictu.
Vidit obliquis oculis volantem
Dextero caelo metuitque latis
Incubans terris draco luridoque
140 Palluit ore.
Tecta tu pernix Nazaraea tangis
Mox et illapsus thalamis pudicae
Virginis mandata refers sereno
Regia vultu.
145 Nostra cui primum hic lyra gratuletur
Haesitat, mundone malis levato,
An deo foetae potius puellae,
An tibi, divae
Conscio mentis meritoque summis
150 Rebus accersi. Tibi tam sacrato

dumbfounded him by announcing that he would have a child so late in life.

Why should we vainly try to sing all your deeds? It is sweet to remember that one message, the most joyful message ever heard by a weeping world.

Once there was no salvation, no hope even of salvation. But rather death, sent forth from the Stygian realms, had seized all mankind, and there was no liberator.

Then the creator devised an unheard-of stratagem, to enter the world himself by becoming man, and to execute this great plan he chose you alone.

'Fly to the earth,' he said, 'and salute the virgin who will soon become my mother. Conceal this mystery lest that wily enemy should learn of it.

'That is what you must do.' He spoke no more, and you descended gently, cutting through the flying clouds and adorning the air with your bright-coloured plumage,

just as Iris, when the sun strikes rain-clouds in the opposite part of the sky, draws her resplendent, many-coloured cloak across the heavens, a memorial of the ancient pact.

With an envious, sidelong glance, the dragon, brooding over the whole expanse of the earth, saw you flying under the favourable heavens, and he felt fear. His ghastly face grew pale.

Swiftly you reach the rooftops of Nazareth and, descending right away to the bedchamber of the chaste virgin, with a serene countenance you deliver the commands of the King.

Here we hesitate in our song, hardly knowing whom to congratulate first: the world, relieved of such evils; or rather the girl, pregnant with God; or you,

who were privy to the thoughts of God and deservedly summoned to carry out the highest

Tamque felici licuit vel uni
    Munere fungi.
Noster, o salve, bone pacifer, qui
Surculum adportans oleae virentem
155 Nuncias primus meliora mersis
    Saecula terris.

De laude Raphaelis

Proxime primis, Raphael, canere,
Ordinis pars non humilis superni,
Tute nam clarum comitem duobus
160 Tertius addis.
O salus ac certa hominum medela
Rebus afflictis, ope cuius olim
Reddito vidit reducem Thobias
    Lumine gnatum,
165 Nec modo salvum, sed et aere largo
Divitem, multa serie clientum
Divitem ac longis gregibus novaque
    Coniuge laetum.
Ethnici Phoebumque genusque Phoebi
170 Saxeos olim coluere divos,
Hos rati morbis dubiis rogatam
    Ferre salutem.
Nos magis nos te colimus, potentem
Vel nigro manes revocare ab Orco,
175 Rursus et pigris animam liquentem
    Spargere venis.
Tu simul membris, simul o medere
Mentibus, praesens opifer, luemque
In tuos euheu male saevientem
180 Exige terris.

De omnibus angelis

Nec tacendi estis, proceres ducesque
Caeteri, nobis, breviterque cuncti
Milites regis ditione late
    Cuncta tenentis,
185 Ambitu quem ter triplici triformem

mission. To you alone it was granted to perform such a sacred, such a happy task.

All hail, our kind bringer of peace! Carrying a green olive branch, you were the first to announce better times to a drowning world.

An encomium of Raphael

Next after the first two, Raphael, you shall be celebrated in song. Far from low is your station among the ranks on high, for you take the third place, an illustrious companion to the other two.

O health, O unfailing cure for the afflictions of mankind, by your help long ago Tobit, his sight restored, saw his son returning

not only safe but also enriched with an abundance of money, enriched with a long train of followers and with herds stretched out in the distance, and taking joy in his new bride.

The pagans once venerated stone statues of Phoebus and the progeny of Phoebus as gods, thinking they would answer their prayers by healing dangerous diseases.

As for us, instead of them we venerate you, who have the power even to call back shades from the darkness of hell and to infuse flowing life into exhausted veins.

Oh, heal both our members and our minds, ever-present bringer of help, and drive from the earth the plague which rages, alas, so fiercely against your charges!

All the angels

Nor should we pass you over in silence, you other nobles and princes and, to put it briefly, all you warriors of the King who rules all things in his wide dominion.

Him in his threefold divinity you encircle with your thrice-three rounds, on the right

Dextera levaque frequentiores
Cingitis quam nocte silente plenam
    Sydera lunam.
O salutandi novies beati,
190 Ocium quorum mala nulla terrent,
Certa quos divi beat intuentes
    Copia vultus.
Invidet vestrae miser ille sorti,
Eminus sedes quotiens ademptas
195 Suspicit frendens et inauspicati
    Poenitet ausus.
Vespero quondam similis rubenti
Inter aeternos rutilabat ignes,
At simul regis diadema miles
200   Ambiit audax.
Iam pares volvens animo cathedras,
Flammeo telo grege cum sequaci
Ictus eiectusque rudem ruina
    Terruit orbem.
205 Excipit partim cava Styx ruenteis,
Abditur lucis bona pars opacis,
Cursitat magnum per inane multo
    Plurima turba,
Densior quam Cecropiis in hortis
210 Tinnulos aeris crepitus secuta
Evolant examina quamque caelo
    Decidit imber.
Pugnat hoc unum haec vigil improboque
Omnis incumbit studio, pios ut
215 Distrahat, tundat geminoque raptos
    Funere perdat.
Ah nefas, quantam daret illa stragem!
Cui salus tandem, nisi frangeretur
Obviis vobis furor et nocendi
220   Dira libido?
Vestra nos tutela fidelis ortos
Excipit nec luce prius relinquit.

hand and the left, more numerous than the stars surrounding the full moon on a noiseless night.

Oh, we must salute you, blessed nine times over! Your peace can never be affrighted by any evil because you are blessed by the unfailing abundance of your vision of the face of God.

That miserable wretch, gnashing his teeth, envies your lot whenever he looks up at the distant abode he has lost, and he rues the audacity of his ill-omened enterprise.

Once he glowed like the red star of evening among the eternal fires, but at the same time the presumptuous soldier coveted the King's crown.

Even as he was turning over in his mind how to get a throne equal to God's, he and his flock of followers were struck by a fiery lightning bolt. He was cast out and the formless world was terrified by his fall.

Some of them fell into the Stygian hollows of hell; a good number are hidden in the dusky woods. A much bigger mob of them flit about in wide, empty space,

denser than the swarms of bees flying forth in the gardens of Attica, drawn by the sound of tinkling bronze, and more numerous than the raindrops falling from the sky.

Ever on the watch, this mob struggles for one thing only: every one of them strives with all his wicked energy to perplex the pious, to buffet them, to snatch them away and destroy them with a double death.

Oh, horrible is the havoc they would wreak! Who, after all, could be saved if you did not stand up to them and crush their rage and their abominable lust for destruction?

When we get up, you undertake to guard us faithfully, nor do you leave off till the daylight disappears. Always trusting in your

Semper hac freti nihili furentem
    Ducimus hostem.
225 Imus hac tuti tumidum per aequor,
Asperas tuti penetramus Alpeis,
Vivimus vestro morimurque demum
    Munere tuti.
Vos parum firmis dare robur, iidem
230 Anxios nostis gemitus levare
Nunciis felicibus ac subinde
    Visere castos.
Caelici cives, adeone vobis
Exules curae sumus, ut vacet sic
235 Obsequi nobis pigeatque nunquam
    Sortis iniquae?
Nuncii crebri volitatis inter
Arduos caelos humilesque terras,
Hinc preces fertis querulas, at istinc
240 Dona refertis.
Porro nos tantis meritis (quod unum
Possumus) gratos memori Camoena
Reddimus cantus ferimusque templis
    Dona dicatis.
245 Ferias anno referente sacras,
Celat hic festus simulacra fumus,
Hic chorus supplex manibus facessit
    Vota supinis.
Quae patris summi penetrent ad aures
250 Semper ac per vos rata sint precamur,
O patroni praesidiumque felix
    Christigenarum.

51 Erasmi Roterodami carmen iambicum, ex voto dicatum virgini Vvalsingamicae apud Britannos [spring 1512 / September 1515]

Ὦ χαῖρ' Ἰησοῦ μῆτερ εὐλογημένη,
Μόνη γυναικῶν θεοτόκος καὶ παρθένος.
Ἄλλοι μὲν ἄλλας σοὶ διδόασι δωρεάς,
Ὁ μέν γε χρυσόν, ὁ δὲ πάλιν τὸν ἄργυρον,
5 Ὁ δὲ τιμίους φέρων χαρίζεται λίθους.
Ἀνθ' ὧν ἀπαιτοῦσ' οἱ μὲν ὑγιαίνειν δέμας,

guardianship, we make light of the furious enemy.

Under your protection we travel safely on the rising seas, we safely cross the rough passes of the Alps. In life, and finally in death, we are safe through your service.

You know how to give strength to the weak, to encourage the troubled and the grieving with words of good cheer, and to look to the chaste time and time again.

O citizens of heaven, are you so concerned about us exiles that you take time to wait on us thus, never wearying of your unfair task?

You fly continually back and forth between the heights of heaven and the lowly earth. From here you carry up our lamentations and prayers, but from there you bring back gifts.

And so we repay such great favours in the only way we can: our muse remembers to sing hymns of thanksgiving and we bring offerings to the churches dedicated to you.

When the year brings around your feast-days, here we envelop your images with solemn incense, here the choir prays to you earnestly, raising its hands in supplication.

We beg that our prayers may always penetrate to the ears of our Father on high and that they may be validated by you, O patrons and blessed guardians of the family of Christ.

51 An iambic poem by Erasmus of Rotterdam, a votive offering to the Virgin of Walsingham in Britain

All hail, blessed mother of Jesus, unique among women as the virgin mother of God. Different people bring you different gifts: one offers gold; another, silver; another honours you with a gift of precious stones. In return, then, some ask you for bodily health, others

Ἄλλοι δὲ πλουτεῖν, καί τινες γυναικίου
Κυοῦντος ἐρατὸν οὔνομ' ἐλπίζειν πατρός,
Πυλίου τινὲς γέροντος αἰῶνας λαχεῖν.
10 Αὐτὸς δ' ἀοιδός, εὐμενής, πένης γ' ὅμως
Στίχους ἐνέγκας, οὐ γὰρ ἔξεστ' ἄλλο τι,
Δόσεως ἀμοιβὴν εὐτελεστάτης, γέρας
Μέγιστον αἰτῶ, θεοσεβῆ τὴν καρδίαν
Πασῶν θ' ἅπαξ ἁμαρτιῶν ἐλευθέραν.

Εὐχὴ τοῦ Ἐράσμου.

52 Epitaphium scurrulae temulenti. Scazon

[summer 1509? / September 1511]

Pax sit, viator, tacitus hos legas versus,
Ut sacra verba mussitant sacerdotes,
Ne mihi suavem strepitus auferat somnum
Repetatque vigiles ilico sitis fauces.
5 Nam scurrula hocce sterto conditus saxo,
Quondam ille magni clarus Euii mystes,
Ut qui bis octo lustra perbibi tota.
Oculis profundus deinde somnus obrepsit,
Ut fit, benigno membra cum madent Baccho.
10 Atque ita peractis suaviter bonis annis
Idem bibendi finis atque vivendi
Fuit. Sed etiam me aliquis ebrium credat
Aut somniare, qui ista dormiens dicam.
Vale, viator. Iam silenter abscede.

53 Encomium Selestadii carmine elegiaco per Erasmum Roterodamum

[1514–15 / August 1515]

Nobile Slestadium, tua quis pomeria primus
  Signans tam dextris condidit auspiciis?

for riches, and some for the fair hope that their wives may conceive and bestow on them the lovely name of father; others ask to obtain the long lifetime of the old man of Pylos. But as for me, a poet well disposed though poor, now that I have brought verses – for that is all I have – in return for this humblest of gifts, I beg you for the greatest of boons: a devout heart, completely free for once from sin.

The prayer of Erasmus

52 An epitaph for a drunken jokester, in scazons

Peace be with you, passer-by. Read these verses silently, the way priests mumble their holy texts, so that the noise does not disturb my sweet sleep and make my throat thirsty once again the minute I wake up. For I, the snoring jokester buried under this stone, was once a famous devotee of the mighty Bacchus, seeing that I drank my way through eight whole decades. Then a deep sleep came over my eyes, the way it happens when one's limbs have been soused by kind Bacchus. And so, having thus lived out my good years in sweet contentment, I came to the end of drinking and living at the same moment. But someone may think I am still drunk or dreaming, since I am saying these things in my sleep. Passer-by, farewell. Now depart silently.

53 A poem in elegiac distichs by Erasmus of Rotterdam in praise of Sélestat

Noble Sélestat, who first laid out your boundaries and founded you under such

Unde tibi genius tam felix tamque benignus?
Sydera nascenti quae micuere tibi?
5 Cum videaris enim neque muro insigne capaci,
Plebe nec innumera divitiisve scatens,
Urbibus in cunctis tamen haud felicior ulla est,
Quotquot Caesarea sub ditione vigent.
Non ego iam memoro, quod fertilis undique campus
10 Adiacet et segetem prosperat alma Ceres,
Quodque hinc vitiferos monteis, hinc ditia Rheni
Flumina prospectas, grata quod aura fovet.
Commoda bella, sed haec tecum communia multis,
Dotibus hisce simul vinceris et superas.
15 Illa tibi propria est, quod et una et parva tot aedis
Virtute insigneis ingenioque viros.
Tot pariter gemmas, tot lumina fundis in orbem,
Quot multis aliis vix genuisse datum est.
Doctrinae proceres tot habes, quot proditor ille
20 Vix belli proceres occuluisset equus.
Quam non Vvimphlingus, quam non Spiegellius urbem,
Quam non Kirherus nobilitare queat?
Unde tibi Sapidus, doctis quoque dignus Athenis?
Unde sacer Phrygio, Storkius unde tibi?
25 Unde tibi Arnoldus, Musis excultus, et unde
Matthias niveo pectore Schurerius?
Ut sileam reliquos, non te satis ille Beatus
Rhenanus, lingua doctus utraque, beat?
Quae tibi cum liquido tacita est cognatio caelo?
30 Num quod Palladia numen ab urbe favet?
Corpora gignit humus, mens aethere manat ab alto.
Membra aliae pariunt, tu paris ingenia.
Quis non invideat tam splendida commoda, ni quod

favourable auspices? Where did you get a tutelar genius so fortunate and so generous? What stars shone at your birth? For, though you make no remarkable showing through capacious walls and you do not have a huge population or abundant riches, still there is hardly a more fortunate city among all those which flourish under the rule of the emperor. I will not mention now the fertile fields which surround you or the crops with which Ceres has bountifully endowed you, the view of the mountain slopes with their vineyards on one side, the sight of the wealthy Rhine on the other, the air so pleasant and salubrious. These are fine advantages, but many cities have them in common with you; in such gifts as these you both surpass and are surpassed.

Your own special gift is this: you alone, small as you are, produce so many men who are extraordinary for their virtue and intelligence. You pour forth into the world at one time so many gems, so many luminaries, that many other cities combined have hardly produced the like. You have so many chieftains of learning that the treacherous horse hardly hid as many chieftains of warfare. What city would not be enobled by Wimpfeling, by Spiegel, by Kierher? Where did you get Witz, a man worthy even of learned Athens? Where did you get the theologian Phrygio? Where Storck? Where Arnold, the refined poet? Where Matthias Schürer, so pure of heart? To say nothing of the rest, is not Beatus Rhenanus, learned in both tongues, enough by himself to beatify you? What secret affinity do you have with the bright skies? Are you favoured by some divinity from the city of Pallas Athena?

The soil generates bodies; the mind flows down from the heights of the sky. Other cities give birth to limbs; you give birth to intellects. Who would not envy such splendid benefits, if

Non tibi sed mundo fertilis ista paris?
35 Gloria te penes est unam, sed fructus ad omneis
Pervenit, humanum qua patet orbe genus.
Haec memor hospitii tibi carmina panxit Erasmus
Haud lepida, at grata qualiacunque cheli.

54 Ad Sebastianum Brant,
archigrammateum urbis Argentinensis.
Phalecium Erasmi [August 1514 / December 1514]

Ornarunt alios suae Camoenae,
Ornas ipse tuas magis Camoenas.
Multos patria reddidit celebres,
Urbem tu celebrem celebriorem
5 Multo constituis, Sebastiane,
Lingua, moribus, eruditione,
Libris, consilio, severitate.
Sic cum foenore plurimo rependis
Acceptum decus, e tuo vicissim
10 Illustrans patriamque literasque.

55 Ad Thomam Didymum Aucuparium, poetam laureatum,
Erasmi Rot. carmen [August 1514 / December 1514]

Quas mihi transcribis, doctissime Didyme, laudes,
Ut sunt maiores quam quas agnoscere possim,
Ni prorsus frons nulla foret, sic rursus eaedem
Sunt adeo doctae talique e pectore natae,
5 Ut minime libeat quas das rescribere, veras
Esse perinde optans quam sunt lepidae atque venustae.
His ego non sane placeo mihi. Tu mihi, vates

it were not that you bestow your fertile births not on yourself but on the world? The glory is in your possession alone, but the fruit reaches the whole human race all over the world. Mindful of your hospitality, Erasmus fashioned these verses for you – hardly elegant but, whatever they may be, composed on the lyre of gratitude.

54 To Sebastian Brant, chief secretary of the city of Strasbourg. By Erasmus, in phaleucian metre

The muses of others have brought them honour, but instead you bring honour to your muses. Many have gained fame because of their fatherland; you have made your famous city much more famous, Sebastian, by your eloquence, character, learning, books, counsel, uprightness. Thus the honour you have received you repay at a high rate of interest, using your own resources in turn to add splendour to your fatherland and to the world of letters.

55 A poem addressed to Thomas Didymus Vogler, poet laureate, by Erasmus of Rotterdam

The praises that you have conveyed to me in your writings, most learned Didymus, though they are too high for me to acknowledge without seeming quite shameless, still, on the other hand, they are so learned and proceed from such a great mind that I am loath to write in refusal of what you have bestowed on me, hoping that it might have as much truth as it has elegance and charm. Indeed I am not pleased with myself because of it; it is with

Lauro digne, places, nam dum me reddere magnum
Carmine magnifico docte conniteris, ipsum
10 Te ostendis vere magnum vereque stupendum,
Ut qui viribus ingenii possis elephantum
Reddere de musca nihilique attollere tricas.
Sed quo iudicium minus approbo, maxime vates,
Hoc mage laetor amore tuo candoreque mentis.

56 Des. Erasmi Roterodami carmen iambicum ad Andream Ammonium Lucensem, invictissimi regis Anglorum a libellis [c 20 October 1511 / March 1518]

Quicunque dotes reputet, Ammoni, tuas
Oculisque totum lustret admotis prope
Oris decus, proceritatem heroicam
Vultuque toto et universo corpore
5 Bene temperatam dignitate gratiam,
Nitentium blandum vigorem luminum
Linguaeque plectrum tam suave tinniens,
Mores dehinc horas ad omneis commodos,
Facileis, amicos, melle melleos magis,
10 Veneres, lepores, gratias, risus, iocos,
Mitem indolem mentisque candorem novum
Mireque mixtam simplicem prudentiam –
His pectus adde sordido aversum lucro
Dextramque quam pro sorte largiusculam!
15 Iam quam benigni vena dives ingeni,
Quot animus unus expolitus literis!
Ac rursus his par addita est facundia,
Demum universa haec rara condit comitas,
Et improbi livoris arcet fascinum
20 Modestiae iucunditas, cum dotibus
In tam superbis nil superbum in moribus –
Haec quisquis, inquam, pensitet tot affatim

you that I am pleased, O poet worthy of the laurel. For while you strive learnedly in your magnificent poem to make me great, you show that you yourself are truly great and truly amazing by using the power of your genius to make an elephant out of a fly, a mountain out of a molehill. But though I cannot approve of your judgment, by the same token, most eminent of poets, I find all the more joy in your love and your kindness of heart.

56 An iambic poem to Andrea Ammonio of Lucca, secretary to the most invincible king of England

Whoever reckons up your endowments, Ammonio, and runs his eyes close up over all of your handsome countenance, whoever notes your heroic height, the fine mixture of grace and dignity in your whole face and your whole body, the charming liveliness of your bright eyes, your sweet voice, ringing as clear as a plucked string, and then your manners suited to all occasions, good-natured, friendly, more honey-sweet than honey itself, your charm, elegance, grace, humour, wit, your easy-going temperament, the unusual kindness of your heart, your marvellous combination of prudence and simplicity – and add to that a mind averse to low money-grubbing and a free-handed generosity (beyond what your lot allows), and then such a rich vein of kindly intelligence, such an integrated mind formed by wide reading, and, on top of that, eloquence on a par with such gifts, and finally a rare affability as a seasoning to all these qualities, and a pleasing modesty that wards off the evil eye of envy (since in spite of such proud endowments you conduct yourself with no pride) – if (I say) someone should weigh all

Congesta in unum, nonne merito dixerit
Soli parentem fuisse naturam tibi,
25 Contra novercam caeteris mortalibus? –
Horum licet tibi ipse debes pleraque.
Restant tuae, Fortuna, iam partes, uti
Dotes ita amplas opibus exaeques tuis,
Nisi vis videri aut caeca plane aut invida.

57 Ad Lucam Paliurum Rubeaquensem, episcopi Basileiensis cancellarium, Eras. Rot. carmen

[c 1515 / March 1518]

Exhaustum immodico novale cultu
Mentitur queruli spei coloni.
Effoetum ingenium labore longo
Nil dignum parit hoc amore nostro,
5 Quo te prosequor unice inter omneis,
Mellitissime Paliure, amicos,
Nec dignum meritis tuis nec ipsi
Quod respondeat eruditioni.
Quod solum licet, hoc in omne tempus
10 Praestabo: ex animo medullitusque
Nostrum (sic meritum est) amabo Lucam.

58 In fugam Gallorum insequentibus Anglis apud Morinum, AN. M.D.XIII. Scazon Des. Erasmi Roterodami. Alludit ad carmen Martialis de Catone.

[autumn 1513 / March 1518]

Audivit olim censor ille Romanus:
'Ludos iocosae quando noveras Florae,
Cur in theatrum, Cato severe, venisti?
An ideo tantum veneras ut exires?'
5 At iure nunc imbellis audiat Gallus:
'Ludum cruenti quando noveras Martis,

these gifts heaped so lavishly on one man, could he not rightly say that nature was a mother to you alone, but a stepmother to other mortals? – though you yourself are responsible for most of these excellencies. All that now remains is that you, Fortune, should match these ample endowments with your riches, unless you wish to appear either downright blind or else envious.

57 A poem to Lukas Klett of Rouffach, chancellor to the bishop of Basel, by Erasmus of Rotterdam

A field worn out by overcultivation disappoints the hopes of the farmer and makes him complain. A mind worn out by long labours brings forth nothing worthy of the love which I feel for you alone, most sweet Klett, among all my friends, and also nothing worthy of your deserts, nothing matching even your learning. All that I can do, I will do for all time: I will love my Lukas, as he deserves, with all my heart and in the very marrow of my bones.

58 On the flight of the French, pursued by the English, near Thérouanne in the year 1513. In scazons, by Desiderius Erasmus of Rotterdam. He is making a playful allusion to a poem by Martial about Cato.

That Roman censor was once told: 'Since you knew what the games of jolly Flora are like, why, O strict Cato, did you come into the theatre? Did you come for no other reason than to leave?' But now the cowardly Frenchman can rightly expect to hear: 'Since you knew what the game of bloody Mars is

Animos ferocis quando noveras Angli,
Quid, quaeso, in aciem, timide Galle, prodisti,
Ferro minaci splendidas agens turmas?
10 An ideo tantum veneras, uti foede
Fugiens sequenti terga verteres hosti,
Ac si pedum certamen esset, haud dextrae?'
Cato foeminas videre non potest, Gallus
Viros. Cato mutare non potest vultum,
15 Gallus nequit mutare pectus ignavum.

59 Cum multos menses perpetuo pluisset et per unam modo dieculam se mundo sol ostendisset rursusque non minus odiose quam antea plueret, ERASMUS Basileam repetens in itinere sic lusit in Iovem, AN. M.D.XV.

[late June 1515 / March 1518]

Menses cum prope Iuppiter per octo
Vota surdus ad omnium pluisset,
Agros iam male perdidisset omneis,
Vexasset segetesque vineasque,
5 Tandem desierat, pudore credo,
Et tandem licuit videre solem,
Quem migrasse polo timebat orbis,
Aeternam ratus imminere noctem.
Vix dum sesquidiem nitere passus
10 Obducit nebulisque nubibusque
Totum qua patet undequaque mundum,
Ac rursum similis sui esse pergit.
Istoc si moderere pacto Olympum,
Nec quicquam es nisi nubium coactor,
15 Quis non officium probet Gigantum
Et cognomina consueta vertens
Pessimum vocet infimumque divum?

like, since you knew the courage of the fierce Englishman, why, I ask you, O fearful Frenchman, did you come out to join battle, marshalling your splendid array of threatening troops and weapons? Did you come for no other reason than to take to your heels so basely and turn your back to the pursuing enemy, as if it were a contest for feet and not for the sword-arm?' Cato cannot bear to look at the women; the Frenchman, at the men. Cato cannot change the expression on his face; the Frenchman cannot change his craven heart.

59 When it had rained continuously for many months and then the sun showed himself to the world for only one short day before it rained once more as disagreeably as before, Erasmus made fun of Jupiter in the following poem as he was on the return trip to Basel in the year 1515.

After Jupiter, deaf to the prayers of everyone, had rained for almost eight months, and had already utterly ruined all the fields and damaged both the crops and the vineyards, he finally stopped (ashamed of himself, I think), and he finally let the sun appear; the whole world was afraid that the sun had departed from the heavens and thought that night would hang over their heads forever. Hardly had he allowed it to shine for a day and a half when he covered everything the whole world over in all directions with fog and clouds, and he proceeded once more just like his old self. If this is the way you govern Olympus, acting as nothing but cloud-gatherer, who would not approve of the Giants' undertaking as a service? And who would not invert your usual titles and call you the worst and the lowest of the gods?

60 Epitaphium Philippi coenobitae Cluniacensis

[1514–15? / March 1518]

Viator Isti cur lubet assidere saxo
Cum toto, Pietas, choro sororum?
Pietas Hic nostrae iacet unicus catervae
Vindex, ille Philippus, ille dudum
5 Coetus gloria prima Cluniaci.
Viator Luctum at pulla solet decere vestis;
Vos albis video nitere totas.
Pietas Cuius tam nivei fuere mores,
Cui tam candida sit peracta vita,
10 Huius funera non puto decere
Aut pulla aut lachrymis nigrandum ⟨amictum⟩.

61 Erasmus Roterodamus Guilielmo Neseno calamum dono dedit cum hoc epigrammate.

[spring 1516? / March 1518]

Calamus loquitur.

Tantillus calamus tot tanta volumina scripsi
Solus, at articulis ductus Erasmiacis.
Aediderat Nilus, dederat Reuchlinus Erasmo,
Nunc rude donatum me Gulielmus habet,
5 Isque sacrum Musis servat Phoeboque dicatum,
Aeternae charum pignus amicitiae,
Ne peream obscurus, per quem tot nomina noscet
Posteritas, longo nunquam abolenda die.

Epigrammatum
Des. Erasmi Roterodami finis

60 An epitaph for Philippe, a monk of Cluny

Passer-by Why have you chosen to sit by this gravestone, Piety, together with the whole band of your sisters?

Piety Here lies the only champion of our troop, that Philippe who was once the pride and glory of the congregation at Cluny.

Passer-by But it is usual and fitting that grief be expressed by black clothing; I see that you are all dressed in shining white.

Piety Since his character was white as snow, since the life he led was shining white, I do not think that his funeral would be fittingly marked by black clothing or garments darkened by tears.

61 Erasmus of Rotterdam gave a reed pen as a present to Wilhelm Nesen, together with this epigram.

The reed pen speaks.

Little reed pen that I am, I wrote so many large volumes all by myself, though I was guided by the finger joints of Erasmus. The Nile produced me, Reuchlin gave me to Erasmus, and now, honourably discharged, I belong to Wilhelm. And he preserves me as sacred to the Muses and dedicated to Apollo, a dear token of eternal friendship, lest I, who made so many names known to posterity, names never to be wiped out in the long course of time, should perish in obscurity.

The end of the epigrams
of Desiderius Erasmus of Rotterdam

POEMS NOT IN THE *EPIGRAMMATA* OF 1518 BUT PUBLISHED ELSEWHERE BY ERASMUS

62 Ad amplissimum patrem Antonium de Berghes, abbatem divi Bertini, de morte fratris episcopi Cameracensis carmen elegiacum Erasmi

[autumn 1502 / 1 April 1503]

Mors, gnata invidiae sed matre nocentior ipsa,
  Taelo eodem cupiens plurima damna dare,
Sustulit eximium generosa ex arbore ramum:
  Berghanae Henricum spemque decusque domus.
5 Sic varios luctus de funere suscitat uno,
  Dum flet patronum patria moesta pium,
Pastoremque bonum dum grex desiderat orbus,
  Dum consultorem principis aula gravem,
Dum Moecaenatem paupertas docta benignum
10 Turbaque subsidium plorat egena suum,
Denique dum pullata suae dispendia stirpis
  Bergica gens iustis prosequitur lachrymis.
Tu quoque iam toties, praesul Bertinice, fratrem
  Luges, heu tanto tercius ex numero.
15 Iusta doles, verum et iusto modus esto dolori;
  Gaude habuisse quod haut semper habere licet.
Non periit, verum precessit ad aethera frater:
  Hoc nivei mores, hoc pia vita meret.

POEMS NOT IN THE *EPIGRAMMATA* OF 1518 BUT PUBLISHED ELSEWHERE BY ERASMUS

62 To the most venerable father, Antoon van Bergen, abbot of St Bertin, an elegiac poem by Erasmus on the death of his brother, the bishop of Cambrai

Death, the daughter of Envy but even more destructive than her mother, wishing to do the most damage she could with one and the same cast of her spear, took away the pre-eminent branch from a noble tree, Hendrik van Bergen, the hope and the splendour of his house. Thus from this one funeral she evokes many different kinds of grief: his grieving fatherland weeps for its loyal protector; his orphaned flock misses its good shepherd; the court of the prince mourns for its weighty counsellor; learned men in their poverty, for their beneficent patron; and the common people, for succour in their indigence; and finally the Bergen family, in black garments, attends with just tears the loss to their lineage. You also, abbot of St Bertin, one of three survivors among so many brothers, have, alas, so often mourned a brother already. Your grief is just, but even a just grief must have its bounds. Rejoice that you have at least had what cannot be had forever. Your brother has not perished but has gone before you to heaven. He deserved this by his pious life, his morals

Vos modo relliquias generis servate perhennes,
20 Numina magnanimis non inimica viris.

63 Illustrissimo principi Philippo reduci Homerocenton

[c February 1504]

Χαῖρε Φίλιππε, πάτρας γλυκερὸν φάος, ὄρχαμε λαῶν.
Ὦ φίλ', ἐπεὶ νόστησας ἐελδομένοισι μάλ' ἡμῖν
Σῶς τ' ἠΰς τε μέγας τε, θεοὶ δέ σε ἤγαγον αὐτοί,
Οὖλέ τε καὶ μάλα χαῖρε, θεοὶ δέ τοι ὄλβια δοῖεν,
5 Καὶ παισὶν παίδων καί τοι μετόπισθε γένωνται.
Ἄλκιμος ἔσσ' αἰεί, καί σου κλέος οὐκ ἀπολεῖται.

64 Illustrissimo principi Philippo foeliciter in patriam redeunti gratulatorium carmen Erasmi sub persona patriae

[c February 1504]

O semper memoranda dies plaudendaque semper,
Quam niveo faciles ducunt mihi vellere Parcae!
Ecquis Erithraeis tam candidus unio conchis
Innitet, ut merita queat huius munera lucis
5 Insignire nota, quae te, optatissime princeps,
Iam lassis desideriis votisque tuorum
Restituit? Nunc nunc videor mihi reddita demum,
Te, mea spes, decus ac votorum summa, recepto.
Scilicet una parum est tam festae gemma diei,
10 Quae semel anteactae novat omnia commoda vitae,
Quae tot laeta simul cumulo mihi congerit uno.
Lingua deest animo, neque enim in sua gaudia pectus

white as snow. O you heavenly powers not hostile to high-minded men, at least preserve for years upon years the surviving members of this race.

63 A cento from Homer, to the most illustrious Prince Philip, upon his return

Hail Philip, the sweet light of our fatherland, leader of the people. O beloved, we sorely longed for you, and now that you have returned safe and valiant and mighty and the gods themselves have brought you back, health and joy be with you! May the gods bestow happiness upon you and upon your childrens' children and those who will be born in after years. Always be brave and your glory will never perish.

64 A congratulatory poem by Erasmus, to the most illustrious Prince Philip, upon his happy return to his homeland, spoken in the person of that homeland

O day ever to be remembered and ever to be applauded, day brought to me by the favourable Fates, spinning snow-white wool! What pearl from Persian shell shines white enough to mark worthily the gifts of this day, which restores you, most longed-for Prince, to the weary desires and longings of your people? Now, now at last I seem to be my old self again, now that I have received you, my hope, my honour, and the sum of my desires. Indeed, one gem is not enough for such a festive day, which renews all at once all the good things of my past life, which heaps together for me all at once so many joys in one pile. My tongue is not adequate to my feelings,

Sufficit, ad iustos desunt sua brachia plausus.
Sospes ab Hispano rediit meus orbe Philippus,
15 Sospes, cunque meo redierunt cuncta Philippo.
Ecce canunt reducem populusque patresque Philippum,
Clamat io reducem laeta undique turba Philippum,
Responsant reducem vocalia tecta Philippum.
Nec fallax ista est iteratae vocis imago:
20 Saxa etiam reducem sentiscunt muta Philippum
Et recinunt reducem minime iam muta Philippum.
Quum procul hinc aberas, squalebant omnia luctu;
Mox ut salvus ades, renitescunt omnia cultu.
Sic ubi tristis hyems Aquilonibus asperat auras,
25 Nuda senescit humus, moerent sine floribus horti,
Torpescunt amnes, languet sine frondibus arbos,
Stat sine fruge seges, marcent sine gramine campi.
Rursus ubi Zephyris tepidum spirantibus anni
Leta iuventa redit, gemmantur floribus horti,
30 Effugiunt amnes, revirescit frondibus arbos,
Fruge nitent segetes, hilarescunt gramine campi.
Sic simul auricomus se condidit aequore Titan,
Mox perit haec nitidi facies pulcherrima mundi,
Pigra quies subit, et nigrantibus horrida pennis
35 Nox operit mortique simillimus omnia torpor.
Rursum ubi purpureis Aurora revecta quadrigis
Rorantes tenero detexit lumine terras,
Cuique repente sua species redit atque renasci
Quaeque putes blandoque magis iuvenescere vultu.
40 Tu ver dulce meum, tu lumen amabile, solus

nor is my heart sufficient to feel its joys, nor are my arms adequate to applaud the occasion worthily. My Philip has returned safe from the land of Spain, safe, and with my Philip all things have returned.

Lo, the people and the nobles sing the return of Philip; on all sides the happy crowd cries 'hurrah' for the return of Philip. In reply the houses lift their voices to cry out for the return of Philip. Nor is this re-echoed voice merely a fictitious figure of speech: even the mute stones feel the return of Philip, and now not mute at all they re-echo the return of Philip. When you were far away from here, everything was unsightly with grief. As soon as you are here safe and sound, everything is bright and neat once again. Just so, when sad winter makes the air harsh with winds from the north, the soil grows bare and old, gardens grieve without flowers, rivers grow sluggish, trees languish without leaves, the stalks stand without grain, the fields shrivel without grass. When the joyous youth of the year comes back again, blowing with balmy western winds, the gardens are begemmed with flowers, the rivers take flight, the trees revive with their green leaves, the stalks are bright with grain, the fields rejoice in their grass. Just so, as soon as golden-haired Titan has vanished beneath the sea, the most beautiful sights of this shining world disappear, sluggish repose takes over, and night, bristling with black feathers, and a stillness much like death itself shroud all things. When Dawn returns once more, brought back by her rosy, four-horse team, and reveals with her tender light the dewy earth, everything suddenly becomes its old self again and you would think that everything is reborn, taking on an even younger and more charming look. O my sweet spring, my lovely light, you

Cuncta rapis fugiens ac redditus omnia reddis.
  Quam misere absentem lugebant cuncta Philippum,
Quam mihi sollicitis trepidabant viscera curis,
Dum tibi nunc iterum peragratur Gallia triplex,
45 Nunc magni lustras soceri latissima regna,
Nunc tumidum visis Rhodanum gelidisque propinqua
Arva iugis, dulci placide regnata sorori,
Nunc rapidum superans Rhenum petis ampla parentis
Imperia et varias gentesque urbesque pererras,
50 Illarum studio ac pro rerum pondere velox,
Ad mea vota tamen lentissimus. Ut mihi segnes
Torpidius solito visi prorepere menses!
Ut geminae noctes, ut tardius ire videri
Invitis sol fessus equis! Quin saepe fathiscens
55 Impatiensque morae pietas haec aeminus in te
Latrabat calidis convicia mixta querelis:
'O nimium saecure mei, iam tertia bruma
Appetit, et cessas etiam lentusque lubensque,
Atque oculos sine fine tuos peregrina morantur,
60 Nec sentis quod sola malisque metuque fatigor.
Num tibi nuper inest adamas in pectore natus?
Nuncubi somniferae gustasti flumina Lethes,
Qui dulcis patriae terraeque altricis alumnus
Non meminisse potes? Tam longo ferreus aevo
65 Non meminisse potes? Sic te regna extera tangunt?'
  Esto bis affinis se tollat in aethera Betis
Et geminis tumeat titulis. Germania iure,
Haud ego diffiteor, magno genitore superbit.

alone take everything away when you leave and give it all back when you return.

How miserably everything mourned the absent Philip, how my heart fluttered with cares and anxieties, while now you were making your way once more through tripartite France, now you were traversing the extensive kingdom of your great father-in-law, now you were visiting the swelling Rhône and the fields near to the icy peaks, ruled tranquilly by your sweet sister, now you were overcoming the swift Rhine and seeking out the ample empire of your father and wandering among various peoples and cities. In your attention to them, you were swift enough, considering the importance of the affairs, but measured by my desires, you were slower than slow. How the lazy months seemed to me to creep more slowly than usual! How the nights seemed to double in length! How the weary sun with his unwilling team seemed to move more slowly! Indeed, faint and impatient with the delay, this loyal love of mine often called out to you from afar, yelling reproaches mingled with feverish laments. 'O Prince too heedless of me, already the third winter is approaching, and still you linger with willing tardiness, and foreign lands endlessly catch and hold your eye, nor do you realize that I, all alone, am worn out by afflictions and fear. Has the heart in your breast recently turned to adamant? Have you somewhere tasted the soporific streams of Lethe, that you cannot remember your sweet homeland, the soil that nursed you like a son? that you, iron-hearted as you are, cannot remember me for such an age of time? Are you so taken with foreign realms?'

So be it, let Spain, doubly related to you by marriage, lift her head on high and swell with her twofold titles. Germany, I will not deny it, is rightly proud of your great father. Not

Nec domina temere Sabaudia leta sorore est.
70 Francia iam tritavos cognataque stemmata centum
Ostentare potest. Uno hoc ego nomine primas
Assero nec cedo socero neque cedo sorori
Nec centum cedo vinclis neque cedo parenti,
Numinibus tantum superisque secunda beatis,
75 Hoc, inquam, titulo quod te mihi protinus uni
Elapsum arcanis uteri Lucina latebris
Tradidit in gremium, quod dulcia murmura primae
Auribus una meis hausi letissima vocis
Reptastique sinu generosus pusio nostro.
80 Qualibus o mihi tum saliebant pectora votis!
Qualibus o mihi nunc saliunt praecordia votis!
Tunc ego plaudebam natum festiva Philippum,
Nunc ego plaudo magis reducem festiva Philippum;
Illo quanta die praesensi gaudia mente!
85 Hoc maiora die persentio gaudia mente.
Vicisti mea vota, bonis gratissime divis,
Optatis mihi maior ades. Nunc thure Sabaeo
Templa vaporentur, nunc omnis luceat ara,
Victima nunc dextro properet votiva tonanti.
90 Is mihi te quondam dederat, mihi reddidit idem;
Et dederat magnum, at maiorem reddidit idem.
Perge, precor, Lachesis, simili de vellere totam
Principis in longumque velis deducere vitam,
Nec pullis unquam vicies bona stamina filis.
95 Tuque, pater, qui digna soles immittere dignis
Eque **πίθοις** misces mortalia fata duobus,
Huic nihil aut certe minimum de tristibus addas,
Sed mihi perpetuo sit, ut est, laetissimus ille.

without reason does Savoy rejoice that it has your sister as its mistress. France indeed can boast of your distant ancestors and a hundred related family trees. For this one reason alone I claim the primacy, neither do I yield to father-in-law nor to sister nor to a hundred bonds of blood, nor to your father. Second only to the gods and the blessed souls on high, I do not yield (I say) for this reason: when Lucina had brought you forth from the secret recesses of the womb, she immediately gave you to me alone, she placed you in my lap; I alone, with the greatest joy, drew into my ears the sweet murmurs of your first words; and as a noble little lad you crept on my bosom. O with what wishes for you my heart then leapt! O with what wishes for you my breast now leaps! Then I applauded in celebration of Philip's birth. Now I applaud even more in celebration of Philip's return. On that day my mind felt premonitions of such great joys. On this day my mind feels in fact even greater joys. You have surpassed my wishes, most pleasing as you are to the kindly gods; beyond my hopes you are here with me.

Now let the churches fume with Sabaean incense; now let every altar shine forth; now let the votive victim hasten to the propitious Thunderer. Formerly he gave you to me; he has likewise given you back to me. And he gave you to me in your greatness; but he has likewise given you back to me even greater than before. Proceed, Lachesis, I beg you, spin out the whole long life of the prince with this same white wool; do not ever spoil the good threads with dark strands. And you, O father, who bestow worthy things on the worthy and mix together the fates of mortals from the two earthenware jars, do not add afflictions to this man's lot, or at least the fewest that can be, but let me forever have him full of joy, as he

Contra ego perpetuo sim, ut sum, letabilis illi,
100 Mutuaque haec nobis ac tam pia gaudia nunquam
Humanis infesta bonis turbaverit Ate.

65 Ad R.P. Guilhelmum archiepiscopum Cantuariensem, Erasmi carmen iambicum trimetrum

[January 1506 / 13 September 1506]

Scite poetas doctus appellat Maro
Cygnos, Guilhelme, praesulum eximium decus.
Res mira dictu, ut cuncta consensu novo
Vati atque holori congruant divinitus.
5 Niveus utrique candor: alter lacteis
Plumis, amico candet alter pectore.
Musis uterque gratus ac Phoebo sacer,
Et limpidis uterque gaudet amnibus,
Ripis adaeque uterque gaudet herbidis,
10 Pariter canorus uterque, tum potissimum,
Vicina seram mors senectam quum premit.
Sed qui tenent arcana naturae, negant
Audiri holorem, ni sonent Favonii.
Nil ergo mirum, barbaro hoc si saeculo
15 Canorus olim obmutuit vatum chorus,
Quum tot procaces undique obstrepant Noti
Boreaeque tristes invidorum et pinguium,
Nulli faventum provocent Favonii.
Quod si bonis clementer ingeniis tuae
20 Benignitatis blandus aspiret favor,
Ita ut facit, tota statim Britannia
Vates videbis exoriri candidos,
Adeo canoros atque vocales uti
In alta fundant astra cygnaeum melos,
25 Quod ipsa et aetas posterorum exaudiat.

now is. May he, on the other hand, forever find me a source of joy, as I now am. And may this interchange of loving joy between us never be disturbed by Ate, hostile to the goods enjoyed by mankind.

65 To the most reverend father, William, archbishop of Canterbury, a poem by Erasmus in iambic trimeters

William, pre-eminent splendour among bishops, the learned Virgil wittily calls poets swans. It is a marvellous thing to relate how all the features of the poet and the swan are strangely matched in a providential correspondence. Both are white as snow: the one has milk-white plumes; the other, a heart shining white with friendship. Both are favourites of the Muses and sacred to Phoebus. Both delight in clear streams; both are equally delighted with grassy river banks. Both are equally melodious, especially when death comes near and presses upon advanced old age.

But those who know the secrets of nature say that a swan is never heard except when the west wind is whispering. Therefore it is not surprising that in this barbarous age the once melodious choir of the poets has fallen silent, since roaring everywhere are the blatant south winds and the dismal north winds of the envious and the dull. No one is roused by the west winds of favouring patronage. But if the sweet favour of your beneficence blows mildly on good minds, as in fact it does, you will very soon see bright-white poets arising all over Britain, so melodious and vocal that they will pour forth swanlike melody up to the lofty stars, melody that will still be heard in the era of coming generations.

William Warham
Copy by Hans Holbein the Younger of his
original portrait of 1527, now lost
Musée du Louvre, Paris

Jérôme de Busleyden
Portrait by a Franco-Flemish master, c 1480–1500
Wadsworth Atheneum, Hartford, Connecticut
Ella Gallup Sumner and Mary Catlin Sumner Collection

66 Epitaphium carmine iambico trimetro D. Iacobi de Croy, ducis et episcopi Cameracensis

[c November 1516? / August 1518]

Utriusque gentis Croicae et Lalaingicae
Decus perenne, Iacobus hoc situs loco.
Praesulne fuerit melior an dux clarior,
Tibi, Camerace, nemo facile dixerit.
5 Evectae ad astra virgini matri sacer,
Cui fuerat usque pectore addictus pio,
Evexit hunc e rebus humanis dies.

67 In hymnos Bernardi Andreae Tolosatis poetae regii Erasmi Roterodami hexastichon

[April 1517? / 7 July 1517]

Maeonius vates ac Thracius Orpheus olim
  Hymnidicis cecinit numina vana modis.
Bernardina chelys veros canit ordine divos,
  Gaudens omniiugis divariare metris.
5 Haec lege, cui pietas, cui sunt coelestia cordi:
  Illa iuvant aures, haec refovent animum.

66 An epitaph in iambic trimeters for Lord Jacques de Croy, the duke and bishop of Cambrai

Jacques, the perennial glory of the houses of Croy and Lalaing, lies buried in this spot. No one would find it easy to tell you, Cambrai, whether he was better as a bishop or more illustrious as a duke. The day consecrated to the taking up into heaven of the Virgin Mother, to whom his pious heart was always devoted, was the day which took him up and away from human concerns.

67 A six-line poem by Erasmus of Rotterdam on the hymns of Bernard André of Toulouse, the king's poet

The Maeonian poet and Thracian Orpheus once sang rhythmic hymns to empty divinities. The lyre of Bernard sings of true saints according to their order [in the liturgical year], taking pleasure in gaining variety by using all sorts of metres. Read these if piety or the things of heaven are dear to your heart. Those poems delight the ear; these refresh the mind.

68 Epitaphium ad pictam imaginem clarissimi viri Hieronymi Buslidiani, praepositi Ariensis et consiliarii Regis Catholici, fratris reverendissimi patris ac domini Francisci, Archiepiscopi quondam Bizontini, qui Lovanii magnis impendiis instituit collegium, in quo publice tres linguae doceantur, Hebraica, Graeca, Latina [c 26 March 1518 / August 1518]

Ἴαμβοι τρίμετροι

Ὁ τήνδε γράψας σώματος μορφὴν καλῶς,
Ὤφελες ἄγαλμα ζωγραφεῖν καὶ τοῦ νοός.
Ἐσιδεῖν ἂν εἴη πίνακος ἐν μιᾶς πέδῳ
Ἀρετῶν ἁπασῶν ἐρατὸν ἐγγύθεν χορόν·
5 Τὴν εὐσέβειαν τὴν ἱεροπρεπῆ πάνυ,
Τὴν σεμνότητα τήν τε σωφροσύνην ἅμα,
Τὴν χρηστότητα τήν τε παιδείαν καλήν –
Καὶ ταῦτα κἄλλα μόνος ὑπῆρχ' Ἱερώνυμος
Ὁ Βουσλεδιακῆς οἰκίας σέλας μέγα.

69 Trochaici tetrametri [c 26 March 1518 / August 1518]

Nominis Buslidiani proximum primo decus,
Itane nos orbas virenti raptus aevo, Hieronyme?
Literae, genus, senatus, aula, plebs, ecclesia
Aut suum sydus requirunt aut patronum flagitant.
5 Nescit interire quisquis vitam honeste finiit:
Fama virtutum perennis vivet usque posteris.
Eruditio trilinguis triplici facundia
Te loquetur, cuius opibus restituta refloruit.

68 An epitaph to accompany a painting of the illustrious Jérôme de Busleyden, provost of Aire and councillor to the Catholic King, brother of the most reverend father and lord François, formerly archbishop of Besançon, who established in Louvain at great expense a college in which public instruction might be given in the three languages, Hebrew, Greek, and Latin

Iambic trimeters

O artist who drew the shape of this body so beautifully, you ought also to have done a portrait of the mind. Then we could have viewed on the ground of this one painting the lovely choral dance of all the virtues: piety full of reverence, dignity linked with self-restraint, honesty and a good education – these things and more were united in the single person of Jérôme, the great shining light of the house of Busleyden.

69 [Another epitaph for Jérôme de Busleyden] Trochaic tetrameters

O Jérôme, all but the highest ornament of the name Busleyden, are you thus snatched away in the prime of life, leaving us orphaned? Literature, your family, the Council, the court, the people, the church either ask to have their star returned to them or demand to have their patron back.

Anyone who has finished an upright life is incapable of perishing: the perennial fame of his virtues will always live for posterity. The three learned tongues will always speak of you with the threefold eloquence which was restored and reinvigorated by your wealth.

70 Erasmus Roterodamus in Brunonem Amerbachium

[November 1519 / March 1528]

Hic iacet, ante diem fatis ereptus iniquis,
Gentis Amerbachiae gloria prima Bruno.
Non tulit uxori superesse maritus amatae,
Turtur ut ereptae commoriens sociae.
5 Hunc blandae lugent Charites Musaeque trilingues
Canaque cum casta simplicitate fides.

71 Erasmi Rot. epitaphium in mortem Martini Dorpii

[8 November 1525 / March 1528]

Martinus ubi terras reliquit Dorpius,
Suum orba partum flet parens Hollandia,
Theologus ordo luget extinctum decus,
Tristes Camoenae candidis cum Gratiis
5 Tantum patronum lachrymis desiderant,
Lovaniensis omnis opplorans schola
Sidus suum requirit, 'o mors' inquiens
'Crudelis, atrox, saeva, iniqua et invida,
Itan' ante tempus floridam arborem secans,
10 Tot dotibus, tot spebus orbas, omnium
Suspensa vota?' Premite voces impias.
Non periit ille: vivit ac dotes suas
Nunc tuto habet, subductus aevo pessimo.
Sors nostra flenda est, gratulandum est Dorpio.
15 Haec terra servat, mentis hospitium piae,
Corpusculum, quod ad canorae buccinae
Vocem resignans optima reddet fide.

70 On Bruno Amerbach, by Erasmus of Rotterdam

Here lies Bruno, the first glory of the Amerbach family, snatched away by the unjust Fates before his time. The husband could not bear to survive his beloved wife, like a turtle-dove that dies at the same time that its mate is snatched away. The charming Graces mourn him, and the trilingual Muses, and venerable Faith together with chaste Simplicity.

71 An epitaph on the death of Maarten van Dorp, by Erasmus of Rotterdam

Now that Maarten van Dorp has left the earth behind him, Holland, like a bereaved mother, weeps for her child; the theological faculty mourns because its glory has been snuffed out; the sad Muses, together with the shining Graces, bewail with their tears the loss of such a great patron; the whole University of Louvain cries out in grief at the loss of its star and begs to have him back, saying: 'O Death, cruel, fierce, savage, wicked, and envious Death, do you thus cut down the flourishing tree before its time, leaving everyone bereft of so many gifts, so many hopes, cutting off the wishes of everyone?'

Suppress such impious words. He has not perished. He lives, and, carried away from this wicked age, he now has safe possession of his gifts. Our own fate is what we should weep for; we should congratulate Dorp. This plot of earth keeps what little is left of his body, which was an inn for his pious mind, and can be completely trusted to keep faith at the sound of the sonorous trumpet by rendering it up and giving it back.

72 Erasmi Rot. in Iacobum, paulo post defunctum

[autumn 1526? / March 1528]

Dum Dorpium assidere mensis coelitum,
Iacobe, gaudes, ille eodem te vocat.
Ita nos vicissim gratulamur et tibi
Datum esse mensis assidere coelitum.

73 Epitaphium Ioannis Frobenii per Erasmum Roterod.

[c November 1527 / March 1528]

Arida Ioannis tegit hic lapis ossa Frobeni,
  Orbe viret toto nescia fama mori.
Moribus hanc niveis meruit studiisque iuvandis,
  Quae nunc moesta iacent orba parente suo.
5 Rettulit, ornavit veterum monumenta sophorum
  Arte, manu, curis, aere, favore, fide.
Huic vitam in coelis date, numina iusta, perhennem;
  Per nos in terris fama perhennis erit.

74 Eiusdem in eundem Graece

[c November 1527 / March 1528]

Ὧδ' Ἰωάννης καθεύδει τυπογράφος Φροβέννιος.
Οὐδέν' ἄλλῳ πλέον ὀφείλει τῶν λόγων σπουδάσματα.
Μὴ νεκρὸν θρηνεῖτε, ζῇ γὰρ καὶ πνέει, πνεύσων ἀεί,
Τῇ τε ψυχῇ τῇ τε φήμῃ τοῖς τε βίβλων λειψάνοις.

72 On Jacob [Volkaerd], who died shortly afterwards, by Erasmus of Rotterdam

While you are rejoicing, Jacob, that Dorp is seated at the table of the saints in heaven, he calls you to come to the same place. Just so, we in turn are now joyful because it has been granted also to you to be seated at the table of the saints in heaven.

73 An epitaph for Johann Froben by Erasmus of Rotterdam

This stone covers the dry bones of Johann Froben, whose fame flourishes throughout the whole world and can never die. He earned it by his spotless morals and his contributions to scholarship, which now lies prostrate with grief, bereft of its father. He restored and adorned the monuments of the wise men of ancient times by means of his skill, manual dexterity, care, money, patronage, and faithfulness. Give to him, O just gods, an endless life in heaven. We will see to it that his fame on earth will be endless.

74 A Greek epitaph for the same man by the same poet

Here the printer Johann Froben is laid to rest. To no other man do literary studies owe more. Do not mourn him as dead. For he lives and breathes, and will do so forever, in his soul, his fame, and the books he left behind him.

75 [c May 1528? / 1529]

Philippus Haneton, clarus auro hic est eques.
Regi Philippo Caesarique Carolo
Cum laude gessit audientiarium.
Sacer ordo, quem vellus decorat aureum,
5 Voluit eundem praeesse thesauris suis.
Virtus in uno hoc vicit invidiam viro,
Tanta erat in omnes et fides et comitas
Animique candor. Maximis et infimis
Desideratus unice, coelum tenet.

76 Des. Erasmus Roterodamus [31 October 1528]

Si cupis astrigeri primordia discere mundi,
Ac mox aethereos implexos orbibus orbes,
Denique quam vario cinctu quae ducitur arte
Linea convexi spatium secet: haec, age, pubes,
5 Perlege, quae triplici Ioachimi cura libello
Tradidit, ac facilem patefecit ad ardua callem.
Surrige te, qui repis humi, patriamque revise,
Astra: levis repete astra, genus qui ducis ab astris.

77 Des. Erasmus Roterodamus [October 1528? / 1530]

Quae vix loquaci disceres volumine,
Brevis en tabella ponit ob oculos tibi.
Labor unius laborem ademit omnibus.

75 [An epitaph for Philippe Haneton]

Here lies Philippe Haneton, renowned as a knight of the Golden Fleece. He did laudable service as audiencer to King Philip and the emperor Charles. The holy order distinguished by the golden fleece chose him to preside over its treasury. In this man alone virtue conquered envy, so great was his trustworthiness and courtesy toward everyone, and the kindness of his heart. A unique loss to great men and lowly, he has his place in heaven.

76 Desiderius Erasmus of Rotterdam [on *Basic Principles of Astronomy* by Joachim Sterck van Ringelberg]

If you want to learn the rudiments of the universe and its stars, and then about their orbits in the heavens, woven one within another, and finally about the varying circumferences cut out by lines artfully constructed in the hollow dome of the heavens, come, young people, read through the three books of this careful work put out by Joachim, who has opened up an easy path for the steep ascent. All you who creep on the ground, rise up and revisit your homeland, the stars: float up lightly to seek once more the stars, since your race has its origins in the stars.

77 Desiderius Erasmus of Rotterdam [on a table in Joachim Sterck's book on astronomy]

What you might find hard to learn from a whole volume of discourse, look, this little diagram places it all right before your eyes. One man's work has made it unnecessary for

Ioachimus haec dat; fruere, lector, ac vale.

78 [1 February 1529 / 1529]

Hoc saxo tegitur celebris heros
Utenhovius ille Nicolaus,
Quo sub praeside Flandriae senatus
Multos floruit unice per annos.
5 Hoc patri orphana turba liberorum
Μνημεῖον posuit, pio quidem illa
Sed casso officio. Quid attinebat
Haec illi monumenta comparare,
Cuius scilicet approbata virtus
10 Haeret mentibus omnium, nec ulla
Illam vis abolebit aut vetustas?

79 [1 February 1529 / 1529]

Τίς εἶ θεάων; Οὔνομ᾽ ἐστί μοι Δίκη.
Τί δακρύεις οὖν; Τὸν δικαίαρχον καλὸν
Τὸν Νικόλαον Οὐθενώβιον ποθῶ,
Ὃς ἦν ἁπάσης Φλανδρίας κλέος μέγα.
5 Τούτου γὰρ οὐδεὶς βελτίων πέφυκ᾽ ἀνήρ.
Φιλῷ θανόντι συναπέθανον, ὡς μοι δοκῶ.
Οὐκ ἦν δίκαιος, ἀλλὰ μᾶλλον ἡ δίκη.

80 [early April 1529 / 1529]

Gallus es, et gallina tibi est; fausto omine dono
Gallum, cui coniunx teneros fovet anxia foetus.

all others to work. Joachim gives you this gift. Enjoy it, reader, and farewell.

78 [An epitaph for Nicolaas Uutenhove]

This stone covers that illustrious hero Nicolaas Uutenhove, under whose presidency the Council of Flanders flourished for many years in an unprecedented way. The orphaned flock of his children set up this *monimentum* to their father – truly a pious and dutiful undertaking but an empty gesture. What good did it do to set up this monument to him? After all, it is to a man whose established virtue sticks fast in everyone's mind and can never be destroyed by any violence or any passage of the years.

79 [Another epitaph for Nicolaas Uutenhove]

'Which of the goddesses are you?'
'My name is Justice.'
'Why, then, are you weeping?'
'I mourn the loss of that good and just magistrate Nicolaas Uutenhove, who was the crowning glory of all Flanders. Never was born a better man than he. With the death of my dear friend, I too have died, as it seems to me: he was not a just man but rather Justice herself.'

80 [A gift of a rooster, a hen, and their chicks to a newly wed couple]

You are a Frenchman [*Gallus*] and you have a sweetheart [*gallina*]. My gift is a good omen: a rooster [*gallus*] whose consort anxiously cares for their tender offspring.

81 [13 April 1529 / 1529]

Iam, Basilea, vale, qua non urbs altera multis
Annis exhibuit gratius hospitium.
Hinc precor omnia laeta tibi, simul illud, Erasmo
Hospes uti ne unquam tristior adveniat.

82 [July 1529 / 1529]

Obsecro, quid sibi vult, ingens quod ab aethere nymbus
Noctes atque dies sic sine fine ruit?
Terrigenae quoniam nolunt sua crimina flere,
Coelum pro nobis solvitur in lacrymas.

83 Epitaphium Corneliae Sandriae, quondam Petri Aegidii coniugis [January 1530 / 1530]

Cornelia hoc sub lapide dormio Sandria,
Olim Petro Gillo beata coniuge,
Cui parentis dulce nomen octies
Mater dedi. Domum atque dulces liberos
5 Fovere et uni casto amore et integra
Fide marito complacere in omnibus
Unica voluptas, cura mi fuit unica,
Solatium hoc, haec summa votorum fuit.
Praepropera mors, quam arctos amores, quam bene
10 Conglutinata distrahis tu pectora!
Per te mihi sextum negatum est, invida,
Peragere lustrum. Quisquis haec, hospes, legis,
I nunc et umbris fidito fugacibus.
Manet una pietas, reliqua fumus avolant.

81 [On his departure from Basel]

Now farewell, Basel. I never found more pleasant hospitality in any other city than I did for many years in you. Hence I pray that all may go well for you and I add this prayer: may no guest ever be sadder at his arrival than Erasmus was at his departure.

82 [On the rainstorms at Freiburg im Breisgau]

I ask you now, what can it mean that such a torrential downpour of rain falls from the sky night and day, with no end in sight? Since earthborn men refuse to weep for their sins, heaven is dissolved in tears on our behalf.

83 An epitaph for Cornelia Sandrien, the former wife of Pieter Gillis

I, Cornelia Sandrien, sleep under this stone. Once I had the blessing to be the wife of Pieter Gillis, on whom, as the mother of his children, I eight times bestowed the sweet name of father. To take care of our home and our sweet children, to please my husband alone in all things with chaste love and unswerving faithfulness, that was my only pleasure, my only concern, that was my consolation, that was the height of my desires. Over-hasty Death, no matter how tightly one love is bound to another, one heart fused with another, how you pull them apart! Malicious Death, you refused to let me live through my third decade. And you, stranger, who are reading this, whoever you may be, go now and place your trust in fleeting shadows. Only piety remains; the rest flies away like smoke.

84 Aliud in eandem [January 1530 / 1530]

Hac sita quae iaceo Cornelia condita petra,
Petro olim Aegidio coniuge clara fui.
Bis quater huic enixa parentis amabile nomen
Donavi toties, non fruitura diu.
5 Nam prius ac sextum licuisset claudere lustrum,
Filum aevi secuit Parca maligna mei.
Cura fuit domus et charissima pignora, fama
Integra et obsequiis demeruisse virum.
Hoc studium fuit, haec votorum summa meorum,
10 Extra haec in vita nil mihi dulce fuit.

85 Epitaphium secundae coniugis [January 1530 / 1530]

Hic ossa Mariae lapis habet Dionysiae.
Digamam digamus hanc Petrus Aegidius sibi
Ascivit, ex qua est filia auctus unica.
Interiit a partu diebus pauculis,
5 Aevo virens, nec est datum diu frui
Charo marito dulcibusque liberis.
Aeterna quaere, tenuis est vita haec vapor.

86 Epitaphium Antonii Clavae senatoris Gandavensis
[January 1530 / 1530]

Quis hic quiescis? 'Clava cognomen mihi est,
Antonius nomen.' Quid audio miser?
Itane occidisti, lux senatus Gandici
Et literarum dulce praesidium ac decus?
5 'Vixi satis, nam lustra quatuordecim

84 Another epitaph for the same lady

I, Cornelia, who lie buried beneath this stone, was once renowned as the wife of Pieter Gillis. Eight times I bestowed on him the lovely name of father by bearing him children, but I was not destined to enjoy them long. For, before I was permitted to conclude my third decade, the malign Fate cut the thread of my life. My concern was our home and our dearest children and to earn the love of my husband by keeping my reputation spotless and serving him well. This was my goal, this was the height of my desires; apart from this nothing in life was sweet to me.

85 An epitaph for his second wife

This stone holds the bones of Maria Denys. Pieter Gillis, her second husband, took her as his second wife, who blessed him with a single daughter. She died a few days after giving birth, still in the prime of life, and she had no chance to enjoy her beloved husband and sweet children very long. Seek things eternal; this life is a thin mist.

86 An epitaph for Antonius Clava, city councillor of Ghent

'Who are you who are resting here?'

'My family name is Clava. My first name is Antonius.'

'It makes me miserable to hear it. Have you set, then, O light of the city council of Ghent, the sweet patron and the glory of learning?'

'I lived long enough, for I had finished my seventh decade.'

Peregeram.' Tibi quidem satis diu,
Sed literis et patriae parum diu.
O coelites, quur talibus saltem viris
Non est perhennis addita immortalitas?
10 Quod restat unum, Clava, tristi carmine
Et lachrymis moesti parentamus tibi.

87 Per Des. Eras. Roterodamum
φιλολόγου καὶ βιβλιοπώλου διάλογος [winter 1530–1 / 1531]

Φιλ. Τί νέον κομίζεις; βίβλον;
Βιβ. Οὐδαμῶς.
Φιλ. Τί δή;
Βιβ. Χρυσοῦ ῥέεθρα.
Φιλ. Ναὶ σὺ πλουσίως λέγεις,
Ταχύτερον εἰπέ.
Βιβ. Τὸν Σταγειρίτην λέγω,
Ὃν ἔλαθεν οὐδὲν τῶν μαθημάτων μέρος.
5 Οὗτός γ' ἀνέζησ' ὡς πρὸ τοῦ πολὺ καλλίων.
Φιλ. Λέγεις ἀληθέως τ' Ἀμαλθείας κέρας.
Βιβ. Οὐ μέν γ' ὀπώρας μεστόν, ἀλλ' ἀμεινόνων.
Φιλ. Καὶ τίς τοσοῦτον πλοῦτον ἡμῖν ἐμφέρει;
Βιβ. Τοῦτόν γε παρέχει φιλόπονος Βεβέλλιος.
10 Φιλ. Χρυσέμπορος γοῦν ἐστιν, οὐ λογέμπορος.
Βιβ. Ναί, κεἴ τι χρυσοῦ καὶ λίθων προφερέστερον,
Θείας δὲ σοφίας οὐδέν ἐστ' ἀντάξιον.

'For you that is long enough indeed, but it is too short for learning and for your country. O inhabitants of heaven, to such men at least why have you not given endless immortality? All that is left for us to do, Clava, is to perform sorrowful rites in your honour with tears and a poem of mourning.'

87 A dialogue between a scholar and a bookseller, by Desiderius Erasmus of Rotterdam

Scholar What's the new thing you are carrying? A book?
Bookseller By no means.
Scholar What is it then?
Bookseller Streams of gold.
Scholar You certainly are using rich language. Do get to the point.
Bookseller I am talking about the Stagirite, who let no branch of learning elude him. He has come to life again much more attractive than before.
Scholar You are right; he is a horn of plenty.
Bookseller Not, however, filled with fruit, but with something better.
Scholar And who is gathering in all these riches for us?
Bookseller They are provided by the industrious Bebel.
Scholar A dealer in gold he is, not a dealer in words.
Bookseller Yes, and in fact, it is something far better than gold or precious stones. For nothing can match godlike wisdom.

88 Des. Erasmi Roterodami divae Genovefae praesidio a quartana febre liberati carmen votivum

[late spring 1531? / 1532]

Diva, pii vatis votivum solvere carmen
Qui cupit aspirans votis sterilem imbue venam
Mentis, et ut te digna canat, tu suggere vires,
Protectrix Genovefa tuae fidissima gentis,
5 Gallia quam late triplici discrimine secta
Porrigitur; sed praecipue tibi pars ea cordi est,
Sequana qua hospitibus factus iam animosior undis,
Matrona quas defert fluvioque admiscet amico,
Pomiferos per agros, per prata virentia perque
10 Vitiferos colles adopertaque frugibus arva
Vitreus incedit et ad amplam Parisiorum
Metropolim properans ad levam pronus adorat
Arcem, virgo, tuam, mox brachia dividit atque
Virgineae matris spatiosam amplectitur aedem,
15 Ac flexu augustam veneratus supplice divam,
In sese redit adque tui cunabula partus
Ac praedulce solum, quo sacra infantula primos
Vagitus dederas, festinat alacrior amnis.
Viculus est humilis, sed tali prole beatus.
20 Huc igitur properans, obiter vicina salutat
Phana dicata tibi, Celtarum lux Dionysi.
Hac regione diu sinuosis flexibus errans,
In se volvitur atque revolvitur, ora subinde
Ad cunas, Genovefa, tuas urbemque relictam
25 Reflectens, dicas invitum abscedere flumen.

88 A poem by Desiderius Erasmus of Rotterdam in fulfilment of a vow made to Ste Geneviève, whose protection freed him from a quartan fever

Look with favour, holy lady, on the desires of a dutiful poet who wishes to fulfil his vow by writing the promised poem; enrich his depleted poetic vein and lend him the power to praise you in a suitable poem, O Geneviève, most faithful protectress of your people, as far as France, divided into three sections, extends, but you are most concerned about that part where the Seine, growing more vigorous as he plays host to the waters which the Marne yields and mingles with his river friend, proceeds glassy-smooth through orchards, through flourishing meadows, through the vineyards on the hillsides and the fields covered with crops, and, as he hurries on to the large metropolis of Paris, he bends down in reverence to your citadel on the left hand, O virgin; then he spreads his arms and embraces the grand sanctuary of the Virgin Mother; and, bending humbly in veneration of that holy and majestic lady, the river gathers himself together again and eagerly hastens on to the cradle of your birth and the most sweet soil where you as a holy little babe gave forth your first cries. The village is a humble one, but it is blessed in having such offspring. And so, hurrying along toward that village, he salutes in passing the nearby church dedicated to you, Denis, light of the Celts. As he pursues for a long time his wandering, winding way in this region, he bends back on himself time and again, turning his head repeatedly toward your cradle, Geneviève, and the city he has left behind; you would say that the river was unwilling to depart.

Est merito cunctis venerabile Namethodorum,
Cui licet hospitibus monumenta ostendere prisca
Ortus, diva, tui fontemque liquore salubri
Undantem. At potius bis terque quaterque videtur
30 Praeside te felix populosa Lutetia, virgo,
Cuius tutelam pariter cum virgine matre
Iugibus excubiis peragis, nec enim illa gravatur
Muneris eiusdem collegam. Tu quidem in alta
Sublimis specula late circumspicis agros
35 Ac mala propulsas charis minitantia Gallis.
Illa fovet gremio miseros mediamque per urbem
Audit egenorum ploratus, hic quoque natum
Clementem mater referens, nihilo secus ac tu
Sponsa tuum, Genovefa, refers mitissima sponsum.
40 Interea paribus studiis defenditis ambae
Germanos Druidas ac maiestate senatum
Regali, sed Christophilum super omnia regem,
Illos qui populo reserent oracula mentis
Divinae, hos variis ut mixtam gentibus urbem
45 Aequo iure regant. Est vestri muneris ergo
Nulla quod hoc aevo respublica floreat usquam
Prosperius.
Sed tempus adest, ut carmine grates
Persolvam, Genovefa, tibi pro munere vitae
Ac paeana canam, multis e millibus unus
50 Quos ope praesenti servasti. Languida febris,
Triste tenaxque malum, quod quarto quoque recurrit
Usque die, miseros penitus pervaserat artus.
Consultus medicus sic consolatur, abesse
Diceret ut vitae discrimen, sed fore morbum
55 Lentum. Mox haec vox me non secus enecat ac si

Nanterre is deservedly venerated by everyone, since it can display to its visitors the ancient monuments of your birth, holy lady, and your spring, flowing with healing waters. But happy indeed, thrice happy and more, O virgin, is populous Paris, which you continuously protect and guard, together with the Virgin Mother. For she takes no umbrage at sharing her office with a colleague. You, to be sure, high in your lofty watch-tower, look around far and wide over the fields and repel any evils that threaten your dear Frenchmen; she fondles the wretched in her bosom and hears the woeful cries of the poor in the midst of the city, a mother who represents here also her merciful son, just as you, Geneviève, espoused to Christ, represent your spouse by your great kindness. At the same time you are both equally diligent in protecting the true teachers of religion and the parliament with its regal majesty, but above all the Christ-loving king: the teachers, so that they can reveal to the people the mysteries of the divine mind; the secular rulers, so that they may rule over the city with equal justice for all its mixed and diverse inhabitants. And so it is a gift from both of you that in this age there is nowhere a more prosperous and flourishing commonwealth.

But now it is time, Geneviève, that I give you thanks in poetry for the gift of my life, time that I sing a paean to celebrate your making me one of the many thousands you have saved by being at hand with your help. An enervating fever, a grievous and persistent affliction, which returned every third day, completely pervaded the limbs of my suffering body. The physician I consulted consoled me by saying that my life was not in danger but added that this was a lingering disease. Thereupon I found those words of his as

Dixisset: 'prius atque quater sol occidat, alta
In cruce pendebis.' Siquidem est renovata cicatrix,
Dum mihi post multos animus reminiscitur annos
Quod puerum toto febris me haec torserat anno.
60 Proin erat in votis mihi mors, quia tristius omni
Morte malum medicus denunciat. Hic mihi numen,
Diva, tuum venit in mentem, simul optima quaedam
Spes animum reficit, tacitoque haec pectore volvo:
'Virgo, sponsa deo gratissima, corpore terram
65 Quum premeres, semper miseris succurrere sueta,
Et nunc plura potes, postquam te regia coeli
Coepit et es Christo sponso vicinior, huc huc
Flecte oculos, Genovefa, tuos et corpore febrim
Pellito. Me studiis, sine queis nec vivere dulce est,
70 Obsecro, restituas, etenim levius puto vitam
Exhalare semel quam lento arescere morbo.
Quod tibi pollicear, nihil est, nec tu indiga nostri es.
Quod superest, grato recinam tibi carmine laudes.'
Vix ea fatus eram nullo cum murmure linguae,
75 Verum intra arcanae mecum penetralia mentis
(Prodigiosa loquar, sed compertissima), stratis
Exilio, reddor studiis, vestigia nulla
Sentio languoris nec inertis taedia febris.
Septima lux aderat, qua se quartana recurrens
80 Prodere debuerat, sed corpus alacrius omne
Quam fuit ante viget. Medicus redit atque quid actum
Miratur, vultum speculatur et ore latentem
Explorat linguam, tum quem vesica liquorem

devastating as if he had said 'before the fourth sun sets you will be hanging high on the cross.' For his words opened up an old wound, as my mind went back to what had happened many years ago when as a lad such a fever as this had tortured me for a whole year. Therefore I desired to die because the physician had pronounced for me a fate worse than any death. At that point, holy lady, your heavenly power came into my mind, which was refreshed by a vague but powerful hope, and I silently turned over in my heart such thoughts as these: 'O virgin, spouse most pleasing to God, when in your body you walked on this earth, you were always helping miserable people, and now you can do even more, now that the royal court of heaven has received you and you are closer to your spouse Christ – hither, turn your eyes hither, O Geneviève, and drive this fever out of my body. Restore me, I beg you, to my studies, without which life itself has no sweetness, for I think it would be easier to breathe out my life all at once than to shrivel away with this slow disease. What I can promise you is nothing, nor do you have need of anything from us. As for the rest, I will compose a poem of gratitude in praise of you.' I had hardly said this – with no murmuring of the tongue, but deep within the secret recesses of my mind – when (what I am going to say is miraculous but quite well established), when, I say, I sprang up from my bed, went back to my studies, felt no trace of exhaustion nor any of the deadening weariness of the fever. The seventh day dawned, when the quartan fever was supposed to return, but my body felt more active and vigorous than it had before. The physician came back and was amazed at what had happened. He looked over my face and examined my tongue in the recesses of my mouth, and then he asked for

Reddiderat poscit, quin brachia denique summis
85 Pertentat digitis. Ubi nullas comperit usquam
Morbi relliquias, 'et quis deus,' inquit, 'Erasme,
Te subito fecit alium? Quis corpore febrim
Depulit ac vatem me, quo de gaudeo, vanum
Reddidit? Is, quisquis divum fuit, arte medendi
90 Plus nostra, fateor, multo valet: haud ope post hac
Nostra opus est.' Nomen medici vis nosse? Guihelmus
Copus erat, iam tum florens iuvenilibus annis
Me quamvis aetate prior, perfectus ad unguem
Dotibus ingenii, sophiaeque mathemata callens
95 Ut si quisquam alius. Senio nunc fessus in aula
Francisci regis, procerum inter lumina, cunctis
Charus adoratur fruiturque laboribus actis.
Hic igitur mihi testis erit gravis atque locuples
Munere, diva, tuo revocatae, virgo, salutis.
100 Quanquam quicquid id est, autori gloria Christo
In solidum debetur honosque perhennis in aevum.
Muneris huius erat, quod viva deo placuisti;
Muneris eiusdem est, quod mortua pluribus aegris
Praesidio es. Sponso sic visum est omnipotenti.
105 Per te largiri gaudet sua munera, per te
Gaudet honorari, veluti lux ignea Phoebi
Per vitrum splendet iucundius, ac veluti fons
Per puras transfusus amat manare canales.
Hoc unum superest, ut te precer, optima virgo,
110 Ne mihi sit fraudi, quod tanto tempore votum
Solvere distulerim. Patere hanc accedere laudem
Tot titulis, Genovefa, tuis: ut castior usquam
Nulla fuit, toto non ulla modestior orbe,

some of the fluid produced by my bladder. Finally he even tested my arms with his fingertips. When he found no remaining traces of the disease, 'Erasmus,' he said, 'what god has so suddenly made you into another person? Who drove the fever out of your body and made me – much to my delight – a false prophet? Whichever god it was, he can do far more, I confess, than my skill in healing. After this there will be no need for my help.' Do you want to know the name of the physician? It was Guillaume Cop, at that time still young and vigorous, though somewhat older than I was, his intellectual endowments honed razor-sharp and conversant with learning and wisdom on a par with anyone. He is now old and weary, at the court of King Francis, among the luminaries of the nobility; beloved and venerated by all, he enjoys the fruits of his past labours. This man, therefore, will be my weighty and substantial witness of how you, O holy virgin, gave me the gift of recovered health.

But whatever it is, the glory of it belongs entirely to its source, Christ; to him be the honour for ever and ever. It was his gift that while you were alive you were pleasing to God. It is his gift that after your death you are the refuge of more sick people. Such was the pleasure of your almighty spouse. He rejoices in dispensing his gifts through you. He rejoices in being honoured through you, just as the burning light of Phoebus shines through glass more pleasantly, and just as a spring delights in pouring itself out through clean conduits.

All that remains, O best of virgins, is for me to beg that I suffer no harm because I put off fulfilling this vow for so long. To your many titles of praise, Geneviève, allow this one to be added: as no one in the whole world was more chaste, no one more modest than you were, so

Sic nec in aethereis clementior ulla feratur.

89 [24 September 1532 / c January 1534]

Lauta mihi, Petre, mittis edulia, sed stomachus deest.
Vis mage quod placeat mittere, mitte famem.

90 [24 September 1532 / c January 1534]

Perfacile est, fateor, proverbia scribere cuivis,
At perdifficile est scribere chiliadas.

91 [March 1533]

Perfacile est, aiunt, proverbia scribere cuivis.
Haud nego, sed durum est scribere chiliadas.
Qui mihi non credit, faciat licet ipse periclum.
Mox fuerit studiis aequior ille meis.

92 Epitaphium D. Udalrici Zasii. Per Erasmum Rot.
[early April 1536 / 1536]

Siccine, mors crudelis et invida, praeripis orbi
Ulrichum Zasium, decus admirabile iuris
Caesarei simul et sacri? Paucissima dixi:
Imo doctrinae totius et artis honestae
5 Thesaurum ac mundum locupletem, cuius ab ore
Manabat sermo vel melle suavior omni.
Quid nunc collaudem summum pietatis amorem

let no one among the saints in heaven be
considered more merciful than you.

89 [Lines to Pierre Du Chastel, who sent him some partridges]

Pierre, you send me elegant edibles, but I have
no stomach for them. If you want to send
something that would please me more, send
me an appetite.

90 [On collecting proverbs]

It is quite easy, I admit, for anyone to write
down proverbs, but it is quite difficult to write
down thousands of them.

91 [On collecting proverbs]

It is quite easy, they say, for anyone to write
down proverbs. I don't deny it, but it is hard to
write down thousands of them. If anyone
doesn't believe me, he can make the
experiment for himself. He will soon have a
fairer appreciation of my efforts.

92 An epitaph for Master Ulrich Zasius by Erasmus of Rotterdam

Cruel and envious Death, are you thus
prematurely snatching away from the world
Ulrich Zasius, the marvellous ornament of both
imperial and canon law? But this says very
little. Indeed he was a treasury and a well-
stocked world of all learning and upright skill;
from his mouth flowed speech sweeter than
any honey. Why should I add to his praises his

Et mentem coelo dignam, quo iam illa soluta
Corporis involucris fruitur sine fine beata?
10 Quod superest: te compello, studiosa iuventus,
Tandem pone modum lachrymis iustoque dolori.
Vocis adempta tibi est Zasianae copia, verum
Extant ingenii monumenta perennia. Quae si
Assidue manibusque teras oculisque frequentes,
15 Spirat in his loquiturque viri pars optima semper.

unmatched love of piety and a mind worthy of heaven, which it now enjoys, freed from the trammels of the body, in unending beatitude? As for the rest, I adjure you, young students, put an end at last to your tears and your justifiable lamentation. The full-throated voice of Zasius has been taken from you, but the perennial monuments of his intellectual genius still stand. If you constantly turn their pages with your hands and read them often with your eyes, in them the best part of the man will always breathe and speak.

POEMS PUBLISHED DURING ERASMUS' LIFETIME WITHOUT HIS CONSENT

From *Silva carminum* ed Reyner Snoy
(Gouda: Aellaerdus Gauter, 17 May 1513)

M. REYNERIUS SNOY LECTORI SALUTEM

Habes, candide lector, primam feturam Herasmi Roterodami, viri undecunque doctissimi. Quum Steynico rure canonicum regularem ageret, has ingenii sui primitias admodum adolescens (nondum annum agebat vigesimum) felicissimo auspicatu delibavit atque prelusit, eximiam animi
5 indolem, precoci suffragante ingenio, palestrae poetices desudatione et instruens et exprimens. Indidem Guielmus noster Goudanus ut alter Theseus cum Herasmo suo in Steynico rure (ubi professione canonici erant regulares) annis ferme decem convixit haud minore animorum observantia atque studiorum similitudine. Profecto felix Steynicum illud rus religione et doctrina
10 conspicuum, quod hos educavit alumnos de litteraria republica optime meritos quosque omnis est admiratura posteritas. Utroque dicendi genere (quod inventu rarum) adeo absoluta itemque elaborata suorum ingeniorum monumenta reliquerunt, ut suffragium Minervae emeritos omnibus in confesso sit. Uter palmariam operam navaverit hisce pauculis poematum eorum
15 lucubratiunculis, candide lector, (ut voles) pro arbitratu percense, nam tibi suffragium supposcens pallium trahit nemo. Sedulo si perlegeris, haud facile diiudicatu estimabis. Hoc carthaceo munere te donamus; propediem plura accepturus si hec aequi bonique consulueris. Sin minus susque deque habendo in spongiam (ut aiunt) incumbent. Vale.

POEMS PUBLISHED DURING ERASMUS' LIFETIME WITHOUT HIS CONSENT

From *A Collection of Poems* ed. Reyner Snoy (Gouda: Aellaerdus Gauter, 17 May 1513)

MASTER REYNER SNOY TO THE READER, GREETINGS

You have here, kind reader, the earliest offspring of Erasmus of Rotterdam, a man richly endowed with all kinds of learning. When he was a canon regular resident at Steyn in the countryside and while he was still a young man (for he was not yet twenty), he gathered these first-fruits of his talent and set forth this prelude, a most happy omen of things to come. Favoured by his precocious talent, he worked up a sweat in the gymnasium of poetry, both training and expressing his outstanding mental gifts. In the same place our friend Willem of Gouda lived about ten years, like another Theseus, with Erasmus in the countryside at Steyn (where they were professed canons regular), joined no less by their regard for each other than by their similar goals. Happy indeed is that country monastery of Steyn, outstanding for religion and learning, since it nurtured these foster-sons, to whom the world of learning owes such a great debt and whom all posterity will admire. In both kinds of composition – and rarely do we find this – they have left us such perfect and carefully finished monuments of their genius that it is clear to everyone that they have earned the accolade of Minerva. Which of them has succeeded in winning the prize in these little poetic products of their midnight oil, judge for yourself, kind reader, just as you please, for no one secretly asks how you voted or uncloaks the choice you made. If you read carefully, you will not find it at all easy to render a decision. We present you with this paper gift; if you look on these with satisfaction and favour, you will soon get more. If not, being considered neither here nor there, they will (as the saying goes) fall on the sponge. Farewell.

93 Apologia Herasmi et Cornelii sub dyalogo lamentabili assumpta adversus barbaros qui veterum eloquentiam contemnunt et doctam poesim derident. Tres primi versus asclepiadei sunt. Quartus est gliconius.

[late winter – May 1489 / 1513]

Herasmus

Ad te, sola michi quem dedit agnitum
Nuper fama tui splendida nominis,
Scribo, docte. Tuas me sine paululum
    Aures questibus impleam.
5 Assuetos numeris, frater, ab ordine
Scribendis calamos cunctaque carmina
Cogit livor edax ponere. Proh dolor,
    Iam pridem posui quidem.
Ex hoc sacra Iovi non tero limina,
10 Non secreta diu visa michi domus,
Doctum qua viridis laurus amat caput.
    Reieci procul omnia.
Demum nulla michi Pieridum sacros
Collustrare choros, non bifidi iuga
15 Montis cura fuit visere, denique
    Non amnes Helyconios.
Dixi, Musa, vale, non sine lachrimis,
Et tu, Phebe pater, perpetuum vale.
Olim nostra quies, noster eras amor.
20 Te nunc desero non volens.
Cogit livor edax, diva poemata
Quod norunt minime, collacerantium.
Cogit (sed pudor est) Archadiae cohors
    Iam stellis numerosior.
25 Hec, semper stimulis acta ferocibus,

93 A defence taken up by Erasmus and Cornelis in the form of a sorrowful dialogue, directed against the barbarous persons who scorn the eloquence of the ancients and deride learned poetry. The first three lines [of each strophe] are asclepiadean; the fourth is glyconic.

Erasmus

Learned sir, until recently I knew you only by the report of your illustrious reputation. I write to you now and beg your indulgence in lending your ear for a little while to my complaints.

It was once my regular practice, my brother, to exercise my pen in ordered metrical composition, but now, alas, consuming envy forces me to abandon poetry completely. Indeed, I abandoned it some time ago, alas and alack!

Since then I no longer step over the threshold sacred to Jove. For a long time I have not visited the secluded abode where the green laurel loves the learned brow. I have put all such things far behind me.

Then finally I lost all desire to observe the holy dance of the Muses, to visit the ridges of the double-peaked mountain or even the streams of Helicon.

I have bid you farewell, O Muse, not without tears. To you also, father Phoebus, farewell forever. Once you were my peace, you were my passion. I leave you now, however unwillingly.

I am forced by the consuming malice of those who in their ignorance tear divine poems to shreds. I am forced (but what a shame!) by a host of bumpkins more numerous even than the stars.

This arrogant herd, always goaded by their

Priscis chara (nephas) carmina seculis
Facundamque stilo Calliopen tumens
    Indignis pedibus terit.
Doctos illa viros invidiae nigris
30 Incandens facibus dente venefico
Nunquam (crede michi) rodere desinit,
    Nunquam carpere desinit.

Cornelius

Hec mecum tacitus sepe revolveram,
Communi cupiens mesticia virum,
35 Divae qui cytharae carperet invidos.
    Te letor comitem michi.
Obstringit (fateor) me vehemens dolor.
Plenos barbariae et pectinis emulos
Mecum, queso, Iovis plangite filiae,
40 Nam fletum locus exigit.
Sacris turba modis inscia detrahit,
Contemnens placidos Castalidum sonos.
O sensu vacuum vel cerebro caput,
    Musa, dum reprobas, eges.
45 En confert furiis, mitigat asperam
Cordis seviciam, demona comprimit.
Tu qum sis similis carmina dilige,
    Placantem repetens lyram.
Sed iam tanta tui pectoris abdita
50 Invasit rabies omne premens iecur,
Ut nec Peonia disperiat manu,
    Nec speranda tibi salus.
Eheu quam miser es! Qui tibi congrua
Contemnens reducis dona malagmatis
55 Corrodis medicum, num medicabere?
    Non vivus capies necem.
Cur torquere (cedo) dum canimus, miser?

fierce passions, tramples under their worthless feet (Oh what a crime!) poems dear to bygone ages; they spurn Calliope, the mistress of eloquent speech.

Burning with the dusky torches of envy, never (believe me) do they cease to bite learned men with their poisonous fangs, never do they cease to snap.

Cornelis

I had often silently reflected on these things, longing for a man to share my grief, someone who would snap back at those who vent their spite at the divine lyre. I rejoice that I have found in you a fellow spirit.

I am afflicted, I confess, by intense grief. O daughters of Jove, join me, I beg you, in bewailing those who are brimming with barbarism and spiteful envy of the poetic plectrum. For the topic is one that calls for tears.

The ignorant mob disparages the holy measures of poetry, scorning the peaceful notes of the Castalian sisters. O brainless blockhead, you have need of the very Muse you reject.

See how she confronts madness, soothes cruel-hearted savagery, subdues the demon. Since all these apply to you, hold poetry dear; take up once more the soothing lyre.

But rage has already pierced so deep into your heart and so totally suppressed your understanding that the malady will not yield to the healing Paeonian hand, nor can you hope for health.

Alas, how miserable you are! You scorn the appropriate gift of a restorative plaster, you find fault with the physician – are you likely to be cured? Lifeless even now, you will utterly destroy yourself.

Come now, why are you in such miserable

En scribens Galatis Paulus apostolus
Infert Meonii diva poemata,
60 Fedantem reprobans gulam.
Quin et moricanis sepius in libris
Aptant laurigeros ecclesiae modos
Doctores nitidi scematibus stili
Lucas, Iheronimus, Leo.

Herasmus

65 Et quid? nonne tibi iusta videbitur
Urgens causa stilum? Nonne per omnia
Dixi vera, comes? Vera per omnia
Dixi, te quoque iudice.
Nusquam grandisonam Virgilii tubam,
70 Nusquam blandisonam Meonii lyram,
Nusquam (crede michi) compta Papinii
Audis carmina concini.
Docto Flaccus ubi, queso, poemate?
Seu Lucanus ubi qui generi necem
75 Scribens Pindarico concrepat organo?
Sordent heu sine nomine.
Phebeae regio lucis in ambitu
Olim non viguit, nec fuit insula
Per quas non ierat conscia carminum
80 Pulchro Calliope pede.
Indus labra tumens et cute decolor,
Qui Phebum liquidis aurea fluctibus
Primus progreditur cornua cernere
Tollentem, coluit modos.
85 Novit Thespiadum carmina Gadium
Tellus, occiduis proxima solibus
Et postrema suos tergere pulveres
Spectans oceano diem.

torment while we are singing? See how the apostle Paul, writing to the Galatians, introduces the divine poems of Homer when he castigates the filthy vice of gluttony.

Indeed, the teachers of the church, such as Luke, Jerome, and Leo, in books that descant on moral matters, very often fit poetic rhythms into the rhetorical patterns of their elegant styles.

Erasmus

What then? Don't you think that the case which impels me to take up my pen is sound? Don't you think, partner of mine, that I have spoken the truth in all respects? I have spoken the truth in all respects, as even you yourself admit.

Nowhere do you hear the lofty sound of Virgil's trumpet, nowhere do you hear the charming tones of Homer's lyre, nowhere (believe me) do your hear anyone chant the elegant verses of Statius.

Where, I ask you, is Horace with his learned poetry? Or where is Lucan, whose verse takes on Pindaric majesty when he writes of the death of the son-in-law? Alas, they are forgotten and despised.

Once there was no flourishing realm under the shining round of Phoebus' course, there was no island, through which Calliope, her mind full of poetry, did not make her way on her lovely feet.

The fat-lipped, dark-skinned Indian, who is the first to go out and see Phoebus lift his golden horns from the flowing waves, cultivated poetry.

The songs of the Muses were known in the land of Gades, nearest to the setting sun, the last place to see the day-star washing off his dust in the ocean.

Et quid plura feram? Novit et ultima
90 Thyle, nec vacua sub Styge pallidi
Manes despiciunt carmina; testis est
    En vates Rhodopeius.
Is raptam numeris Euridicen querens
Mulcebat placidis infera cantibus.
95 Commovisse ferunt Tartareum caput
    Plutonem cytharae modis.

Cornelius

Plus dicam. Rapidis Strymona fluctibus
Spumantem numeris flexit Eagrides.
Auditus superis, manibus insuper,
100 Sedem commeruit poli.
Vates Bistonius nuper Apolline
Compertam genito dante sibi lyram
Traxit percutiens pectine barbiton
    Silvas et nemorum deas.
105 Advenere ferae cantibus excitae
Contractisque iubis colla ferocia
Summittunt manibus dum canit Orpheus
    Mansuescuntque viri iugo.
Pastus immemorem tardat et alitem,
110 Escas dum soboli querit amabili
Suspensisque volis captat in ethere
    Argutos cytharae modos.
Auget dicta stupor: velivolam ratem
Immotam validis tractibus omnium
115 Plectris elicitum solvit a littore
    Ad puppim veniens mare.
Plus dicam: superos regnaque pallida
Idem blandisono gutture carmina
Placavit recinens et Sisiphi grave
120 Fixit concrepitans onus.

Why should I add any more? Their songs are known to outermost Thule, nor are they despised by the pale shades beyond the insubstantial Styx; to that, lo, the Rhodopeian poet can testify.

Lamenting in song for the kidnapped Eurydice, he softened the underworld with his soothing songs. They say that by the music of his lyre he shook the heart of Pluto, lord of Tartarus.

Cornelis

I will add to that: with his verses the son of Oeagrus turned back the foaming rapids of the river Strymon. Heard by the gods on high as well as by the deities of the underworld, he earned a place in the firmament.

The Thracian bard, when Apollo gave the recently discovered lyre to his son, drew to himself the trees and the goddesses of the groves by plucking the lyre with his plectrum.

Stirred by his singing, the beasts came to him. While Orpheus sings, they smooth down their manes, subject their wild necks to his hands, and grow tame to the yoke of the man.

He slows down the bird and makes it forget its feeding, even while it is seeking food for its beloved offspring. Stopping its wings, it catches in the air the melodious music of the lyre.

Amazement leads me to say more: when everyone was strongly tugging to launch an unmoving sail-winged ship, the sea, drawn by the plectrum, came up to the ship and floated it away from the shore.

I will add to that: the same bard, re-echoing his sweet-throated songs, won over the gods above and the kingdom of the pale shades; with his loud music he stopped in its place the heavy burden of Sisyphus.

Ad sacros venio commemorans libros.
Victor fit Gedeon dum resonat tuba,
Et David Saulem carmine mitigat
    Et flammas posuit rogus.
125 Hec, ut rite probem cantibus omnia
Placari, recito. Proh genio fruens
Tantum desipuit, pergat ut inclita
    Demens spernere carmina.

Herasmus

Quid ni? Vera refers, proh dolor et pudor!
130 Ipsis constat homo crudior inferis;
Flecti dulcisono carmine non valet,
    Sed dulces refugit modos.
Nunquam quinetiam desinit insequi
Torva bile, lupis peior edacibus
135 Et quae plumifera pascitur undique
    Preda sevior alite.
Conculcata iacent docta poemata.
Lumen Pegasei Calliope chori
Iam neglecta locis exulat omnibus,
140 Rupes incolit invias.
Regnat barbaries horrida, regio
Sublimis solio ridet Apollinis
Artem laurigeram. Carmina rusticus
    Docto barbarus imperat.
145 Et quid cuncta meis crimina persequar
Stultorum numeris? Ante diem, puto,
Ornans syderium luminibus polum
    Vesper subripiet michi.
Nec si quot placidis ignea noctibus
150 Scintillant tacito sydera culmine,
Nec si quot tepidum flante Favonio
    Ver suffundit humo rosas,
Tot sint ora michi, tot moveam sonos,

To come now to events recalled from the Holy Bible: Gideon was victorious when the trumpet blew; through song David soothed Saul and the funeral pyre put down its flames.

These things I recount to demonstrate fitly that all things are appeased by songs. Alas that a man of talent should be so insane as to go on spurning the glories of poetry!

Erasmus

Why not? You are telling the truth, alas, to our shame and grief! Mankind persists in having less feeling even than the inhabitants of the underworld. Men are incapable of being moved by the sweet sounds of poetry. Instead they flee from such sweet music.

Even more, they never cease to attack with bitter anger. They are worse than voracious wolves, more savage than a bird of prey that feeds indiscriminately on its feathered victims.

Learned poems lie trampled underfoot. Calliope, the shining light of the Pegasean choir, is everywhere scorned and banished. She lives among inaccessible crags.

Bristling barbarism holds sway, mocking from its lofty regal throne the skill of Apollo's laurel. The ignorant barbarian orders poems from the learned bard.

And why should I list in my verses all the offences of fools? Before I could do so, I think that the evening, adorning the heavens with the light of the stars, would deprive me of daylight.

Now even if I had as many mouths or could speak with as many voices as there are burning stars sparkling in the silent firmament on calm nights, or as many as there are roses overspreading the ground when the west wind blows in the warm springtime,

Nunquam (crede) tamen sufficiam queri,
155 Quantis pressa diu sacra poemata
    Hoc seclo iaceant malis.
Hinc venere michi tedia carminum,
Vates, pars animae non tenuis meae,
Hinc, inquam, studium destitui meum,
160   Musarum tepuit calor.

Cornelius

Quod nunc Aonidum negligitur chorus,
Hoc vesana facit mens sine litteris.
Insanire putat, carmina qui canunt,
    Ridens ac digito notans.
165 En rara invidiam provocat ars sibi,
Sed vincet superans. Cedite, pallida
Confecti macie, ponito turgidum
    Fastu, livor edax, caput.
Dic quaecunque voles: dummodo carmina
170 Oblectare suo nos properent sono,
Tu ride, nichil est; pluris habebimur,
    Et frons excipiet decus.
Buccis parce tuis! Hactenus, invide,
Nil sacris dedimus carminis edibus,
175 Sed iam sceptra michi Davidis in vicem
    Melchom de spoliis feram.
Gomer Debelaym coniugio fruar,
De scorto generans Israhel inclitum,
Quo semen domini pulchrius emicet
180   Dulci Lybetridum sinu.
In nos ore fero, livide, garrias,
Consumens proprios invidia sinus.
En summos sequimur per studium viros,

still I would not measure up (believe me) to the task of lamenting the indignities that have long been heaped on venerable poems in this age of ours.

This is the reason I have grown weary of writing poems, O my poetic friend, you who are no small part of my soul; this is the reason, I say, that I have given up my poetic pursuits, that the fire of the Muses has died down.

Cornelis

The neglect of the Aonian choir springs from an insane and illiterate mentality. Such a person thinks anyone who writes poetry is mad; he points his finger at him and laughs him to scorn.

Know that a skill which is rare draws malice upon itself, but it will overcome and conquer. Depart, you wretches, pale and emaciated. O consuming Envy, hang down your head, swollen with pride.

Say whatever you like. As long as poetry is ready to delight us with its sounds, go ahead and laugh. It makes no difference to us. We will gain more recognition and our brows will be crowned with honour.

Stop your angry sputterings. Up to this point, you malicious wretch, we have offered no song to the sacred temple. But now, like David, I will bear a sceptre taken from the spoils of Melchom.

I will enjoy in marriage Gomer, the daughter of Debelaim. On a whore I will beget a glorious Israel, so that the seed of the Lord may shine forth more beautifully from the sweet bosom of the Muses.

With your beastly mouth, you spiteful wretch, you may babble away against us, eating your own heart out with envy. But see how we, through our pursuits, are following in

Nec sentit pulices equus.
185 Nostro sub studio plus cruciabere,
Vel nunc destituas carmina persequi,
Ne cantatus eas carmine pessimo,
Confusas referens genas.
Quod si perstiteris nostra ciconia,
190 Tantum feda potes rostra reducere.
Serpentes comedas per nemus aspidum,
Nec sacras aquilas vora.

Herasmus

Nunc olim calamos ut Rhodopeios
Musam non aliter (crede michi) meam,
195 Tu Tyrinthius hic alter in omine
Torpentes animos moves.
Sacrarum rediit Meonidum calor,
Et quam sepe dolens mestaque reppulit,
Nunc (quamquam tenuis) Musa tamen mea
200 Exultans repetit lyram.
Et quis, rere, fuit leticiae modus,
Qum post dicta deae grandia denique
Versus dulcisonos lumine candido,
Vates, aspicerem tuos?
205 Ingens fama quidem, sed meritis minor,
Ingens fama quidem, iudice me tamen
Vincunt et, fateor, carmina gloriam
Et docti numeri tuam.
Reddis Virgilium versibus alterum,
210 Seu prosam libuit texere liberam,
Iam prosa (fateor) Tullius alter es:
Tantum scripta placent tua.
Ceptos ergo, precor, pergito tramites,
Nostri non tenuis gloria seculi
215 Et spes una mei flammaque pectoris,
Vatum reliquiae prium.

the footsteps of the greatest men. A horse pays no attention to fleas.

By our endeavours you will feel even more tormented. Stop attacking poetry immediately lest you have lampoons sung about you and go away covered with blushes of shame.

But if you persist in stabbing away at us like a stork, you will only succeed in drawing back a battered beak. Go eat snakes in the wild woods. Do not feed on sacred eagles.

Erasmus

Now, as Hercules once enlivened the Rhodopeian pipes, just so here, like a second Hercules of good omen, you arouse my muse, believe me, you arouse my sluggish spirits.

The heat of the sacred Muses returns, and now my muse, however slight, joyfully takes up again the lyre that she often rejected in her sorrow and grief.

And what bounds do you think there were to my joy when finally, after the lofty pronouncements of the goddess, I could clearly see with my own eyes, O poet, those sweet-sounding verses of yours?

Indeed your fame is immense, but it is less than you deserve. Indeed your fame is immense, but if I am any judge, even your glory is surpassed, I confess, by the learned verse of your poems.

In poetry you are a second Virgil, or if you choose the unfettered language of prose, you are in prose (I acknowledge it) a second Cicero – so great is the pleasure given by your writings.

Therefore I implore you, the glory – and no minor one – of our age, the only hope and shining light of my heart, the remaining heir of the ancient poets, go forward on the course you have begun.

Aspirent studiis Pierides tuis,
Te nobisque diu fata superstitem
Servent, et spacii stamina plurimi
220 Producat Lachesis tibi.
Et cum lethificus te tulerit dies,
Nobis perpetuum tu nichilominus
Preclari titulis ora per omnium
Vives ingenii. Vale.

May the Muses inspire your endeavors, and may the Fates long keep you alive for us, and may Lachesis draw out a long thread for you.

And when the fatal day takes you from us, you will still be forever alive for us, you will live on the tongues of all men by virtue of your illustrious genius. Farewell.

Herasmi·
·Roterodami·

Silua carminū antehac nūq̄ impressorū.

Satyre tres.

¶Satyra prima in errores hoīm degenerātiū
et p sūmo celestiq; bono varias falsorū bonorū species
amplectētiū.

¶Satyra secūda In iuuenē luxuria defluentē
atq; mortis admonitio.

¶Satyra tercia in diuitē auarū.

Metrū phalenticū de Nūmo.

Apologia Herasmi sub dyalogo lamētabili as-
sūpta aduersus barbaros q̄ veterū eloquentiā cōtem-
nūt et doctā Poesim derident.

Guielmi Goudani.
Prosopopeia Hollandie. bello penuria morbo factioib9 iamdiu vexate de suorū calamitate lamē-
tantis.

Erasmus *Silva carminum* ed R. Snoy, title-page
Gouda: A. Gauter 1513
Gemeentebibliotheek, Rotterdam

PROGYMNAS
MATA QVAEDAM PRI-
mæ adolescentiæ Erasmi.

Louanii apud Theodoricum Martinũ
Alostensem, Anno. M. D. XXI.

Erasmus *Progymnasmata quaedam primae adolescentiae*, title-page
Louvain: Dirk Martens 1521
Gemeentebibliotheek, Rotterdam

From *Progymnasmata quaedam*
primae adolescentiae Erasmi
(Louvain: Dirk Martens 1521)

ERASMUS ROTERODAMUS STUDIOSAE IUVENTUTI S.D.

Impudenter faciunt, qui mea me vivo publicant formulis typographorum, sed multo impudentius, qui pueriles etiam naenias meas evulgant. Omnium autem impudentissime, qui nugis alienis meum praefigunt nomen, id quod nuper fecit nescio quis, qui libellum emisit de ratione conscribendi epistolas,
5 in quo praeter pauculas voces furtivas nihil est meum. Nec unquam mihi quisquam notus fuit, cui nomen esset Petro Paludano. Olim puer quia minus valebam carmine elegiaco, caeperam excercere me ceu declamatiunculis aliquot in eo genere, et has semel atque iterum evulgatas video. In quibus non intelligo quid sit quod mereatur publicum, nisi forte ut exemplo pueri pu-
10 erorum ingenia provocentur, ut malint excercere stilum in argumentis huiusmodi quam, quod quidam eruditi pulchrum ducunt, in decantandis amoribus suis. Sed tamen hoc, quicquid est nugamenti, recognovimus ac rursus excudi sumus passi. Quid enim aliud possum? Bene vale, lector, et si quid me audis, melioribus incumbe.

Elegiae protrepticae, detestantes errores mortalium,
et adhortantes ad veram pietatem,
Erasmi Roterodami

94 Elegia prima, in errores hominum degenerantium et pro summo caelestique bono varias falsorum bonorum species amplectentium, incipit. [winter 1490–1 / 1513]

Heu quantum caecae mortalia pectora noctis,
  Heu quam terrigenas noxius error habet!
Vera quibus cum sint et coelica danda, perhenni
  Invigilant vacuis anxietate bonis,
5 Nec summum novere bonum quo fluxit ab uno

From *Some Poetic Exercises*
Written by Erasmus in His Early Youth
(Louvain: Dirk Martens 1521)

ERASMUS OF ROTTERDAM TO YOUNG STUDENTS, GREETINGS

It is shameful for anyone to issue my writings in print while I am still alive, but it is much more shameful to publish my youthful ditties. It is most shameful of all, however, to put out someone else's trifles under my name, as somebody or other recently did when he issued a little book on the method of writing letters, in which nothing was by me except a few plagiarized words. Nor have I ever known anyone by the name of Petrus Paludanus. Long ago, when I was a youth, I was not very good at writing elegiac distichs, and so I began to practise that verse form in some little declamations (as it were), and these, I see, have been published once or twice. I do not understand what merit they can have in the eyes of the public, except that perhaps as a youthful precedent they might stimulate talented youths to employ their pens on subjects of this sort instead of composing sing-song love poems (which some learned men think to be such a fine thing to do). But I have revised this material, however trifling, and have permitted it to be republished. For what else could I do? Farewell, reader, and if you value my opinion at all, devote your energies to something more worthwhile.

Hortatory elegies, denouncing the delusion of mortals
and urging them to pursue true piety,
by Erasmus of Rotterdam

94 The first elegy, against the delusions of degenerate men, who embrace various appearances of false goods instead of the highest good in heaven, begins as follows.

Alas, what a blinding darkness possesses the hearts of mortals! Alas, what a destructive delusion holds earthborn men in thrall! Though true and heavenly goods are there to be given to them, they are constantly and anxiously on the lookout for empty goods, and they know nothing of the highest good from which alone

Quicquid inest pulchri, quicquid in orbe boni.
Ecce sed hic Stygiis admotas effodit umbris
Condit et effossas insatiatus opes.
Mollibus hic studet illecebris, indulget amori
10 Blandaque mortiferae gaudia carnis amat.
Ambitione tumens fasces petit ille superbos
Et quaerit summum summus habere gradum.
Est quem sydereos iuvet apprendisse meatus
Et rerum causas edidicisse novas.
15 Hic petit hoc, ille illud; agit sua quenque libido,
Navigat et ventis in freta quisque suis.
Quo raperis, mortale genus, vacuoque labore
Dona quibus pereas quid peritura legis?
Quae (cedo) cum stolidis tibi sunt commercia terris,
20 Cui coelum patria est, cui pater ipse deus?
Quaeris in exilio patrio tibi condita coelo:
Non hic quas sequeris inveniuntur opes.
Quid per squamigeros saxosa cacumina pisces
Sectare et leporem per freta vasta vagum,
25 Quaeris et in sterili flaventia mala salicto,
Quaeritur incultis fertilis uva rubis?
Gaudia nequicquam reperire quid angeris illic,
Nil nisi moeror ubi est, nil nisi planctus ubi est?
Et quid amas molles luctus in carcere luxus?
30 Nil nisi (crede mihi) flebile mundus habet.
Ast bona, te quorum vexat male sana cupido,
Ah tibi (si credes) nil bonitatis habent.
Sed quae te totum tegit ignorantia veri,
Haec bona cum non sint, ut videantur agit.

sprung all that is beautiful, all that is good in the universe. But look, one man digs up riches buried in Stygian darkness and once they are dug up he hides them away, never satisfied. Another man pursues voluptuous pleasures, gives himself up to love, and loves the alluring joys of the death-dealing flesh. Another man, swelling with ambition, seeks the proud appurtenances of high office, and even at the top he still seeks the top level. Some find pleasure in comprehending the courses of the stars and learning new causes for natural phenomena. One man seeks this, another that; each is driven by his own passion, each steers toward the straits, driven by his own winds.

O mortal mankind, where are you rushing to? And why do you lose all your labours by choosing gifts that will perish, in the pursuit of which you yourselves perish? Tell me now, what business do you have with the stolid earth, since heaven is your fatherland and God himself your father? In exile you seek what is stored up for you in your native country, heaven. The wealth you pursue is not to be found here. Why do you chase scale-coated fish on the rocky peaks or the backtracking hare on the vast seas, and why do you seek the yellowing fruit on sterile thickets of willow, why look for fruitful grapevines among wild brambles? Why do you vainly torment yourself to find joys in a place where there is nothing but grief, nothing but lamentation? Why do you love soft luxury in a prison full of sorrow? The world, believe me, has nothing that does not deserve our tears. But those goods about which you plague yourself because of your unwholesome craving, ah, they bring you (if you will take my word for it) no good at all. But you are so totally enveloped in ignorance of the truth that these things, which are not good, seem so to you. Far from it, indeed; they

35 Quin mage verorum sunt haec simulachra bonorum,
Et fallax oculos fascinat umbra tuos.
Gaudia (nonne vides?) stimulis viciantur amaris,
Vertitur in lachrymas risus et iste graves.
Mixta labore quies, nulla est syncera voluptas
40 Nec diuturna nihilve anxietatis habens.
Et quid opes, quid honor, quid purpura, quid diadema?
Quid nisi sunt animi pondera pulchra tui?
Adde quod ista levi fortunae agitata tumultu
Fallant et dominis sint male fida suis.
45 Haec bona carpis, homo, multo nocitura periclo,
Nulla sed est summi sollicitudo boni,
Nulla dei, sed cuique deus sua dira cupido,
In mala quisque, suus quo trahit error, abit.
Iam tandem resipisce, precor, radiisque receptis
50 Hanc noctem ex oculis discute, quaeso, tuis.
Sursum duc oculos: illic patriamque patremque
Suspice quo mentem, quo tua vota feras.
Illic cerne tui generosos sanguinis ortus,
Illic cerne animi semina prima tui.
55 Non es enim indigena stolidae licet incola terrae,
Coelica progenies aethereumque genus.
Conditor, ignifluo cuius procedis ab ore,
(Quid maius?) statuam te vocat ipse suam.
Ergo, homo, terrenis quid inhaeres degener istis
60 Oblitusque dei nec memor ipse tui?
Terrea terrigenis age linque caduca caducis,
Tu pete perpetuas non moriturus opes.
Sydera scande levis et inertes despice sedes,
Iam pudeat collo sustinuisse iugum.
65 Est illic quod ames, est illic rite quod optes,

are false images of what is truly good and they bewitch your vision with their deceptive appearances. Joys – don't you see it? – are spoiled by bitter goadings, and this laughter of yours turns to tears of sorrow. Repose is mingled with labour; no pleasure is unalloyed, or lasting, or unmixed with anxiety. And what is wealth, what is honour, or royal purple, or a crown? What are they but beautiful clogs weighing down your mind? Moreover, these things, stirred up by the unstable agitation of Fortune, are deceptive and prove treacherous to their masters. These goods that you grasp for, O man, are very dangerous and harmful, but you have no concern for the highest good, none for God. Rather, everyone makes a god of his own fierce desire; everyone ends in the disaster to which his own delusion carries him.

Now at last come to your senses, I beg you, dispel this darkness from your eyes, I pray you, and take in the rays of light. Cast your eyes upward; look up there to your fatherland and your Father, where you should focus your attention and your desires. See there the noble source of your lineage. See there the first seeds of your mind. For you are not a native, though you are an inhabitant, of the stolid earth; your race springs from the skies, your ancestry is from heaven. Your creator himself, from whose fiery breath you proceed, calls you – what could be greater? – an image of himself. Therefore, O man, why have you degenerated from your origin, bogged down in earthly matters, not mindful of God and forgetting even yourself? Come, leave the fleeting things of earth to the fleeting creatures of earth. You who will never die, seek lasting treasure. Climb up unburdened to the stars and look down on the inert regions below; now be ashamed that you bore the yoke on your neck. What you love is there. What you rightly hope for is

Illic sunt votis omnia plena tuis.
Gaudia vera illic et amari nescia luctus,
Et placida est nullo mixta labore quies,
Pax secura, procul strepitus bellique tumultus.
70 Exundant quae non attenuentur opes,
Invidiae securus honor, diademata, sceptra
Ignibus astrigeri splendidiora poli.
Denique cunctorum finisque et origo bonorum,
Ut videas, aderit, ut potiare, deus.
75 Quod si nulla movet tantarum gloria rerum,
Nec capiunt animum praemia tanta tuum,
Vindicis extimulent saltem tormenta gehennae:
Quem non ducit amor vel trahat ipse timor.
Suspicere aethereum si mole vetaris Olympum,
80 Saltem Tartareae despice regna Stygis.
Aspice quam maneant sceleratos horrida manes
Supplicia, aeternus quos Herebi ignis edit.
Quos pendant brevibus pro luxibus aspice luctus,
Quorum hic in vitiis mortua vita fuit.
85 Vita manet, fugiat ne sensus et ipse malorum,
Sed mors morte carens tempus in omne premat.
Aspice quam rapido volvantur tempora lapsu,
Quam veniat celeri mors inopina pede.
Dura heus conditio nimium miserandaque, pandat
90 Altera ut alterius mors tibi mortis iter.
Nostra sed, ut video, surdis canit auribus ista
Musa, levis monitus dissipat aura meos.
Quid causae stolidis mortalibus obstruit aures?
Colligo, luminibus iam liquet illa meis.
95 Quippe sibi duram promittunt fallere mortem,

there. There all your desires will be fulfilled. True joys are there, with no trace of bitter grief; calm repose is there, with no admixture of hardship. Secure peace is there, far from the noise and the uproar of war. Inexhaustible wealth abounds there, honour safe from envy, crowns, sceptres brighter than the stars emblazoned on the firmament. And finally God, the goal and the source of all good things, will be there for you to see and to possess.

But if you are unmoved by such great glories, if your mind is not taken with such great rewards, at least be goaded by the avenging torments of hell: whoever is not led on by love, let him be drawn on by fear itself. If you are hindered by your heavy grossness from looking up to the high reaches of heaven, at least look down at the Stygian realms of the underworld. Look at the horrible punishments that are in store for the wicked souls who are eaten up by the everlasting fire of hell. Look at the grief for their brief pleasures, to be suffered by those whose lives here were dead because of their vices. Life remains, so that the very awareness of their afflictions should not disappear but rather that the death which never dies should weigh upon their minds for all time. See how quickly time rolls on and slips away from us, how swiftly and unexpectedly death creeps up on us. Mark this: it is a cruel and all too miserable state of affairs, that one death should open up for you the road to another death.

But I see that my muse is preaching these things to deaf ears; the lightest breeze disperses my warnings. What is the reason that the ears of stupid mortals are blocked? I have puzzled it out; now my eyes see it clearly. It is this: they hold out for themselves the idea that they can deceive cruel death; they hope that

Sperant perpetuos vivere posse dies.
Hic iuvenis valido fidit temerarius aevo,
Divitiis locuples nititur ille suis,
Fallit purpureos invicta potentia reges.
100 Acrius ergo mihi quisque monendus erit.

95 Elegia secunda, in iuvenem luxuria defluentem atque mortis admonitio [winter 1490–1 / 1513]

Stulte, quid imberbi spem tu tibi fingis ab aevo
Et gaudes tremulos iam procul esse dies,
Longevae numerans restantia tempora vitae,
Et spondes capiti tempora cana tuo,
5 Luxibus interea iuvat indulgere cupitis,
Gaudia lascivae carnis amica sequi?
'Dextra,' inquis, 'dum fata sinant, dum floreat aetas,
Pascamus placidis mollia vota modis.
Adsint laetitiae, choreae, convivia, lusus,
10 Plausus, complexus, basia grata, Venus
Gaudiaque et Veneris tenerique Cupidinis ignes,
Adsint innumeris ludicra mixta iocis.
Tibia nec desit, adsint citharaeque lyraeque;
Cura dolorque procul, tristia cuncta procul.
15 Ut curent superis permittite caetera divis,
Et stimulet vacuos sollicitudo deos.
Ocia nos tenerae peragamus blanda iuventae,
Tradatur tumidis noxia cura fretis.
Utamur, ne frustra abeat torpentibus, aevo,
20 Dum vernat teneris laeta iuventa genis.'

the days of their lives can go on forever. This rash young man has confidence in the strength of his youth; that rich man relies on his own wealth. Invincible power deceives kings in their royal purple. Therefore, I must admonish each of them all the more sharply.

95 The second elegy, against a young man dissipating himself in lust, and a warning about death

Fool, why do you imagine you can base your hope on your beardless youth, and why do you rejoice in the notion that the days of trembling old age are far away, counting up the remaining years of a long lifetime, and why do you assure yourself that the hair of your temples will grow white, pleasing yourself in the meantime by indulging in the sensual excesses your heart desires and pursuing the pleasing joys of the wanton flesh?

'While the propitious fates allow it,' you say, 'while we are in the bloom of youth, let us gratify our voluptuous desires in agreeable ways. Let there be delights, dances, banquets, games, applause, embraces, charming kisses, lovemaking, both the joys of Venus and the fires of young Cupid, let there be dalliance intermingled with countless jests. Let flutes not be lacking. Let there be guitars and harps. Away with care and sorrow, away with everything gloomy! Let the gods above take care of everything else and let the gods, who have time for it, be driven by responsibility. Let us get on with the blandishing leisure of tender youth. Let destructive cares be consigned to the swelling seas. Let us make use of this time in our lives, while joyful youth still blooms on our tender cheeks, lest we lose it in vain through our own lethargy.'

Dic quid arundineae, infelix, innitere cannae,
  Qua scissa pereas, qua recidente cadas?
Tune iuventuti fidis, male sane, fugaci,
  Qua nil mobilius maximus orbis habet?
25 Illa Noto levior celerique volucrior Euro,
  Labilior liquidis quas habet Hebrus aquis,
Ocyor emissa nervo crepitante sagitta,
  Illa magis veris flore caduca novi,
Vanior et nebula et tenui fallacior umbra
30 Et nive quae in liquidas sole tepescit aquas
Quaeque secat medium pernicior alite coelum.
  Flos velut illa viret, ut levis aura perit.
Illa perit, tenueis rapitur ceu fumus in auras
  Et standi nullam servat amata fidem.
35 Si levis autor ego, natura disce magistra.
  En docet illa breves temporis esse vices.
Aspice purpureis ut humus lasciviat omnis
  Floribus, in campos ver ubi molle venit.
Luxuriat vestita suis tum frondibus arbor,
40 Et rediviva novis cingitur herba comis,
Mollia sanguinei pingunt violaria partus,
  Induitur placidis aspera spina rosis,
Multicolore nitent densissima gramina flore,
  Denique resplendent cuncta decore novo.
45 At mora parva, cadunt redolentia tempora veris,
  Et properat nymbis horrida bruma suis.
Iam neque prata virent, moeret sine frondibus arbos,
  Et ponit virides languida sylva comas.
Iam non purpurei pingunt violaria flores,
50 Iam riget elapsis aspera spina rosis.

Tell me, unhappy fellow, why do you lean on a reed cane, which, when it breaks, will destroy you – when it falls, will let you fall? Madman, do you rely on fleeting youth, than which nothing in the whole wide world is more volatile? It is more light-footed than the south wind, more fleet-winged than the swift east wind, more rapid than the flowing waters of the Hebrus, faster than an arrow shot from a twanging bowstring. It is more perishable than the flowers of early spring, more insubstantial than mist, more illusory than an empty shadow or the snow that melts into flowing water in the warmth of the sun, more quick than a bird cutting through the air up in the sky. Youth flourishes like a flower, perishes like a mere breath of air. It perishes like smoke, vanishing into thin air, and however much it is loved, it never keeps its promise to stay.

If you think I am a lightweight authority, let Nature be your teacher and learn from her. Lo, she teaches that the vicissitudes of time are rapid. See how the ground wantons everywhere with its crimson flowers when the gentle spring comes to the fields. Then the luxuriant trees are clad in their own foliage, and the reviving vegetation is wreathed in fresh tresses. The soft violet-beds are coloured with blood-red offspring. The harsh thorns are clothed with gentle roses. The grass at its full thickness is bright with many-colored flowers. In short, everything is resplendent with new beauty. But after only a short pause, the fragrant season of spring falls away, and winter, bristling with his rainstorms, hastens onward. Now the meadows are no longer green. The trees, bereft of their foliage, are in mourning, and the languishing forest puts off its green tresses. Now the crimson flowers do not colour the violet-beds, and the harsh thorn stands stiff, now that the roses have fallen

Turpes dissimilesque sui sine gramine campi,
  Atque omnis subito flosque venusque cadit.
Sic sic flos aevi, sic sic male blanda iuventa
  Labitur, heu celeri non reditura pede.
55 Tristior inde ruit ac plena doloribus aetas,
  Inde subit tremulo curva senecta gradu,
Et gravibus curis et tristibus aspera morbis,
  Luctibus et centum conglomerata malis.
Haec tibi temporibus canos sparsura capillos,
60 Haec tibi pendentem contrahet hirta cutem.
Corpora tum subito linquit moribunda voluptas,
  Omnis et ingenii visque calorque cadit.
Forma perit, pereunt agiles in corpore vires,
  Et rosa purpureis excidit ista genis.
65 Finditur annosis subito frons aspera rugis,
  Decrescunt oculis lumina fusca cavis.
Pro mento fit leve caput, fis simia tandem,
  Ignotusque tibi dissimilisque tui.
I modo, confide, infelix, iuvenilibus annis
70 Et sponde votis gaudia longa tuis,
Si tamen et salvam tribuent egisse iuventam
  Maturosque sinent fata videre dies.
Sed gaudet tenerae fera mors primordia vitae
  Saepius atque ortus praesecuisse rudes.
75 Lurida Tartareis circumvolat omnia pennis,
  Quam circum tenebris nox spatiosa cavis,
Mille neces circum et morbi genus omne tremendi,
  Mille humeris succo spicula tincta nigro.
Dentibus infrendet horrendum semper ahenis,
80 Insanam cupiens exaturare famem.
Haec te loetiferis sequitur metuenda sagittis,
  Haec sequitur laqueis insidiosa suis.

away. The fields without their grass are ugly and unlike their former selves, and suddenly all bloom and beauty perish. Just so, just so the flower of our lifetime, just so the false blandishments of youth slip away, alas, at a rapid pace, never to return. Then age, sad and full of griefs, rushes upon us. Then crook-backed old age, tottering along, creeps up on us, calamitous with both heavy cares and miserable diseases, encompassed by griefs and hundreds of afflictions. She will sprinkle your temples with grey hair; she will make your hairy skin hang down in folds. Then pleasure suddenly abandons your dying body and all the force and vitality of your mind fail. Beauty dies, the nimble strength of the body dies, and those roses fade from your ruddy cheeks. Suddenly your forehead is rough and furrowed with the wrinkles of old age. The light in your sunken eyes grows dim. Your head, instead of your chin, grows smooth. Finally you become a monkey, quite unlike what you were and unrecognizable even to yourself.

Go on now, unhappy fellow, rely on the years of your youth and assure yourself that you will long enjoy the fulfilment of your desires – if, that is, the fates permit you to get safely through youth and allow you to see the days of your maturity. But fierce Death often delights in nipping tender life in the bud and cutting off the fruit unripe. Ghastly, she flits around all things on her infernal pinions, surrounded by a vast darkness of enveloping shadows; a thousand deaths surround her, and every kind of terrible disease, and a thousand arrows dipped in a black potion are on her shoulders. She always grinds her bronze teeth horribly, longing to satiate her raging hunger. Fearsomely she pursues you with her death-dealing arrows. Insidiously she pursues you with her snares. She knows nothing of sparing

Parcere nec formae nec parcere gnara iuventae,
  Sed vorat imberbes insatiata genas.
85 Quid dubitas, male sane, meis confidere verbis?
  Sis vel luminibus credulus ipse tuis.
Nonne vides passim ut pereant iuvenesque senesque,
  Fervidus effoeto cum genitore puer?
Hic perit ante diem clauso praegnantis in alvo,
90 Sarcophagum miserae viscera matris habens.
Ille cadit dulci genetricis ab ubere raptus,
  Hic infans moritur, tollitur ille puer.
Multos iam calidos mediis a luxibus ecce
  Abrumpit iaculis mors truculenta suis.
95 Tum dic, vane iocis adolescens dedite vanis,
  Gaudia carnis ubi pristina, luxus ubi?
Spes ubi, quaeso, modo longaevae prisca senectae
  Temporaque in seros iam numerata dies?
Omnia nonne brevis subito necis abstulit hora?
100 Non sequitur dominum gloria vana suum.
Cuncta levis nebulae vanique simillima somni
  Effugiunt, ut iam nulla fuisse putes,
Et tu, perpetuis luiturus crimina flammis,
  Mitteris in Stygios flebilis umbra lacus.
105 Clauditur hoc mundi levis oblectatio fine,
  Et sequitur risum aeterna querela brevem.
Ergo age, dum liceat, tibi consule: nautica sera est
  Fluctibus elisa sollicitudo rate.
Sed prius ac veniat venturam prospice mortem.
110 Sic facis ut veniat non metuenda tibi.

beauty or sparing youth, but insatiably devours beardless cheeks.

Madman, why do you hesitate to place your trust in my words? At least believe your own eyes. Don't you see how both young and old are dying everywhere, the hot-blooded boy together with his debilitated father? One person perishes before his time, shut up in his pregnant mother's womb, having for his tomb the womb of his miserable mother. Another is snatched by death from the sweet breast of his mother. One dies in infancy, another in boyhood. In the heat of youth, lo, many are torn away in the very midst of their debauchery by the shafts of grim death. Tell me then, O vain youth, devoted to vain jesting, where are the previous joys of the flesh? Where is the lust? Where now, I ask you, is your former hope of an advanced old age and of seasons reckoned upon seasons down to the latest days? Has not the brief hour of death taken all this away at one stroke? Empty glory does not follow its master. Exactly like a light mist or an empty dream, everything flees away, so that you would think it had never existed. And as for you, you are sent as a lamentable shade to the Stygian lake, where you will pay for your sins in unending flames. To such an end comes the petty pleasure of the world, and brief laughter is followed by eternal lamentation.

Come then, look out for yourself while you still can. Too late is the sailors' concern when the vessel has been broken up by the waves. Look ahead to your coming death before it comes. Thus you will make it come with no fear for yourself.

96 Elegia tercia, in divitem avarum [winter 1490–1 / 1513]

Tu quoque, nescio qua rerum spe lusus inani,
  Cogis, avare, tuas insatiatus opes,
Ausus et ipse tibi vitam spondere beatam,
  Tantum si votis arca sit aequa tuis.
5 Hinc domus, hinc teneri chara cum coniuge nati
  Linquuntur, patrium linquitur ergo solum.
Quaeritur Aeoo quaecunque est proxima soli,
  Quaecunque occiduo terra sub axe latet.
Temnuntur scopuli et ratibus metuenda Charybdis,
10 Temnitur hymbriferis acta procella Notis.
Mille per undarum, per mille pericula terrae,
  Per phas perque nephas, per necis omne genus,
Quaeritur innumeris nocitura pecunia curis,
  Quaeque queat dominum perdere parta suum.
15 Stulte, quid attonita refugis nova nomina fronte?
  Lumina cur tollis cum 'nocitura' legis?
Hac nihil est (neque enim mirere) nocentius, inquam,
  Saevius haud ullum Styx dedit atra malum.
Ipsa est cunctorum genitrix et alumna malorum,
20 Fomentum vitii, saeva noverca boni.
Illa peregrinos prima intulit horrida mores
  Primaque vipereum sparsit in orbe malum.
Haec docuit tacitis aliena capessere furtis
  Cognataque feras tingere caede manus.
25 Suasit adulterium, periuria, bella, rapinas;
  Lenonem illa facit, prostibulum illa facit.
Sit facit illa suo malefidus amicus amico,
  Rectaque ne iudex censeat illa facit.

96 The third elegy, against a greedy rich man

You also, O man of greed, deluded by some empty hope you place in possessions, you gather in your riches insatiably, and you even dare to promise yourself a happy life if only you can fill your money-chest up to the level of your desires. For this you leave your home, your dear wife and young children; for this you leave the soil of your native land. You seek out whatever lands lie close to the rising sun, whatever countries lie hidden under the setting sun. You scorn reefs and Charybdis, a fearful danger to ships; you scorn storms driven by the rain-laden winds of the south. Through countless dangers at sea, through countless perils on land, through fair means or foul, through all sorts of slaughter, you take infinite pains to seek out money, which will harm you and which, once it is gotten, can destroy its master. Fool, why do you wrinkle your brow in amazement and rejection when you hear this new way of putting it? Why do you roll your eyes upward when you read 'which will harm you'? Nothing, I say, is more harmful than money – no need to wonder at it – no crueler affliction has been sent forth by the darkness of hell. She is the very mother and nourisher of evils, the fomentor of vice, the cruel stepmother of virtue. She was the horrible creature who first introduced exotic ways of life, she was the first to bespatter the world with the snake venom of wickedness. She taught how to purloin what belongs to others and how to dye savage hands with the blood of kinsmen. She persuaded people to commit adultery and perjury, to make war and to pillage. She makes pimps, she makes prostitutes. She makes friend betray friend, and she keeps judges from making rightful decisions. She teaches cruel stepmothers how

Illa docet saevas miscere aconita novercas,
30 Illa beat reprobos, deprimit illa pios.
Schisma aurum parit, ambitio quoque nascitur auro,
Iurgia, proditio, livor et ira nocens.
Illius humanos caecat caligine sensus,
Fascinat atque oculos insatiata fames.
35 Hac Achar populo dominum succendit Hebraeo,
Hac Giesi lepra ceu nive tectus abit.
Ipsa Philisteo Sampsonem prodidit hosti,
Coniuge delusos ingeminante dolos.
Hac quoque tu, innocui saevissime venditor agni,
40 Complexo medius guttura fune crepas.
Et quid cuncta feram? Haec est totius una vorago
Criminis, inferni ianua, mortis iter.
Id quoque natura didicisse docente licebit,
Quae tanto nocuas obice clausit opes.
45 Surgere flava Ceres praecepta patentibus arvis,
Laetaque pampineo palmite vina fluunt,
Et mala in patulis flavescunt mollia ramis,
Dives mille palam munera fundit humus.
At natura, olim cunctarum praescia rerum,
50 Noxia terrigenis dona latere iubet.
Terrae visceribus nocitura recondidit auri
Pondera, et obscoenas in Styga mersit opes.
Gemmea marmoreo latitare sub equore saxa
Iussit et obscurum gurgite clausit iter.
55 Nec latuisse licet quantumlibet abdita: avari
Effodit e latebris improba cura suis.
Quo non dira fames? Stygias penetratur ad umbras

to brew poisons, she blesses the wicked, she oppresses the pious. Gold causes factions. Ambition is also born of gold, and so are quarrels, treachery, envy, and destructive anger. Insatiable greed for gold blinds human perceptions with its dark fumes and bewitches the eyes. Greed was the reason that Achar inflamed the Lord against the Jewish people; it was the reason that Gehazi went away covered with leprosy white as snow. It betrayed Samson to his Philistine enemies, as his wife redoubled her wiles, which had been mocked by Samson's guile. It also caused you, most cruel seller of the innocent lamb, to tie the rope around your neck and burst asunder. But why should I bring up every instance? Greed alone is the abyss of all crime, the gateway to hell, the road to death.

We can also learn this lesson from Nature, who shut up harmful riches behind such formidable barriers. The yellow grain has been taught to spring up in the open fields; so too the happy grapes on the tendrilled vine-stalks are flowing with wine, and the soft, yellowing fruit ripens on the spreading branches. The rich ground openly pours forth thousands of gifts. But Nature, who long ago knew all things in advance, commanded that her harmful gifts be hidden from the children of earth. She hid the heavy mass of gold, which would do harm, in the bowels of the earth, and she sunk ill-omened riches down into the lower world. She directed that precious stones should be hidden under the marmoreal surface of the sea, and she closed off the way to them in the murky depths of the sea. But however well concealed, they are not allowed to remain hidden: the wicked solicitude of the greedy man digs them up out of their hiding places. To what lengths will dreadful greed not go? It penetrates to the shades of the underworld and it reaches down

Inque procellosi tenditur ima freti.
Promuntur tecti preciosa pericula census,
60 Pernicies hominum materiesque mali.
Mentior at forsan. Sed tu quae commoda lucris
Experiare, miser, profer (amabo) tuis.
Nulla, reor, nisi forte tuas tu commoda curas
Dixeris. Et quid enim, quid nisi cura tuum est?
65 Arca beata quidem; miserum te copia rerum
Strangulat, innumeris accumulata malis.
Sollicito quaesita metu, querenda fatigat
Curis, te miserum spesque metusque premunt.
Lux est, assiduo mens anxia fluctuat estu.
70 Nox venit, ipsa quoque est irrequieta quies.
Nec tam crediderim Titii derodere fibras
Vultura, quam pectus improba vota tuum,
Ut iam haud immerito divesque vocere miserque,
Ille velut quondam perditus aere Midas.
75 Omnia cui quamvis fulvum vertantur in aurum,
Vota tamen votis damnat avara novis
Moxque perosus opes sylvas et rura colebat,
Grande docens opibus grandibus esse malum.
Adde quod ingenti congesta pecunia cura
80 Nec sopire famem nec relevare potest.
Auri dira sitis crescit crescentibus arcis,
Et cum iam tulerit plurima, plura cupit.
Utque solum omne salum in sinuosam congerit alvum,
Undique collectis nec satiatur aquis,
85 Nutrit et ut pinguis rapidas alimonia flammas,
Noxia sic avido crescit edendo fames.
Quid iuvat immenso disrumpere scrinia censu,

to the depths of the stormy sea. The precious perils of covered riches are brought forth to destroy mankind and to provide the stuff of wickedness.

Still, perhaps I am mistaken. But reveal, you wretch, the advantages you experience from your riches – I will be obliged to you if you do. None, I think, unless perhaps you say that your anxieties are advantages. For what belongs to you, what besides the anxiety? Your money-chest is rich indeed, but you are miserably suffocated by an abundance of possessions, accumulated with countless afflictions. You seek it with anxiety and fear; since it must be sought with sorrow, it wears you out. You are miserably squeezed by hope and fear. It is daylight: your mind is in a continuous turmoil of anxiety. Night comes: even your rest is also restless. I would not imagine that the vulture gnaws away the entrails of Tityus any more painfully than your wicked desires eat away at your heart, so that it is quite fitting to call you rich and wretched in the same breath, as Midas once was destroyed by money. Though everything turned into yellow gold for him, still his new wish condemned his former greedy wish and he soon enough came to hate riches, living among the forests and fields, teaching that great wealth is a great affliction.

Add the fact that money gathered up with enormous pains cannot alleviate greed or put it to rest. The dreadful thirst for gold grows as the money-chests grow, and when it has already got much it wants more. And as the earth gathers together all the water of the sea into its winding gulfs and is not satiated by the waters it collects from all directions, and as oily fuel feeds a raging fire, so the noxious hunger of a greedy man grows by feeding. What good does it do him to have chests bursting with

Cum satis esse animus nesciat ipse sibi?
Omnis eget cupidus nec habet quod habet, sed et ipsas
90 Inter opes medias degit avarus inops.
Esurit et plenis patitur ieiunia mensis,
Irritant rabidam fercula visa famem,
Non secus ac refugis cruciatur Tantalus undis
Et sitit in mediis guttura siccus aquis,
95 Illeve ieiuno qui devorat omnia ventre
Et proprios artus insatiatus edit.
Ergo quid argentum, quid inutile congeris aurum,
Perdite, quod dominum non beat, immo gravat,
Loraque quod captis innectens vincula collis
100 Te servum statuat, qui modo liber eras?
Servus enim, servus rerum est, mihi crede, suarum,
Obsceno quisquis victus amore iacet.
Custos, non dominus, nec habet, sed habetur ab illis,
Nilque in eas dives iuris avarus habet.
105 Mox etenim ut volucrem fortuna revolverit orbem,
Quae tua sunt hodie, cras subito huius erunt,
Teque Irum ex ipso faciet lux unica Craeso.
Plenus eras opibus, iam moriere fame.
Finge sed immensas votisque capacibus aequas
110 Et semper stabili finge manere gradu.
Quid tum, cum veniet mors, meta novissima rerum?
Defunctum faciles iamne sequentur opes?
Quid tum contulerit largarum copia rerum?
Tartara tu nudus nec rediturus adis,
115 Sudoresque tuos peregrinus devorat haeres,
Te velo in tumulum vix comitante brevi.
An te forte putas non exorabile fatum

untold wealth if his own mind never knows how to be sufficient unto itself? Everyone who desires something is needy and does not have what he has, but even in the very midst of his riches the greedy man lives in want. He starves and suffers hunger when the table is loaded with food. The very sight of the dishes drives him mad with hunger. He is not unlike Tantalus tortured by the retreating water, and with water all around him his throat is dry and thirsty; or he is like the one who devours everything into his lean belly and insatiably eats his own limbs. Why then, O ruined man, do you heap up silver, why gather useless gold, which does not make its master happy but rather weighs you down and, by fastening reins like bonds on your captive neck, decrees that you, who were once free, are a slave? For a man who is abjectly subject to his own filthy desire is a slave, believe me, a slave of his own possessions. He is their guardian, not their master; he does not possess them but is possessed by them, and a greedy rich man has no power over them. For as soon as Fortune turns her whirling wheel, what is yours today will be someone else's tomorrow, and a single day will change you from a Croesus to an Irus. You abounded in riches; now you will die of hunger.

But imagine enormous wealth, enough to match your capacious desires, and imagine that it will always stay fixed and never go away. What will happen when death comes, the final goal of all things? Will riches be so agreeable as to follow the dead man then? What good will a lavish abundance of wealth do then? You go naked down to the underworld, never to return, and a stranger inherits and devours all that you sweat for, while you have barely a little rag to go with you into the tomb. Or do you think, perhaps, that you can evade

Mortis et extremum fallere posse diem?
Posse puta, sperare licet, si tempora quenquam
120 Invenias opibus perpetuasse suis,
Et si quid Crasso, si quid sua copia Craeso
Profuit et cineres ille vel ille fugit,
Si mors felici Solomoni saeva pepercit,
Si non et Phrygium Laomedonta tulit.

Finiunt elegiae tres.

97 Ad Lesbium metrum phaloecium hendecasyllabum, de nummo themation [1490–1? / 1513]

Ut quicquid cupis assequare, Lesbi,
Non magnos opus est pares patronos,
Si rubris tumeat crumena nummis.
Nummo non melior patronus ullus.
5 Sin vero tibi desit ille tutor,
Nequicquam (mihi crede), amice Lesbi,
Facundus Cicero patrocinetur.
Persuadet citius nihil beata,
Impetrat citius nihil crumena.
10 Hac quodcunque voles eris repente:
Facundus, generosus atque bellus,
Invictus, sapiens amabilisque.
Hac et consul eris et imperator,
Haec te si cupies deum creabit
15 Aequabitque Iovi. Sed ut tumentes
Cessabit loculos gravare nummus,
Fies rursus, eras quod ante, Lesbi.
Tam gratus venies tuis amicis
Quam primum puto parsimoniarum
20 Adventare diem his, madens lagena
Quos et semper olens iuvat culina.
Sic sic dum loculos habere, Lesbi,
Cessas, desinis esse charus. Aera
Desisti dare? Desiisti amari.

inexorable fate and put off the final day when you must die? Think that you can, hope for it if you like, if you can find anyone who has achieved perpetual life through his wealth, or if Crassus or Croesus got any good from their riches, or if the one or the other could escape from turning to ashes, or if cruel death spared Solomon in all his good fortune and did not carry away even Laomedon of Troy.

The end of the three elegies

97 A little set piece addressed to Lesbius, in phalaecian hendecasyllabics. On money

Whenever you want to get something, Lesbius, there is no need to get powerful backers, if your purse is bulging with ruddy gold coins. There is no better backer than money. But if you lack that protector, the eloquent backing of Cicero himself, believe me, my friend Lesbius, would do you no good at all. Nothing persuades more quickly, nothing wins over more quickly, than a well-filled purse. With it you will suddenly be whatever you want: eloquent, noble, and handsome; invincible, wise, and lovable. With it, you will be both consul and emperor. If you want, it will make you a god, the equal of Jove.

But, when your bulging pockets stop being heavy with coins, Lesbius, you will become once more what you were before. When you come you will be as welcome to your friends, I imagine, as the first day of short rations when it comes to those who have always enjoyed a brimming wine jar and a kitchen full of good smells. Just so, Lesbius, just so, when your pockets are empty, you will cease to be beloved. Have you stopped giving money? You have stopped being loved.

POEMS PUBLISHED AFTER ERASMUS' DEATH

Poems from Gouda MS 1323

98 Erasmus magistro Enghelberto Leydensi

[summer 1489? / 1930]

Ethere quot placidis rutilant sub noctibus ignes
  Siderei, guttas quot capit unda freti,
Quot flavae segetes Cereris, quot pocula Bacchi
  Et quot verna virens gramina campus habet,
5 Tantas et plures, vates divine, salutes
  Exoptat vitae nostra Camena tuae.
Fama loquax, populos late diffusa per omnes,
  Ignarum quemquam non sinit esse tui.
Qui licet usque loco maneas immotus eodem,
10 Hac tamen immenso notus in orbe volas.
Hec facit ut nil te dubitem me noscere, quamquam
  Non unquam facies sit tua visa mihi.
Illa meas quoniam delapsa est nuper ad aures
  Laudis et ingenii nuncia multa tui,
15 Insigni virtute virum Musis et amicum
  Praedicat ac superi tollit ad astra poli.
Ingens fama quidem atque viro bene digna perito,
  Sed longe meritis est minor ipsa tuis.
Nam (nunc suspectae dubitem ne credere linguae)

POEMS PUBLISHED AFTER ERASMUS' DEATH

Poems from Gouda MS 1323

98 Erasmus to Engelbert of Leiden, Master of Arts

As numerous as the fiery stars shining in the sky on calm nights, or the drops contained in the waters of the sea, or the rows of grain belonging to yellow Ceres, or the cups of Bacchus, or the blades of grass in a green field at springtime, so many blessings and more, divine poet, my muse wishes for you in your lifetime. Loquacious Fame, spreading her news far and wide among all nations, does not allow anyone not to know of you; even if you should always remain immobile in the same place, nevertheless your fame makes the knowledge of you fly forth throughout the whole wide world. This Fame makes me have no doubt whatever that I know you, even though I have never set eyes on your face. Recently, after she dropped down to my ear to bring me many tidings of your merits and your genius, she proclaimed you to be a remarkably virtuous man and a friend of the Muses and she praised you up to the stars in the heavens above. Indeed, vast is your fame and well worthy of a learned man, but it is far less than you deserve. For lest I should hesitate to believe

20 Hauserunt versus lumina nostra tuos.
In quibus oppressae lucet spes multa Camenae,
Quae misere toto, proh pudor, orbe iacet.
Ergo, precor, ceptos fac perge, vir optime, calles,
Inque dies crescat haec tua cura tibi.
25 Barbaries indocta cadat, facunda poesis
Te duce sublime tollat in astra caput.
Iamque vale, eternos dent numina vivere in annos,
Atque immortales det tibi Parca dies.

99 Elegia Erasmi de collatione doloris et leticiae [1487? / 1930]

Nimbus et obscurae pellantur ab aethere nubes:
Pectoribus nostris cura dolorque cadat.
Affricus aequoreos cesset sustollere fluctus:
Pectoribus nostris cura dolorque cadat.
5 Frondiferae Boreas agitare cacumina sylvae:
Pectoribus nostris cura dolorque cadat.
Cura dolorque cadat, surgant nova gaudia, cedant
Luctus et Eumenides, cura dolorque procul.
Cura dolorque procul: viridem solet ille iuventam
10 Ante diem rugis commaculare suis.
Ante diem solet ille gravem celerare senectam,
Ille solet dulces abbreviare dies.
Ille rapit vires, vorat ossibus ille medullas,
Fronte perempta perit forma dolore suo.
15 Pectoribus sensum furor aufert pessimus ille,
Eripit ingenium pessimus ille furor.
Ergo procul Stigias, procul hinc demigret in undas

spoken reports, which are suspect nowadays, my eyes drank in your verses. In them shines great hope for the oppressed Muse, who lies miserably downtrodden (Oh the shame of it!) all over the world. Therefore, I beg you, best of men, go forward on the path you have begun to follow, and may this devotion of yours to poetry grow day by day. Let ignorant barbarism fall; let eloquent poetry under your leadership lift its head high up to the stars. And now farewell. May the gods make you live endless years and may the goddess of fate give you immortal days.

99 An elegiac poem by Erasmus comparing sorrow and joy

Let the rainstorms and dark clouds be driven from the sky: let care and sorrow fade away from our hearts. Let the south-west wind stop raising up waves on the surface of the sea: let care and sorrow fade away from our hearts. Let the north wind stop shaking the leafy treetops of the woods; let care and sorrow fade away from our hearts. Let care and sorrow fade away; let joys arise renewed; let grief inspired by the Furies depart. Away with care and sorrow! Away with care and sorrow; before their time they always mar the bloom of youth with their wrinkles. Before their time they always speed up burdensome old age; they always cut short the sweet days of youth. They snatch away our strength; they eat away the marrow of our bones; our good looks diminish and disappear because of sorrow. That ruinous turmoil of passion robs our hearts of understanding; that passionate and ruinous turmoil takes away the talents of our minds. Therefore, away with it! Let it depart far hence to the waves of Styx and the vast darkness of

Tartareumque cahos, cura dolorque cadat.
Adsit leticia: pulchram decet illa iuventam,
20 Qua sine nil pulchrum, nil queat esse bonum.
Corporis illa iuvat vires seniumque moratur
Tristius, et letos protrahit illa dies.
Leticia maior est forma, serenior est frons,
Leticia ingenium clarius esse solet.

100 Elegia Erasmi de praepotenti virtute Cupidinis pharetrati. [1487? / 1930]

Nunc scio quid sit amor: amor est insania mentis,
Ethna fervidior pectoris ignis amor.
Nutibus et signis teneri pascuntur amores,
Inter blanda oritur suavia stultus amor.
5 Lumina mollis amor primum subit, inde medullis
Figitur atque potens ossa penetrat amor.
Ossa penetrat amor tacitisque edit intima flammis,
Ima suis facibus viscera torret amor.
Viscera torret amor, mentem vetat esse quietam
10 Atque adimit somnos irrequietus amor.
Non requiescit amor, sed mutua victor amantum
Corpora si nequeat, pectora iungit amor.
Sit licet unus amor, nectit duo corda duorum;
Ut duo iam non sint efficit unus amor.
15 Quem ferus urit amor, in amati pectore totus;
Absens ipse sibi est, quem ferus urit amor.
Quem ferus urit amor, nil dulce ubi desit amatum,
At qum rursus adest, nil grave sentit amor.
Omnia vincit amor: adamantea claustra relaxat,

Tartarus; let care and sorrow fade away. Come hither joy, which befits the beauty of youth, joy without which nothing can be beautiful, nothing can be good. It makes our bodies strong and fends off gloomy old age, and it prolongs our days of joy. Joy increases our beauty and makes our faces more cheerful; joy tends to make our mental endowments more brilliant.

100 An elegiac poem by Erasmus on the overmastering power of Cupid with his quiver

Now I know what love is: love is a madness in the mind; love is a fire in the heart hotter than Aetna. Young love affairs are nourished by nods and signals; from sweet kisses foolish Love takes his origin. Tender Love first enters the eyes; then with full force Love sticks in the marrow and pierces the bones. Love pierces the bones and eats away the innards with silent flames; with his torch Love inflames the very depths of the entrails. Love inflames the entrails, he forbids the mind to be at rest, and Love in his restlessness takes away sleep. Love does not rest, but rather, if he cannot join together the bodies of lovers after his victory, Love joins their hearts. Although Love himself is single, he fastens together the two hearts of two lovers; this single Love causes them to be no longer two. Whoever is inflamed by fierce Love lives entirely in the heart of the beloved; absent from himself is the man who is inflamed by fierce Love. Whoever is inflamed by fierce Love finds nothing sweet when the object of his love is away; but when the beloved is present once more, nothing seems burdensome to Love.

Love conquers all: he unbars adamantine

20 Ferrea ceu stipulam vincula rumpit amor.
Omnia vincit amor sine cede et sanguine certans,
Et domat indomitos non domitandus amor.
Mollia nodosae valido pro robore clavae
Alciden trahere pensa coegit amor.
25 Praelia Mavortis quem non potuere cruenti
Magnanimum Eaciden vincere, vicit amor.
Denique quid vastus Sampsone valentius orbis
Edidit? Hunc potuit sternere solus amor.
Quidve tulit totus Salomone peritius orbis?
30 Hunc quoque quo lubuit victor abegit amor.
Doctus amor vigiles custodum fallere curas,
Noctis et excubias ludere doctus amor.
Cardine doctus amor nullum faciente tumultum
Scit reserare fores, claudere novit amor.
35 Omnia vertit amor: facit insipidos sapientes,
Atque Argi cecus lumina cecat amor.
Omnia vertit amor: mutum facit esse disertum,
In puerosque senes vertit amarus amor.
Fortia frangit amor, fragiles docet esse potentes,
40 Audaces timidos reddere novit amor.
Vulnera dirus amor temnit crudelia, ventis
Turbida nymbriferis aequora temnit amor.
Quid non fortis amor? Et morte valentior ipsa est:
Mortem quam trepidant omnia vincit amor.
45 Didonis egit amor miserae per viscera ferrum,
Insanus laqueo Phillida strinxit amor.
Per te, fortis amor, moritur Babilonia Tysbe,
Pyramus et per te sub Styga pergit, amor.
Singula quid memorem? Vincit puer improbus ille
50 Omnia, tu pueri tu quoque seva parens.

doors, and iron chains are broken like straw by Love. Love conquers all in a battle without slaughter or bloodshed, and the unconquerable are conquered by never-to-be-conquered Love. Instead of wielding the tough oak of his knotty club, Hercules was forced by Love to spin out the soft thread. The great-hearted Achilles, who could not be conquered in the battles of bloody Mars, was conquered by Love. And then, what has the whole wide world ever produced that was stronger than Samson? Single-handed, Love was able to lay him low. Has anyone in the whole world ever been wiser than Solomon? He, too, was driven to do whatever victorious Love wanted. Love is skilled in circumventing vigilant and careful guardians; and Love is skilled in outwitting watchmen posted by night. Love is skilled in opening doors without any creaking of the hinges; Love knows how to close them too.

Love transforms everything: he makes the wise stupid, and the eyes of Argus are blinded by Love, who is blind. Love transforms everything: he makes the eloquent dumb, and old men are changed to striplings by bitter Love. Love shatters what is strong and teaches the frail to be mighty; Love knows how to make the timid bold. Fell Love scorns cruel wounds; Love scorns the sea churned up by windswept rainstorms. Is there anything Love is not powerful enough to do? He is even stronger than death itself: death, which is feared by everything, is conquered by Love. Love drove the sword into the entrails of wretched Dido; mad Love tightened the noose around Phyllis' neck. Because of you, mighty Love, Babylonian Thisbe died, and Pyramus went down to the Styx because of you, O Love. Why should I recount single examples? That wicked boy conquers all, and you, O mother of the boy, you are also cruel. Which is

Seva parens pueri magis an puer improbus ille?
Improbus ille puer, tu quoque seva parens.

101 Elegia Erasmi querula doloris [1487? / 1930]

Qum nondum albenti surgant mihi vertice cani,
Candeat aut pilis frons viduata suis,
Luminibusve hebetet aciem numerosior aetas,
Aut dens squalenti decidat ore niger,
5 Atque acuant rigidae nondum mihi brachia setae, aut
Pendeat arenti corpore laxa cutis,
Denique nulla meae videam argumenta senectae,
Nescio quid misero sorsque deusque parent.
Me mala ferre senum teneris voluere sub annis
10 Iamque senem esse volunt nec senuisse sinunt.
Iam quae canicie spergant mea tempora tristi
Praevenere diem cura dolorque suum.

102 Carmen buccolicum Ἐράσμι [1487? / 1538]

Rosphamus insano Gunifoldae captus amore
Stridenti tacita solus sub nocte cicuta
Rumpebat longo lucubrantia sidera questu.
Quem circum simeae, quondam unica cura, capellae
5 Errant et gelidis neglecti in vallibus agni.
Nec stabulis egisse pecus nec culmina tecti
Vel sera meminit deserta revisere nocte.
Rore procul tantum madida proiectus in herba

greater, the cruelty of the boy's mother or the wickedness of the boy? That boy is wicked, and you, his mother, are also cruel.

101 An elegiac poem by Erasmus complaining about grief

Although gray hair has not yet begun to whiten the top of my head and fallen hair has not left me with a shining forehead, although advanced age has not dimmed my eyesight and no blackened tooth has fallen from a rotten mouth and stiff bristles have not yet made my arms prickly and my skin does not hang loose on a withered body – in short, although I see in myself none of the signs of old age, the lot assigned me by God is contrived to make me miserable, I know not how. He has decided to make me bear the afflictions of old age during my tender years, and he wants me to be already old, and yet he does not allow me to grow old. Care and sorrow, which would sprinkle my temples with sad gray hair, have come before their time.

102 A pastoral poem by Erasmus

Rosphamus, seized by a mad passion for Gunifolda, was playing his shrill pipes alone in the silence of the night, piercing with a long lament the stars, which shone like lamps in the dark. Wandering around him were his snub-nosed goats, once his only concern, and his lambs, neglected in the cold valleys. He forgets to drive his flock to their stables and, late as it is at night, he neglects to see once more the roof of his deserted hut. Far from home, stretched out on the grass wet with dew, he

Crudeles querula meditatur arundine flammas:
10 'Huc ades, o Gunifolda, mei medicina furoris,
Huc ades extremum vel visere funus amantis.
Rosphamus ecce vocat tuus, o Gunifolda, peritque,
Et tu flammivomae duris in collibus Ethnae
Mollibus indignum refoves Poliphemon in ulnis.
15 Ah tibi setosi ne candida colla lacerti,
Barba ah ne tenerum tibi conterat hispida mentum.
Huc ades, o Gunifolda, hic vitrea flumina iuxta
Gramine florigero viridi recubabimus umbra.
'Rosphame, quid sterili iuvat indulgere labori?
20 Desine: non tanto certasse licebit amanti.
Et certasse tamen (quid tum si vertice Ciclops
Sidera sublimi feriat?) licet; audiat ipse
Quantuscumque, nec illi cessero carmine, sola
Voce velit, velit arguta cecinisse cicuta.
25 Molle pecus, nivei sunt et mihi vallibus agni.
Corpore Dametas, voltu mihi cedit Amyntas.
Non mihi taurinis cervix riget horrida pilis,
Pectora sunt nobis candentia, levia nobis
Ora: quid amplexus, quid amas, insana, caninos?
30 'Rosphame, litus aras, aversis aspera (cerne)
Auribus effusas refugit Gunifolda querelas.
Quid speras? Sed et esto velit, vetat ille volentem.
Quin morere et longos componito morte dolores.
Extremum hoc, Gunifolda, tui cape munus amantis.
35 Eternum, Gunifolda, vale, dirae necis auctrix.'
Sic ait, et pulsae referebant carmina rupes.

thinks only of the cruel flames of his passion, lamenting the while on his pipes:

'Come hither, O Gunifolda, healer of my madness, come hither at least to see the end of your lover in death. Lo, your Rosphamus is calling you, O Gunifolda, and he pines away, while on the hard ridges of flame-spewing Aetna you are fondling the unworthy Polyphemus in your soft embraces. Ah, do not let his hairy arms chafe your white neck or his bristling beard, ah, brush your tender chin! Come hither, O Gunifolda, and here next to the glassy river we will lie back on the flowery grass in the green shade.

'Rosphamus, what good can it do to indulge in this futile task? Cease, you cannot compete with such a huge lover. But yes, you can compete – what does it matter if the head of the Cyclops strikes the stars on high? Let him hear me – however big he is – I will not yield to him in song, whether he chooses to sing with unaccompanied voice or to play on the pure-toned pipes. I have soft sheep and snow-white lambs in the valleys. In bodily build I surpass Dametas; my face is handsomer than Amyntas'. My neck is not bristling with hair standing up like that of a bull. My chest is white, my face is smooth. Why, oh why, are you madly enamoured of doggish embraces?

'Rosphamus, you are ploughing the seashore. See how the cruel Gunifolda closes her ears and flees from the plaintive pleas you pour out to her! What do you hope for? Even granted that she wished to comply, he frustrates her wishes. No, die instead and by death put an end to this long-drawn-out pain. Take this ultimate gift, Gunifolda, from your lover. Farewell forever, Gunifolda, the cause of my cruel death.' This is what he said and the rocks, struck by the sound, re-echoed his song.

Omne nemus 'Gunifolda' sonat, sonat arduus aether.
  Thetidos interea Titonis ab aequore coniunx
Paulatim croceis subvecta iugalibus alto
40 Iam rarescentem pellebat ab aethere noctem.
Et iam Phebeae ferientia sidera rupis
Culmina vix dubio cepere rubescere sole,
Cinctus et ecce senex viridanti tempora mirto
Letus agit teneras ad pascua nota capellas
45 Drales, pastorum quo non annosior alter,
Cui iam depositis niteat frons nuda capillis,
Qui iam tergeminos cum Nestore computet annos.
Una viro serae requies et cura senectae,
Tortilis hirsuto pendebat fistula collo.
50 Hic ubi roranti resupinum Rosphamon herba
Conspicit, his miserum dictis compellat amantem:
'Quaenam sub gelido tenuit Iove, Rosphame, causa
Teque pecusque tuum? fluitas quia totus, et ecce
Nocturno madet omne pecus sua vellera rore.'
55 'Si vacat, o Siculum pastorum gloria Drales
Una, tibi nostros referam moriturus amores.
Qum sol hesternus medium transmensus Olympum
Ureret ignivomis arentes aestibus herbas,
Atque ego, ne noceat quicquam calor ille capellis,
60 Condensi nemoris capto sicientibus umbram,
Illic forte sacrae video sub tegmine lauri
Naiades Aonidesque simul Driadesque puellas
Ducere solemnes cantu modulante choreas.
Pan calamo, pulcher cythara ludebat Apollo,
65 Omnis et in numeros agitabat brachia cetus
Pulsabatque humiles pedibus salientibus herbas.
  'Viderunt oculi, rapuerunt pectora flammae.

The whole grove resounds with 'Gunifolda'; 'Gunifolda' resounds high in the air.

Meanwhile the spouse of Tithonus, rising from the level surface of the sea, slowly conveyed by her saffron team, was already driving the thinning darkness from the upper air, and now the sky-grazing peaks of the crag sacred to Apollo were hardly beginning to grow red in the faint sunlight, when, lo, an old man, his temples wreathed with green myrtle, joyfully drives his young goats to their familiar pasture. It is Drales, the oldest of the shepherds; the hair has already fallen from his bare, shining brow. He has lived like Nestor through three generations. From his hairy neck hung a flute with a twisting design, the man's only solace and concern in his declining years. This man, when he saw Rosphamus lying on his back on the dewy grass, addressed the miserable lover in these words: 'What keeps you out in the cold air, Rosphamus, you and your flock? You are dripping wet and, look, the fleece of your whole flock is drenched with the dew of the night.'

'If you have time, Drales, O sole glory of Sicilian shepherds, I will tell you of my love as my death draws near. Yesterday, when the sun had traversed half its course through the sky and was scorching the parched grass with its beams of raging fire, after I sought out the shade of a thick grove for my thirsty goats to keep the heat from harming them, there by chance, under the canopy of the sacred laurel, I saw naiads and the Aonian Muses together with dryad maidens, dancing in their customary circle to the tune of their song. Pan played on his pipes, the beautiful Apollo played on his lyre, and the whole band swayed their arms in time with the music, leaping and beating on the short grass with their feet.

'My eyes saw it, my heart burst into flame.

'Ibat formosis formosior addita nymphis
Et gracilis toti extabat Gunifolda coronae,
70 Digna dea facies, ipso dignus Iove voltus.
Non illi igniferi Citherea parens pueri (me
Iudice), non illi certarit pulchra Dyana.
'Viderunt oculi, rapuerunt pectora flammae.
'Germanam quantum Phebi lux aurea Pheben,
75 Luciferum roseo quantum Phebe aurea voltu,
Caetera quam radians praecellit Lucifer astra,
Tam forma socias vincit Gunifolda puellas.
'Viderunt oculi, rapuerunt pectora flammae.
'Caesaries capitis fulvo crispantior auro
80 Undique cervicem circumvolitabat eburnam,
Ardentes oculi, liquido caro levior amne
Candidiorque nive, superis rutilantior astris.
'Viderunt oculi, rapuerunt pectora flammae.
'Adfuit et mediis puer improbus ille choreis,
85 Nudus membra, genas levisque et captus ocellis,
Armatus facibus levibusque volatilis alis.
Adfuit et medius medio stetit improbus orbe.
'Viderunt oculi, rapuerunt pectora flammae.
'Is mihi fulgenti promens sua tela pharetra
90 Flammifera stupidum traiecit arundine pectus.
Pectora traiecit, calidumque per ossa cucurrit
Virus, et in medias serpsit furor ille medullas.
Serpsit, et insuetis caluerunt intima flammis.
Hinc perii, atque gravis cepit mihi vita videri.
95 Et iam virgineas me conspectante choreas
Ibat supremi spacia ultima Phebus Olympi.
Quid facerem? Iam tempus erat quo septa capellae,

'Among the beautiful nymphs, herself more beautiful, went Gunifolda, and in her slender elegance she stood out from the whole ring of dancers, with a figure worthy of a goddess, a face worthy of Jupiter himself. If I am any judge, not Venus, the mother of the torch-bearing boy, not the beautiful Diana could vie with her.

'My eyes saw it, my heart burst into flame.

'Just as the golden light of Phoebus outshines his sister Phoebe, just as golden Phoebe with her rosy face conquers the morning star, just as the radiant morning star excels the other stars, so Gunifolda in her beauty surpassed her maiden companions.

'My eyes saw it, my heart burst into flame.

'The locks of her head, her curls, more sparkling than yellow gold, flew all around her ivory neck; her eyes were shining, her flesh smoother than a limpid stream and whiter than snow, more radiant than the stars above.

'My eyes saw it, my heart burst into flame.

'That wicked boy was also in the midst of the dancers, his limbs naked, his cheeks smooth, his eyes blind, armed with his firebrands, hovering on his rapid wings. He was there, that wicked boy, standing in the very middle of the circle.

'My eyes saw it, my heart burst into flame.

'Taking out his weapons from his flashing quiver, he pierced my stunned heart with a fiery arrow. He pierced my heart and the hot poison ran through my bones and the madness crept into their very marrow. It crept and burned deep within me with unfamiliar flames. From that time on I was lost and my life came to seem a burden to me. And then, while I was gazing at the dancing circle of maidens, Phoebus was travelling the last stretch of the western sky. What was I to do? It was now time for the goats to return to their pens, for

Quo repetant pasti praesepia nota iuvenci.
Me dirus retinebat amor, sequor invia saltus
100 Perditus et questu Gunifoldam sector inani
Et vano clamore voco: fugit illa vocantem.
Nil lacrimas miserata meas, nil flexa querelis,
Cautibus Hismariis immotior, aspide seva
Surdior, aereae summis in rupibus Ethnae
105 Immani sese Polyphemi condidit antro.
Hinc perii, atque gravis cepit mihi vita videri.
Tum redeo tandem, sequitur grex tristis euntem,
Atque hic, qum iam spes misero mihi nulla supersit,
Mortem oro superos, certe aut (quod gratius esset)
110 Improba permutent Gunifoldae pectora nostrae.'

Finis eglogae buccolicae

the full-fed bullocks to return to their familiar stalls. Cruel love held me fast. Devastated, I follow through the trackless glades, I pursue Gunifolda with futile lamentation, I call her with vain cries; she flees from me as I call. Taking no pity on my tears, unmoved by my plaints, more unyielding than the crags of Ismarus, more deaf than the fierce viper, she hides in the vast cave of Polyphemus high in the cliffs of lofty Aetna. From that time on I was lost and my life came to seem a burden to me. Then at last I returned, my sad flock followed me as I went, and here, since there is no hope left for wretched me, I beg the gods for death or at least – what would be more pleasant – a change in the cruel heart of my Gunifolda.'

The end of the pastoral eclogue

Tartareumque chaos: cura dolorque cadat.

Adsit leticia, pulchram decet illa iuventam:
Qua sine nil pulchrum, nil queat esse bonum.
Corporis illa iuvat vires, seniumque moratur
Tristis: et letos protrahit illa dies.
Leticia maior est forma, serenior est frons:
Leticia ingenium clarius esse solet.

Elegia erasmi de prepotenti virtute cupidinis pharetrati.

Nunc scio quid sit amor: amor est insania mentis.
Ethna ferventior pectoris ignis amor.
Nutibus et signis teneri pascuntur amores:
Inter blanda oritur suavia stultus amor.
Lumina mollis amor primum subit: inde medullis
Figitur, atque potens ossa penetrat amor.
Ossa penetrat amor, tacitisque edit intima flammis:
Ima suis facibus viscera torret amor.
Viscera torret amor, noctem vetat esse quietam:
Atque adimit somnos irrequietus amor.
Nec requiescit amor: sed mutua victor amantum
Corpora si nequeat, pectora iungit amor.
Sit licet unus amor, nectit duo corda duorum:
Ut duo iam non sint, efficit unus amor.
Nunc ferus urit amor, in amati pectore totus

Gouda MS 1323, f 9r, showing
Elegia Erasmi de praepotenti virtute Cupidinis pharetrati
Streekarchiefdienst Hollands Midden

Tum redeo tandem, sequitur grex tristis euntem.
Atque hic cum iam spes misero mihi nulla supersit,
Mortem oro superos, certe aut (quod gratius esset)
Improba permutent Galateae pectora nostrae.

Finis.

Oda amatoria. Primus versus hexameter, secundus est Iambicus.

Hei mihi quae flamma puer ille sagittifer unquam
Crudeliore torruit?
Sol cadit, et feras inducit vesperus umbras,
Somnum ferens mortalibus.
At mihi sollicito pectus tamen aestuat igne,
Nec accipit somnos amor.
Plurima labitur ecce dies, nox multa vicissim
Nigris profecta manibus.
At iecur usque mihi lasso sub pectore siccum
Aegris anhelat ignibus.
Atqui ego cuncta ratus mollescere stultus amore,
Ultro simul fio tuus,
Victaque dedo tuis stultissimus ora capistris,
quas.

MS Scriverius, f 4v, with the end of
Carmen buccolicum and the start of *Oda amatoria*
Katholieke Universiteit Brabant, Tilburg

Poems from MS Scriverius

103 **Oda amatoria. Primus versus hexameter, secundus est iambicus.** [1487? / 1706]

Hei mihi, quem flamma puer ille sagittifer unquam
Crudeliore torruit?
Sol cadit, et seras inducit vesperus umbras,
Somnum ferens mortalibus.
5 At mihi sollicito pectus tamen aestuat igne,
Nec accipit somnos amor.
Plurima labitur ecce dies, nox multa vicissim
Nigris profecta manibus.
At iecur usque mihi lasso sub pectore siccum
10 Aegris anhelat ignibus.
Atqui ego cuncta ratus mollescere stultus amore
Ultro simul fio tuus
Victaque dedo tuis stultissimus ora capistris.
Quas non dedi supplex preces!
15 Testis luna meis aderat taciturna querelis
Totusque syderum chorus.
Conscius ipse quibus, quibus heu nostrosque tuosque
Sinus rigarim lachrimis –
Frustra, nam scopulis tu surdior usque marinis,
20 Tu rupe quavis durior,
Nec prece nec lachrimis miseri mollescis amantis,
Tormenta te iuvant mea.
O doliture mea multum virtute Menalca,
Nam virium si quid mihi est,
25 Sis licet et Venere et Ganymede nitentior ipso
Totusque spires balsama
Isque color tibi sit, tenero quo vere videmus
Flores rubere punicos,
Quem vel Apelleas memorant habuisse tabellas
30 Viva exprimentem corpora:
Ut tamen haecce tuis subduxero colla cathenis
Spem praeter omnem strennuus,

Poems from MS Scriverius

103 An amatory ode. The first verse is a hexameter; the second is iambic.

Woe is me! Who has ever been burned by that bow-boy with a crueler flame? The sun is setting, and the evening star, leading on the shadows of twilight, is bringing sleep to mortals. But for all that, my heart still rages with the flames of anxiety, and love receives no sleep. Many a day has slipped by and many nights in their turn have taken up their journey from the dark underworld. But always my withered heart within my weary breast pants with fevered fire. And yet I, who foolishly thought that all things could be softened by love, have not only willingly become yours; overcome, I have also most foolishly taken your bit in my mouth. How have I humbly pleaded with you! The silent moon and the whole choir of the stars were present as witnesses to my laments. You yourself are aware of the tears, alas such tears, that moistened my breast and yours – in vain, for you are always deafer than any sea cliff, harder than any crag; no prayers or tears of a wretched lover can soften you; you enjoy my torments. O Menalcas, you will one day be greatly grieved by my power, for if there is any strength in me, even though you are more radiantly beautiful than Venus or Ganymede himself, though your whole person breathes forth balm, even though your complexion has the deep red colour that we see on the flowers in the tender springtime, the very colour that they say could be seen in the paintings of Apelles, a colour that made the bodies seem alive, nevertheless, once I have found strength beyond what could ever be hoped for and have withdrawn this neck of mine from your chains,

Heu heu, te nimium domiti tedebit amoris
    Nimisque sani pectoris,
35 Mutatumque tuum subito maerebis Amyntam,
    Egoque flocci pendero.

104 Elegia de mutabilitate temporum ad amicum

[late autumn 1489? / 1706]

Aspicis ut densas ponant arbusta coronas
  Et linquant virides vitis et herba comas,
Arida purpurei fugiant violaria flores,
  Horreat elapsis aspera spina rosis,
5 Cernis et ut nudi iaceant sine gramine campi,
  Quos florum quondam pinxerat ampla Venus.
Pro placidis Zephiris audis Aquilona frementem,
  Audis nymbriferi flamina saeva Nothi.
Nec solitum placidus blanditur in aethere Phaebus,
10 Pendet in oceanas quin mage pronus aquas,
Succedentis ubi brumae vice labitur aestas
  Tristeque sorte venit vere cadente gelu.
Sic sic flos aevi, sic, dulcis amice, iuventus
  Heu properante cadit irreparata pede.
15 Forma perit, pereunt agiles in corpore vires,
  Et subito ingenii visque calorque cadit.
Tristior inde ruit ac plena doloribus aetas,
  Inde subit propero curva senecta pede.
Haec tibi canicie est flavos, formose, capillos
20 Sparsura et frontem findet amara tuam.
Candida deformi pallore tibi induet ora,
  Et rosa purpureis excidet ista genis.
Iamque abient nunquam redeuntia gaudia vitae,

then, alas, alas, you will be sorry that you tamed your love too well and kept your heart too sound, and you will grieve that your Amyntas has suddenly changed – and I will not care a whit.

104 An elegiac poem on the mutability of time, to a friend

You see how the trees have put off their thick-leafed crowns and the vines and the meadows have lost their green tresses, how the crimson flowers have fled from the arid violet beds and the harsh thorns bristle now that the roses have fallen away. And you perceive how the fields lie bare of grass, where once Venus had bountifully bedecked them with flowers. Instead of gentle western winds, you hear the raging wind from the north, you hear the savage blasts of the rain-laden wind from the south. Nor does mild Phoebus smile as usual in the sky, but rather he leans down low toward the waters of the ocean, now that summer slips away and winter follows in turn and melancholy frosts, after the end of spring, have taken their allotted place.

Just so, my sweet friend, just so the flower of our lifetime, youth, hastens away, alas, and fails, never to be recovered. Beauty dies, the nimble strength of the body dies, and suddenly the force and vitality of the mind fail. Then age, sad and full of griefs, rushes upon us; then crook-backed old age steals upon us all too swiftly. Beautiful lad, she will sprinkle your yellow locks with gray; she will bitterly plough furrows in your brow. She will cast an ugly pallor over the fair white of your face, and those roses will depart from your ruddy cheeks. The joys of life are already about to go

Succedent quorum morsque laborque locis.
25 Ergo ferox dum Parca sinet, patiantur et anni,
Dum vireat vicibus laeta iuventa suis,
Utamur, ne frustra abeat torpentibus, aevo,
Carpamus primos, dulcis amice, dies.

105 Elegia de patientia, qua sola vincuntur omnia, atque de dolore mortalium, quomodo non tam fugiendus, quam fortiter patientia vincendus sit [1490? / 1706]

Quo fugis, o nimium tener impatiensque doloris?
Te quocunque fugis quem fugis insequitur.
Ne confide fugae, rapitur pernicibus ille
Alis, nec dubitat te fugiente sequi.
5 Otyor est iaculo Partho quod mittitur arcu
Et vincit volucres mobilitate Nothos.
Cum iam a calce omnem gaudes liquisse dolorem,
Ocyor ille Euro tum tua terga tenet,
Et male securi iam gaudia inania ridens,
10 Incumbit misero durior inde tibi.
Stulte, quid extremas iuvat evasisse per oras?
Omnibus in terris te prior ille videt.
Quid frustra varia rapit in diversa cupido
Sollicitatque animum perdita cura tuum?
15 Quid totiens mutare locum, mutare gradumque
Vitae et inexpertum te nova adire iuvat?

away, never to return, and their places will be taken by hardship and death.

Therefore, while the fierce goddess of fate still permits it, while the years still allow it, while youth rejoices and flourishes in its own season, let us make use of this time in our lives, lest we lose it in vain through our own lethargy. Let us seize, sweet friend, the days of our youth.

105 An elegiac poem on patience, which is the only way to conquer all things, and on the tribulation of mortals, which is not so much to be shunned as bravely conquered by patience

Whither are you fleeing, O you who are too sensitive and unwilling to be patient under tribulation? Wherever you flee, what you flee from follows you. Do not place your trust in flight, for your pursuer rushes on rapid wings, and when you flee from him he does not hesitate to follow. He is swifter than an arrow shot from a Parthian bow, and he moves faster than the rushing wind from the south. And when you rejoice that you have finally outrun tribulation and left him completely behind, then he comes swifter than the east wind and takes hold of you from behind and, from then on, laughing at the empty joy of your overconfidence, he oppresses you even more cruelly in your misery. Fool, what good is it to run away to the ends of the earth? Everywhere in the world he spies you first.

Why are you vainly distracted by manifold desires? And why is your mind so taken with a hopeless cause? Why do you so often delight in going from one place to another and in changing your state in life? And why in your ignorance are you so eager to seek out new

Curas ditari, cupis in sublime levari,
Tanquam te solvant ista dolore tuo.
Non, inquam, non etsi Craeso opulentior esses
20 Aut ditioni sint subdita cuncta tuae.
Anne putas regum vacua esse palacia curis?
Credo equidem excelsis has magis esse locis.
Tu quamvis summe in cunctis mirere beatos,
Tristes saepe animos ostra superba tegunt.
25 Eumenides circumvolitant laquearia tristes
Aurea, perlustrant tecta superba ducum.
Nil curant plenis spirent convivia mensis
Despumentque vetus pocula abunda merum
Milleque dulcisonum moduletur carmina plectrum
30 Spargat et innumeros tibia blanda modos,
Quin inter luxus sedet, illaetabile virus
Plausibus immiscens, anxia cura, suum.
Aequa lege dolor summos sortitur et imos,
Involvens misere regem humilemque simul.
35 Neve puta, cum iam te opibus fortuna bearit,
Nil fore quod cupidum temptet amare animum.
Tum primum curae, dolor et suspiria surgent,
Tum primum angores experiere graves.
Sic etenim fortuna suis sua munera miscet,
40 Ut fel non modicum paucula mella tegant.
Candida et impexi cingunt ut lilia vepres
Spinaque purpureum gignit acuta decus,
Tristia sic laetis, sic dulcia miscet amaris,
Et coeunt iuncto spesque metusque pede,
45 Gaudia cum maerore gravique tripudia luctu,
Libertas curis, mixta labore quies.
Hoc volvunt Parcae, hoc ineluctabile fatum

experiences? You take pains to get rich, you long to rise to the top, as if these things could free you from your tribulation. No, I say, not even if you were richer than Croesus or if all things were subject to your sway. Do you imagine that the palaces of kings are devoid of cares? Indeed, I think, cares are more likely to be found in high places. Though you may have unlimited admiration for those who have everything going for them, haughty robes of purple often cloak minds oppressed with sadness. The harsh Furies flit about under golden-coffered ceilings; they wander everywhere in the proud palaces of rulers. They do not care what aromas rise from the fully laden banquet tables or what vintage wines foam in full cups or what an abundance of song is plucked from melodious strings or what endless airs float about from lovely flutes. No, restless anxiety sits at the luxurious feast and mingles her joyless poison with the flattering applause. With an even hand tribulation assigns the lots of low and high alike, wrapping both king and clown in misery.

And do not imagine that, even when Fortune has blessed you with wealth, there will be no bitterness to try your greedy soul. That is the very time when cares, tribulations, and sighs will emerge; that is the very time when you will experience grievous anguish. For Fortune intermingles her gifts to her followers in such a way that a bit of honey masks a deal of wormwood. And just as the white lilies are surrounded by tangled briers and the sharp thorn brings forth the crimson glory, so Fortune mixes sorrow with joy, the sweet with the bitter, and hope marches linked in an even pace with fear, delight keeps step with grief, and dancing is mingled with heavy-hearted mourning, freedom with cares, repose with hardship. This is the will of the Fates; this is

Archanique animi sic voluere deum.
Certandum ergo tibi est contendendumque palaestra;
50 Hostis erit feritas hac superanda via,
Victoque ingentem referes ex hoste triumphum,
Nominis emittens seculum in omne decus.
Nonne vides toto Iob ut venerabilis heros
Cuncta per ora volans orbe celebris eat?
55 Funera post sua vivit adhuc super aethera notus,
Atque illi aeternum haec fama superstes erit.
Et dubitamus adhuc consistere cominus hosti?
Verte gradum et vires experiare tuas.
Ne dubita, in manibus pendet victoria nostris,
60 Tute modo advertas aurem animumque mihi.
Pandam ego queis telis, qua sit res arte gerenda,
Haec etenim ad palmam non mediocre ferent.
Est nova luctandi species, nova Martis imago,
In qua non frameis, non opus est iaculis.
65 Sta tantum intrepido et fidenti pectore firmus,
Nec moveant animum tela cruenta tuum.
Ille fremat sine more furens frustraque laboret,
Irritus in ventum et sudet inane diu.
Sive petat iaculo seu certet cominus ense,
70 Ne moveare cave; sta modo, tutus eris.
Temne simul iaculo, temne et simul ense petentem;
Hostem si poteris temnere, victor eris.
Ne tamen eliso vitalia pectore ferro
Sauciet et letum toxica spicla ferant,
75 Apta humeris thoraca prius atque omnia denso
Ordine squamarum ferrea texta tegant.
Ne rursum assiduo iacientis ab imbre fatiscant

ineluctable destiny; and it has been so willed by the unsearchable minds of the gods.

Therefore you must contend and struggle on the wrestling mat. This is the way to overcome the fierceness of the enemy, and once the enemy is defeated you will gain an enormous triumph, extending the glory of your name to all future ages. Do you not see how the name of the venerable hero Job flies about on the tongues of everyone, celebrated all over the earth? After his death he still lives, well known in the heavens above, and this fame of his will survive forever. And do we still hesitate to grapple with the enemy? Turn around and find out how strong you really are. Do not hesitate: the victory lies in our own hands, if you will only lend me your ears and give me your attention. I will reveal to you with what weapons, with what strategy, the battle is to be waged, for these things contribute not a little to the winning of the palm. This is a new sort of struggle, a new image of warfare, in which there is no need for javelins or spears. Simply stand firm with a fearless and confident heart, and do not let your mind be moved by bloody weapons. Let the madman rage beyond all reason, let him labour in vain, let him sweat at length but to no purpose, frustrated and fighting against the wind. Whether he attacks you with a spear or engages you at close quarters with his sword, take care not to be moved; just take your stand, you will be safe. Whether he attacks with his spear or with his sword, scorn him equally; if you can scorn the enemy, you will be the victor. But, lest his sword should pierce your heart with a fatal wound, lest the poisoned point of his spear should seal your fate, first fit a cuirass to your shoulders and let the thickly woven rows of iron platelets cover your whole body. Then too, lest the ceaseless hail of spears should

Aera, perita sibi dextera scutum habeat,
Scutum quo quicquid furiato emittitur hoste
80 Irritet et vigilem ludat inane manum.
Pectore letum abigat agili omnibus obvia motu,
Improbitate prior iam cadet ipse sua.
Sed quid te moror obscura sub imagine verbi?
Corporea neque enim haec res peragenda manu est.
85 Rem nude referam potius sine nubibus omnem;
Tu cape dicta memor, me duce victor eris.
Muniat intrepidam virtus patientia mentem
Contra fortunae tela sinistra deae,
Ipsaque ne crebro nimium duroque malorum
90 Concidat impulsu, quo tueare cape.
Inviolabile erit manui prudentia scutum,
Opportunius hac in patiente nihil.
Hanc capiat comitem fortis patientia fidam,
Non timeat casus hac comitata graves.
95 Languet enim et tenues nequicquam in grandia vires
Obiicit et facilis lucta oriente cadit.
Deficit ut tumidis sine clavo puppis in undis,
Et sine honore manet si incomitata manet.
Ipsa quidem virtutum acies firmatque tegitque
100 Fortis et in tota dux legione praeit.
Cedet prima tamen saeva turbante procella,
Hanc nisi sedula sit concomitata ducem.
Denique vis modico complectar ut omnia verbo?
Prudens disce pati cuncta: beatus eris.
105 Nullum prorsus enim quod non patientia fortis
Leniat et vincat in sapiente malum.

open up chinks in your armour, hold a shield in your skilful right hand, a shield with which your hand can render useless whatever is hurled by your outraged enemy and can mock his hand as it vainly looks for an opening. Let your hand stave off death by nimbly moving to check all his thrusts; he will fall all the sooner through his own audacity.

But why do I detain you with this shadowy metaphor? For this battle is not to be waged by a bodily hand. Rather I will set forth the whole matter bare and unclouded. And, as for you, grasp and remember what I say, and under my leadership you will be victorious. Let the virtue Patience arm your fearless mind against the sinister weapons of the goddess Fortune; and to keep Patience herself from falling under the relentless and all too fierce assault of afflictions, take it from me how you may protect her. Your hand shall hold the inviolable shield of Prudence; nothing can be more fit for the afflicted than this virtue. Let valiant Patience take her as a faithful companion; with this companion, she need have no fear of grave calamities. For Patience grows faint and her powers are too weak to ward off great assaults; and when the struggle begins she easily gives in and falls. She gives way like a ship without a rudder in swelling seas, and she remains without honour if she remains without this companion. Patience does indeed strengthen and protect the battleline of the virtues and advances before the whole legion as its brave commander. But she is the first to yield when the storm of battle rages unless zealous Prudence accompanies this commander. Finally do you want me to put the whole matter in a nutshell? Learn to bear all things with prudent patience; then you will be blessed.

For there is no affliction which valiant Patience in a wiseman cannot alleviate and

Mobilibus neque enim fortunae subiacet ille
  Casibus aut patitur se ditione premi.
Navigat in tuto fortuna immotus utraque,
110 Nec ditante tumet nec retrahente dolet.
Numinis ardentes ridet securior iras
  Nec metuit trepidus quid vaga fata parent.
Omnia perpetitur sapiens atque omnia vincit
  Et fruitur mediis perpete pace fretis.
115 Non tam praevalidi temnunt vaga flamina montes
  Aut rident nymbos aequora vasta leves,
Quam verus dominae sapiens tonitru omne sinistrae,
  Saeviat in toto concita felle licet.
Dic age, dic toto quid eo faelicius orbe?
120 Laetior usque manet nec miser esse potest.
Nos fera fortunae saevis turbata procellis
  Aequora et assidue concutit unda salis.
Assidue tumidis miseri iactamur in undis,
  Nec sinimur placidi visere tuta soli.
125 Erramus pelago flatumque movemur ad omnem,
  Nil haeret mediis anchora missa vadis.
Blanditur si quando serenum et lenior aura,
  Fallimur, incautis turba inopina venit.
At ponti nihil esse minas, nil flamina ventum
130 Curat: adit salva littora amata rate.
Solus enim ille potest frendentibus undique fatis
  In tranquilla aevum ducere pace suum.

conquer. For he is not subject to the chops and changes of Fortune, nor does he suffer himself to be oppressed by her dominion. He sails safely, undeflected by either extreme of Fortune, neither puffing himself up when she enriches him nor lamenting when she withdraws her favours. Self-confident he laughs at the burning wrath of the goddess, and undaunted he has no fear of what the wavering Fates have in store for him. The wiseman suffers all things steadfastly and conquers all things; and even in the midst of turbulent straits, he enjoys continual peace. The unconquerable mountains have no more contempt for the wandering blasts of wind, the vast oceans find no more to mock in light showers of rain, than the true wiseman does in all the thunderclaps of the sinister lady, even if she should rage to the full heights of her fury. Tell me, I pray, tell me who in the whole world is happier than he? He is constantly joyful and can never be miserable. As for us, we are continually buffeted by the wild oceans, stirred up by the fierce storms of fortune; we are continually struck by the waves of the salty sea. We wretches are continually tossed about on the swelling waves, and we are never allowed to visit the safety of the placid shore. We wander on the ocean main, driven about by every blast; the anchor we throw out in the midst of the sea does not catch hold. If a clear sky and a gentle breeze smiles on us, we are deceived; unprepared, we are overtaken by an unexpected storm. But the wiseman cares nothing for the threats of the sea, nothing for the gusts of the winds: his vessel safely approaches the beloved shore. For he alone is able to lead his life in peace and tranquillity, however the Fates gnash their teeth all around him.

Tu quoque, quicunque es cui pax et gaudia curae,
  Discito quicquid erit temnere, disce pati.
135 Ferto aeque gelidam veri succedere brumam,
  Inque vices redeant noxque diesque suas,
Donec supremam (subducens tristia) metam
  Ponat et aethre deus te sine fine beet.

106 Certamen Erasmi atque Guielmi de tempore vernali, quod per viridantia prata alternis ex tempore luserunt anno eorum decimo nono. Nota, candide lector.

[spring 1488? / 1706]

Guielmus incipit.

Tristis hyems abiit quae flores abstulit, at nunc
  Purpureo tellus vere decore nitet.
Eras. Ipsa suo cum bruma gelu cadit horrida tristi,
  Iam properant vicibus tempora laeta suis.
5 *Guiel.* Iam violas, iam terra rosas suffundit, et omnis
  Iam viret et flore stat redimitus ager.
Eras Iam per prata novo pinguntur gramina flore,
  Arboribusque redit quam posuere comam.
Guiel. Vere nemus, volucres, campus, flores quoque cuncti,
10 Frondet, dulce canunt, ridet, olentque bene.
Eras. Frondes arboribus, ver reddit gramina campis

You also, whoever you are, who care for peace and joy, learn to scorn whatever happens, learn to suffer it patiently. Bear with equanimity the icy winter which succeeds the spring, and let the days and nights come and go in succession, until God brings the race to its close and, removing all sorrow, makes you happy forever in heaven.

106 A contest between Erasmus and Willem about springtime, which for fun they composed in alternating extemporaneous couplets out in the green meadows when they were eighteen years old. Note this point, fair-minded reader.

Willem begins.

Sad winter, which took away the flowers, departs, but now in springtime the ground is resplendent with crimson beauty.

Erasmus Now that winter fails, for all his bristling and gloomy ice, a time of joy hastens to take its turn.

Willem Now the earth strews violets, now she pours forth roses; and all the fields flourish with greenery and stand wreathed with flowers.

Erasmus Now the grass throughout the meadows is coloured with fresh flowers, and the trees regain the locks which they shed.

Willem In the springtime the groves, the birds, the fields, and also all the flowers, are putting forth leaves, singing sweetly, laughing, and smelling sweet.

Erasmus Spring brings leaves back to the trees, grass to the fields, and it

Et laetam multo flore venustat humum.
Guiel. Purpurea capite cinctum venit ecce corona
Ver, in quo gaudet terra decore novo.
15 *Eras.* Iam nova per vacuos consurgunt gramina campos,
Vestiturque modo terra decore novo.
Guiel. Omne suum per triste gelu posuit decus arbos,
Sed postquam rediit ver, rediere comae.
Eras. Dura quibus viduarat hyems, cum flore virentes
20 Arboribus redeunt vere tepente comae.
Guiel. Propter triste rubis frigus decor omnis abibat,
Ast ubi ver venit irrubuere rosis.
Eras. Arida quae longo latuit sub frigore tellus
Vere refert vultu florida quaeque novo.
25 *Guiel.* Arboribus fluxere comae prae frigore, sed ver
Flores atque comas reddidit arboribus.
Eras. Frondibus arentes renovantur in arbore rami,
Caepere ut vicibus verna nitere suis.
Guiel. Stabat operta nive, sed veris tempore laeto
30 Fronde stat et densis arbor amicta comis.
Eras. Triste abeunte gelu telluris amaena iuventus
Iam redit et flore fit rediviva novo.

adorns the happy soil with abundant flowers.

Willem Lo, spring comes, his head wreathed with a crimson crown; in springtime the earth rejoices in fresh beauty.

Erasmus Now the fresh grass springs up in the bare fields, and the earth is now clothed with fresh beauty.

Willem During the melancholy frosts the trees shed all their beauty, but now that spring has returned their locks have returned.

Erasmus The verdant locks and the blossoms of the trees, stripped away by harsh winter, return with the warmth of spring.

Willem Because of the gloomy cold all beauty departed from the blackberry bushes, but when spring came they flushed with rosy blossoms.

Erasmus The dry ground, which long lay hidden under the cold, looks renewed in the springtime and restores all kinds of flowers.

Willem Their locks drifted away from the trees because of the cold, but spring has brought back blossoms as well as locks to the trees.

Erasmus The dry branches of the trees are renewed with leaves as the springtime begins to take its turn to shine.

Willem The trees stood covered with snow, but now in the joyous spring season they stand covered with foliage and clad in their own thick locks.

Erasmus Now that the gloomy ice is disappearing, the ground is restored to its lovely youth and is again enlivened with fresh flowers.

Guiel. O quam dulcisono resonant iam murmure sylvae!
  Quos posuit cantus vere resumit avis.
35 *Eras.* Per maestum taciturna gelu, iam tempore verno
  Dulce resumit avis exhilarata melos.
Guiel. Caeruleis citius Phaebus consurgit ab undis
  Atque mari lassos tardius abdit equos.
Eras. Iam dirae cessere hyemes, laetissima terris
40 Lux redit et vacuis gramina reddit agris.
Guiel. Iam nox caeruleis citius caelo avolat alis,
  Et Phaebi citius promitur axis aquis.
Eras. Vere leves Zephiris spirant melioribus aurae,
  Clarius et roseum lux agit alma diem.
45 *Guiel.* Quae nuper nive tecta fuit, iam vere tepenti
  Solvitur et tellus stat redimita comis.
Eras. Rursum sylva comis vestitur, gramine tellus,
  Invisit clausam vernus ubi imber humum.
Guiel. Qui concretus erat bruma amnis solvitur, at nunc
50 Vestitur nuda ripa decore novo.
Eras. Flumina iucundo currunt resoluta susurro,
  Frigore quae quondam strinxerat acris hyems.
Guiel. Alma Venus, nunc gignit humus gratos tibi flores,

Willem Oh, how the woods are now resounding with sweet-sounding murmurs! The birds, which had ceased to sing, take up their song again in the springtime.

Erasmus The birds, which fell silent in the cheerless cold, now grow merry in the spring season and take up their sweet tunes once more.

Willem Phoebus rises earlier from the dark-blue waves and drives away his weary steeds later into the sea.

Erasmus Now cruel winter has gone away: most joyful light returns to the earth and restores the grass to the bare fields.

Willem Now night flies more swiftly from the sky on her dark-blue wings, and Phoebus' chariot arises sooner from the waters.

Erasmus In the springtime the mild west wind wafts his light breezes, and the cherishing light brings forth the rosy day more brightly.

Willem The earth, which was formerly covered with snow, now thaws in the warm springtime and stands wreathed in its tresses.

Erasmus Once more the woods are garbed with their tresses, as is the ground with grass, when the spring showers have visited the ice-bound soil.

Willem The stream that was frozen by winter has melted, and now the bare bank is clothed with fresh beauty.

Erasmus The rivers, which harsh winter had once bound with its cold, are loosened and flow with a pleasant whispering sound.

Willem Bountiful Venus, the soil now brings forth your favourite flowers, and the

		Verque tuas roseo pingit honore genas.
55	*Eras.*	Iamiam florigero redimitur gramine pratum,
		Miratur frondes sylva decora novas.
	Guiel.	Ha, quam grata mihi sunt veris tempora, quae pro
		Grandine dant imbrem, pro nive rosque cadit.
	Eras.	Cui non vere graves curae sit ponere curas?
60		Ecce decore nitent cuncta creata novo.
	Guiel.	Quas clausas servavit humus ver elicit herbas,
		Et gaudet campus tectus honore novo.
	Eras.	Vere tepet tellus nivibus laetata solutis,
		Quae latuit matris panditur herba sinu.
65	*Guiel.*	In sylvis cantus ferit aethera, prata nemusque
		Sparguntur flore, rore aperitur humus.
	Eras.	Vere novo terris sese exerit herba solutis,
		Purpureum fundit aspera spina decus.
	Guiel.	Veris ubi tellus persensit nuda teporem,
70		Exiliunt terris gramina picta rosis.
	Eras.	Vere patescit humus partu faecunda virenti,
		Summittit gremio florida pressa suo.
	Guiel.	Nondum solis equi consurgunt aequore vasto,

spring tints your cheeks with rosy beauty.

Erasmus Now the meadow is wreathed in grass and flowers; the beautiful woods are amazed at their fresh leaves.

Willem Ah, how charming I find the springtime, which gives us showers instead of hail, when dew falls instead of snow.

Erasmus Who does not take care to put aside heavy cares in the springtime? Behold, all creatures are resplendent with fresh beauty.

Willem The spring brings forth the green blades which had been shut up in the soil, and the fields rejoice, covered with fresh beauty.

Erasmus In the springtime the ground grows warm, rejoicing that the snow has melted; the green shoot which lay hidden in its mother's bosom springs forth.

Willem In the woods, song strikes the sky, the meadows and groves are sprinkled with flowers, the soil is loosened by the dew.

Erasmus In the fresh springtime the green shoots thrust up out of the loosened earth; the harsh thorn pours forth its crimson glory.

Willem When the bare ground feels the warmth of spring, the grass, coloured with roses, springs from the earth.

Erasmus In the springtime the fertile earth opens up in a birth of greenery, and she brings forth the flowers concealed in her own womb.

Willem The horses of the sun have not yet risen from the vast expanse of ocean,

Et iam sub summo culmine cantat avis.

75 *Eras.* Tempore veris humus blanditur olentibus herbis,
Et tegitur foliis arbor onusta suis.

Guiel. Flora tepore suo tam delectat roseum ver,
Tristis nos hyemis reddat ut immemores.

Eras. Mortua sese aperit redivivo germine tellus,
80 Cessit ubi pulsum vere tepente gelu.

Guiel. Arboribus coma, agris flores, avibus quoque cantus
Vere redit, tristis vere recedit hyems.

Eras. Pingit gramineum florum decus undique campum,
Candida purpureis lilia mixta rosis.

85 *Guiel.* Sylva comis et terra rosis redimitur, et amnis
Qui gessit currus en modo vela gerit.

Eras. Vere novo apricus vestitur gramine campus
Et florum venere multicolore nitet.

Guiel. Quae brumae sub luce solet vix linquere nidum,
90 Iam cantu volucris praevenit ecce diem.

Eras. Ver placidum cunctis sparsit sua munera terris;
Gramine prata virent, gramina flore nitent.

Guiel. Vere suum citius Phaebus caput exerit undis,
Gratior et laetum lux agit alma diem.

and already the birds are singing from the highest eaves.

Erasmus In the season of spring the soil allures us with fragrant herbs, and the trees are covered and burdened by their own leaves.

Willem Flora so delights the rosy spring with her warmth that she makes us forget the gloomy winter.

Erasmus The dead ground opens up as the sprouts come alive again, once the ice has been forced away by the warmth of spring.

Willem In the springtime, tresses return to the trees, flowers to the fields, and songs to the birds; in the springtime gloomy winter withdraws.

Erasmus The beautiful flowers colour the grassy fields on all sides; the white lilies are mingled with the crimson roses.

Willem The wood is wreathed with its tresses and the earth with roses; and the stream that bore wagons, lo, it now bears sailboats.

Erasmus In the fresh springtime the sunny fields are clothed with grass and are resplendent with the many-coloured beauty of the flowers.

Willem The bird that hardly left its nest in the winter light, lo, now it anticipates the daytime with its song.

Erasmus The mild spring scatters its gifts over the whole earth; the meadows are green with grass, the grass is resplendent with flowers.

Willem In the springtime Phoebus lifts his head sooner from the waves, and the cherishing light brings forth the joyful daytime more charmingly.

95 *Eras.* Gramine terra viret, leni ruit unda susurro,
Ac apis in flore mella legendo strepit.
⟨*Guiel.*⟩ Flore nitet campus, ornatur frondea sylva,
Ac volucrum cantu tecta nemusque sonant.
Eras. Frondet vere nemus, vestitur et herbida tellus,
100 Picta canit volucris, florida lustrat apis,
Gratius et roseo sol inficit aethera curru,
Blanditur liquida vitreus amnis aqua,
Mitior aura strepit. Cui florida ducitur aetas,
Tu quoque pone animos vere monente graves.

107 Metrum asclepiadeicum coryambicum, constans quarto glyconico, in laudem beatissimi Gregorii papae

[early 1491? / 1706]

Nunc et terra simul caelicus et chorus
Gaudens hymnisonis concinat organis,
Cum lux grata refert festa Gregorii
Mundo gaudia praesulis.
5 Et tu, summe, tuis, pastor, ab aethere
Adsis o placidus rite canentibus.
Laudes lingua foris nostra sonet tuas,
Intus mens iubilet pia.
Tu primum ingenui sanguinis immemor,
10 Secli temptor, opum spretor inanium,
Abiectis croceis prodigus omnium
Christo nudulus advolas.
Te quum Roma petit anxia praesulem,
Tu tantum fugiens culmen ad invia

Erasmus The earth is green with grass, the waters run with a gentle whisper, and the bee hums as it gathers honey among the flowers.

⟨*Willem*⟩ The fields are resplendent with flowers, the woods are adorned with leaves, and the rooftops and groves resound with the song of the birds.

Erasmus In the springtime the grove puts forth leaves, the ground is clothed with green shoots, the brightly coloured bird sings, and the bee roams among the flowers, and the sun in his rosy chariot charmingly tints the air, the glassy river allures us with its clear water, the breeze murmurs gently. You also who are in the flower of your lifetime, admonished by the spring, put away feelings of melancholy.

107 A poem in asclepiadean metre, with choriambs, every fourth line being glyconic, in praise of the most blessed Pope Gregory

Now let the earth and the heavenly choir together sing hymns with joyful tongues, now that the cheerful light brings to the world once more the happy feast of Pope Gregory.

And you, O exalted shepherd, look gently from heaven on your servants duly singing their hymns. May our tongues sound your praises outwardly; inwardly may our devout minds rejoice.

First of all, you ignored your aristocratic birth, scorned the world, spurned empty riches, and throwing off your saffron garments, giving up everything, you fled to Christ naked and simple.

When Rome in her distress sought you out to be her bishop, you shunned such a lofty

15 Saltus antra volas, sed minime lates,
Flamma proditus indice.
Ergo summa quidem scandis humillimus,
Non extollit honor, non diademata,
Sed te cura gregis sedula, maxime
20 Pastor, sollicitat tui.
Cui pratis fidei nulla salubria
Vitae deficiunt te duce pabula,
Dum quem voce doces mystica disserens
Et vita simul erudis.
25 Plebem, summe, tuam protege, praesulum,
Praedonemque cavis qui tua faucibus
Quaerens quem rapiat lustrat ovilia,
Ne cuiquam noceat, veta.
Sit laus digna patri patris et unico,
30 Almo sit parilis gloria pneumati,
Indivisa quibus numinis unitas
Est sub nomine triplici.

108 Epigramma de quatuor novissimis [early 1491? / 1706]

Mortis amara dies, metuendi iudicis ira
Et Phlegetontei stridula flamma lacus,
Denique Iherusalem luctus ignara supernae
Gaudia, non finem, non habitura modum:
5 Haec si sollicito semper sub pectore volvas,
Non capient animum turpia quaeque tuum.
Quicquid et ante tibi grave et intolerabile visum est,
Iam dices facile, iam tibi dulce putes.
Ipsa sed et nebula citius fugientia mundi
10 Gaudia tristitiam duxeris esse gravem.

pinnacle and fled to a cave in the pathless woods, but you did not succeed in hiding, for a flame betrayed you and pointed you out.

And so you climbed to the heights by being the most humble. What exalted you was not honour or crowns; but rather your concern, O greatest of shepherds, was the zealous care of your flock.

Under your leadership, in the meadows of the faith, they had no lack of the wholesome food of life, for you taught them with your voice, explaining the sacred mysteries, and at the same time you instructed them by your life.

O greatest of bishops, protect your people and prevent anyone from being harmed by the beast of prey that prowls among your sheepfolds with gaping jaws, seeking someone to seize.

Fitting praise be given to the Father, and to the only begotten of the Father, and equal glory be to the Spirit, the giver of life, who are united indivisibly in their divinity under the diversity of a triple name.

108 An epigram on the four last things

The bitter day of death, the anger of the dreadful judge, the hissing flames of the lake of Phlegethon, and finally the joys of the heavenly Jerusalem, joys beyond all sorrow, joys which have no end, no bounds: if you carefully and constantly turn these things over in your heart, your mind will not be invaded by shameful desires. And what before seemed to you burdensome and intolerable, you will then say it is easy, you will then find it sweet. But the joys of the world, which flee even more swiftly than mist, you will think to be sad and burdensome.

109 Carmen asclepiadeum coryambicum, quarto glyconico. Ad amicum suum

[early 1488? / 1706]

Non semper faciem nubila caelicam
Abscondunt madidis obvia molibus,
Non usque implacido defluus aethere
    Imber vexat humum gravis.
5 Nec semper crepitans Africus excita
Attollit tumidis aequora fluctibus,
Sed nec continue mota procacibus
    Stridet sylva Aquilonibus.
Nec semper steriles nix tegit alta agros,
10 Aut totis gelidae flumina mensibus
Constringunt glaties, aut viduum suis
    Maeret triste nemus comis.
Dura abscedit hyems florigeri vice
Veris, prisca redit post Boream asperum
15 Arbustis species et solitus vagis
    Cursus redditur amnibus.
Horrentem placidus lumen amabile
Post umbram revehit Phaebus, et aethera
Alternis vicibus nox habet et dies
20   Pacti faedere perpeti.
Aequis cuncta modis, astra, salum et solum,
Alterna ut maneat quod requies levat,
Natura atque deus provida temperat,
    Mulcens quod gravat otio.
25 Me vero usque dolor, me furor et labor
Consumunt miserum, nec requiem meis
Nec, proh, saeva modum fata sinunt malis,
    Addunt tristia tristibus.
Quo nam, quo superum nescio tam gravi
30 Olim magna deum numina crimine
Offendi, ut Stygium vel puerum improba
    Cogant supplicium pati.

109 A poem in asclepiads, with choriambs, every fourth line being glyconic. To his friend

Clouds charged with masses of water do not always hide and block off the face of the heavens; heavy rain falling from the relentless sky does not constantly torment the ground.

The whistling south-west wind does not always disturb the surface of the sea and raise up swelling waves, nor do the woods continually shake and scream in the arrogant blasts of the north wind.

Deep snow does not always cover the barren fields, and the icy cold does not fetter the rivers for whole months on end, nor does the sad grove mourn endlessly for its lost tresses.

A hard winter departs with the return of spring and its flowers; after the harsh north winds the trees regain their former beauty, and the rivers wander once more in their accustomed courses.

After the frightful shades of night, mild Phoebus brings back the lovely light, and night and day claim the air by turns, holding to a perpetual convenant.

God and provident nature temper all things in equal measure – the stars, the sea, and the earth – relieving with rest what is burdensome, so that they may be permanently sustained by intervening periods of relief.

But as for me, I am continually consumed by grief; in my misery I am consumed by mad passion and hardship. The cruel Fates allow no relief and, alas, no end to my afflictions; they heap sorrow upon sorrow.

I know not by what crime, by what grievous crime in the past I have so offended the mighty powers of the gods above that they should unjustly impose the torments of hell on such a youth as I.

Post umbrosa dies reddita milies
Succeditque frequens bruma caloribus
35 Et campis gelidae saepe patentibus
Surgunt ac pereunt nives.
Nec fit nostra suo tempore mitior
Cura, aut mente cadunt sollicitudines
Maestae, aut luminibus tempore lachrymae
40 Discunt parcere turgidis.
Et iam deficerem ni, iuvenum optime,
O spes, o animae dimidium meae,
Lenimen miseris dulce doloribus,
Me praesens recrees. Vale.

110 Ode dicolos tetrastrophos hendecasyllaba sapphica. Paean divae Mariae, atque de incarnatione verbi

[April–May 1499 / 1706]

Huc ades pernici, age, Musa, gressu,
Callida aurato resonare plectro.
Mitte dilectas Heliconis oras
Castaliamque.
5 Pone serpentes hederas, odoram
Liliis nectens niveis coronam:
Quaeritat, frondes fugiens prophanas,
Lilia virgo.
Tu Sophoclaeo potius cothurno
10 Digna quae pleno recinaris ore,
Ne lyrae nostrae tenuem repelle,
Diva, Camenam.
Cuncta te celso residentem Olympho et
Prole divina decies beatam
15 Concio cantu celebrat canoro
Caelicolarum.
Te pii vates et apostolorum
Regius laudat dominam senatus,
Te sacerdotum chorus et phalanges
20 Sanguine clarae.
Candidae te unam, dea, virginum quae
Praevium semper comitantur agnum

Time after time, day returns after the dark, and winter repeatedly follows upon hot summer days, and icy snow often builds up in the open fields and then vanishes.

But my anxiety never has its time of relief, gloomy cares never leave my mind, no season teaches my swollen eyes to cease from weeping.

I would long since have wasted away, if you, best of youths, O my hope, O half of my soul, the sweet solace of my misery and grief, did not by your presence restore me. Farewell.

110 A sapphic, hendecasyllabic ode, containing two kinds of lines, in four-line strophes. A paean to St Mary and on the incarnation of the Word

Come hither, O Muse, come fleet-footed, O Muse skilled in making music with your plectrum of gold, leave behind the Castalian fountain and the beloved clime of Helicon.

Put aside the winding ivy and weave a fragrant crown of lilies white as snow. The Virgin shuns fronds that are profane and looks for lilies.

Though you are worthy of the buskin of Sophocles so that you might be celebrated in full and lofty song, do not, O holy lady, refuse the thin strain of my lyre.

In your dwelling-place in the heights of heaven, the whole host of heavenly inhabitants celebrates you in resounding song as the thrice-blessed mother of divine offspring.

The holy prophets and the royal senate of the apostles praise you as their lady – so too the chorus of priests and the ranks of those who are illustrious for shedding their blood.

The white chorus of the virgins, who always attend the lamb going before them, praises

Caeteris psalli vetito choreae
    Carmine laudant.
25 Cuncta quid pergam memorare? Flexo
Poplite aeternis modulantur hymnis
Angeli te caelicolaeque cuncti
    Caeligenaeque.
Quin et invisi nigra Styx Averni
30 Plebe cum tota Phlegetontis atri
Te tremit, per te populata mortis
    Bellua pallet.
Laudat invito Rhadamantus ore
Gnosius, centum tumidae colubris
35 En tuum numen metuunt sorores,
    Virgo Maria.
Flecte age huc, quaeso, faciles ocellos.
Non vel in toto (meritoque sane)
Mutus hymnorum superest tuorum
40   Angulus orbe.
Ustus Eoo Nabathaeus axe,
Qua recens ponto exerit ora Titan,
Dedicat supplex tibi grata fumis
    Vota Sabaeis.
45 Luteae tellus propior quadrigae
Cerulum Phaebi subeuntis aequor
En suis blandas tibi promit odas,
    Virgo, sacellis.
Arduus nec qua radiat borei
50 Syderis vertex, neque semper Austro
Permadens tellus tacita est modorum,
    Diva, tuorum.
Quippe tu summi decus unum Olymphi,
Tu potens vindex necis atque ademptae
55 Seculo toti, dea, vendicatrix
    Unica vitae.
Tuque nequicquam saniem trilingui,
Luridum virus, iacientis ore
Candidis calcas pedibus colubri
60   Sibila colla.
Aureum vincis speciosa solem,
Astra divino superas decore,

only you, O divine lady, in a song that others are forbidden to chant.

Why should I go on to include every group? On bended knee the angels and all the inhabitants and all the progeny of heaven sing eternal hymns to you.

Indeed, the black Styx down in hateful hell and all the masses in dark Phlegethon tremble before you. The monster of death whom you despoiled grows pale at the thought of you.

Rhadamanthus of Crete praises you with an unwilling voice; lo, the sisters swollen with numberless serpents fear your divine power, O Virgin Mary.

Come, turn your kind eyes hither, I beg you. Nowhere in the whole world – and rightly so – is there a nook or cranny that is silent, singing no hymn to you.

The Arab, burned dark by the oriental sun where Titan first lifts up his face from the sea, humbly offers you his prayers, sweetened with fumes of Sabaean incense.

The lands quite near to where the rose-streaked chariot of Phoebus goes down under the dark-blue ocean, lo, in their chapels they send forth sweet hymns to you, O Virgin.

And where the north star shines high in the heavens, and where the wet south wind keeps the ground forever moist, there is no lack of melodies sung, O holy lady, to you.

For you are the unique glory of the highest heavens; you alone, O divine lady, had the power to revenge our death and to claim redress for the life that was stolen from the whole world.

And you are the one who treads with white feet on the neck of the hissing serpent, vainly spitting gore and yellowish poison from his triple-tongued mouth.

In your beauty you surpass the golden sun; in your divine splendour you overcome the

Roscidae cedunt tibi luculenta
    Cornua Phaebes
65 Ipsa, quam celsus speculator ille
Viderat lunam pedibus prementem,
Syderum ingenti rutilam corona
    Soleque cinctam.
Providi quondam cecinere vates
70 Te novum casto genus edituram
Ventre, collapsis nova quo redirent
    Secula terris.
Regis aeterni fore te parentem
Deliae cantant liquido Sybillae
75 Scripta, membranis temere caducis
    Credita, virgo.
Legis obscuro veteris ab aevo
Praeviis iam tunc venientis umbris
Multa te patrum minimeque mendax
80 Lusit imago.
Sylva monstrabat humilis rubeti
Non adurenti glomerata flamma
Te dei salvo fieri parentem,
    Virgo, pudore.
85 Caelicum quae clauserat arca manna
Te deum castae docuit sub alvi
Pabulum vitae fore conditurам,
    Diva, sacello.
Virga te partu nimis insolenti
90 Et ferax gratae nucis atque florum,
Rore te siccis madidum notabat
    Vellus in arvis.
Et tui quondam tulit Hester umbram,
Mille Iudeis mala molientis
95 Splendide vindex, et in omne Iudith
    Nobilis aevum.
Porta te vatis notat irreclusa,
Fronte quae terras renitens Eoas
Spectat adversa, minime nisi uni
100 Pervia regi.
Hisce te, virgo, voluit figuris
Praecini vasti fabricator orbis,

stars; even the bright horns of dewy Phoebe yield to you,

whom that lofty seer beheld pressing the moon beneath your feet, shining under a vast crown of stars, and robed with the sun.

Prophetic bards long ago sang of how you would bring forth a new manner of offspring from your chaste womb, one which would bring back a new age to a world in decay.

The writings of Apollo's Sibyl, which were rashly entrusted to fallen leaves, clearly chanted that you would be the mother of the eternal king.

In the dim era of the Old Law many altogether truthful images of the fathers alluded to you, foreshadowing your coming even then.

The thicket of the low bush, encompassed by a flame which did not burn it, showed that you would become the mother of God, O Virgin, while still keeping your chastity.

The ark which enclosed the manna from heaven taught that you, holy lady, would hide God, the food of life, in the chapel of your chaste womb.

The rod which, by an extraordinary birth, brought forth flowers and handsome nuts, the fleece soaked with dew though the ground around it was dry, these things were signs of you.

Both Esther, who took splendid vengeance on the man who was plotting to inflict numberless woes on the Jews, and Judith, famous throughout all ages, foreshadowed you long ago.

The prophet's unopened gate, which shone out over against the lands of the east and was to be entered only by the king, is a sign of you.

In these figures the maker of the whole wide world desired that you, O Virgin, should be

Non quidem vanis, comitante vero
    Ocyus umbras.
105 Namque dum scisso periens Olympho
Lucifer praeceps grege cum tumenti
Fulminis ritu rueret sub atrae
    Tartara noctis,
Aetheris tantae miserens ruinae
110 Conditor 'lapsum decet' inquit 'agmen
Suffici, prorsus reparanda secti
    Portio caeli.'
Fingitur rubro rude plasma limo:
Viva divino bonus ille flatu
115 Indidit post haec opifex inerti
    Semina massae.
Inde per sedes nemorum beatas
Iussit apricis habitare campis,
Dulcibus quae quadrifluus scatebris
120   Irrigat amnis.
Illic aeternum redolente vere
Dulcibus semper renitet rosetis,
Mollibus semper violis iniquae
    Nescia brumae
125 Terra, nec gratis viduantur unquam
Frondibus sylvae nimium feraces,
Nec deest unquam viridis tumenti
    Pampinus uvae.
Spiritum spargit folium suavem, et
130 Cinnamum et nardus patulis amica
Naribus; semper lachrymant virenti
    Balsama surclo.
Hisce praefecit pater ille regnis
Quem modo fingens hominem crearat:
135 'Haec tuis, Adam, moderanda trado,'
    Dixit, 'habenis.
Liber ad quidvis tulerit libido
Dexteram mittas dominam licebit,
His modo ramis fuge fac nocivos
140   Carpere faetus.
Haec tibi duram paritura mortem
Mala tu quaqua violaris hora,

foretold, and they are not empty shadows, since the foreshadowings were quickly linked with the reality.

For when Lucifer, who destroyed himself by splitting heaven into factions, had fallen with his proud flock like a lightning bolt down to the black night of Tartarus,

the creator, struck with pity at the loss caused by such a great downfall in heaven, said: 'The fallen ranks must be replenished; the part of heaven that was cut off must immediately be restored.'

He formed a rough shape out of red clay, and afterwards with his divine breath that good workmaster implanted the seeds of life in the inert mass.

Then he bade him live in his dwelling-place among happy groves and sunny fields, watered by the sweet freshets of a fourfold river.

Forever spring gives off fresh odours there. There the earth, always decked with bright beds of sweet roses, always adorned with tender violets, knows nothing of harsh winter;

the groves, hung with superabundant fruit, are never stripped of their handsome leaves; green tendrils never fail to support the swelling grapes.

The leaves dispense lovely fragrance, and also the cinnamon and the nard, which pleases the flaring nostril; the green boughs always weep their balm.

Over this realm the Father set the man he had just shaped and created, saying: 'These things I give to you, Adam, to curb and rule them under your sway.

'I permit you to extend your lordly right hand freely wherever your desires lead you. Only from these branches make sure that you do not pluck the harmful fruit.

'In whatever hour you break this command and eat these apples, they will bring forth cruel

Ah tegunt quantos tibi blandienti
    Cortice luctus.'
145 Non tulit tantos stomachans honores
Viperae livor; vetuisse mira
Arte contendit male perdito suc-
    cedere caelo.
'Usque quo,' dixit, 'miseri dolosis
150 Creduli iussis similem supremo
Numini vitam fugitis daturos
    Carpere fructus?'
Subdolis, eheu, facilis colubri
Suasibus coniunx nimiumque mollis
155 Credidit, vidit, tenuit, momordit,
    Occidit atque.
Falsa tum post haec socium fefellit
Coniugem coniunx; tenero ille amori
Cessit, accepit, tenuit, momordit,
160 Occidit atque.
O dies atro numeranda semper
Calculo, o semper lachrymanda, toti
Quae potes seclo, potes una tantos
    Aedere luctus.
165 Nam dehinc totam vitiata radix
Serpit in prolem, male temperantum
Posteri iam morte luunt avorum
    Facta nepotes.
Et quibus caelos opifex pararat,
170 Iam (dolor) saevis sua colla loris
Demonum nexi rapiuntur imas
    Mortis ad umbras.
Quid pater tanto faceret tumultu?
Plasmatis certe proprii benignum
175 Paenitet plasten, hominis gementem
    Flebile fatum.
'Ecce dum caelum reparare terra
Pergimus,' dixit, 'simul hanc et illud,

death. Ah, what grief lies concealed for you under the seductive rind!'

The envious serpent, angry and grudging the great honours bestowed on mankind, strove with marvellous skill to prevent them from succeeding to the place in heaven which he had wickedly lost.

'How long,' he said, 'will you continue to be miserably taken in by this deceitful command and to refrain from plucking fruit that will give you life like that of the highest Godhead?'

Easily persuaded, alas, by the cunning words of the serpent, Adam's wife was all too compliant; she believed, looked, held, bit, and fell.

After that, the spouse who had been deceived deceived the spouse who was her companion; out of tender love he yielded, accepted, held, bit, and fell.

O day always to be reckoned as black, always to be remembered with tears, you alone had the power, you alone were able to bring down on the whole world such a heap of misery!

For from then on, the vitiated root spread its infection through all its offspring: the descendants of these unrestrained parents now pay with their deaths for the deeds of their ancestors.

And those for whom the workmaster had prepared heaven, now (Oh the sorrow of it!) they have their necks bound with the cruel thongs of the devils and are dragged down to the deepest shadows of death.

What was the Father to do about this great rebellion? Certainly the kind maker was displeased with what he himself had made; he groaned at the lamentable fate of mankind.

'Behold, while I was proceeding to restore heaven by means of earth,' he said, 'sin, alas,

Veh, parens mortis, simili ruina
180 Noxa peremit,
Dispari longe tamen hic ministro
Hausit infandum colubro venenum,
Ambitus alter stimulante nullo
Auctor iniqui
185 Factus, aeternum meritas necesse est
Ut luat paenas: scatet e medullis
Abditum vulnus, fugit huius omnem
Plaga medelam.
Porro quem stravit peregrinus astus
190 Non sua iustum est ope surrigatur:
Arte pellectus redimendus arte
Aeque aliena.'
Summus hic summi genitus parentis,
Fons inexhaustus sophiae perhennis,
195 Prompsit arcanos patrio latentes
Pectore census.
'Arte subreptus revehendus,' inquit,
'Arte, non dextra dominante, mortis
Ortui respondeat ut salutis
200 Forma reductae.
Et caro sane redimenda carne.
Dira ligno pernicies profecta est:
Sanitas aeque reditura ligno ac
Stipite sacro.
205 Aedidit vero quia sibilante
Vipera lethum mulier, decenter
Faemina rursus revehenda flante
Numine vita.
Mors item adversa populanda morte est,
210 Atque curandus dolor est dolore,
Denique obiecto merito fugandum
Vulnere vulnus.
Sed quid? En omnis vitio laborat
Aemulans patrem soboles avito,

the progenitor of death, destroyed both one and the other by a similar downfall;

'but the downfall of man was far different, since he drank in the abominable poison through the ministry of the serpent; the other was not instigated by anyone else but became the source of his own wicked pride.

'Thus it is necessary that he should suffer his deserved punishment for all eternity: his hidden wound festers in the very marrow, his gash refuses all remedies.

'Moreover, it is not right that one who fell through the wiles of a stranger should be lifted up through his own resources; he who was entrapped by cunning should be redeemed by cunning likewise not his own.'

At this point the almighty Son of the almighty Father, the inexhaustible fountain of unending wisdom, brought forth the secret riches hidden in his Father's heart.

'He who was artfully snatched away must be brought back artfully, not by the power of a lordly right hand, so that the manner in which salvation is restored may correspond to the origin of death.

'And flesh should surely be redeemed by flesh. Cruel death came from a tree; health will rightly be restored by the wood of a sacred trunk.

'But because a woman, tempted by the hissing serpent, brought forth death, it is fitting that a woman, through the breath of the divine Spirit, should bring back life again.

'Likewise, death should be undone by having a death set against it, and pain should be cured by pain, and finally wounds should rightly be put to flight by confronting them with wounds.

'But what about this? See, the entire offspring, by imitating their father, labour under the ancestral vice. And God does not

The Annunciation
Painting by Jan van Eyck on the outer wings of the Ghent altarpiece
Photo ACL, by permission of Institut Royal du Patrimoine
Artistique, Brussels

215 Nec mori novit deitas, acerbi
Nescia fati.
Ergo cui partes scelus expiandi
Demus humanum? Pereat necesse est
Plasma, ni certe Deus ipse tollat
220 Vincula mortis.
Et quid? An nostri moriens imago
Noctis aeternas luitura paenas?
Quid Dei mentem fuit indidisse
Ore capacem?
225 Illa de multis via restat una:
Carne miscenda est deitas caduca.
Summus humani deus ambiendus
Corporis umbra.'
Filii blando pater ore dictis
230 Annuens, 'qui consilium,' inquit, 'aequum
Protulit, facti sit et author idem
Auxiliique.'
Hic tui, virgo, thalamum pudicum
Ventris aeterni sibi dedicavit
235 Numinis sermo, placido pudoris
Captus odore.
Ocior vento aut celeri sagitta
Labitur caelo paranymphus alto
Moxque secrete veneranda visit
240 Tecta puellae.
Hinc novas adfert Gabriel salutes.
Illa suspecto tremefacta vultu
Paululum insuetas tacito volutat
Pectore voces.
245 Ille sed vultu radians amico,
Proprio signans Mariae vocablo,
Lenibus dictis trepidos ademit
Virginis aestus.
'Cur,' ait, 'faelix, rapit ora, virgo,
250 Anxii pallor socius timoris?

know how to die, knows nothing of that bitter fate.

'Therefore, to whom can we assign the mission of expiating the sin of mankind? What God has shaped must certainly perish unless God himself takes away the bonds of death.

'What then? Shall our own image die and be punished by a never-ending night? What did it signify that the mouth of God breathed into him a mind capable of understanding?

'Of the many ways only this one remains: the Godhead must be mingled with fleeting flesh. Almighty God must be encompassed and shadowed by a human body.'

Agreeing with the words spoken so persuasively by his Son, the Father said: 'Let him who proposed the just plan likewise put it into action by giving the help needed.'

At this point, O Virgin, the Speech of the eternal Godhead, much taken by the gentle fragrance of your chastity, consecrated to himself the chaste bridal-chamber of your womb.

Faster than the wind, swifter than an arrow, the best man of the bridegroom swept down from the heights of heaven, and soon he secretly paid his visit to the venerable house of the girl.

Then Gabriel made his unparalleled salutation. The maiden, trembling as she looked up at his face, was silent for a little while, turning over in her heart the extraordinary words.

But he, his face shining with friendship, addressed her by her own name, Mary, and with mild words calmed the tumult in the virgin's breast.

'Why,' he said, 'is your face, blessed virgin, suddenly overspread by pallor, the companion of uneasy fear? Why, I beseech you, are your

Cur decens, oro, teneras reliquit
　　Purpura malas?
Ne time, iussus venio superni
Patris interpres. Capies in alvo
255 Perditi Iesum generis salutem
　　Tuque vicissim
Ipsius mundo paries parentem,
Regiae stirpis generosa proles,
Tu Nazareum paritura Iesse
260 　　Virgula florem.
Quo, rogas, pacto? Fuge suspicari
Carnis amplexus geniive nexus,
Illecebrosi fuge suspicari
　　Faedera lecti.
265 Finge ne taedas tibi nuptiales,
Casta sed verbum paritura verbo es.
Spiritus fies rutilante sancti
　　Numine faeta.
Virgo faecunda et genitrix pudica,
270 Nec tibi faetus rapiet pudorem,
Crede, nec salvus pudor abnegabit
　　Matris honorem.
Ut iubar solis liquidum penetrat
Nec secat vitrum, penetrabit alvum
275 Filius, sed non temerabit aucti
　　Claustra pudoris.
Fundit ut suaves redolens vapores
Lilium laeso minime nitore,
Haud secus divam pariēs, Maria,
280 　　Integra prolem.'
Credit oraclo facili superno
Aure. Natalem repetens Olymphum
Gabriel pictis liquidum secabat
　　Aethera pennis.
285 Nil morae, summis citus en ab astris
E sinu Christus rutilat superno,
Labitur sacram in tacitus fidelis
　　Virginis alvum.
O stupor mentis novitasque rerum!

tender cheeks bereft of the crimson colour which so becomes them?

'Do not be afraid. I come as a messenger at the command of the Father above. You will receive in your womb Jesus, the salvation of mankind that is lost, and then in turn

'you will bring into the world its very creator. Noble offspring of royal stock, rod of Jesse, you will put forth the flower of Nazareth.

'By what means? you ask. Have no fear of fleshly embraces or generative couplings. Have no fear of the contractual duties of the alluring bed.

'Do not imagine that there will be bridal torches for you. Still chaste, you are to bring forth the Word by a word. You will conceive by the divine light of the Holy Spirit.

'O fertile virgin and virgin mother, the fruit of your womb will not take away your chastity, believe me, nor will the preservation of your chastity deprive you of the honour of motherhood.

'As a sun-ray penetrates clear glass without breaking it, so the Son will penetrate your womb, but he will not violate the gates of your exalted chastity.

'As a fragrant lily pours forth sweet odours with no injury to its shining beauty, just so will you, Mary, remain inviolate when you bring forth your divine offspring.'

She readily believed the oracle she had heard from above. Gabriel, returning to his native home in heaven, clove the liquid air with his bright-coloured pinions.

Behold, with no delay, from the highest stars Christ flashes swiftly down from the bosom of his Father above and silently alights in the sacred womb of the faithful virgin.

How it boggles the mind! What an unprecedented state of affairs! Do you realize

290 Scisne quid clausa teneas in alvo?
Scisne, ter faelix, tua quid recondant
    Viscera, virgo?
Ipse qui solo quatit astra nutu,
Qui fretum saevis tumidum procellis
295 Temperat, dextra prohibens inertem
    Sidere terram,
Ipse qui quicquid viget orbe summo,
Manium quicquid gelido sub Orco est,
Quicquid in terris, moderatur aequis
300 Unus habenis,
En tui, mater, latitat sub antro
Pectoris rerum dominus sacello,
Ventre circundans gracili, rotundus
    Cui minor orbis.
305 Nunc graves, Adae miseranda proles,
Pone singultus, populique duras
Barbaro passi duce sub cathenas,
    Tollite vultus.
En adest nobis sator ille rerum,
310 Non quidem saevo minitans furore
Nec memor noxae aut inimica mittens
    Fulmina dextra,
Sed puer lenis, puer a vetustis
Imminens seclis, face qui secunda
315 Secla iamdudum miseris daturus
    Aurea terris.
Emica caecis uteri latebris,
Pusio dulcis, trepido tumultu
Cerne nutantem fabricam, sacratam
320 Exere frontem.
O dies omni venerandus aevo
Quo, patris Iesu soboles superni,
Carne vestitus lutea silenti
    Proderis orbi.
325 O, tui quantum iubili tulere,
Nate, vagitus; redeuntis illi
Nuntii vitae, reducis fuere
    Signa salutis.

what you hold shut up in your womb? Do you realize, O virgin thrice blessed, what your womb conceals?

The very one who shakes the stars with a mere nod, who calms the sea when it swells with raging storms, who with his right hand keeps the unmoving earth from subsiding,

the very one who alone rules with his level reins whatever flourishes in the world above, whatever shades there are down in the cold of hell, whatever there is on earth,

lo, the lord of all things lies hidden in the shrine beneath the hollow of your breast, O mother, enclosing within your slender womb one who is greater than the wide round of the world.

Now, O wretched offspring of Adam, put an end to your grievous sobs; and all you peoples who have suffered under the cruel chains of a barbarous victor, lift up your heads!

Behold, he who planted all things is present with us, not indeed threatening us with his fierce anger, not mindful of our sins, not throwing thunderbolts with hostile hand,

but as a gentle boy, a boy whose birth has been impending since ancient times, who with auspicious light will very soon bestow a golden age on the wretched world.

Shine forth from the dark recesses of the womb, sweet little boy! See how the frame of the world is tipping over, ready to fall in fearful ruin! Bring forth your holy forehead.

O day to be revered for all ages to come! O day on which you, O Jesus, the offspring of the Father on high, came forth, clothed in fleshly clay, to the silent world!

O newborn babe, what shouts of joy were aroused by your cries: they announced the return of life; they were the signs of salvation restored.

En tibi vultu iubilant sereno
330 Cuncta nascenti, prope iam recisam
Excitat lucem meliore currens
Tramite Phaebus.
Nubibus caeli chorus e supernis
En modos gaudens ciet insolentes,
335 Orbis extremi duce te requirunt
Sydere Chaldi.
Te pecus prono veneratur ore
Bruta, te cantu modulans agresti
Laudat, exultat pietas relictis
340 Rustica bubus.
Quin et umbrosas subito renatis
Frondibus sylvas videas et omne
Floribus densis viruisse pratum et
Gramine laeto.
345 Iam fluunt amnes celeres Lyaei
Dulcibus rivis, sapit unda vitem,
Rore iam stillant hilares benigno
Balsama caeli.
Iam ferunt duri nova mella scopli,
350 Ismarae cautes redolente nardo
Iam calent, Syrum spatiosa sudat
Quercus amomum.
Inter haec quanto saliisse rere
Gaudio castae tenerum puellae
355 Pectus, immensi impedientis orbis
Gaudia pannis?
Prolis o salve veneranda tantae
Mater, abs cuius niveis papillis
Pendet et terrae Deus et supremi
360 Rector Olymphi,
Lacteo cuius alitur liquore,
Cuncta qui pascit, vehit aura quicquid,
Quod capit tellus, natat inquieto
Aequore quicquid,
365 In sinu cuius recubat pudico
Ambitus quem nec sinuosus aethrae
Concipit, cuius roseis propinat
Oscula malis

Behold, at your birth all things rejoice with untroubled countenances. Phoebus, driving on a better course, enlivens the light, which was almost cut off.

Behold, a heavenly choir from the clouds above is singing songs of joy never heard before. From the furthest edge of the earth the Magi are following the star to find you.

The brute beasts worship you, bowing their heads down low; in rural song the pious country people sing your praises; leaving their oxen behind, they leap for joy.

Indeed, you can see how the dark woods have suddenly put forth new foliage again and how all the meadows flourish, thickly strewn with flowers and gaily clad with grass.

Now the swift brooks flow with sweet streams of wine, the water tastes of the grapevine, the cheerful sky drips down a kindly dew of balm.

Now the hard crags bear unheard-of honey, the Thracian peaks now grow warm with the fragrance of nard, the spreading oak sweats drops of Syrian cardamom.

Amidst these things, what joy, do you suppose, leapt up in the tender breast of the chaste girl as she wrapped in swaddling clothes him who is the joy of the boundless universe.

Hail, O venerable mother of such mighty offspring! On your breasts, white as snow, hangs the God of the earth and the ruler of highest heaven.

Your flowing milk nourishes him who feeds all things, whatever is borne along by the air, whatever the earth contains, whatever swims in the restless sea.

On your chaste bosom lies one who cannot be encompassed by the winding orbits of the heavens. On your rosy cheeks kisses are planted

Ille pre natis hominum decorus,
370 Patris exemplar superi, ac tenellis
Dulce subridens recipit vicissim
    Pressa labellis.
Quid neget, mater, tibi iam rogatus
Filius? Seu quid nequeat roganti
375 Ferre, quam tanto veneratur unam
    Tantus honore?
Ergo te cuncti querulis fatigant
Iure mortales precibus, dolore
Quolibet pressi, veriti tremendi
380 Iudicis ora.
Qui cavis tentant trabibus minaces
Adriae fluctus rabidasque Syrtes,
Certa tu nautis, duce qua ferantur,
    Stella refulges.
385 Cumque iam scissis Aquilone velis
Concitae cymbam rapiunt procellae,
Te vocant unam, prece tu cieris
    Supplice, diva.
Te petit votis, dea, quem lacessit
390 Noxius languor, domini petit te
Barbari saevis miseranda vinctus
    Colla cathenis.
Tu levas cunctos miserans et aures
Admoves votis faciles precantum,
395 Tu reis placas trepidis, dearum
    Maxima, regem.
En ego morbis animi laborans,
Mersus immani scelerum baratro,
En ego vinclis premor impeditus
400 Colla pudendis.
Tu meos, virgo, miserare fletus,
Te mei unam suspiciunt ocelli,
Tu meos audi lyrico vocata
    Carmine questus.

by one more beautiful than all the sons of men, the pattern of his Father on high; and smiling sweetly he receives kisses in turn, pressed on him by your tender lips.

Can your son, O mother, refuse you anything you ask for, and is there anything you can ask for that he does not have the power to provide for you, whom one so great has singled out and venerated with such a great honour?

Therefore all mortals rightly wear you out with their complaints and prayers, whenever they are crushed by any kind of suffering, fearing the countenance of their terrible judge.

For sailors who brave the threatening waves of the Adriatic or the raging Syrtes in their hollow wooden ships, you shine out as a fixed star by which to set their course.

And when their sails have already been split by the north wind and their skiff is in the grip of the onrushing storm, they cry out to you alone, they invoke you, O holy lady, with their humble entreaties.

Anyone stricken by a consuming disease seeks you out, O divine lady, with his prayers. Anyone whose miserable neck is bound with the cruel chains of a barbarian overlord seeks you out.

In your compassion you lift up everyone and you are quick to give ear to the prayers of those who beseech you. For fearful sinners, O greatest of goddesses, you placate the king.

Behold, I struggle with diseases of the mind; I am drowned in a boundless abyss of sins; behold, my neck is shackled and weighed down with shameful chains.

Take pity, O Virgin, on my tears. My eyes look up to you alone. As I invoke you in these lyric strains, hear my laments.

111 Carmen de monstrosis signis Christo moriente factis. Metrum primum est asclepiadeicum coryambicum. Secundum est archiloicum iambicum dimetrum. [summer? 1499 / 1706]

'Quis tam turbo ferox tantus et omnia
Repente concutit tremor?
Nostra et non modico mens trepidat metu,
Vultumque pallor occupat.
5 Vix Phaebus medium contigit aethera
Nonam recurrens lineam,
Et iam nunc hyemis noctibus atrior
Caligo texit sydera.
Terra ingente tremit concita turbine,
10 Seseque saxa dissecant,
Convexoque poli pondere machina
Pendet recliva in inferos.
Unde hic insolitae noctis ab aethere
Toti horror incubat solo?
15 Tantum, ah, ne vetulis territa concidat
Natura ruptis legibus
Et totam properent solvere machinam
Rerum soluta faedera,
Neu caeleste iubar Tartareum cahos
20 Terrae rescindens obicem
Involvat tenebris triste nigrantibus
Rumpatque luminis vices
Confundatque gravans omnia Tartarus
Umbris creata informibus!
25 Quod si nunc superum conspiciant diem
Manes recluso carcere,
Nil huius reliquum (credite) machinae
Dies videbit crastina.
At tu tale veta, summe deus, nefas,
30 Magni creator aetheris,
Quin iam salvet opus ipsa quod aedidit
Invicta virtus dexterae.

111 A poem on the preternatural signs that occurred at the death of Christ. The first line of each couplet is asclepiadean, with choriambs; the second is in archilochean iambic dimeters.

'What whirlwind, raging so fiercely, what massive tremor suddenly shakes everything? My mind, too, is shaken by no small fear, and pallor overspreads my face. The sun barely touched the midpoint of his course in the sky, circling back to the ninth hour-line, and just at that moment a darkness blacker than winter nights covered the sky. The earth shakes, agitated by an enormous [underground] whirlwind; and rocks split in two of their own accord, and the frame of the universe, under the weight of the curving heavens, hangs tilted downward toward the underworld. What caused this strange and horrible night to descend from the heavens and brood over the ground everywhere? Ah, if only nature does not collapse in terror at this rupture of her ancient laws and if only the breaking of the compact which holds things together does not hasten the dissolution of the universal frame, and if only the darkness of the underworld does not tear open the barrier of the earth and wrap the light of heaven in dark shadows and gloom, if only it does not break the successive returns of light, and if only hell does not oppress and confound all creatures in shapeless shadows! But if now the shades of the dead have their prison opened and behold the daylight above them, tomorrow, believe me, will see nothing left of this universal frame. But may you, almighty God, creator of the vast heavens, forbid such a horror. Nay rather, let the same invincible power of the right hand that produced this work now save it.

'Sed quid deterius in dubiis sibi
Mens usque praesumit tremens?
35 Noctem hanc forte vagans et male cognitus
Poposcit ordo syderum.
Phaebe forte gravi noxia corpore
Fratris recondidit facem.
Huc huc quotquot habet Graecia, quotquot et
40 Chaldaea nutrit regio,
Qui nostis varios aetheris ordines,
Cursum et recursum syderum,
Et quo luna meet menstrua tramite,
Adeste, ne moremini.
45 Collustrate polum, sydera discite,
Quo quaeque volvantur gradu,
Et monstrate novae noctis originem,
Si forte deprendi queat.'
'Vae terrae indigenis, piscibus et feris,
50 Quicquidque caelo clauditur.
Triste heu, triste nimis fata parant opus
Saevo sinistra numine.
En mox pressa cadet pondere non levi
Tellus ruentis aetheris.
55 Nil haec nox aliud, nil sibi vult tremor:
Solvenda clamant secula
Et dirupta canunt vincula faederis
Quo cuncta strinxerat deus.
Nam nec luna quidem crassa tegit diem,
60 Solis morata lampadem,
Quae iam nunc rosei luminis inscios
Completa lustrat inferos.'
Heus! Quo tota strepit murmure concio?
Quis tantus in turba timor?
65 Quo tanto trepidat turba fugax metu?
Quis nam ruentium pavor?
O caecam rabiem, proh furor impudens!
Heu gentis horrendum scelus!
En plebs ausa deum perdere perfida,
70 Caecis citata furiis!
Qui caelum atque solum, qui mare et omnia
Potente condidit manu,

'But why does the mind, when it trembles in doubt, always presume the worst? Perhaps the orderly wandering of the heavenly bodies, which is not well understood, requires this darkness. Perhaps Phoebe does the damage by hiding her brother's light with her massive body. Hither, come hither, all you astronomers claimed by Greece or raised in Chaldea, you who know the various patterns of the heavens, the comings and goings of the stars, and how the moon moves in its monthly course, come, do not delay! Sweep through the heavens, discover the path of each star turning in its orbit, and show the reason for this strange darkness, if it can be at all understood.'

'Woe to the inhabitants of earth, to the fish and the beasts, and to whatever is enclosed in the heavens! The hostile Fates, with their cruel power, are preparing some grievous, alas, too grievous deed. Lo, the earth will soon fall, weighed down by the enormous weight of the falling sky. This darkness, this earthquake have one meaning and one only: they proclaim that the world is to be dissolved; they forebode the breaking of that compact in which God has bound all things together. For it is doubtless not the gross body of the moon that is blocking out the day by hindering the light of the sun, for the moon, having reached fullness, now makes her way in the underworld, among those who know not the rosy light.'

Hark, how the whole assembly rustles and murmurs! How the crowd is stricken with terror! How the crowd bustles about in great fear and flees in panic! How they rush about in terror! O blind frenzy! Ah, the arrogant madness! Alas, the horrible wickedness of that nation! Lo, this faithless people, driven by blind fury, has dared to kill God! The one who with his powerful hand made heaven and earth, who made the sea and all things, is now

Confossus lacero est in cruce corpore,
Iam morte pallet insuper.
75 Duram heu vita necem mortua pertulit,
Sol ille verus occidit!
Quid ni cuncta nefas expaveant novum
Turbis patratum pessimis
Authorique suo condoleant deo,
80 Orbata quippe iam patre?
Hinc plane, hinc subitae funereum polo
Diem tulere tenebrae.
Pressis obstupuit lucida cornibus
Phaebi videntis orbita
85 Obduxitque suam nube nigra facem,
Ne indigna cernat funera.
Et tellus oneris impatiens gravis
Imis tremit radicibus,
Ah, quam pene suum tota per infera
90 Regem sequuta Tartara!
Verum quicquid id est, nil cadit omnium
Christi necem gementium.
Non solum solidum perdere non venit,
Verum imbecille ut roboret.
95 Quae te, quae maneat iudicis ultio,
Gens caeca, saxo durior!
En sol turpe scelus tectus abhorruit,
Tellusque sensit stolida,
At tu, sola animis caeca procacibus,
100 Quem perdis ignoras deum.

112 Carmen heroicum de solemnitate paschali atque de tryumphali Christi resurgentis pompa et descensu eius ad inferos [summer? 1499 / 1706]

Clara serenati laetentur sydera caeli,
Sydera quae quondam domino moriente choruscos
Condiderant radios caligine turbida tristi,
Laetentur referantque obtectos ocyus ignes.
5 Umbris ut quid enim nox usque nigrantibus omnem

on the cross, his body torn and pierced, already overspread with the pallor of death. Alas, Life has cruelly perished and is dead. That true sun has set. Why should not all things shudder at the unheard-of crime perpetrated by the most wicked mob? And why should they not share the grief of their creator and their God, orphaned as they now are and fatherless? This is clearly the reason, this is why sudden darkness has removed the grieving daylight from the sky. Astounded at the sight Phoebus has drawn his horns within his bright disk and covered his light with a black cloud lest he see such an undeserved death. And the earth, incapable of bearing such a heavy burden, trembles to its inner depths – how close the entire earth came to following her king through the darkness of the underworld! But however that may be, none of all the things that groaned at the death of Christ actually falls. Not only does he not come to destroy what is firm but rather that he might strengthen what is weak. What kind of avenging judgment awaits you, O blind nation, harder than rock! Lo, the sun covered himself in horror at this foul crime and the stolid earth felt it, but you alone have minds so brazenly blind as not to know that the one you kill is God.

112 A heroic poem on the feast of Easter and on the triumphant procession of the risen Christ and on his descent into hell

Let the bright stars rejoice in the clear heavens, the same stars that formerly hid their flashing rays at the death of the Lord, expressing their grief in gloomy darkness, let them rejoice and speedily reveal once more their covered fires. For why do the black shadows of dark night

Occupat atra polum? Fugiens petat infera nox haec.
Ecce etenim iamiam, tetris male amica tenebris,
Nascitur ecce dies, lux surgit amabilis orbi,
Lucis et immo opifex verusque Diespiter ille
10 Nascitur, horrentis pulsurus nubila noctis.
Florida plaudat humus, fundat sua munera tellus,
Squallorem excutiat, blandis se floribus ornet.
Incipiat steriles dudum componere ramos
Sylva virente coma et festa se fronde coronet,
15 Missaque plumigeri repetant sua carmina caetus.
Dulce susurrantes modulentur in aethere voces,
Et freta inaequales ponant pacata procellas,
Nimbosusque Nothus longe concedat et Auster
Grandisonus, tumidos cessent attollere fluctus,
20 Et natura novos omnis iam denique vultus
Laetior assumat seque in nova gaudia solvat.
Nec desit superum tantis solemnibus ordo.
Huc huc quin mage quot habet regio illa beata
Aetheris indigenas properent penetralibus omnes
25 Sydereis caelumque leves et mollia rumpant
Nubila iamque oras veniant invisere nostras.
Terris haec celebranda dies; nova gaudia terris
Christus agit, superis nondum gustata vel ipsis.
Sed pater esse modo communia cuncta benignus
30 Terrigenis superisque iubet, veteris mala quando
Semina dissidii patris unicus ipse rubenti
Sanguine diluerit moriens; iam nulla simultas,
Materies iam nulla odii, limum quia nostrum
Assumpsit deitas, reddens divina vicissim.

still continue to occupy the whole sky? Let this night flee to the underworld. For behold, even now the day, the enemy of dismal shadows, is being born; the lovely light is dawning on the world; indeed, the very maker of light and the true lord of the day is being born and is about to drive away the mists of dreadful night.

Let the soil with its flowers applaud, let the ground pour forth its gifts, let it shake off its ugliness and adorn itself with charming blossoms. Let the forest begin to arrange green tresses on its branches, long bare, and let it put on its festive crown of leaves, and let the feathered flocks take up once more the songs they had ceased to sing. Let their twittering voices make sweet melodies in the air, and let the sea be peaceful and put down the storms which roughen her waters; and let the rainy south wind, let the howling southwester depart far hence; let them stop stirring up the swelling waves. And in short, let all nature in her happiness put on a new face now and find release in new joys.

Also let not the ranks of those above be lacking to this great celebration. Nay rather let them come hither, let all the denizens of that blessed region of heaven hasten hither from their inner sanctum beyond the stars. Let them swiftly break through the firmament and the soft clouds and come now to visit our climes. On earth this day should be celebrated; for earth Christ is causing new joys never yet tasted even by those on high. But the beneficent Father commands that the inhabitants of earth and heaven alike should now have all things in common, since the only begotten Son of the Father by dying has himself washed away with his red blood the evil seeds of the ancient dissension. Now there is no conflict, no reason for hatred now, because the Godhead has taken on our clay,

35 Nostra tulit suaque ille dedit, mortalia caepit,
Rettulit aeterna, per enim haec commertia carnem
Conciliat patri, commiscuit infima summis
Caelumque et terram vinclo connexuit uno.
Ergo homini ne dedignetur adesse vocatus
40 Spirituum sacer ille chorus, demissus Olympho
Sedibus in nostris nobis se misceat una
Laetificum celebrare diem ac post fortia bella
Victorem festo deducere carmine regem.
Ille canat caeleste melos, nos terrea terra
45 Plaudentes fragili miscebimus organa voce.
Ille lyram feriat, hic plectra sonantia pulset,
Ille canat cythara, hic agitet salientia sistra,
Hinc ventosa tonet tuba, misceat inde suaves
Tibia blanda modos, domini modulata tryumphos.
50 Sed nec nostra quidem, quicquid tenui ipsa valebit
Carmine, Musa novos parcet cantare tryumphos
Victoris domini et solemnes ducere pompas.
Ergo age iam fidibus quodcumque, Camaena, sonoris,
Nostra, potes, nunc hora monet, nunc incipe carmen.
55 Incipe, magnificos Iesu cantemus honores.
Fronte leves discinge hederas et tempora lauro
Cinge sacra atque imbellis amica pacis oliva:
Palma pii recinenda ducis, recinenda trophaea,
Vicerit ut nostram moriente in corpore mortem,
60 Ut quoque Tartareae colliso principe noctis
Regna tryumphali populaverit infera ligno

making us godlike in turn. He took what is ours and gave what is his. He took what is mortal and gave back what is eternal, for by this exchange he reconciled our flesh to the Father, mingling the lowest with the highest, and bound heaven and earth together in a single bond. Therefore, let that sacred choir of spirits deign to answer our call and be present with mankind; let them be sent down from heaven and intermingle with us where we live so as to celebrate this joyful day and after the hard fight to escort the royal victor with festive song. Let that choir sing a heavenly melody; we on earth will applaud and mingle our earthly instruments with our weak voices. Let one strike his harp; let another pluck the resounding strings. Let one sing to the lyre; let another shake the jiggling tambourine. From one side let the blown horn sound; from another let the sweet flute blend its smooth notes, making music for the triumphant procession of the Lord.

But my muse, too, whatever contribution her thin song can make, will not refrain from celebrating in song this marvellous triumph of our victorious Lord, accompanying the solemn procession. Come then, my muse, whatever music you can make on the resounding strings, now is the time, now begin your song. Begin, let us sing in honour of the great deeds done by Jesus. Remove from your brow the trifling ivy; encircle your temples with the sacred laurel and with the peace-loving olive, enemy to war. We must sing the palm won by our faithful leader; we must sing his victory, how he conquered our death through his own bodily death, how he also crushed the prince of Tartarean darkness and despoiled the kingdom of hell through the triumphant wood of the cross and removed the hard chains of

Duraque captivae dimorit vincula gentis,
Vincula quae canos religabant carcere patres.
  Ergo ubi triste iugum et veteris durissima lethi
65 Imperia ipse ferens indigna morte peremit,
Protinus arrepto post praelia dura bacillo,
Livida quo torvi contriverat ora colubri,
Victor perpetuis squalentia castra tenebris
Laetus adit properatque ereptam abducere praedam.
70 Ast tenebrosa cohors et noctis amica silentis,
Eminus ut sensere diem radiare serenum
Insolita et noctem rarescere luce profundam
Prospiciuntque novi radiantia signa triumphi,
Concusso subitis tremuerunt pectore monstris,
75 Moxque umbrosa specus dubio tremebunda tumultu
Verticibus summis imisque a sedibus omnis
Concutitur; stetit unda Stygis Phlegetontis et amnis,
Cocytique vagos tenuerunt flumina cursus.
Umbrarum tremuere duces, tremuere rigentes
80 Centumque Eumenides subito intumuere colubris,
Et cecidere manu radiantia sceptra minaci,
Ac trepidans premit ora trifaucia ianitor ingens,
Cunctaque praeterea teter quae plurima Averni
Carcer habet gelido pallebant monstra timore.
85 Nec non interea valido ter turbine quassae
Tartareae tremuere domus, mirabile dictu,
Ter sunt mugitus per opaca silentia turpes
Horrendum ex imis visi resonare cavernis.
Flebat enim absorptam rabido qui gutture praedam
90 Eriperet propius fera bellua figere gressus

the captive people, the chains which bound the white-haired fathers in prison.

And so, after he had borne the sad yoke and the most cruel dominion of death, decreed in ancient times, and had destroyed them by his undeserved death, immediately after the hard battle he seized the staff with which he had crushed the envious head of the grim serpent, and he approached in joyful triumph the squalid camp, enshrouded in perpetual darkness, hastening to rescue and lead away his booty. But, when the dark cohort, friends of noiseless night, saw the serene daylight shining in the distance and perceived that the deep night was thinning in the unfamiliar light, when they beheld the shining sign of this strange triumph, these sudden prodigies struck their hearts with shuddering fear, and then the whole shadowy cavern trembled in doubtful confusion, shaken from its uppermost regions to the lowest; the waters of the rivers Styx and Phlegethon stopped flowing and the streams of Cocytus ceased in their wandering course. The princes of the shades trembled, and the Furies, stiffening, trembled and suddenly swelled up with their numberless snakes, and the radiant sceptres fell from threatening hands, and the huge guardian of the threshold shut his threefold jaws in fear, and all the many other monsters besides that are kept in the foul prison of hell grew pale with chilling fear. And also, at the same time, the mansions of hell, struck by a powerful whirlwind, quaked three times, and three times (marvellous to say!) ugly bellowing was heard resounding horribly through the dark silence from the very depths of the caverns. For the savage beast wept at the thought that the one who would snatch the prey swallowed by his rabid throat was planting his footsteps nearer and nearer, and he was howling because Christ's triumph,

Et iamiam veritos ululabat adesse triumphos.
Pectore quinetiam trepidanti maximus ipse
Arbiter umbrarumque deus paulum ore represso
Pallidus obriguit animoque exterritus haesit.
95 Nam quid tanta novis portendant omina monstris
Nec prorsus latuit neque certius omnia novit.
Mente legit veterum studiosa carmina vatum,
Venturum qui carne deum miserabile sacra
Morte piare genus mundo et succurrere lapso
100 Legis adhuc dubia positi cecinere sub umbra;
Anxius atque refert, quae monstra potentia quondam
Infirma testata deum sub carne latentem
Hauserit ipse suis non longe amotus ocellis,
Utque viro in ligno vitam expirante supremam
105 Legibus antiquis subito natura remissis
Tota perhorruerit mortem et damnarit iniquam.
Iamque iterum furiis inter praecordia ceptis
Frigidus intremuit gemitumque e pectore duxit.
Haud mora longa fuit, moxque alta silentia rupit
110 Affaturque suam maesto sermone cohortem:
'Saepe quidem mentem turbarunt haec mala nostram,
O fortes socii, cum perfidus ille aliena
Subrepens specie nova tam miracula mundo
Proderet assiduus faceretque ingentia signa.
115 Quin etiam ipse adii variatis artibus olim
Explorare virum dubiosque resolvere sensus.
Ille sed occuluit sese mixtusque fefellit
Infirmus virtute dolor, nam more parentum
Alsit et esuriit, sed et infans ubera suxit,
120 Vagiit, excrevit, nunc haec super omnia et ipsam

which he had feared, was now finally at hand. Indeed, with fear in his heart, even the supreme ruler himself, the god of the shades paled, stiffened, and kept his mouth shut for a little while, his mind frozen with terror. For what ominous events were portended by these strange prodigies was neither entirely concealed from him nor did he know all about them for sure. He carefully ran over in his mind the songs of the ancient prophets who predicted, while they were still placed under the doubtful shadow of the Old Law, that God would come in flesh to atone for miserable mankind by his holy death and would bring succour to the fallen world. And he anxiously remembered those mighty wonders that he himself had formerly taken in with his own eyes as he stood not far away, miracles testifying that God was concealed under the weak flesh; he recalled how, when the man breathed his last on the cross, all nature suddenly departed from her ancient laws, in horror and condemnation of his unjust death. And now once more his breast began to be tormented by the Furies; chilled and shivering, he groaned from the bottom of his heart. Soon, after a short delay, he broke the deep silence and addressed his cohorts in sad speech:

'Often indeed, O brave companions, our mind was disturbed by such afflictions as these, when that treacherous man, hiding under a false appearance, constantly displayed to the world such unheard-of wonders and performed such mighty miracles. Indeed, I myself also approached him once with various strategies to test him and resolve my doubts. But he concealed himself and deceived me by mixing weakness and pain with his power, for like his parents he felt cold and hunger, as a baby he sucked at the breast, he cried, he grew up, and now, over and above all this, he

Mortem obiit fuditque extremam in funere vitam.
At nunc sero quidem tectas nunc novimus artes,
Novimus heu victi nunc sero dolumque virumque
Nequicquamque crucis radiantia cernimus arma.
125 Laedit et id nostram gravius super omnia mentem,
Tela quod haec hosti male sani cudimus ipsi
Nostram in pernitiem: nostris heu vincimur armis.'
Cominus interea gradiens se lumine victor
Admovet immenso media inter verba loquentis.
130 Iam trepidatus adest, validas nec multa moratus
Impulit in valvas, vectes confregit ahenos
Divinoque graves disiecit numine moles.
Inde profunda subit saevi penetralia Ditis,
Sceptra ferens erecta manu radiantia dextra,
135 Pallida et ingenti perfundit fulmine tecta.
Protinus immissum reserata sub atria manes
Obstupuere diem, mirantur lampada Phaebi
Deductam, roseis penitus ingressa quadrigis.
Quis tibi tunc, Pluto, cernenti talia sensus?
140 Quosve dabas fremitus cum Tartara luce nitere
Protinus insolita aspiceres totumque videres
Misceri ante oculos tantis fulgoribus Orcum?
Est specus extremum barathri devexa sub antrum
Immensumque cahos tetris sine lumine flammis
145 Aetnae more calens, tormenta ubi dira perenni
Igne ferunt animaeque luunt sua crimina sontes,
Bis tantum in praeceps tantumque sub infera tendens
Quantus syderei suspectus ad ardua caeli.

suffered death itself and expired, shedding all his blood. But now indeed, when it is too late, now we recognize his deceptive tricks; too late, alas, now that we are vanquished, we recognize the man and his deception, and in vain we perceive the shining weapon of the cross. Above all, our mind is pained by this: that we ourselves insanely forged for the enemy the very weapon of our own destruction; we are conquered, alas, by our own arms.'

Meanwhile, even as he is speaking these words, the victor, walking in an immense aura of light, is drawing near. The dreaded figure is now at hand; with no delay he strikes the strong doors, breaks the bronze bars, and by his divine power dashes the heavy mass to pieces. Then he enters the deep inner regions of cruel Dis, holding erect in his right hand his radiant sceptre, which engulfs the pale mansions in an enormous flash of light. Immediately the shades of the dead are stunned that the daylight has flooded into the unlocked halls; they marvel that the lamp of Phoebus has been brought down, at the light which has entered into the depths on his rose-streaked chariot. What was your reaction then, Pluto, when you saw such things? How did you growl when you beheld hell suddenly illuminated by such unheard-of light and saw, before your very eyes, all the underworld thrown into confusion by such dazzling flashes?

There is a cave which is hollowed out at the very bottom of the abyss, an immense confusion of darkness, burning like Aetna with hideous and lightless flames, where guilty souls suffer the fierce punishment of eternal fire and pay for their sins. It reaches sheer down into hell twice as far as the distance to the starry heights of heaven which we see

Ocius huc omnis denso ruit agmine facto
150 Luciferi tremefacta cohors, neque tanta ferentes
Fulgura mobilibus mire vibrantia flammis,
Ultro sulphureis sese immersere caminis.
Ille autem placido per inania regna meatu
Arduus incedit, vasti sedes et Averni
155 Squallentes legit hinc illincque stupentibus umbris.
Tum facili Phlegetonta gradu flammantibus undis
Horrentem piceoque tumentem gurgite victor
Transilit et summam barathri citus astat ad oram.
At dirae subita deprensae luce sorores
160 Praecipites imam valido cum turbine abyssum
Ultro petunt alta seseque voragine condunt.
Hi vero quos iam tormenta et vincula captos
Longa fatigarunt, ut primum lumine tanto
Adventasse deum didicere sub infera summum,
165 Spem frustra caepere animis gemituque represso
Nequicquam aeterna torpentia lumina nocte
Attollunt praebentque arrectas ocyus aures,
Si metam, si forte modum daret ille malorum.
Grande sed horrisono iustissimus arbiter ore
170 Desuper increpitans stolidissima pectora quondam
Intonat et meritos caepisse haec omnia pandit.
Inde potente ferum dominus verbo alligat hostem,
Alligat et valido pavitantem sauciat ictu,
Ferrea captivis innectens vincula collis,
175 Posthac mortiferum tentet ne spargere virus
In famulos famulasque dei faucesve cruentas
Imbuat effuso laniatae sanguine praedae.
Haec ubi complevit, grave olentia limina linquit,

extending above us. Swiftly the whole quaking cohort of Lucifer closes its thick ranks and rushes down to this cave. Unable to bear such great bolts of wondrously darting and flashing light, they willingly plunge into the sulphurous furnace. But Christ, holding his head high, walks calmly through the bodiless kingdom and passes through the vast and filthy mansions of hell, as the shades look on in amazement, now from one side, now from another. Then the victor easily leaps over the Phlegethon, whose waters bristle with peaks of flame and gurgle with surges of pitch, and soon he stands on the very brink of the abyss. But the dreadful sisters, surprised by the sudden light, of their own accord hurl themselves headlong in a great uproar down to the bottom of the abyss and hide in the depths of the chasm. But those who had already been worn down by the torments and bonds of their long captivity, as soon as they perceived from the great light that almighty God had come down into hell, were seized by a futile hope and stopped groaning; in vain they lift up their eyes, grown dim in the eternal night, and quickly prick up their ears, to learn if perhaps he would place some limit, some end to their afflictions. But the most just judge, speaking lofty but horrible-sounding words, thunders down rebukes on those who once completely hardened their hearts, and he makes it clear that they have earned all their punishments. Then the Lord binds our savage enemy with a word of power, binds him and wounds the cowering devil with a strong blow, wrapping his captive neck in iron chains lest he later try to spread his deadly poison among the men and women who serve God or to steep his gory jaws in the blood poured out by his mutilated victims. When he has finished these things, he leaves the foul-smelling brink

Rursus et illusis spes mentibus excidit omnis,
180 Et maesti posuere caput gemituque resumpto
Tota simul tristi complebant Tartara voce,
Incipit et gravius late increbrescere planctus.
Sic tibi sic visum, dux inclyte Christicolarum,
Ut videant doleantque magis. Iam reddere charis,
185 Christe, tuis: videant laeti et suspiria ponant.
Ocyus ergo recurrit iter quo venerat et iam
Limina prima tenet Erebi sedesque supremas.
Hic quos a prima nascentis origine mundi
Ipsos recta quidem Moysique aedicta sequentes
190 Patria sub noctem detraxit culpa profundam.
Spe longa labefacti animis ingentibus usque
Fletibus ora rigant, nec non suspiria maesto
Pectore longa trahunt umbroso carcere clausi,
Dum veniat tandem tenebris qui, morte soluta,
195 Tristibus eripiat superasque educat in auras.
Ut primum ergo crucis victricia signa choruscae
Molibus adversisque domus portis et ahenis
Obiecit, cecidere fores, et carceris ingens
Machina terrifica sonuit concussa ruina.
200 Detectae patuere domus, patuere cavernae,
Mox et discussis nox atra evanuit umbris.
Hic primum ille sacer populus dilata serenum
Conspexit post vota diem, post nubila solem
Laetus, et optatum viderunt lumina lumen.
205 Quae tum, quae subitas rapuerunt gaudia mentes?
Quem tum laeticiae trepidis, quem plausibus illic

behind him, and the souls who had been deceived lost all hope again and hung their heads in grief and took up their groaning once more; they filled all hell at once with their sad voices and began to send forth even more frequent and heavy lamentation far and wide.

This, this is what was pleasing to you, O glorious commander of Christians, that they should see you and grieve all the more. Now go back to your dear ones, Christ, let them see you with joy, let them put an end to their sighs. And so he returns more swiftly the way he had come and now he reaches the outer threshold of hell and the highest mansions. Here are those who from the very dawn of the world had been drawn down into the depths of darkness by our forefather's guilt, even though they themselves had followed the rule of right and the commands of Moses. Their minds are worn out by hope long deferred, their faces are continually wet with copious tears, and from heavy hearts they draw deep sighs, shut up in their shadowy prison, until the one should finally come who would break the bonds of death, rescue them from the gloomy darkness, and lead them forth into the air above. Accordingly, as soon as the victorious ensign of the glittering cross faced the massive mansion with its bronze gate, the doors fell and the huge framework of the prison was smashed, collapsing with a terrifying crash. Uncovered, the mansion lay open, the cavern was exposed. And immediately the shadows were dispersed and black night vanished. Now for the first time, after prayers so long drawn out, that holy people saw the clear light of day; after clouds they joyfully saw the sun, and their eyes took in the light they had longed for. What joy, what sudden joy then flooded their minds? What limit then, do you suppose, could there

Rere fuisse modum? Tandem o, post tristia tandem
Vota datum admotis coram qui salvet ocellis
Cernere victorem, iam non sub imagine, Iesum,
210 Iesum, quem veterum cecinerunt provida vatum
Carmina, quem sacri, nascens ubi caeperat orbis,
Usque adeo ardenti clamabant pectore patres.
Nec mora multa fuit, mox ferrea claustra resolvit,
Rumpit et indignis circundata vincula collis.
215 Libera scandentis sequitur post terga magistri
Candida turba, ducis comitans vestigia tanti.
Atque hinc ne qua domus maneant monumenta nefandae
Ille levi penitus disperdidit omnia flatu,
Immanisque brevi structura evanuit ictu.
220 Nunc age magnarum stimulant fastigia rerum,
Nunc age grandiloquum (si quid potes) incipe carmen.
Incipe, Musa, opus est totos intendere nervos.
Dicito laeta quibus procedant agmina pompis
Utque ipse ante alios victor clarissimus omnes
225 Praevius incedat praedamque sub aethera ducat.
Tuque ades, o cantande, tuo tu suggere vati,
Ut te digna canat tibi carmina, et abdita pande.
Agmine prima praeit veterum veneranda parentum
Canities, ac dein superno numine mentem
230 Plena prophaetarum series, quos legis amantum
Purpureus regum sequitur longo ordine caetus.
Iungit adulta quibus se animoque aevoque valentum
Turba virum, nec non agili laetissima gressu

be to the rejoicing of these anxious souls; what bounds, in such circumstances, to their applause? At last, after such sad prayers, oh at last it was granted to them to see in person with their own eyes the conqueror who would save them, to see him no longer under foreshadowings but to behold Jesus himself, Jesus who had been foretold by the prophetic songs of the ancient seers, Jesus who had been invoked with such a burning heart by the holy patriarchs from the very origin and birth of the world. He does not delay any longer; he soon releases the iron bars and breaks the chains which had undeservedly been placed round their necks. Free, the white-robed multitude follow behind their master as he climbs upward, keeping pace with their great commander. Moreover, so that there would henceforth be no remains of that evil mansion, with a single breath he utterly destroyed all of it, and the immense structure vanished at his slightest blow.

Now come, we are hurried along up to the heights of our great theme. Now come, lift the strains of song as high as you possibly can. Begin, O Muse – you need to strain with all your strength. Tell how the joyful ranks parade onward and how the most illustrious conqueror himself goes before all the others and leads his booty up into the sky. And you also, the subject of my song, come, reveal the hidden mysteries and inspire your poet to sing of you worthily. Ahead in the first rank go our venerable, white-haired forefathers and then the full series of prophets, whose minds were inspired by God from above. They are followed by the band of kings who loved the Law, clad in royal purple and stretched out in a long line. They are joined by a crowd of grown men, mature in mind and years, and then come the young people, full of joy and

Accedit pubes, pueri teneraeque puellae,
235 Chara nec amplexae desunt sua pignora matres.
Par cunctis studium, laudis vox omnibus una,
Omnibus unus amor, una exultatio cunctis.
Qui taceat nemo est: cantant memoranda potentis
Bella manus praedamque gravem atque insigne tropheum,
240 Solemnique ducem plaudentes carmine clarum
Concelebrant, animis omnes atque ore faventes.
At novus ille novo victor praeit agmina cultu,
Nec tegitur solito insolitus bellator amictu.
Fulminis in morem, Phaebeae lampadis instar
245 Cingebat diadema caput totumque serenat
Lumine purpureo regem. Velut ignis in igne
Ille micat, medioque refulget lumine lumen;
Ex humerisque fluens talos dependet in imos
Murice palla rubens roseoque ardentior ostro
250 Auroque et multa gemmarum luce choruscans.
Quomodo si adversis aestivo lumine flammis
Obiicias soli speculorum levia centum
Vitra refulgentum, conceptis aequore plano
Ignibus emittunt radios impulsa receptos
255 Et nova vibranti simulant sese aedere luce
Fulmina concertantque vel ipsum vincere solem:
Talis erat lapidumque decor flaventis et auri,
Talis erat species, rutili dum fulmine miro
Desuper exceptos revomunt diadematis ignes
260 Scintillantque rubra velut aethere sydera bysso.
Regia nec desunt tantis vexilla triumphis,
Invicta tollebat enim radiantia dextra
Vivificae vexilla crucis, iam nescia lethi,

walking with nimble steps, the boys and the young girls. Nor is there any lack of mothers embracing their dear children. They all have one purpose, they all sing with one voice of praise, they all share the same love, they all share the same exultation. There is no one who is silent: they sing the power of his hand in battle, never to be forgotten, the abundant booty and the glorious trophies, they sing and clap, celebrating their illustrious commander in festive song, everyone praising him with heart and mouth.

But that new conqueror goes before his ranks clad in new raiment, and such an unheard-of warrior does not wear the garb we usually hear of: a crown as bright as lightning or the rays of the sun binds his temples and bathes the whole body of the king with clear, bright light. He flashes through it like fire surrounded by fire or light shining in the midst of light. And from his shoulders down to his ankles hangs a flowing robe, dyed a deep red, brighter than the scarlet sea-dye, glittering with gold and the many-faceted light of gems. Just as if you were to set up the smooth glass of a hundred gleaming mirrors to face the flaming light of the summer sun, the level surfaces are struck by the rays they take in, giving off the beams they have received, and they look as if they themselves with their shimmering light were giving off their own original flashes and trying to outdo the sun himself; such was the beauty of the gemstones and of the yellow gold, so gorgeous were they when their brightness cast back in marvellous flashes the fire they received from the crown up above, glowing on the fine linen like red stars against the sky. Nor does such a great triumph lack its royal ensign, for in his invincible right hand he carries the radiant standard of the life-giving cross, no longer a symbol of death, no longer

Nescia dedecoris solitique ignara pudoris,
265 Tota sed effuso innocui distincta cruore
Agnelli summique sacrato nomine regis
Picta nitent, oleae fixis in vertice sertis.
Hoc gradibus victor redimitus honore superbis
Ad superos Phlegetonte procul post terga relicto
270 Scandit ovans seseque iacenti reddere mundo
Concitus accelerat, ne spes dilata dolentes
Frangeret, hymnisona longe comitante caterva.
Iamque iter emensus ipsis in faucibus astat
Liminibusque quibus superas via ducit in auras.
275 Interea oppressis confuso turbine terris
Humanum trepidare genus caecasque volutat
Noctes atque dies perplexo pectore curas,
Ne qua timens visis graviora pericula monstris
Perferat inveniantque suos sua crimina sontes.
280 Nec dictu facile est, quae cura, quis angor amantum
Corda agitet, quae vota, quibus suspiria flentum
Anxia perpetuo vexent singultibus ora.
Nulla quies oculis, fletur noctesque diesque,
Lumina nec dulci capiuntur fessa sopore.
285 Quid mirum? Cruciabat enim prolixa calentes
Spes animos onerata metu, triduumque per omne
Nequicquam (triduum hoc toto productius anno)
Plangitur, et lachrymae miseris volvuntur inanes,
Amissumque gemunt tristi quem funere mersum,
290 Algida quem caeci frigentem saxa sepulchri
Condere conspiciunt. Ingens exanguia rupes
Ossa premit, signantur et ostia, milite duro

linked with ignominy, divorced from its usual associations of shame. But rather, adorned everywhere with the blood poured out by the innocent lamb and brightly painted with the sacred name of the highest king, it shines forth, surmounted by an olive wreath. His proud steps leaving Phlegethon far behind him, the victor, adorned with this honour, ascends rejoicing to the upper earth and hurries eagerly to present himself to a downcast world, lest hope deferred should crush them in their grief; and the long procession accompanies him singing their hymns. And now his journey brings him to the point where he stands at the very jaws of hell, at the threshold where the way leads to the upper air.

Meanwhile, the human race is disturbed at how the earth had been afflicted by turmoil and confusion, and they moil over their dark cares day and night in perplexity of heart, fearing that, having seen these prodigies, they might suffer even graver dangers and that their own sins should find them out in their guilt. It is not easy to describe the sorrow, the anguish that afflicts the hearts of those who love him, with what desires, sobs, and sighs of anxiety their tearful faces are perpetually disturbed. Their eyes have no rest, they weep night and day, their weary eyelids never find sweet repose. How can that be surprising? For their feverish minds are tormented by hope deferred, hope burdened with fear, and for three whole days (three days longer than a whole year) they lament in vain, and futile tears roll down their wretched faces, and they groan for the one they have lost, the one now extinguished by dismal death, whose cold corpse they saw laid away in the chilly stones of the dark sepulchre. A huge stone conceals the bloodless bones, and the entrance is sealed,

Stipantur, servatque fores custodia clausas
Ensibus et ferro servat noctesque diesque.
295 His prodire queat, haec tantane rumpere claustra?
Rumpat at esto, virum poterit superare furorem?
Custodesque queat medius transire per omnes?
His agitata malis miserum in diversa labat mens.
Iam spes victa timore cadit, iamiamque cadentem
300 Tollit amor; iam saeva timent, iam prospera sperant.
Tertia lux roseo iam rarescentibus umbris
Caeperat irradiare polo, caeloque voluto,
Sera quidem et tardis tandem prolixior horis,
Tandem aderat votiva dies. Ire ocyus ergo
305 Noctis adhuc dubia mixtis cum luce tenebris
Ad monimenta parant, usquam si forte magistri
Occurrat facies, lachrymarum aut ubere saltem
Frigida (quandoquidem miseris spes caetera languet)
Imbre et odorata perfundant corpora myrrha,
310 Exhibeant vel hoc exangui munus amico
Funeris et maestum fletu solentur amorem.
  Quid tibi, Christe, morae est? Quid te, regum optime, tardat?
Quid tibi cum Phlegetonte, quid est, quid te atria longum
Atra tenent? Iam redde fidem: sol tertius ecce.
315 Aspice convexo nutantem pondere mundum,
Aspice, Christe, tuo recreentur ut omnia vultu.
Orbis enim, dum lentus inania Tartara lustras,
Heu prope totus abit, heu pene resolvitur ingens
Machina, pene suos liquerunt sydera cursus.

guarded by a troop of cruel soldiers, who keep the entryway blocked with their swords and keep it so night and day with their weapons. Can he get out through such obstacles? Can he break through such formidable bars? Even if he could break through them, can he overcome the rage of the men? Can he pass through the midst of all the guards? Tormented by such afflictions, the minds of these miserable people waver in manifold doubts. Now hope falls, conquered by fear; now again love raises their falling hope. Now they fear cruel suffering; now they hope that all will be well. In the thinning darkness the dawn of the third morning was already beginning to light up the rosy sky, and as the heavens revolved the longed-for day was finally coming – though it seemed late indeed, delayed by the slow passing of the hours. Accordingly, they quickly prepare to go to the monument, while the shades of night are still mixed with the doubtful light, to see if somewhere perhaps they can encounter their master's face or, since in their misery all other hope is growing faint, at least to lave his cold body with copious showers of tears and anoint it with sweet-smelling myrrh and at least pay these last respects to their dead friend and console with tears their grief for the dead man they love.

What is keeping you, Christ? What is delaying you, O best of kings? What do you have to do with the Phlegethon? Why do the dark halls hold you so long? Keep your promise now. Lo, the third sun is here. Look upon the world bowing under the weight of its dome, look upon it so as to re-create everything by your glance. For while you are slowly making your way through the bodiless regions of hell, the world, alas, has almost totally perished; alas, the frame of the universe is almost dissolved; the stars have almost

320 Ipsa etenim vastam minitat tremefacta ruinam
Tellus et monstris mortalia corda sinistris
Concutit, et (quid triste magis?) caligine crassa
Nox operit nebulosa animos, dum te infera verum
Claudunt regna diem. Iam nemo salubria, nemo est
325 Qui teneat tua facta memor; totum avius orbem
Error habet, quoniam si te doctore quid unquam
Crediderant penitus te longum absente remittunt.
Ipsis quin etiam ceciderunt spesque fidesque
Discipulis. Refer, alme, diem, placidum exere vultum.
330 Nubila pelle animis, squallentem discute noctem.
Surge age, vel moveant inconsolabile flentum
Te propter gemitus maesti lachrymaeque tuorum.
Otyus ergo fores extremaque limina linquens,
Vota animo aspiciens miserum miserante, superbis
335 Progreditur rex haud multa sine luce triumphis
Ad superum sedes; lustrataque protinus illum
Sensit et immenso gradientem lumine tellus,
Sensit et effusis subito se vestiit herbis.
Sumpsit sylva comas dudum viduata virentes,
340 Res mira, et blandis subito se floribus omnis
Pingit ager laetusque deum molli excipit herba.
Nec latuit Titana novo se sydere vinci;
Sensit et ad superos properabat concitus ortus.
Authorique suo quicquid viget aethere, tellus
345 Quicquid habet, quidque aura vehit, natat aequore quicquid
Applaudit reduci et festo veneratur honore.

abandoned their paths. Even the quaking earth itself threatens to collapse in a vast ruin and strikes the human heart with sinister prodigies; and (what could be sadder?) a thick and misty darkness has descended on our minds, while you, our true daylight, are shut in by the kingdom of hell. Already there is no one, no one who remembers your salutary deeds. The whole world is in the grip of aberrant delusions, since, if they ever did believe anything when you were present to instruct them, they have completely given it up now that you have been absent so long. Indeed, even your disciples have lost their hope and faith. Bring back the daylight, O bountiful one, bring forth your peaceful countenance. Disperse the clouds from our minds, dispel the murky night. Come, arise! at least be moved by the sad groans and the inconsolable tears which your followers shed for your sake.

And so, quickly leaving behind the doors and the outermost threshold, looking with pity in his heart upon the prayers of his piteous followers, the king makes his lofty and triumphant progress, with no lack of brilliant light, back to the upper world, and immediately the earth felt him passing over her, stepping over her surrounded by boundless light, felt him and suddenly clad herself in vast stretches of grass. The trees, formerly bare, put on their green tresses – a wonder to see – and all the fields suddenly adorned themselves with pretty, bright-coloured flowers and joyfully received their God with soft grass. The sun was not unaware that he was surpassed by a new sun. He felt it and hastened eagerly to rise into the upper world. Whatever flourishes in the heavens, whatever the earth contains, whatever is borne by the air, whatever swims in the seas, they all applaud the return of their creator and

Ipse autem festinus oves regione virenti
Pergit et apricis paradysi condere pratis,
Donec corporea in vitam iam carne resumpta
350 Charorum maestum sese soletur amorem,
Edoceat solidetque suos, ad sydera demum
Quem sumpsit de matre hominem praedamque sequentem
Transvehat, aeternum victurus in aethere victor.

113 Epitaphium Bertae de Heyen [late October 1490? / 1706]

Hac qui carpis iter fixo haec lege carmina gressu.
Ecce hic sarcophagus, quem cominus aspicis, almae
Ossa tegit Bertae. Porro penetralia caeli
Celsa tenent animam, meritorum digna metentem
5 Praemia; quippe illi praesens dum vita maneret
Pupillis pia mater erat, solamen egenis,
Nutrix his quos dura premebat inedia, cunctis
Unica spes miseris, famula officiosior aegris.
His quondam illa suos partita est prodiga census,
10 Ut caperet superos multo cum faenore census.

114 Aliud epitaphium, metro anapestico [late October 1490? / 1706]

Huc lumina flecte, viator,
Numeros age perlege nostros.
Tumulum, quem conspicis istic,
Molli levis attere planta:
5 Bertae tegit ossa beatae
Meritaeque perennibus annis.
Quam postera praedicet aetas
Hymnisque ad sydera tollat,
Donec ferat arbuta tellus,

venerate him with festive honours. But he proceeds quickly to put his sheep away in green places and in the sunny meadows of paradise, until, having once more taken on and revived the flesh of his body, he consoles by his presence the loving grief of his dear ones, teaches and strengthens his followers, and finally conveys up to the stars the humanity he received from his mother, followed by the booty from hell, to live forever victorious in heaven.

113 An epitaph for Berta van Heyen

You who are passing along this way, stop and read these verses. Behold, this tomb, which you see close up, covers the bones of a bountiful lady, Berta. Henceforth the lofty inner courts of heaven possess her soul, which reaps rewards worthy of her merits. For while her life lasted here, she was a kind mother to orphans, a consolation to the needy, a giver of food to those who suffered from cruel starvation, the only hope of all the wretched, a very dutiful servant to the sick. To these she lavishly distributed her treasure so as to receive heavenly treasures together with high interest.

114 Another epitaph, in anapestic metre

Turn your eyes hither, traveller. Come, read these verses of mine. Tread with a light and gentle step on the grave which you see there. It covers the bones of blessed Berta, who deserves praise throughout endless years. May future ages praise and lift her up to the stars in their hymns, for as long as the earth bears

10 Dum sydera lucidus aether,
Roseum dum sol agat orbem,
Phaebe dum roscida noctem.
Hac namque superstite nusquam
Vasti regionibus orbis
15 Pietatis amantior ulla
Fuit atque tenacior aequi.
Mater fuit omnibus illa,
Ope quos studioque parentum
Furor illachrimabilis Orci
20 Fatis viduarat iniquis.
Nutrix fuit omnibus illa
Quos dira premebat egestas,
Spes una dolentibus, una
Aegris reparatio vitae.
25 Humili licet aggere terrae
Lateant modo lucis egena
Et nescia sanguinis ossa,
Ea secula sed tamen olim
Venient, quis prisca revisens
30 Vivax habitacula sensus
Putribus rediviva sepulchris
Secum super aethera tollat.

Poems from MS Egerton 1651

115 Carmen extemporale [autumn 1499 / 1856]

Quid tibi facundum nostra in praeconia fontem
Solvere collibuit,
Aeterna vates, Skelton, dignissime lauro
Casthalidumque decus?
5 Nos neque Pieridum celebravimus antra sororum,
Fonte nec Aonio
Ebibimus vatum ditantes ora liquores.
At tibi Apollo chelim
Auratam dedit, et vocalia plectra sorores,
10 Inque tuis labiis

trees, or the sky is bright with stars, or the sun makes his rosy rounds, or Phoebe brings dewy nights. For while she was alive there was no one in all the regions of the vast world who loved kindness more or was more intent upon justice. She was a mother to all those whom the unjust fates and the ruthless fury of death had deprived of their parents' support and care. To all who suffered from cruel poverty she gave food. For those who mourned she was their only hope. To the sick she was their only source of life-giving help. Though her bones, hidden under this low mound, are now destitute of life and deprived of blood, nevertheless the time will one day come when her living soul will revisit the former habitation of its consciousness and, raising it to life from the mouldering grave, will take it with her up to heaven.

Poems from MS Egerton 1651

115 An extemporaneous poem

Why did you deign to set the spring of your eloquence flowing to proclaim my praises, O Skelton, O poet fully worthy of the eternal laurel, O glory of the Castalian Muses? I have not frequented the grotto of the Pierian sisters, nor have I drunk from the Aonian spring those waters that enrich the mouths of poets. But to you Apollo has given a golden lyre, and those Sisters have given you a sonorous plectrum, and the goddess Persuasion, sweeter than the

Dulcior Hybleo residet Suadela liquore.
Se tibi Calliope
Infudit totam, tu carmine vincis olorem,
Cedit et ipse tibi
15 Ultro porrecta cithara Rhodopeius Orpheus.
Tu modulante lyra
Et mulcere feras et duras ducere quercus,
Tu potes et rapidos
Flexanimis fidibus fluviorum sistere cursus,
20 Flectere saxa potes.
Grecia Meonio quantum debebat Homero,
Mantua Virgilio,
Tantum Skeltono iam se debere fatetur
Terra Britanna suo.
25 Primus in hanc Latio deduxit ab orbe Camenas,
Primus hic edocuit
Exculte pureque loqui. Te principe, Skelton,
Anglia nil metuat
Vel cum Romanis versu certare poetis.
30 Vive valeque diu.

116 In castigationes Vincentii contra Malleoli castigatoris depravationes

[February? 1498 / 1923]

Plus sibi quam Varo volui Tuccaeque licere
In musam sumit turba prophana meam.
Hic lacerat mutilatque, hic pannos assuit ostro,
Sordibus et mendis pagina nulla vacat.
5 Vel nuper quanta horrebam rubigine, scabro
Malleolo vexor dum miser atque premor!
Hic sordes mihi dum male sedulus excutit auxit,
Dumque agitat veteres addidit ipse novas.
Reddidit ereptum Vincenti lima nitorem,
10 Ornavit variis insuper indicibus.
Vivat ut usque meus vindex Vincentius opto,
Flagret malleolis Malleus ille malis.

honey of Hybla, sits on your lips. Calliope has bestowed on you her fullest inspiration. In song you surpass the swan, and even Rhodopeian Orpheus yields to you and freely offers you his lute. When you make music on your lyre, you have the power both to soothe wild beasts and to make hard-hearted oaks follow you. With your soul-stirring lute you can make swift rivers stop flowing; you can move stones. What Greece owed to Maeonian Homer, what Mantua to Virgil, the land of Britain now owes to Skelton, as she openly professes. He was the first to bring the Muses hither from the world of Rome. This man was the first to teach men refined and pure speech. Under your sway, Skelton, England need not fear to contend in song even with the poets of Rome. Live long and fare well.

116 On Vincentius' corrections of the corruptions introduced by the corrector Hemmerlin [meaning 'little hammer.' The book, an edition of Virgil, speaks.]

In handling my muse, the unholy mob takes upon itself more than I wanted to grant to Varius and Tucca. One rips and mutilates, another sews rags onto my purple, leaving no page without its filthy errors. Just recently, what horrid rust was deposited on me while I was held down and miserably tormented by the scabrous Hemmerlin! In his misguided eagerness to beat the filth out of me, he increased it; and while he pounded away at old blotches he added new ones. The file of Vincentius restored the polish that had been lost, and he also adorned me with various indices. I wish a long life to Vincentius, my vindicator. May that plaguy hammerhead Hemmerlin be mauled with hammer and tongs.

117 Contestatio salvatoris ad hominem sua culpa pereuntem. Carminis futuri rudimentum [winter 1490–1? / 1923]

Qum mihi sint uni si quae bona terra polusque
    Habet, quid hoc dementiae est
Ut malis, homo, falsa sequi bona, sed mala vera,
    Me rarus aut nemo petat?
5 Forma capit multos: me nil formosius usquam est,
    Formam hanc amat nemo tamen.
Sum clarissimus et generosus utroque parente:
    Servire nobis qur pudet?
Dives item et facilis dare multa et magna rogatus,
10 Rogari amo: nemo rogat.
Sumque vocorque patris summi sapiencia: nemo
    Me consulit mortalium;
Preceptor: mihi nemo cupit parere magistro;
    Eternitas: nec expetor.
15 Sum via qua sola celi itur ad astra, tamen me
    Terit viator infrequens.
Auctor qum ego sim vitae unicus ipsaque vita,
    Qur sordeo mortalibus?
Veraci credit nemo, fidit mihi nemo,
20 Qum sit nihil fidelius.
Sum placabilis ac misereri pronus, et ad nos
    Vix confugit quisquam miser.
Denique iustus ego vindexque severus iniqui:
    Nostri metus vix ullum habet.
25 Proinde, mei desertor homo, socordia si te
    Adducet in mortem tua,
Preteritum nihil est. In me ne reiice culpam,
    Malorum es ipse auctor tibi.

117 The Saviour's earnest entreaty to mankind, perishing by its own fault. The first draft of a future poem

Since whatever good is to be found in the earth and sky belongs to me alone, what is this madness, O mankind, that you prefer to pursue false goods which are truly evils, while few or none seek out me? Many are taken with beauty: nothing anywhere is more beautiful than I am, but no one loves this beauty. I am most illustrious and noble-born both on my Father's and my mother's side: why are people ashamed to serve me? I am rich as well and I am quick to give many and great gifts to anyone who asks – I love to be asked: no one asks. I am and I am called the wisdom of the highest Father: no one among mortals asks me for advice. I am a teacher: no one wishes to submit himself to me as his master. I am eternity: and yet I am not longed for. I am the only way that leads up to the stars in the heavens: but rarely am I trodden by any traveller. Since I am the only source of life, since I am life itself, why do mortals think me so paltry? Though I speak the truth, no one believes me; no one trusts me, though no one is more trustworthy than I. I am forgiving and quickly moved to mercy, and yet hardly anyone in his misery takes refuge in me. Finally, I am a just and severe punisher of evil; hardly anyone is constrained by fear of me. And so, O mankind, if you desert me and stupidly cause your own death, there is nothing I have not done. Do not put the blame on me; you yourself are the source of your own afflictions.

Poems from other sources

118 Erasmi precatio 'Salve, regina' [spring 1499? / 1538]

O regina, reum miseratrix maxima, salve,
  O spes, dulcedo vitaque nostra simul,
Ad te clamamus nati miserabilis Hevae,
  Quos lachrymae et gemitus vallis et ista premunt.
5 In miseros ergo miserantia lumina flecte,
  Ostendas natum post mala secla tuum.
Nam pia, nam dulcis, nam clementissima quum sis,
  Fac dignos fructu, virgo Maria, tuo.

119 Carmen iambicum [late spring 1511? / 1925]

Ut examussim quadrat in te Iulii
Nomen secundi! Plane es alter Iulius.
Et pontifex fuit ille quondam maximus,
Et ille arripuit per nefas tyrannidem.
5 Nec secius illi, quam tibi modo placet,
Violata placuit gratia regni fides.
Contempsit ille deos, et hoc es Iulius.
Orbem universum cede, bello, sanguine
Miscebat ille, et hoc es alter Iulius.
10 Tibi Nicomedes unus haut sat est seni,
Iam nomine isto plus eris quam Iulius.
Vexator ille Galliarum maximus,
Es et ipse pestis Galliarum maxima.
Nihil illi erat sacrum, nisi morbus sacer.
15 Et pectus illi Erinnys ultrix criminum
Furiis agebat, mensque scelerum conscia.
Torva erat et illi frons minaci lumine,
Et ille quovis histrione vafrior.
Et his et aliis non silendis dotibus
20 Refers et equas, imo superas Iulium.
Tantum una ab illo levicula differs nota
Quod, gente nulla, vinum amas pro litteris.
Unum illud ergo totus ut sis Iulius
Superest, ut aliquis Brutus obtingat tibi.

Poems from other sources

118 Erasmus' prayer 'Hail, Holy Queen'

Hail, O queen most merciful to sinners, O our hope, our sweetness, and also our life, to you do we cry, children of piteous Eve, overburdened in this valley of tears and groans. Turn, then, your merciful eyes upon us wretches; after this evil world show us your son. For since you are loving and sweet and most compassionate, make us, Virgin Mary, worthy of the fruit of your womb.

119 An invective in iambics

How perfectly the name of Julius II fits you – to a tee! You are clearly a second Julius. He too was once the chief pontiff. He too snatched his tyrannical power by foul means. It pleased him, just as it recently pleased you, to break faith in order to extend his rule. He scorned the gods; in this too you are Julius. He filled the whole world with slaughter, war, and bloodshed; in this too you are a second Julius. One Nicomedes is not enough for you, even in your old age. In that respect, now, you are something more than Julius. He was the greatest scourge of the French; you yourself are also the greatest plague of the French. Nothing was holy about him except the holy sickness. His mind too was tormented for his crimes by the avenging Fury, and his conscience was full of guilt. He too had a grim brow and a threatening eye. He too was craftier than a stage player. In these and other ways, which ought not to be passed over in silence, you resemble and equal – nay, you surpass – Julius. There is just one tiny difference between you: low-born as you are, you love wine, not literature. Only one thing remains, then, that would make you a complete Julius: that some Brutus should turn up for you.

Carmen Iambicum.

Ut examussim quadrat i[n] te Julii
Nomen [illegible]. plane es alter Julius.
Et pontifex fuit ille quondam maximus
Et [illegible] accepit ille [illegible]
Nec servus ille, quam tibi modo places.
Violata placuit gratia regni fides.
Contempsit ille deos, et hoc es Julius.
Orbem universum caede bello sanguine
Miscebat ille. et hoc es [illegible] Julius.
Vexator ille Galliarum maximus.
Et pestis ipse es Galliarum maxima.
Nihil illi erat sacrum. nisi morbus sacer
Et pectus illi Erinnys ultrix [illegible]
Furiis agebat, mensque scelerum conscia.
Tonsa erat et illi frons [illegible] lumine
Et ille quovis histrione vafrior.
Et his et aliis non silendis dotibus
Refers et aequas, imo superas Julium.
Tantum una ab illo leviuscula differs nota
Et gente nulla, vinum amas pro litteris
Unum illud ergo [illegible] ut sis Julius,
Superest, ut aliquis Brutus [illegible] tibi.

+ Tibi [illegible] haud [illegible] sem.
Iam nomine isto plus eris quam Julius

Autograph copy of Erasmus *Carmen iambicum,* bound in before the title-page in his *Moria* (Basel 1676)
Fondation Custodia, Institut Néerlandais, Paris

Pope Julius II
Portrait by Raphael
Galleria degli Uffizi, Florence
Photo: Alinari

120 Desi. Erasmus Rotero. lectori [early 1517? / 1540]

Enituit (proh grande nefas) post saecula multa
Nobilium rerum series et velleris almi
Inclyta Romanos contemnens fama triumphos.
Et nullam Aoniae, nullam Parnasidos undae
5 Sensit opem, nullo se evexit in astra cothurno,
Donec Hesperio spectatus sanguine Gomez,
Clarus avis opibusque potens, sed carminis alti
Divitiis caelsaque et magniloquente Camoena
Nobilior, tantae miserans oblivia laudis
10 Ac prima intactum repetens ab origine carmen,
Splendida grandiloquo reserans exordia versu
Ordinis et causam, ter magno et maxima Charlo
Decretis promissa deum venturaque fata
Asseruit tetris illustria gesta tenebris,
15 Ausonii lucem eloquii sacrumque furorem
Carminis Hispani succendens flatibus oris.
Non hic mendaci commendat Iasona versu,
Nec vigilem Medaea parat sopire draconem,
Aut mentita novo prorumpunt praelia sulco.
20 Fulgida sed sacri miracula velleris udi
Arenti tellure prius, ac mox vice versa
Undantem pluviis sudo iam vellere terram,
Et Gedeoniacos ausus divinaque bella
Tercentum pugnata viris, quos more ferarum
25 Dira sitis liquidas non adpronavit in undas,
Dulcia sed gerulis rapuerunt flumina dextris,

120 Desiderius Erasmus of Rotterdam to the reader [of Álvar Gómez's poem on the Order of the Golden Fleece]

Oh what a great shame, what a crime it is that only now, after so many ages, the history of these noble matters shines forth, illuminating the glorious fame of the bountiful fleece, which can scorn the triumphs of Rome. The order found no help from the Heliconian or Parnassian springs; no lofty poet praised it to the sky until Gómez, a Spaniard of noble blood, a man famous for his forebears and mighty in his wealth, but even nobler because of his rich vein of lofty poetry and the full-throated eloquence of his soaring muse, was struck with pity that such great and praiseworthy deeds were hidden in oblivion, and so he sang the untold story, going back to its first beginnings. Displaying in grandiloquent verse the splendid origin and cause of the order and revealing the great things decreed by the gods for the thrice-great Charles and prophesying his destiny, he saved illustrious deeds from the dark shadows of oblivion, enkindling the light of Ausonian eloquence and the sacred fury of Spanish song with the breath of his mouth. His verse gives no lying praise to Jason, nor does Medea prepare to put the watchful dragon to sleep, nor do fictitious warriors spring up from the newly ploughed furrow. But rather, with the voice of a swan he sings of the shining miracles of the holy fleece, first wet while the ground around it was dry and then dry in turn while the earth around it was saturated with rainwater, and he sings of the daring deeds of Gideon's men and the wars fought for God by the three hundred men whose fierce thirst did not cause them to lie down and drink from the clear stream like wild beasts but who instead carried the sweet water

Ac precibus superata piis furiata Sathanum
Agmina et innumeris turgentia castra maniplis
Militiamque sacram generosique ordinis amplum
30 Eximiumque decus cygnaeo gutture cantat,
Martia flammato celebrans praeconia versu.
Scilicet ut mutae longo iam tempore laudes
Non nisi ab Hispano rupere silentia cantu,
Sic erit armipotens virtus tua, maxime Charle,
35 Tum demum foelix, toto spectabilis orbe,
Cum dabit infractas vires et robora firma
Addita Burgundis Hispanica lancea gesis.

121 Erasmi Roterodami theologi in commentarios D.B. Andreae Tholozani poetae regii super opus Aurelii Augustini De civitate dei

[April 1517? / 1939]

Doctor Augustine, sacrae celebris author paginae,
Tua gravi scalebat antehac Civitas caligine
Et parum liquebat oculis impericioribus.
Ecce Bernardus labore plurimarum noctium
5 Luculentis sic retexit cuncta commentariis,
Ut queant vel lusciosis perspici dilucide.

122 Erasmus de concordia Caroli imperatoris et Henrici regis Angliae et Franciae

[July 1520 / 1882]

Sidera si quando in caelis coiere benigna,
Id maximo fit gentis humanae bono.

rapidly to their mouths with their cupped right hands, and he sings of the devils' enraged battle lines conquered by pious prayers and of the camp swarming with innumerable squadrons and of the holy chivalric order and of the abundant and extraordinary glory of the noble order, proclaiming in fiery verse their martial exploits. Thus, just as these praiseworthy deeds had already remained unsung for a long time until the silence was broken by the song of a Spaniard, so too, greatest Charles, your military valour will finally bear fruit and be revealed to the whole world when the lance of Spain adds unbreakable power and unshakable strength to the pikes of Burgundy.

121 [A poem] by the theologian Erasmus of Rotterdam on the commentary by the Reverend B[ernard] André of Toulouse, the king's poet, on the work by Aurelius Augustine called *The City of God*

O Augustine, great teacher and famous expounder of the Bible, hitherto your *City* was so grievously defaced and darkened by errors that to unlearned eyes it was quite obscure. Behold, Bernard has laboured through many a night to make it all visible again by means of his lucid commentary so that now it is perfectly clear even to the purblind.

122 Erasmus on the concord between the emperor Charles and Henry, king of England and France

Whenever beneficent planets have formed a conjunction in the heavens, that turns out to be of the greatest benefit to mankind. Now,

Nunc quia summorum duo candida pectora regum
  Tam rarus ecce iunxit in terris amor,
5 Haud leviora sibi promittit commoda mundus,
  Henricum ubi videt faederatum Carolo,
Quam si vel Veneri Solem se iungere, vel si
  Solem benigno cernat adiunctum Iovi.

123 Idem in substructionem Caletiensem [July 1520 / 1882]

Miraris hospes unde moles haec nova?
Templum est, dicatum regiae concordiae,
Quod hunc in usum condidere Gratiae.

124 In laudem divae Mariae Magdalenae [August 1520? / 1882]

Impotenti amoris oestrO | Haec beata percitA
Nardicum profudit ungueN, | Eluit lacrymis pedeS,
Mox capillis tersit; eccE | Rex Olympi, qui semeL
Illecebras sprevit ac suB- | Egit, istis ampliteR
5 Capitur oblectaculis. ProcH, | Daemonis technis malI
Eva capta est: ista lacrymiS | Tincta culpas diluit.

125 Erasmi Roterodami [c September 1522 / 1933]

Non absque causa celebris est mortalibus
Sive est Catonis sive vox testudinis:
Felicitatis portio non infima est
Habitare belle. Quisquis autem iunxerit
5 Amoena tutis, sic ut adsit puritas,
Is sibi pararit commodam plane domum.
Tibi, hospes, his arrideo si dotibus,
Agnosce dominum qui tenet me et condidit.

because the sincere hearts of two most mighty kings are joined in such a rare conjunction of love here upon earth, the world, seeing Henry in league with Charles, promises itself benefits no less substantial than if it should perceive either the sun in conjunction with Venus or beneficent Jupiter joined with the sun.

123 The same poet on a substructure at Calais

Do you wonder, stranger, what is the reason for this novel structure? It is a temple dedicated to royal concord, constructed by the Graces for this purpose.

124 In praise of St Mary Magdalen

This saint, driven by the gadfly of vehement love, poured out an ointment of nard, washed his feet with her tears, and then dried them with her hair. Behold, the king of heaven, who before scorned and rejected such allurements, was much taken with these delights. Alas, Eve was taken in by the wiles of the wicked devil; this woman washed away her guilt with her streaming tears.

125 [Meersburg Castle] by Erasmus of Rotterdam

Not without good reason is the saying oft repeated among mortals – whether the source be Cato or a tortoise – that not the smallest part of happiness is to have a handsome place to live in. But whoever combines beauty with safety and adds spotlessness too has gotten himself a thoroughly fine home. If these gifts make me attractive to you, visitor, you should recognize in them the master who built and

Mores suos expressit hac imagine,
10 Fidis amicis fidus et cautus sibi.
Tutum ergo reddit a dolis et hostibus
Coniuncta fortitudini prudentia,
Pietasque purum, comitas amabilem;
Ac talem in opere semet expressit suo.
15 Is me novavit, auxit, expoliit, meo
Baro Iohannes inclytus cognomine.
Si cupis et illud nosse, Merspurgum vocor.

M.D.XXIII

126 [autumn? 1527 / 1628]

Hic Theodoricus iaceo, prognatus Alosto;
  Ars erat impressis scripta referre typis.
Fratribus, uxori, soboli notisque superstes
  Octavam vegetus praeterii decadem.
5 Anchora sacra manet, gratae notissima pubi.
  Christe, precor, nunc sis anchora sacra mihi.

127 [early April 1536 / 1939]

Est pomum pede quod dependet ab arbore curto,
  Atque hinc cognomen Gallica lingua dedit.
Huius si posses sex, octo decemve parare,
  Iam pranso stomacho clausula grata foret.

maintains me. In this image he expressed his own character: to his true friends he is true and he is careful to protect himself. Thus prudence joined with courage makes him safe from open or underhanded enemies, piety makes him spotless and courtesy makes him amiable; and these are the traits in him which he expressed in this work of his. The one who renovated, expanded, and put the finishing touches on me is Baron Johann, renowned because I am his surname. If you want to know it too, I am called Meersburg.

1523

126 [An epitaph for Dirk Martens]

Here I lie, Dirk, born at Aalst. My craft was to print writings with pieces of type. Having survived my brothers, wife, offspring, and friends, I have lived hale and hearty past my eighth decade. The sheet anchor still remains, well known to a grateful public. I beg you, Christ, be my sheet anchor now.

127 [A request for dates]

There is a fruit which hangs from the tree by a short foot, and from this fact it gets its name in French. If you can get six, eight, or ten of them, it would be pleasant to have them as an after-dinner dessert.

POEMS EMBEDDED IN ERASMUS' PROSE WORKS (EXCLUDING TRANSLATIONS)

128 From *Conflictus Thaliae et Barbariei* [latter half of 1489? / 1684]

Barbaries Swollenses tales quod eorum Theutonicales
Nomen per partes ubicunque probantur et artes
Et quasi per mundum totum sunt nota rotundum,
Swollensique solo proferre Latinica solo
5 Discunt clericuli nimium bene verba novelli.

En ii versiculi in poematibus quam sim diserta declarant.

Thalia Ha ha hae. Tot barbarismos numero, quot voces. Patria certe haec vox est: Chironis videlicet. Hui, quam digesta poemata! Non differam iis laudes referre suas:

10 Tale sonant insulsa mihi tua carmina, vates,
Quale sonat sylvis vox irrudentis onagri,
Quale boat torvus pecora inter agrestia taurus,
Qualeque testiculis gallus genitalibus orbus
Concinit; haud vocem humanam, sed dico ferinam.

POEMS EMBEDDED IN ERASMUS' PROSE WORKS (EXCLUDING TRANSLATIONS)

128 [The Latinity of the school at Zwolle, from *The Conflict between Thalia and Barbarism*]

Barbarism The students at Zwolle are such
what their name and their skills be
approved throughout the whole
Teutonical regions. And just like it is
knowed through the whole round
world, solely on the soil of Zwolle
do the young scholarlings learn to
produce Latinian words real good.

See, these verselets show how smart I am in poems.

Thalia Ha, ha, ha! I count as many barbarisms in them as there are words. You certainly talk your forebear's language – Chiron's, that is. Oh, such well-composed poetry! Without delay I will give them their due praise:

Poet, your witless verses sound to
me like the braying of a wild ass in
the woods, like the bellowing of a
mad bull among the cattle in the
country, like the singing of a rooster
that has had its generative testicles
cut off. You speak like a wild
animal, I say, not like a human being.

15 Hanc, celebres, laudate, viri, et doctissime Florum
Author, ades: gratos in serta nitentia Flores
Colligito meritaeque coronam nectito divae.
Urticae viridi graveolentem iunge cicutam,
Talia nam tali debentur praemia vati.
20 Annue, Barbaries: tuque hanc sine cornua circum
Inter candidulas laurum tibi nectier aures.

129 From the colloquy *De lusu: Ludus sphaerae per anulum ferreum* [March 1522]

Plaudite victori, iuvenes, hic quotquot adestis,
Nam me qui vicit, doctior est nebulo.

130 From the colloquy *Convivium poeticum* [August 1523]

The colloquy begins as follows:

Hilarius Levis apparatus, animus est lautissimus.
Leonardus Coenam sinistro es auspicatus omine.
Hilarius Imo absit omen triste. Sed cur hoc putas?
Leonardus Cruenti iambi haud congruunt convivio.
5 *Crato* Euge, certum est adesse Musas, effluunt carmina imprudentibus.

Celebrated men, praise this voice, and you too, most learned author of *The Flowers*, come hither. Gather charming flowers into a bright garland and weave for the goddess the wreath she deserves. Join the green nettle with the ill-smelling hemlock, for such a poet deserves such a reward. Bow your head, Barbarism, and let this sort of laurel encircle your horns and be attached between your pretty white ears.

129 [From the colloquy 'Sport': 'The game of sending a ball through an iron ring.' Gaspar, the loser in a game resembling croquet, pays his forfeit, a couplet in praise of the winner.]

Let all the young people who are here applaud the winner! The one who beat me is first-rate – a first-rate bastard!

130 [From the colloquy 'A Poetic Banquet']

[The colloquy begins as follows:]

Hilary The fare is slight; the intentions, very elegant.

Leonard You open the dinner with an unlucky omen.

Hilary Far be it from me to suggest a bad omen. But why do you think so?

Leonard Harsh iambics are hardly suitable to a banquet.

Crato Bravo! The Muses must certainly be lending their aid: unconsciously you speak in flowing verse.

Hilarius Si rotatiles trocheos mavelis, en accipe:
Vilis apparatus hic est, animus est lautissimus.
Quanquam et iambi olim ad rixas ac pugnas
10 nati, post didicerunt omni servire materiae.

Toward the end of the colloquy the friends compete in poetic variations on the theme that it is more important to cultivate your mind than your garden:

Hilarius Cui renitet hortus undiquaque flosculis,
Animumque nullis expolitum dotibus
Squalere patitur, is facit praepostere.

Leonardus Cui tot delitiis renidet hortus,
15 Herbis, floribus arborumque foetu
Et multo et vario, nec excolendum
Curat pectus et artibus probatis
Et virtutibus, is mihi videtur
Laevo iudicio parumque recto.

20 *Carinus* Cura cui est, ut niteat hortus flosculis ac foetibus,
Negligenti excolere pectus disciplinis optimis,
Hic labore, mihi ut videtur, ringitur praepostero.

Eubulus Qui studet, ut variis niteat cultissimus hortus
Delitiis, patiens animum squalere nec ullis
25 Artibus expoliens, huic est praepostera cura.

Hilary If you prefer tumbling trochees, come then, take this: Here the fare is bad; the intentions, very elegant. Although iambs were originally born for quarrels and fights, they later learned to serve for all sorts of subject-matter.

[Toward the end of the colloquy the friends compete in poetic variations on the theme that it is more important to cultivate your mind than your garden:]

Hilary Whoever has a garden bright with flowers on all sides but who allows his mind to be ugly and unadorned with any accomplishments, he has his priorities backwards.

Leonard Whoever has a garden resplendent with many delights – grass, flowers, and trees laden with abundant and diverse fruits – but takes no care to cultivate his mind both with virtues and commendable intellectual pursuits, such a person seems to me to display perverse and erroneous judgment.

Carinus Whoever takes care to have a garden resplendent with flowers and fruit but neglects to cultivate the mind with the finest disciplines, that man, it seems to me, is clenching his teeth with misdirected effort.

Eubulus Whoever strives to have a beautifully tended garden, resplendent with manifold delights, but allows his mind to be ugly and unadorned by the liberal arts, that man has his aims arsy-versy.

	Sbrulius	Cui vernat hortus cultus et elegans, Nec pectus ullis artibus excolit, Praepostera is cura laborat. Sit ratio tibi prima mentis.
30	*Parthenius*	Quisquis accurat, variis ut hortus Floribus vernet, neque pectus idem Artibus sanctis colit, hunc habet prae- postera cura.
 35	*Leonardus*	Ὧι κῆπός ἐστιν ἄνθεσιν γελῶν καλοῖς, Ὁ δὲ νοῦς μάλ᾽ αὐχμῶν τοῖς καλοῖς μαθήμασι, Οὐκ ἔστι κομψός, οὗτος οὐκ ὀρθῶς φρονεῖ, Περὶ πλείονος ποιῶν τὰ φαῦλ᾽ ἢ κρείττονα.

131 From the colloquy Πτωχοπλούσιοι [March 1524]

Hospes, in hac mensa fuerint quum viscera tensa,
Surgere ne properes, ni prius annumeres.

132 From the colloquy *Epithalamium Petri Aegidii* [c 1514 / September 1524]

Clio

Candida laurigero nubit Cornelia Petro;
Auspiciis adsint numina dextra bonis.

Sbrulius Whoever has a blooming, well-tended, and elegant garden and a mind uncultivated by the liberal arts, is devoting himself to inverted values. Your first thought should be for the mind.

Parthenius Whoever takes care that his garden should bloom with different kinds of flowers but does not also cultivate his mind with lofty intellectual pursuits, that man has his priorities upside down.

Leonard Whoever has a garden smiling with fine flowers but a mind quite dry and devoid of fine learning, he is not refined; such a man does not think straight, placing as he does more value on the trivial than on what is more important.

131 [A sign in the common room of an inn, from the colloquy 'The Well-to-do Beggars']

Guest, at this table, when you have filled your guts till they're ready to burst, don't be in a hurry to get up until you have paid your bill.

132 [An epithalamium for Pieter Gillis, from the colloquy of the same name]

Clio

The dazzling beauty Cornelia is marrying Pieter, crowned with laurel. May the powers above graciously grant them good fortune.

Melpomene

Contingat illis turturum concordia,
Corniculae vivacitas.

Thalia

5 Ille charitate Gracchum Tiberium praecesserit,
Qui suae vitam anteposuit coniugis Corneliae.

Euterpe

Illa charitate superet coniugem Admeti ducis,
Quae volens mortem mariti morte mutavit sua.

Terpsichore

Ille non flagret leviore flamma,
10 Attamen fato meliore, quam olim
Plaucius, raptae sociae gravatus
Esse superstes.

Erato

Illa non flagret leviore flamma,
Attamen longe meliore fato,
15 Casta quam sanctum deamavit olim
Portia Brutum.

Calliope

Sponsum moribus undiquaque sanctis
Nec Nasica probatus antecellat.

Urania

Uxor moribus undiquaque castis
20 Vincat Sulpiciam Paterculanam.

Polyhymnia

Laudetur simili prole puerpera,

Melpomene

May they be granted the loving harmony of turtle-doves, the long and vigorous life of crows.

Thalia

May his love surpass that of Tiberius Gracchus, who valued the life of his spouse, Cornelia, more than his own.

Euterpe

May her love exceed that of King Admetus' wife, who willingly exchanged her own life for that of her husband.

Terpsichore

May he burn with no lesser flame, but with a happier destiny, than Plautius once did, who could not bear to survive the wife that had been snatched away from him.

Erato

May she burn with no lesser flame, but with a far happier destiny, than chaste Portia once did in her passionate love for the upright Brutus.

Calliope

May the husband's character be so thoroughly upright that even the tried and true Nasica could not outdo him.

Urania

May the wife's character be so thoroughly chaste as to surpass Sulpitia Paterculana.

Polyhymnia

May she be praised for bearing children who

Accrescat domui res simul et decus,
Sed livore vacet, si fieri potest,
Factis egregiis debita gloria.

133 The introit and sequence from *Virginis Matris apud Lauretum cultae liturgia* [November 1523]

Introitus

Laurus odore iuvat, speciosa virore perhenni,
Sic tua, virgo parens, laus omne virebit in aevum.

Sequentia

Sume nablum, sume citharam, virginum decens chorus.
Virgo mater est canenda virginali carmine,
5 Vocemque referent accinentes angeli,
Nam virgines amant et ipsi virgines.
Iunget carmina laureata turma,
Vitae prodiga sanguinisque quondam.
Martyr carnificem vincit, et edomat
10 Carnem virgo: decet laurus et hunc et hanc.
Coelitum plaudet numerosa turba,
Virginem sacram canet omne coelum,
Nato virginis unico
Nulla est cantio gratior.
15 Ut cedrus inter arbores, quas Lybanus aedit, eminet,
Sic inter omnes coelites virgo refulget nobilis.
Ut inter astra Lucifer emicat,
Sic inter omnes lucida virgines.
Inter cunctorum stellantia lumina florum
20 Lilia praecellunt candore rosaeque rubore,

resemble her. May their home prosper both in wealth and honour. But, if such a thing is possible, may the glory due to their extraordinary accomplishments provoke no envy.

133 [The introit and sequence from *A Liturgy of the Virgin Mother as She is Venerated at Loreto*]

The Introit

The laurel has a pleasing fragrance and delights the eye with its perennial green. So too, O Virgin Mother, your praise will be forever green.

The Sequence

Take up the harp, take up the lute, O seemly choir of virgins. A hymn to the Virgin Mother should be sung by virgins, and the angels will add their voices, singing along with you, for they love virgins, being virgins themselves.

The band of those who once freely gave up their lives and blood will join the song, wearing their laurel crowns. A martyr conquers those who kill the flesh, and a virgin subdues the flesh itself. Both the one and the other deserve the laurel.

The whole heavenly host will applaud. All heaven will hymn the holy Virgin. To the only son of the Virgin no song is more pleasing.

As the cedar stands tallest among the trees growing on Mount Lebanon, so the noble Virgin shines among all the inhabitants of heaven. As the morning star shines brightest among his fellows, such is the lady of light among all the virgins.

Among all the flowers, bright like stars, the lily is the whitest, the rose the most red: and

Nec gratior ulla corona
Iesu niveae genitrici.
Inter odoriferas non gratior arbor ulla lauro,
Pacifera est, dirimens fera praelia, fulmen arcet ardens,
25 Baccas habet salubres,
Iugi nitet virore.
Esto, virgo, favens, qui modulis te celebrant piis,
Iram averte dei, ne feriat fulmine noxios.
Laurus esto gaudeasque
30 Usque Lauretana dici,
Licet in vasti finibus orbis
Plurima passim fumiget ara.

Amen.

134 From *Responsio ad Petri Cursii defensionem, nullo adversario bellacem* [c August 1535]

Nihil igitur superest, nisi ut Alvianum inter bellaces deos relatum hoc carmine consalutemus:

Alviane, dii beent
Te qui beasti Oenotriam.

no other crown is more pleasing to the snow-white mother of Jesus.

Among the fragrant trees none is more pleasing than the laurel. It is the tree of peace, putting an end to savage battles. It wards off the fiery thunderbolt; it has healing berries; it is always bright green.

Grant your favour, O Virgin, to those who celebrate you in loving melodies. Turn away God's wrath, lest he strike the guilty with his thunderbolt. Be a laurel and rejoice always in being called the Virgin of Loreto, though many an altar sends up its fragrant fumes throughout the whole wide world.

Amen.

134 [A sarcastic couplet about the Venetian general, Bartolomeo d'Alviano, from Erasmus' *Reply to Pietro Corsi's 'Defence'*]

Therefore all that is left for me to do is to salute Alviano, now that he is taken up among the gods of war, with this poem:

May the gods bless you, Alviano;
you certainly blessed Italy.

POEMS DUBIOUSLY ASCRIBED TO ERASMUS

135 Quum Erasmus et Cornelius inter se carminibus mutuis questi essent de stultitia barbarorum, qui veterum eloquentiam contemnunt et poesim derident, Cornelius tandem inducit divum Hieronimum de poesi colenda sententiam ferentem tanquam sequestrum. [c May 1489 / 1706]

Hieronimus loquitur.

Iussisti causae sim providus arbiter huius:
Pondera iudicii gratanter suscipe nostri.
Collaudo veterum legisse poemata vatum
Et deridentes acri configere metro.
5 Ecce per altiloquas currunt Proverbia Musas,
Versibus alludunt Sapiens, Iob, Cantica sponsae,
Concrepat et metricis David sua carmina plectris.
Sed quaedam vicia tibi dico iure cavenda.
Prospice ne maculet damnanda superbia mentem,
10 Neve pios spernas qui nondum carmina norunt,
Attamen haud vates temnunt, sed amant venerantes.
Si stilus ipse placet, placet et sententia vernans,
In quibus Aoniae renitent (me iudice) Musae,
Non reprobo studium, veniam concedo legenti.

POEMS DUBIOUSLY ASCRIBED TO ERASMUS

135 After Erasmus and Cornelis had complained in alternating strophes about the stupidity of the barbarians who scorn the eloquence of the ancients and deride poetry, Cornelis finally brings in St Jerome as an arbitrator, so to speak, to give his decision about cultivating poetry.

Jerome speaks.

You have required that I should be the prudent arbitrator in this case. Be pleased, then, to accept my well-considered judgment. I think it is praiseworthy to read the poems of the ancients and to satirize with sharp verse those who deride them. See how Proverbs runs the gamut of the grandiloquent Muses, how Wisdom, Job, and the Canticle of the Bride play with poetical lines, and how David renders his songs in metrical rhythm, resounding to the harp. But I say to you that some faults are rightly to be avoided. Watch out that your mind is not stained by damnable pride and that you do not scorn holy men who are not yet familiar with poetry – though they do not condemn poets but venerate and love them. If the style itself is pleasing and pleasure is also to be found in the vigorous content – for in both, if I am any judge, the Aonian Muses shine forth – I have nothing against such studies; I grant permission for such

15 Dum tamen ex aequo scripturas pondere sacras
Pensans, imo magis venerans, te dedis amori
Pierio, quo vel nitidum tuus induat alto
Scemate sermo stilum, aut Aegipti fulgida tollens
Vasa, pares domino pulchrum aedificare sacellum,
20 Non culpandus eris, sed laudem laude mereris.
Sic, puto, primitias mellis, quod consona legis
Verba iubent domino devota mente dicare,
Offers et placito placabis munere Christum.
Si tamen iis nimium curas adhibere laborem,
25 Mel bene libasti, sed sal non apposuisti,
Quo sine nil sapidum acceptumque deo perhibetur.
Musam non damno, sed tantum sobrietatis
Te satis admoneo ne dogmata sacra refutes.
Si quae gesta legis veterum ratione soluta,
30 Haec vis in numeris pedibusque ligare disertis,
Ingenium veneror et dulci carmine laetor.
Historias imitare sacras quum scribere tentas;
Ornet Musa stilum, scriptura paret tibi sensum.

Cornelius concludit assentiens:

Ieronimi dictis assentio, dulcis Erasme:
35 Sic faciamus in his quae nutrit amaena poesis.

reading. Indeed, as long as you grant equal, nay even greater, emphasis to the study of Holy Scripture, devoting yourselves to the Muses in order to raise your style to a high level of polished expressiveness or to build up and beautify the chapel of the Lord by appropriating the shining vessels of Egypt, you are not to be reproached but rather your praises are to be praised. In this way I think that you offer the first-fruits of the honey which some consonant words in the Law require to be offered to the Lord in a spirit of devotion, and you please Christ with a pleasing gift. But if you expend too much effort and concern on such things, you will have poured out the honey indeed, but you will not have added the salt, without which nothing can be offered to God with an acceptable savour. I do not condemn the Muse, but rather I only urge upon you moderation sufficient to keep you from conflict with sacred dogmas. If you read about the deeds of the ancients written in prose and you desire to reproduce them in the learned confines of metrical composition, I honour your talent and delight in your sweet song. Imitate the histories in Holy Scripture when you try to write; let the Muse elevate your style, let Scripture provide your meaning.

Cornelis concludes by agreeing:

My sweet friend Erasmus, I agree with what Jerome has said. This is the way we should proceed in applying the pleasures provided by poetry.

136 Erasmus cantoribus Maximiliani [1493–4? / 1615]

Ex minimis, vitium, coelum, medicamina, castra,
Surgit, alit, penetrat, mitigat, exuperat,
Seditio, requies, oratio, coena, favilla,
Maxima, longa, brevis, semibrevis, minima.

137 An epitaph for Hendrik van Bergen, bishop of Cambrai [autumn 1502 / 1853]

Hic premitur tumulo Henricus, cui clara propago
Bergentum redolet claraque facta magis.
Sidere felici cum natus surgit in annos
Amplexus studia est libera, iura simul.
5 Hiisque insignitus lauris perrexit ad urbem,
Primus et ob merita scriba creatus erat.
Antistesque simul gratus fulsit Cameraci,
Ut summo ad patrium versus honore solum est.
Dulce refrigerium orbatis luxit viduisque
10 Cum populatae edis tum reparator erat.
Celitis hic instar mentem corpusque ferebat
Intactum maculis, sydera ceu alta petens.
Noverat hic pariter componere faedera regum,
Velleris aurisoni praeses ob acta fuit.
15 Sepulchrum Domini, Hesperii quoque templa Iacobi,
Paulique et visit limina sacra Petri.
Et dubitamus adhuc virtutem extollere ad astra,
Rumpere et in vocem grandia facta viri?
Hic vir, hic est qui stellifero demissus Olimpo
20 Rexit ovesque suas tempore quo illud ait:

136 Erasmus to the singers of Maximilian

From smallest things, vice, heaven, medications, camps,
Arises, nourishes, penetrates, lessens, conquers,
Sedition, idleness, prayer, dinner, spark,
The greatest, long, a short, a very short, the smallest.

137 [An epitaph for Hendrik van Bergen, bishop of Cambrai]

Here, buried in his grave, lies Hendrik, who emitted and increased the good odour of the illustrious Bergen lineage. Born under a happy star, when he grew older he embraced liberal studies, and also the law. Adorned with these laurels, he proceeded to the city and because of his merits he was made the chief clerk. He also shone as the beloved bishop of Cambrai as soon as he returned with the highest honours to his native soil. He grieved with orphans and widows, providing sweet relief for them, and he also repaired the ruined church. He behaved himself in mind and body like a saint here on earth, untouched by any stain, like one striving to reach the stars above. He was equally knowledgeable in drawing up treaties between kings; because of his accomplishments he became chancellor of the Golden Fleece. He visited the sepulchre of the Lord and also the church of St James in Spain and the sacred thresholds of Paul and Peter. And are we still hesitant to praise his virtue to the skies and to burst into speech to praise the great deeds of the man? This man, this man sent down from the starry heavens, ruled his sheep at the time indicated by this:

eCCe saCerdos MagnVs qVI In dIebVs
sVIs pLaCVIt Deo. 1480
Et referens merita meritis, repetivit ad astra
Inclite ad Hesperia tempore quo sequitur:
25 et InVentVs est IVstVs.
Ergo si fecere fidem tot tantaque certam,
Degere in ethereis quisque rogate pium.

138 In Europae a monachis subactae picturam, E.R. [1509? / 1544]

Iuppiter Europam, vera est si fabula, tauri
Lusit mentita callidus effigie.
Quam monachi falsa sub imagine simplicis agni
(Pro pudor, haec non est fabula) nunc subigunt.

139 Ad eandem [1509? / 1544]

Spurca sacerdotum meretrix, Europa, puella
Inclita quae fueras unius ante Iovis,
Dic, precor, effigies ubi prisca, ubi candida vestis?
Cur luxata modo, cur ita senta iaces?

140 Europa respondet. [1509? / 1544]

Nonne vides, qui me grex stipat? Hic oris honorem
Abstulit et dotes quas Deus ante dedit:
Foelices Asiae terras Libyesque, procorum
Turba quibus non tam flagitiosa nocet.

Behold the great priest, who pleased God
in the days of his life. 1480
And so, acquiring what he had earned through his merits, he returned gloriously to the western stars at the time indicated by this:
And he was found to be just.
Therefore, if so many and such great achievements are firmly believed in, let everyone beg that this pious man may live in heaven.

138 On a picture of Europa assaulted by monks, E.R.

Jupiter cleverly deceived Europa, if the fable is true, by disguising himself as a bull. Nowadays the monks assault her under the false appearance of innocent lambs, and that – alas, what a shame – is no fable.

139 To the same person

You dirty whore of the priests, Europa, you were once the renowned sweetheart of Jupiter alone. Tell me, I beg you, where are the looks you had then? Where is your white robe? Why are you now so disjointed, why are you lying there so ragged?

140 Europa replies.

Don't you see what a crowd of them is hemming me in? That is what has taken away my fine appearance and the gifts which God once gave me, the prosperous lands of Asia and Africa, which are ravaged by a mob of suitors who are not so outrageous [as the priests are to me].

141 In eundem Iulium II Ligurem [November 1511? / 1901]

O medice verpe, cui vel uni Iulius,
Caput atque princeps Christiani nominis,
Vitam ac salutem contuendam credidit,
Quod belle Hebraeo conveniat et ebrio,
5 Dic per sacrum illum Messyan Callipedem,
Quid, iam tot annos dissipato podici
Atque ulceroso dum mederis inguini,
Et artem et operam ludis, infoelix, tuam?
Quin tu malis obnoxium furiis caput
10 Sanas vel herba, si quae nascitur magis
Potens veratro, sive magico carmine?
Valere utroque gentis est dos ac tua.
Quod si via quacumque peste tam gravi
Orbem levaveris, grata perenni vice
15 Plebs Christiana publicis precabitur,
Recutite, votis mentulam tibi integram.

142 Chorus porcorum [July 1519]

Nos portamus ad sepulchrum
Unam Musam quod videtur nobis pulchrum,
Quae est causa maxima
Quod sophistica nunc dicitur pessima.
5 Propterea volunt eam magistri nostri sepelire
Nec eius defensionem audire,
Et ideo dicunt eum esse hereticam,
Quia spernit theologiam peripateticam,
Quam incipiunt nunc eciam contemnere isti moderniores,
10 Cum tamen hec sola confundit hereticos contumaciores.

141 On the same Ligurian, Julius II

O circumcised physician, the one and only doctor to whom Julius, the chief and prince of the Christian domain, entrusts the care of his life and health (because there is a good fit between a Hebrew and an inebriate), tell me, by that holy Messiah of yours who is forever on his way but never gets anywhere, tell me, unhappy man, why are you fooling away both your skill and your labour, trying to cure an asshole that has been spread around for so many years and a groin full of sores? Why don't you try instead to cure a head plagued by the wicked Furies, either with an herb (if any can be found that is stronger than hellebore) or some magical incantation? To do both of these well is the gift of your race and of you personally. But if you should relieve the world of this plague in any way at all, the Christian people in their gratitude will forever offer up public prayers, my circumcised fellow, that you might have a whole dick.

142 [The chorus of the Porkers]

We are carrying an Muse to a grave, which seems to us pretty, who is the greatest reason why sophistic is nowadays said to be the worst. For that reason Our Learned Professors want to bury her and won't hear her defence. And therefore they say that her is a heretic because she spurns peripatetic theology, which these moderns also are now beginning to scorn, when in fact it is the only thing that confounds contumacious heretics.

143 An epitaph for Nicolaas Baechem of Egmond

[November–December 1526 / 1635]

Hic iacet Egmondus, telluris inutile pondus,
  Dilexit rabiem, non habeat requiem.

144 Upon hearing of the death of John Fisher and Thomas More

[August 1535 / 1611]

Henrici laudes vis versu claudier uno,
  Eque Mida facias eque Nerone virum.

143 [An epitaph for Nicolaas Baechem of Egmond]

Here lies the man from Egmond, a useless weight on the ground. He loved to rage; may he never find rest.

144 [Upon hearing of the death of John Fisher and Thomas More]

If you want the praises of Henry to be summed up in one verse, combine Midas and Nero into one man.

INDEX OF FIRST LINES

A LIST OF THE POEMS IN CHRONOLOGICAL ORDER

INDEX OF METRES

INDEX OF MEDIEVAL AND NEO-LATIN WORDS

TABLES OF CORRESPONDING NUMBERS

Index of First Lines

References are to the poem numbers in this edition.

Greek poems

Latin poems

A List of the Poems in Chronological Order

In this index the poems are arranged in the order in which they appear to have been composed.

7	In morbo de fatis suis querela	spring? 1496
14	Episcopo Traiectensi David	May? 1496
15	Eidem	May? 1496
13	Epitaphium Margaretae Honorae	1497–9?
30	In fronte Odarum Guilielmi	c January 1497
38	Ioanni Okego musico summo epitaphium	c February 1497
19	Duo salina argentea	autumn 1497?
20	In sex tintinabula	1497–1501?
41	In magnatem quendam qui laudes suas exiguo munusculo pensarat	1498–1500?
116	In castigationes Vincentii contra Malleoli castigatoris depravationes	February? 1498
9	Epitaphium Odiliae	July 1498?
10	Querela de filio superstite	July 1498?
11	Respondet filius	July 1498?
118	Erasmi precatio 'Salve, regina'	spring 1499?
110	Paean divae Mariae, atque de incarnatione verbi	April–May 1499
111	De monstrosis signis Christo moriente factis	summer? 1499
112	De solemnitate paschali atque de tryumphali Christi resurgentis pompa et descensu eius ad inferos	summer? 1499
4	Ode de laudibus Britanniae	late September? 1499
115	Carmen extemporale	autumn 1499
18	In tergo codicis Battici	before 1502
12	In filiam Bekae	1502–4
16	Iacobo Batto	1502
17	Iidem Latini versus	1502
39	Henrici episcopi Cameracensis epitaphium	autumn 1502
40	De eodem	autumn 1502
137	Epitaph for Hendrik van Bergen, bishop of Cambrai	autumn 1502
62	Ad amplissimum patrem Antonium de Berghes	autumn 1502
34	Sub pictura vultus Christi	1503?
29	In fronte libelli de imperatoria maiestate	c February 1503
36	In fronte Enchiridii	c February 1503
28	In fronte libelli dono missi episcopo Atrebatensi	autumn 1503
31	In fronte libelli Buslidio dono missi	November 1503?
32	In fronte alterius	November 1503?
63	Homerocenton	c February 1504
64	Illustrissimo principi Philippo foeliciter in patriam redeunti	c February 1504
35	Agit carmine gratias pro misso munere	1505–6
37	Libellus dono missus	1 January 1506?
65	Ad R.P. Guilhelmum archiepiscopum Cantuariensem	January 1506
8	Arx vulgo dicta Hammensis	June 1506?
2	Carmen de senectutis incommodis	August 1506
33	In caecum tragoediarum castigatorem	autumn 1506

21	In aulicum quendam	before 1507
22	In eundem	before 1507
23	In eundem	before 1507
24	In picturam fabulae Giganteae	before 1507
25	In eosdem fulmine depulsos	before 1507
26	In tabulam Penthei trucidati	before 1507
27	In picturam Europae stupratae	before 1507
138	In Europae a monachis subactae picturam	1509?
139	Ad eandem	1509?
140	Europa respondet	1509?
52	Epitaphium scurrulae temulenti	summer 1509?
43	Expostulatio Iesu cum homine	1510–11?
44	Carmen iambicum	1510–11
45	Sapphicum	1510–11
46	Imago pueri Iesu in ludo literario, quem nuper instituit Coletus	1510–11
47	Carmen phalecium	1510–11
48	Aliud	1510–11
119	Carmen iambicum	late spring 1511?
56	Ad Andream Ammonium Lucensem	c 20 October 1511
141	In eundem Iulium II Ligurem	November 1511?
51	Carmen ex voto dicatum virgini Vvalsingamicae	spring 1512
49	Christiani hominis institutum	1513–14
58	In fugam Gallorum	autumn 1513
53	Encomium Selestadii	1514–15
60	Epitaphium Philippi coenobitae Cluniacensis	1514–15?
132	From the colloquy *Epithalamium Petri Aegidii*	c 1514
3	Ad Ioannem Sapidum suum	August 1514
54	Ad Sebastianum Brant	August 1514
55	Ad Thomam Didymum Aucuparium	August 1514
57	Ad Lucam Paliurum Rubeaquensem	c 1515
59	Cum multos menses perpetuo pluisset	late June 1515
61	Erasmus Guilielmo Neseno calamum dono dedit	spring 1516?
66	Epitaphium D. Iacobi de Croy	c November 1516?
120	Lectori	early 1517?
67	In hymnos Bernardi Andreae Tolosatis	April 1517?
121	In commentarios D.B. Andreae Tholozani super opus Aurelii Augustini De civitate dei	April 1517?
68	Epitaphium ad pictam imaginem Hieronymi Buslidiani	c 26 March 1518
69	Trochaici tetrametri	c 26 March 1518
142	Chorus porcorum	before July 1519
70	In Brunonem Amerbachium	November 1519
122	De concordia Caroli imperatoris et Henrici regis Angliae et Franciae	July 1520
123	In substructionem Caletiensem	July 1520
124	In laudem divae Mariae Magdalenae	August 1520?
129	From the colloquy *De lusu*	before March 1522

125	Meersburg Castle	c September 1522
130	From the colloquy *Convivium poeticum*	before August 1523
133	From *Virginis Matris apud Lauretum cultae liturgia*	before November 1523
131	From the colloquy Πτωχοπλούσιοι	before March 1524
71	Epitaphium in mortem Martini Dorpii	8 November 1525
72	In Iacobum, paulo post defunctum	autumn 1526?
143	Epitaph for Nicolaas Baechem of Egmond	November–December 1526
126	Epitaph for Dirk Martens	autumn? 1527
73	Epitaphium Ioannis Frobenii	c November 1527
74	In eundem Graece	c November 1527
75	Epitaph for Philippe Haneton	c May 1528?
76	On *Basic Principles of Astronomy* by Joachim Sterçk van Ringelberg	before 31 October 1528
77	On a table in Joachim Sterck's book on astronomy	October 1528?
78	Epitaph for Nicolaas Uutenhove	1 February 1529
79	Greek epitaph for Nicolaas Uutenhove	1 February 1529
80	A gift of a rooster, a hen, and their chicks	early April 1529
81	On his departure from Basel	13 April 1529
82	On the rainstorms at Freiburg	July 1529
83	Epitaphium Corneliae Sandriae	January 1530
84	Aliud in eandem	January 1530
85	Epitaphium secundae coniugis	January 1530
86	Epitaphium Antonii Clavae	January 1530
87	Dialogue between a scholar and a bookseller	winter 1530–1
88	Des. Erasmi divae Genovefae praesidio a quartana febre liberati carmen votivum	late spring 1531?
89	To Pierre Du Chastel, who sent him some partridges	24 September 1532
90	On collecting proverbs	24 September 1532
91	On collecting proverbs	before March 1533
134	From *Responsio ad Petri Cursii defensionem*	c August 1535
144	Upon hearing of the death of John Fisher and Thomas More	August 1535
92	Epitaphium Udalrici Zasii	early April 1536
127	A request for dates	early April 1536

Index of Metres

In Allen I 3:19–20 / CWE Ep 1341A:69–70 Erasmus boasts that there is no form of poetry that he did not attempt. The following table, which lists the metrical patterns of his extant verses, shows that he came as close as any poet to exhausting the metrical possibilities of classical Latin verse. Of the metrical combinations here listed one is unparalleled: a dactylic hexameter followed by a catalectic iambic dimeter, used in the 'Poem about the troubles of old age' (2).

The numerals refer to the poems and, where necessary, the lines. Greek poems are marked with an asterisk.

Index of Medieval and Neo-Latin Words

This index lists words that occur neither in *Thesaurus Linguae Latinae* nor in Forcellini's *Lexicon totius Latinitatis*. Words that are found in dictionaries of medieval Latin, in the sense indicated here, are marked with an asterisk.

References to Erasmus' poems are by poem and line number. References which are preceded by 4d indicate line numbers of Erasmus' dedicatory letter to Prince Henry printed before poem 4; those preceded by F indicate line numbers of Froben's preface to the *Epigrammata* of 1518; those preceded by P indicate line numbers of Erasmus' preface to poems 94–7; and those preceded by S indicate line numbers of Snoy's preface to poems 93–7.

Tables of Corresponding Numbers

These tables give the corresponding numbers of Erasmus' poems in C. Reedijk's edition (Leiden 1956) and the CWE edition.

TABLE I

Reedijk	CWE
1	102
2	99
3	100
4	101
5	103
6	109
7	104
8	105
9	106
10	13
11	98
12	113
13	114
14	93
15	135
16	36
17	107
18	108
19	110
20	111
21	112
22	1
23	94
24	95
25	96
26	97
27	19.1–2
28	19.3–4

TABLE II

CWE	Reedijk
1	22
2	83
3	97
4	45
5	38
6	39
7	40
8	82
9	29
10	30
11	31
12	73
13	10
14	41
15	42
16	62
17	63
18	61
19	27–8
20	50–7
21	58
22	59
23	60
24	68
25	69
26	70
27	71
28	75

Reedijk	CWE	CWE	Reedijk
29	9	29	67
30	10	30	43
31	11	31	76
32	38	32	77
33	42	33	49
34	50.1–96	34	72
35	50.97–156	35	81
36	50.157–80	36	16
37	50.181–252	37	48
38	5	38	32
39	6	39	64
40	7	40	65
41	14	41	74
42	15	42	33
43	30	43	85
44	116	44	88
45	4	45	90
46	115	46	86
47	117	47	87
48	37	48	89
49	33	49	94
50	20.1–4	50	34–7
51	20.5–6	51	92
52	20.7–8	52	84
53	20.9–10	53	98
54	20.11–12	54	95
55	20.13–14	55	96
56	20.15–16	56	91
57	20.17–18	57	101
58	21	58	93
59	22	59	102
60	23	60	99
61	18	61	103
62	16	62	66
63	17	63	79
64	39	64	78
65	40	65	80
66	62	66	104
67	29	67	Not in Reedijk
68	24	68	106
69	25	69	107
70	26	70	108
71	27	71	113
72	34	72	114
73	12	73	116
74	41	74	117

Reedijk	CWE	CWE	Reedijk
75	28	75	120
76	31	76	118
77	32	77	119
78	64	78	121
79	63	79	122
80	65	80	125
81	35	81	123
82	8	82	124
83	2	83	126
84	52	84	127
85	43	85	128
86	46	86	129
87	47	87	130
88	44	88	131
89	48	89	132
90	45	90	133
91	56	91	134
92	51	92	135
93	58	93	14
94	49	94	23
95	54	95	24
96	55	96	25
97	3	97	26
98	53	98	11
99	60	99	2
100	118	100	3
101	57	101	4
102	59	102	1
103	61	103	5
104	66	104	7
105	120	105	8
106	68	106	9
107	69	107	17
108	70	108	18
109	122	109	6
110	123	110	19
111	124	111	20
112	125	112	21
113	71	113	12
114	72	114	13
115	126	115	46
116	73	116	44
117	74	117	47
118	76	118	100
119	77	119	Appendix II-2
120	75	120	105

Reedijk	CWE
121	78
122	79
123	81
124	82
125	80
126	83
127	84
128	85
129	86
130	87
131	88
132	89
133	90
134	91
135	92
136	127
Appendix I-1	128
Appendix I-2	132
Appendix I-3	129
Appendix I-4	130
Appendix I-5	131
Appendix I-6	133
Appendix I-7	134
Appendix II-1	138–40
Appendix II-2	119
Appendix II-3	142
Appendix II-4	143
Appendix II-5	144

CWE	Reedijk
121	Not in Reedijk
122	109
123	110
124	111
125	112
126	115
127	136
128	Appendix I-1
129	Appendix I-3
130	Appendix I-4
131	Appendix I-5
132	Appendix I-2
133	Appendix I-6
134	Appendix I-7
135	15
136	Not in Reedijk
137	Not in Reedijk
138	Appendix II-1 (a)
139	Appendix II-1 (b)
140	Appendix II-1 (c)
141	Not in Reedijk
142	Appendix II-3
143	Appendix II-4
144	Appendix II-5